The Monumental Andes

THE MONUMENTAL ANDES

Geology, Geography, and Ancient Cultures in the Peruvian Andes

ROSEANNE CHAMBERS

THE UNIVERSITY OF UTAH PRESS
Salt Lake City

Copyright © 2024 by The University of Utah Press. All rights reserved.

 The Defiance House Man colophon is a registered trademark of the University of Utah Press. It is based on a four-foot-tall Ancient Puebloan pictograph (late PIII) near Glen Canyon, Utah.

LIBRARY OF CONGRESS CATALOGING-IN-PUBLICATION DATA
Names: Chambers, Roseanne, 1953- author
Title: The monumental Andes : geology, geography, and ancient cultures in the Peruvian Andes / Roseanne Chambers
Description: Salt Lake City : The University of Utah Press, [2024] | Includes bibliographical references and index.
Identifiers: LCCN 2024016336 | ISBN 9781647691714 (cloth) | ISBN 9781647691721 (paperback) | ISBN 9781647691738 (ebook)
Subjects: LCSH: Geology—Andes Region—History. | Archaeological geology—Peru. | Archaeological geology—Andes Region. | Indians of South America—Andes Region—Antiquities. | Andes Region—Historical geography. | Peru—Historical geography. | Andes Region—Antiquities. | Peru—Antiquities.
Classification: LCC F2212 .C4296 2023 | DDC 980/.01--dc23/eng/20240801
LC record available at https://lccn.loc.gov/2024016336

Errata and further information on this and other titles available at UofUpress.com

For Eric and Andrea

Contents

List of Figures and Tables		viii
Preface		xi
Acknowledgments		xv

PART I — SETTING THE STAGE

1	Young Mountains and Ancient Cultures	3
2	Rocks	16
3	Tectonics	24
4	Earthquakes	32
5	Volcanoes	46
6	Landforms	59

PART II — CULTURE COMES TO THE ANDES

7	Migrations	73
8	Animals	83
9	Water	92
10	Agriculture	103
11	Plants	116
12	Monuments	127
13	Ritual Drugs and Sacrifices	146
14	Metals	156
15	Mining and Metallurgy	166
16	Decorative Arts	180

PART III — THREE MONUMENTAL AND UNIFYING CULTURES

17	Water and Power	197
18	The Top of the World	212
19	The Inca Builders	230

PART IV — PACHACUTI: AN OVERTURNING OF THE WORLD

| 20 | After the Incas | 251 |
| 21 | Looking Ahead | 262 |

Notes	273
Bibliography	309
Index	333

Figures and Tables

FIGURES

Figure 1.1. Curved stone block wall of the Coricancha.	4
Figure 1.2. South America satellite photo.	6
Figure 1.3. Inca walls at Pisac.	9
Figure 1.4. Schematic chronology for the major ancient Andean cultures described in this book.	13
Figure 1.5. Map of maximum extent of Inca, Tiwanaku, and Chavín influence.	14
Figure 2.1. Granitic blocks at Machu Picchu.	19
Figure 2.2. Limestone blocks at Sacsayhuaman.	21
Figure 3.1. Map of Pacific Ring of Fire.	26
Figure 3.2. Schematic of the subduction zone along the Central Andes.	27
Figure 3.3. Aconcagua, the tallest mountain in the Americas at 22,838 ft (6,961 m), view of south wall.	30
Figure 4.1. Seismicity of the South American coastal and Andean regions from 1900–2000.	35
Figure 4.2. Scarp on the Cordillera Blanca fault east of Huaraz.	37
Figure 4.3. Map showing Peru-Chile Trench and cross sections of flat slab and steeply dipping subduction zone segments.	38
Figure 4.4. Aerial view of the 1970 Huascarán avalanche that destroyed Yungay, Peru.	42
Figure 4.5. Huascarán as seen from Yungay.	43
Figure 5.1. Map of four volcanic zones along the west coast of South America.	49
Figure 5.2. Volcanic rocks showing areas where gas-fill bubbles formed and obsidian, Panum Dome, California.	51
Figure 5.3. Map showing ancient obsidian quarries and active volcanoes mentioned in text.	53
Figure 5.4. Misti volcano and the city of Arequipa in 2009.	57

Figure 6.1. Map of mountain ranges and the Altiplano-Puna
plateau in the Central Andes. 60
Figure 6.2. Alpacas grazing near Ausangate southeast of Cuzco. 61
Figure 6.3. Topography of Bolivian Orocline, Arica Bend, and Altiplano-
Puna plateau. 65
Figure 7.1. Map of the oldest archaeological sites mentioned in text. 76
Figure 8.1. Reconstruction of animals around a lagoon in
central Chile during the late Pleistocene. 85
Figure 8.2. The four types of camelids in the Andes. 87
Figure 8.3. Llama residents of Machu Picchu. 89
Figure 9.1. Overview of the Central Andes near Cuzco in 2021. 93
Figure 9.2. Lake Titicaca. 95
Figure 10.1. Puquios built by the ancient Nazca culture near the
city of Nazca, Peru. 108
Figure 10.2. Terraces built by the Incas in the Sacred Valley. 109
Figure 10.3. Muyu terraces at Moray, Peru. 113
Figure 11.1. Chuño from a market near Cuzco. 121
Figure 11.2. Maize from Latin America used in the Germplasm
Enhancement for Maize (GEM) project. 122
Figure 11.3. Shicra bags at Caral archaeological site. 124
Figure 11.4. Inca rope bridge across Río Apurímac. 125
Figure 12.1. Map showing locations of monuments mentioned in text. 129
Figure 12.2. Terraced Pyramid at Caral in the Supe Valley. 133
Figure 12.3. Hummingbird geoglyph by Nazca artists. 136
Figure 12.4. Terraces at Machu Picchu. 141
Figure 13.1. Chavín carved stone sculpture of an anthropomorphic jaguar
bearing a San Pedro cactus in the right hand. 147
Figure 13.2. Pacific thorny oyster (*Spondylus crassisquama*). 151
Figure 13.3. Inca shrine at the top of Llullaillaco (22,110 ft/6,739 m),
border of Argentina and Chile. 155
Figure 14.1. Map showing extent of principal metals found
in the Central Andes. 158
Figure 15.1. A mythical condor or eagle from a hammered
gold sheet by a Chavín artist. 167
Figure 15.2. Reconstruction of the tomb of the Lord of Sipán
in Huaca Rajada, Peru. 169

Figure 15.3. Hammerstones found at Machu Picchu. 172
Figure 15.4. Ceremonial tumi knife of gold, silver, and turquoise. 176
Figure 16.1. Mantle for the mummy of a man, Paracas culture, fabric of camelid hair. 183
Figure 16.2. Quipu of cotton string, Inca, 1400–1600. 184
Figure 16.3. Chavín stirrup-spout vessel with feline (jaguar?) and San Pedro cactus. 192
Figure 16.4. Moche stirrup-spout vessel with portrait head. 193
Figure 17.1. Overview of Chavín de Huántar. 201
Figure 17.2. Temple architecture and sculpted tenon heads at Chavín de Huántar, ca. 1901. 204
Figure 17.3. View of Chavín de Huántar and near-vertical bedrock fins in Chimú Formation. 206
Figure 18.1. Akapana pyramid at Tiwanaku. 219
Figure 18.2. Sunken temple at Tiwanaku. 220
Figure 18.3. Gateway of the Sun at Tiwanaku. 222
Figure 18.4. Tiwanaku (or Tiahuanaco), ca. 1907. 228
Figure 19.1. Map of the Inca Empire showing the four quarters and the road system. 234
Figure 19.2. Kachiqhata quarry above Ollantaytambo. 238
Figure 19.3. Map of faults at Machu Picchu. 245
Figure 19.4. Granitic quarry at Machu Picchu. 246
Figure 20.1. Cerro Rico del Potosí in the first image shown in Europe. 254
Figure 20.2. Street in Cuzco with colonial structures built above Inca walls. 258
Figure 21.1. Alpamayo in the Cordillera Blanca and lake held back by unstable glacial moraines. 265
Figure 21.2. Celebration of Inti Raymi at Sacsayhuaman. 270

TABLE

Table 1.1. Prominent Ancient Andean Cultures and Approximate Age Ranges. 12

Preface

My fascination with the Andes Mountains began in 2006, when I first traveled in Peru as a tourist. The highlight of this trip was hiking for several days through the mountains to the archaeological site of Machu Picchu. Although I had hiked in many mountain ranges and knew that the snow-covered Andean peaks would be spectacular, I was unprepared for the experience of walking in this landscape. If I hadn't already been laboring to breathe in the thin air, the sight of these majestic mountains would have taken my breath away.

During that two-week trip, I climbed for many miles on steep stairways and through tunnels carved into solid rock, traveling along paths paved with cut stone blocks and built many centuries ago by Andean people who made this region their home. Beneath my feet as I walked, I could see different types of rock, reflecting the changing geology of the surrounding terrain. Looking out over the landscape, I recognized the distinctive shapes of volcanoes and the scars that enormous landslides had left behind. My heart pounded hard, and I would struggle to catch my breath as I pondered the challenges faced by all who carved out a living in such a rugged environment. I touched cool surfaces of stone block structures constructed by long-ago builders, admired the closely fit seams between blocks, wondered where the builders quarried the heavy stones they used. The ancient buildings, now roofless and open to the vast sky, had a timeless quality as an ever-changing pattern of clouds drifted above.

It is these awe-inspiring vistas, these rarely seen monuments to long-vanished cultures, that I hope to reveal to readers in *The Monumental Andes*.

My 2006 adventure in Peru began unexpectedly. A friend invited me to join a small group on a visit to that country. Thrilled, I learned that the highlight of the trip would be to hike for four days through the mountains to the archaeological site of Machu Picchu. Squarely in middle age, I had been an enthusiastic hiker for decades. I am an avid traveler, especially to mountains, deserts, and other wild natural places. I have spent some of my happiest days wandering through wild regions of California, Nevada, Wyoming, Utah, and even the Sahara Desert in Egypt, with much of it as part of my professional work as a geologist evaluating earthquake hazards.

So, when the invitation came to hike in the Andes Mountains, I readily accepted. South America, and specifically the geology of the Andes, intrigued me. I wanted to know more. I was unprepared, however, for what I ultimately experienced on this trip: the immense size and sweeping majesty of the Andes; the vast and diverse environments ranging from arid deserts to glacier-covered mountains and Amazon jungles; the archaeological remnants of Indigenous cultures that flourished, displaying accomplishments that amaze so many of us today.

I had a few concerns about the Peru trip. The foremost one: could I really walk many miles of rugged trails to Machu Picchu? I spent most of my time sitting in front of a computer, and a birth defect had led to having an artificial hip implanted eleven years earlier. Now that hip was becoming increasingly cranky. I knew that the plastic and metal parts keeping me moving were wearing out and that I was on a downward slide, heading toward more surgery. But the lure of such a magnificent destination as the Andes was strong and fueled my determination to do whatever I could to prepare for the trip.

Every weekend I hiked for several hours up and down the steep hills near my home—and then I'd limp for the next few days. Over several months, as the muscles supporting my weak leg strengthened, my gait smoothed out. The problem was solved (temporarily) by persistence; my artificial joint was ready to handle many more miles ahead. My other concerns—including responsibilities for my aging and ailing parents, boundary-pushing teenaged children, a faltering marriage, and a day job as a geologist—weren't as easily appeased. Still, I pressed on in my preparations for the upcoming adventure.

The trip turned out to be transformational. I successfully hiked to Machu Picchu, renewing my confidence not only in my physical abilities but also in how I could change the direction of other aspects of my life. The sheer beauty of the Andes, coupled with the powerful geologic forces that have been and are continuing to shape this landscape, captivated me. Learning more about the exceedingly long and rich cultural history of the region was remarkable as well. The remote Inca archaeological sites we hiked to and explored, far from any roadway, renewed my long-held interest in archaeology.

The Incas reigned for a relatively short time, yet they left behind so much that we marvel at today. One of the first Spaniards to see Cuzco, the capital city of the Inca Empire, was Pedro Sancho. In 1534, he wrote that the city was "so large and so beautiful that it would be worthy of admiration even in Spain."

How did the Incas accomplish so much so quickly? The answer: They built the achievements of the empire on the broad cultural and infrastructure features developed over millennia by earlier Andean societies.

Shortly after returning home, I wanted to learn more about Peru. I planned another trip. Just a year later, in 2007, I joined a small group for a strenuous ten-day trek along a high and rugged loop through the Cordillera Blanca in northern Peru. Once again, I trained to have the strength and endurance to tackle the hikes, and again, it was a memorable journey. The folded and varied rocks surrounding us, the glaciers, and snowfields above the ancient paths we walked, the small hamlets where we saw mountain people herding sheep and llamas, the glimpses of fossils of extinct marine creatures entombed in rocks now high in the mountains, my exhaustion from hiking over 15,000-foot mountain passes day after day—the rich tapestry of the Andes environment was extraordinary.

Early in the trip, our trekking guide, Ian, learned about my professional background and asked if I knew of a geology book about Peru. I needed to admit that, regrettably, I did not. Although I had skimmed through many scientific papers with details about obscure topics in Andean geology, I had found no book for general audiences with a focus on geology. Indeed, despite all the information available about the Andes Mountains, and the Incas and their ancestors, there was no book that specifically traced the geologic history of the landscape and how this history helped to shape ancient Andean cultures.

Now there is: the book you are reading.

In the years since my unpredicted, life-changing visit to Peru, I have learned much about this remarkable region of South America. Gaining a greater understanding of the geology and geography of the Andes and how this influenced the cultural development of the Indigenous inhabitants became my focus, and the journey has been fascinating. The earliest Andeans coped with one of the most complex and varied environmental systems on earth. The Incas' achievements, and those of their ancestors for thousands of years before, are unmatched.

The geology sculpting the western edge of South America ultimately controlled the lives of the Andeans. By understanding the geologic processes that formed the Andes Mountains, we can better recognize and appreciate the adaptations made by Indigenous societies. Carving out a living in high mountains takes great effort. Isolated by high mountains, deep valleys, and arid coastal deserts, the Andean people had to develop their own unique solutions for environmental and societal challenges. They were remarkably successful.

Geology and geography, the interaction between people and their environment, strongly influence human cultures. Geology creates the landscape, affects the climate, focuses settlement patterns, determines agricultural and mineral production, shapes the natural history of plants and animals, and controls natural hazards such as volcanoes and earthquakes. The relationships between human societies, the natural resources available to them, and the weather patterns they experience—along with the soil, water, landforms, and other aspects of their environment—are the realm of geography.

Different from the many other books that report on the social history, political systems, and religious practices of the ancient Andeans, I focus on the relationship between Andean cultures and the geology and geography of their world. We will look at the area's geologic volatility, learning about the earthquakes, volcanoes, and landslides, and the practices the Andeans developed to cope with these natural hazards. We will examine the associations between rocks, quarries, and the construction of monumental structures. We will consider climate, topography, and agricultural practices that fed millions of people. And we will explore the mineral resources and metal use for producing exquisite art objects.

Approaching this wide range of topics as a North American observer, but also as a professional geologist and an avid traveler, I will share what I have learned about ancient Andean cultures and how their world shaped their societies and their fate.

So, let's take a walk together through the grandeur, majesty, and amazing history of the monumental Andes Mountains.

Acknowledgments

This book would not have been possible without the collective wisdom of countless archaeologists, geologists, and other researchers who published their Andean studies. The University of California at Berkeley libraries, Google Scholar, and Wikipedia provided essential information for my research.

I deeply appreciate the support of family members and friends over the years that I worked on this book. Hiking friend J. P. Torres organized the 2006 trip to Peru and invited me to join, igniting my fascination with the Andes Mountains. In 2007, I trekked through the Cordillera Blanca on a trip arranged by Mountain Travel Sobek (Emeryville, California). During the trek, my idea for this book originated in conversations with Ian Lewis, our superb Peruvian guide. For my 2009 trip, Explorandes (Miraflores, Peru) arranged the logistics, including the accompaniment of guide Ian Lewis. J. Ross Wagner and Frank H. (Bert) Swan, my favorite geology fieldwork partners from my Woodward-Clyde Consultants days, joined me on the 2009 trip and supplied an abundance of useful information, as did my friend Joe Balciunas, biologist.

Enormous gratitude to geologist and good friend Doris Sloan, who gave inspiration and helpful suggestions throughout all the years of this project. Deep appreciation for the valuable help of Suzanne Sherman, book consultant and memoir coach. Suzanne provided many beneficial editorial recommendations, including how to organize and best present a vast amount of information, plus excellent advice as I worked to develop a suitable writing style.

I gratefully acknowledge several individuals who reviewed the text and supplied important questions and comments. Archaeologist Michael Malpass (Professor Emeritus, Ithaca College) read the complete draft and identified gaps that this geologist missed. John Hanc, writer and publishing consultant (Enhanced Communications), reviewed an early draft and suggested beneficial improvements. While my writing was in progress, three reviewers generously read either large sections or the entire manuscript: Doris Sloan, Eric Perman, and Ann Derry. Each of these individuals saved me from making many errors; any remaining are my own.

I thank the many friends and family who provided valuable support and input. Those who were especially helpful include Christopher Chambers-Ju,

Peter Crigger, Melanie Haiken, Moya Melody, Edward (Al) Merewether, Elizabeth Nesbitt, Marjorie Wilkens, Linda Wright, and the late Ray Perman. I learned essential information about writing and the publishing process from Carla King, Andy Ross, and Susan Shillinglaw. Peer reviewers Gregory Knapp and Wayne Ranney provided helpful comments on the book. Graphics artist Javier Chalini, a talented colleague from my consultant days, expertly prepared the original maps and figures.

I am grateful to Justin Bracken, University of Utah Press acquisitions editor, whose wise recommendations and patience significantly improved the book. I appreciate the support of other staff associated with the Press. These include Rebecca Rauch, who expressed interest initially in my project, and Anya Martin, copy editor, who carefully reviewed and improved my writing. All, but especially Justin Bracken, helped to turn my dream for this book into reality.

Special thanks to my husband, Robert C. Davis, who gave invaluable reviews of my writing and unwavering encouragement.

Part I

Setting the Stage

I

Young Mountains and Ancient Cultures

High in the Andes Mountains of Peru stands a remnant of a curved stone wall that was covered in sheets of gold during the height of the Incas, the powerful empire that ruled over a vast region of the Andes from at least 1438 to 1533. Built as part of a great Inca sanctuary called the Coricancha, this wall is now surrounded by the modern city of Cuzco. The blocks that form the wall are smooth, uniform, and fit tightly together. Inca builders are renowned for their stonework, and the workmanship in the curved stone wall is exquisite, probably the most superb ever constructed at the height of this formidable empire. The wall has stood solidly for almost 600 years, even as structures around it have crumbled in the earthquakes that frequently rock this region. Clearly, the ancient builders understood their materials and environment.

When I first saw the curved wall, surrounded by the noise and bustle of modern Cuzco, I was mesmerized. Ignoring the ornate façade of the Spanish church attached above, I imagined the Coricancha during the height of the Inca Empire and the riches held within the enclosing stone walls. The elegance and artistry of the smooth and even stonework, and the solidity of the remaining wall, appear as if rooted in the ground for millennia. Learning the history of this magnificent structure, and understanding its strength and resilience, was even more impressive.

The Coricancha was once an elaborate ceremonial complex occupying the geographical and spiritual center of the Inca Empire.[1] The curved wall has withstood the test of both time and earthquakes. How could the Incas, who mainly used stone tools and did not have a written language, have accomplished this

CHAPTER 1

FIGURE 1.1. The curved stone block wall of the Coricancha beneath the Church of Santo Domingo. Photograph by author.

feat? Their creations provide mute testimony to the knowledge and ingenuity of the ancient builders.

Spanish conquistadors traveled to the heart of Inca territory in 1532, when they set into motion the collapse of this great empire. A few decades later, the Spanish Dominicans chose the location of the Coricancha for the construction of their Church of Santo Domingo. They ordered much of the curved wall dismantled, with a single large section preserved to form part of the facade of the church.[2] A powerful earthquake shook Cuzco in 1650. The estimated size of this event was magnitude 7.7, followed by more than one hundred strong aftershocks. Many people died, and the shaking reduced the Church of Santo Domingo and many other Spanish colonial structures in the city to rubble. The curved stone wall remained unscathed,[3] as the heavy blocks carefully trimmed to fit tightly together and sloped slightly inward create an extremely sturdy structure.

The Incas ruled for only a short time, but they could base their technological superiority on cultural experience developed over thousands of years in the Andes. Perhaps the ghosts of Inca builders laughed at the construction blunders made in their homelands by the ignorant European newcomers who had invaded so brashly?

Following the 1650 collapse of the Church of Santo Domingo, the Dominicans ordered it to be rebuilt, again anchored above the solid Inca wall. In 1950 another strong earthquake shook Cuzco, this one with estimated magnitude 7.0. More than half of the buildings in Cuzco collapsed,[4] including the Church of Santo Domingo.[5] And once again, the curved stone block wall stood firmly. Later, builders restored the Church of Santo Domingo for yet a third time using the solid Inca foundation (Figure 1.1). The Incas planned for this structure to last indefinitely, and they had the skill and knowledge to accomplish this feat.

The Dynamic Andes Mountains
The Incas and their ancestors inhabited distinctive lands. The Andes Mountains extend along the entire western edge of the South American continent, from the humid tropics of the Caribbean on the north to the ice fields of Patagonia on the south (picture the approximately 4,000 mi, or 6,440 km, span of these mountains next to the 2,800 mi, or 4,500 km, east-to-west width of the United States). This procession of majestic snow-covered Andean peaks and deep valleys forms the longest continental mountain chain on earth and the highest outside of Asia (Figure 1.2). Arranged in a series of distinct mountain ranges separated by basins, dozens of Andean peaks exceed 20,000 ft (6,096 m) above sea level in height. Only the soaring Himalayas, crowned by Mount Everest, are higher. The millions of years of geologic history that created this dramatic landscape became the foundation for human achievements in the Andes. We will explore those achievements, but first, examining these mountains through the lens of time will provide an important viewpoint.

The modern Andes Mountains began to rise around 25 million years ago. To put that timeframe in perspective, keep in mind the earth has an age of approximately 4.6 billion years. Complex life forms grew in the oceans around 540 million years ago and primitive land plants started diversifying and covering the continents around 420 million years ago. These immense spans of time and the scales by which we measure them can be difficult to grasp. Framed in a

FIGURE 1.2. South America satellite photo by NASA.

more familiar way, the Andes took shape during roughly the last one-half percent of the earth's history. The mountains are continuing to rise today, which is why, viewed from a geologic perspective, they are young mountains. In contrast, the Appalachian Mountains in the eastern United States, with their rounded shapes and low peaks of similar heights, show signs of a long history, and first formed around 480 million years ago.

In my travels through the Andes Mountains, much of it on foot along hiking trails, I have admired the variety and abundance of geologic activity. Today, powerful forces shape these majestic mountains. The region is among the most geologically active places on earth, and the marks of natural processes are visible everywhere in this dynamic landscape. The signs include jagged scars left by landslides; long lines of steep scarps, or small cliffs, showing ground broken in strong earthquakes; enormous piles of rock rubble left behind by retreating glacial ice; and stair-steps of broad terraces surrounding rivers that are downcutting into bedrock as the mountains grow taller. The landscape is remarkably diverse.

High mountain environments present challenges for many types of life. In the Andes Mountains, torrential rains and heavy snowfalls alternate with multiyear droughts. Andean volcanoes periodically erupt fiery hot ash and rock that engulf the surrounding region, and powerful earthquakes slice across the landscape. Unstable soils and ice fields can trigger devastating landslides and avalanches. At high altitudes, oxygen concentration drops along with decreased atmospheric pressure. In Cuzco, with an elevation about 11,200 ft (3,414 m), the air contains oxygen levels only 60 to 70 percent that of Lima, on the Pacific Coast. Low oxygen availability, or anoxia, makes rest and manual labor more strenuous and energy demanding. This was demonstrated vividly when I first flew into Cuzco from Lima—pulling my heavy bag off the baggage claim conveyer belt in the airport left my heart pounding from the unusually taxing effort required.

Yet despite the extreme conditions, despite the ground changing, literally, beneath their feet, for thousands of years ancient Andean cultures adapted to the challenges of their environment and thrived. Over millennia, the Indigenous people refined the skills and infrastructure that culminated in the solid curved stone wall of the Coricancha and the many other impressive accomplishments of the Inca Empire.

Unraveling Andean Cultural History

When I first visited Peru, I was only vaguely familiar with the great cultures that rose and fell in the Andes long before the Incas. This may be partly because the "world history" of my early education (now many decades past) emphasized the more widely shared European heritage of the surrounding community. Also, many in our modern society view Andean cultures as undeveloped and inferior. After all, the Andeans did not have a writing system that we recognize, leaving us to piece together the record of their accomplishments only from the material remains they left behind. For these and probably more reasons, I had an incomplete view of world history, and one in which ancient Eurasian cultures crowded in to gather most of the glory.

The focus on the Incas rather than on the cultures that preceded them, could be due to the sheer abundance of impressive archaeological sites in the

Cuzco region in comparison with the often poorly preserved and isolated sites of the earlier Andean cultures. Another reason no doubt originated with Hiram Bingham III, an American historian who happened upon the solid walls of the spectacular archaeological site of Machu Picchu in 1911. Subsequently, funded by Yale University and the National Geographic Society, Bingham organized several archaeological expeditions to that Inca city.[6] Researchers collected thousands of artifacts from the site, including mummies, stone and metal tools, and ceramics. Bingham's reports and photographs, published in *National Geographic* magazine and widely distributed, revealed the stunning beauty and complexity of Machu Picchu. The spectacular finds focused attention on Cuzco and the surrounding region, helping to turn it into the world-famous tourist destination that it continues to be today.

While remarkable sites such as Machu Picchu and remnants of fine masonry walls in the city of Cuzco still exist, signs of much of Inca culture have vanished, obliterated during the ravages associated with the Spanish conquest. Most of the conquistadors were illiterate and their primary interest in Indigenous culture was the loot they could gain.[7] Only a few early Spanish colonialists left written records about various aspects of Inca life and history. As chroniclers typically favored observations from nobility over those of commoners, accuracy likely suffered. Many of the early accounts are also contradictory, in part because of translation complications and difficulties inherent in fitting oral histories into a European-style framework.[8] Nonetheless, the sixteenth- and seventeenth-century reports provide valuable descriptions of Inca traditions that were rapidly disappearing. Hundreds of years after the conquest, travelers also wrote narratives about the region. They often based their stories on idealized and exaggerated historical reconstructions—such as describing precious gems embedded in the walls of the Coricancha despite no evidence for this—which limits their usefulness as historical records.

Fortunately, by analyzing the remains of ancient settlements and cultural relics, researchers have pieced together reconstructions of the lives of the Indigenous Andeans. The arid coastal deserts and the freezing temperatures on lofty mountain peaks have preserved normally highly perishable textiles, plant remains, and mummies. Together with the remains of elite architecture, constructed to last by many Andean cultures, these finds reveal the rich history of the Incas and their ancestors (Figure 1.3).

FIGURE 1.3. Inca walls at Pisac. Photograph by author.

Defining Monuments and Ancient Cultures

The citadel of Machu Picchu, sited on a narrow mountain ridge with graceful wide and flat terraces, buildings with fine stonework, and stunning views of the surrounding landscape, has enthralled millions of visitors. This spectacular place memorializes the vision and skill of the Inca builders, and people widely acknowledge it as a monument—a location with enduring evidence of a notable and historically significant achievement.

References to the monumental Andes have two major and overlapping meanings in this book. The towering, icy white peaks that span the length of the South American continent are massive and imposing, evoking awe from those who spend time in their shadows. They are truly monumental mountains. Similarly, the complex and frequently enormous structures of adobe brick and shaped-stone blocks built by the ancient Andeans astonish those who view them with their power and the tremendous efforts spent on construction. The social and political significance of monumentality in ancient societies intrigues many researchers. While we may not understand all the meanings that these monuments held for the ancient people, we can admire their enduring presence in the landscape.

Why, in this book, are Indigenous cultures referred to as ancient when we're talking about a time as recent as the sixteenth century? Definitions of the term ancient include "as relating . . . to a time early in history" and as "the civilized people of antiquity."[9] I refer to Andean cultures, from the earliest hunter-gatherer societies to the Incas, as ancient Andeans because the people practiced ancient technologies and no longer exist in the form that they did previously. None of these Indigenous societies used wheeled vehicles, and they domesticated no draft animals capable of pulling plows or carts. They did not use iron tools. Although the Andeans collected data and kept records on string devices called quipus, they had no written language that we recognize. Nonetheless, the Incas created one of the greatest empires in history, and we can see a splendid record of their accomplishments today.

A surprise for me when I first visited Peru, and perhaps for many others: The Inca Empire was in power for only about one hundred years. Many individuals, including some of my family members, have lived as long as or longer than this extraordinary empire existed. What accounts for its rapid rise, its immense success, and its precipitous fall?

Knowledge of the foundations of the Inca Empire provides the key to understanding how it could expand and flourish in such a short time. The Incas built their empire on the cultural developments of their ancestors, who provided a strong social and technological foundation developed over thousands of years of experimentation. And the exceedingly rich and varied environments of the Andes Mountains made these advances possible.

The rugged topography of the Andes effectively separated societies, so that they developed independently. Several great civilizations rose and fell in regions far to the north of the Andes. In what is now central Mexico, the Aztec Empire existed during the same time that the Incas reigned.[10] In Central America, the height of the Maya civilization, known as the 500-year-long "Classic Period," ended about 600 years before the rise of the Inca Empire. Exchanges between these cultures of the Americas were minimal.[11] In contrast, early in human history people established cultural connections in the Old World among African, Asian, and European cultures. These interactions occurred primarily over long-distance trade routes,[12] including the Silk Road, or Silk Routes, that emerged around 2,000 years ago across Asia, the Middle East, East Africa, and Europe.[13]

Things changed in the Americas during the sixteenth century when small wooden ships carrying European fortune seekers sailed across the Atlantic Ocean. Both the Aztec and Inca cultures collapsed shortly after the Spanish conquistadors brought with them their diseases, horses, guns, and lust for precious metals. During the colonial period that ensued,[14] much of the rich cultural heritage of the Indigenous Andean cultures was destroyed. Fortunately, aspects of these ancient societies live on in the languages and practices of modern Andeans, as well as in the fabulous artifacts and archaeological sites that remind us of the remarkable Incas and their ancestors.

Thousands of Years of Andean Cultural Development

Over human history in the central Andes Mountains, many unique ancient cultures rose to prominence at different times between the Pacific Coast and the highlands. Clear evidence of human settlements in South America, including hearths with charcoal and food fragments, extends to at least 14,000 years ago. Preserved footprints and cultural remains suggest people were in the Americas several thousands of years earlier, although most traces of these societies are lost in time (see Chapter 7). The earliest people hunted, butchered, and cooked large mammals, including giant ground sloths and mastodons, creatures that were largely extinct by 10,000 years ago.[15] In the cold and high mountains, they collected obsidian, volcanic glass that is valuable for tools,[16] and in the icy water of sparkling streams, they searched for nuggets of gold, fashioning it into jewelry to accompany their dead into the afterlife.[17]

Facing environmental challenges ranging from earthquakes and volcanoes to changing climates, the ancient Andeans developed ways to adapt to their surroundings (described in Chapters 2, 3, 4, 5, 6, 7, 9, and 13). They domesticated plants and animals, built large and impressive ceremonial complexes, developed sophisticated agricultural methods, and created exquisite textiles, ceramics and art objects in gold and silver (described in Chapters 8, 10, 11, 12, 14, 15, and 16). All these achievements, and many more, millions of people admire today.

I list the names of the prominent Andean societies described in this book and their approximate date ranges below in Table 1.1. A chronological diagram of the overlapping time ranges spanned by the major South American cultures according to region follows (Figure 1.4). Since the Quechua spoken by the Incas was not a written language, people have used many variations in the spelling of Quechua words since Spanish colonial times. In this book, I have tried to use the spellings that are the most common in American English.

Many of the age dates for events described in the following chapters are deliberately approximate, since collection and reporting of age-dating information from archaeological sites are subject to complications and published results are updated inconsistently. Specific dates I cite are calibrated dates, which are corrected for variations in radiocarbon amounts through time.[18] Also note that the terms Before Common Era (BCE) and Common Era (CE) are alternative and secular names for the numerically equivalent time periods designated by BC and AD.

Table 1.1. Prominent Ancient Andean Cultures and Approximate Age Ranges.

Prominent Ancient Andean Cultures	Approximate Age Range
Inca Empire	1438–1532 CE
Chimú, Killke	900–1470 CE
Tiwanaku, Wari	500–1000 CE
Moche	100–700 CE
Nazca	100 BCE–700 CE
Paracas	800 BCE–100 BCE
Chavín	1200 BCE–500 BCE
Norte Chico	2500 BCE–1800 BCE
Guitarrero Cave	ca. 10,000 BCE
Monte Verde site	ca. 14,000 BCE or earlier

Note: Adapted from Michael A. Malpass, *Ancient People of the Andes* (Cornell University Press, 2016).

The rugged geography of the Andes Mountains has isolated communities throughout the long period of human occupation. Socially independent societies, with different languages and customs, developed as a response to this environment. Remarkably, the Inca Empire grew to unite and control hundreds of distinctive societies along two-thirds of the length of western South America.

Young Mountains and Ancient Cultures 13

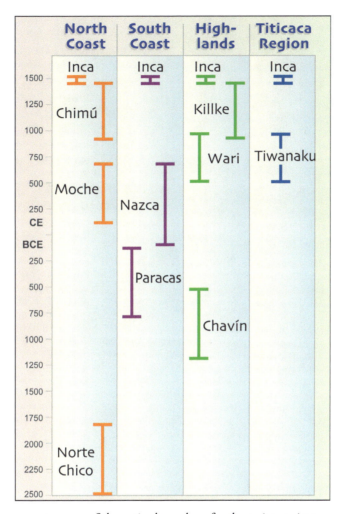

FIGURE 1.4. Schematic chronology for the major ancient Andean cultures described in this book. Age ranges from Michael A. Malpass, *Ancient People of the Andes*, 2016; modified from Michael E. Moseley, *Incas and Their Ancestors* (2001): Figures 6–9.

Centuries before the Incas, two earlier extraordinarily successful cultures also had a far-reaching cultural influence in the Andes Mountains: the Chavín, in modern northern Peru, and the Tiwanaku, in the high plateau region near Lake Titicaca. The geographic extent of each of those cultures can be seen in

FIGURE 1.5. Map of maximum extent of Inca, Tiwanaku, and Chavín influence. Modified from John Haywood, *Penguin Historical Atlas of Ancient Civilizations* (2005): 131–135.

the Figure 1.5 map. In this book, I describe the remarkable accomplishments of these three unifying societies and others with notable achievements, along with the geography of their lands (see Chapters 17, 18, and 19).

The societies that preceded the Incas lived primarily on territory now in modern Peru and northern Bolivia, a region referred to as the Central Andes. Not surprisingly, modern political boundaries rarely correspond to Indigenous cultural zones. I use the broad geographic term of Central Andes throughout this book, defined as the region between about 5–27° south latitude. The name refers to the entire range of environments extending from Pacific Ocean waves breaking along the arid coastline, up into the cold high mountains, and then down into the humid jungle-covered slopes above the Amazon Basin.[19]

What We Can Learn from Andean History
The achievements of the ancient Andeans were extraordinary. We gain valuable knowledge by exploring the legacy of the Andean cultures and the relationships they had with their environment. We can benefit also from the lessons in resiliency these past societies learned. The influence of the natural world on the trajectory of human history has always been important. This dynamic is as true today as it has been for thousands of years. And the more we understand this interplay, the better prepared we are to face the future.

Now, traveling back through time, we will look at the natural environment the ancient people encountered many thousands of years ago as they spread out and explored the Central Andes.

2

Rocks

As a geologist, whenever I venture out into the world, I like to check out the rocks in my environment. I find interesting rocks in natural outcrops and layered onto buildings. In tiles on the floor or in wall panels, on counters in reception areas in office buildings and hotels, in elevators, and even the stall dividers in public bathrooms, one can find an intriguing variety of rough and polished rock. In the past, when I have inspected beautiful marble floor tiles filled with fossils, hotel staff have asked if I have lost something. I attract puzzled glances when I stand in an elevator with my nose almost touching a polished granite wall panel. While hiking, I survey the rocks around me and try not to pick up too many samples to add to my ever-growing collection.

Ultraviolet light and exposure to oxygen affect human skin, as we know, and they also affect rocks, especially in high altitude mountain environments like the Andes. Most rocks that are exposed to our atmosphere for any length of time become weathered by wind and water, and an outer crust with a slightly different color and hardness develops (same for human skin). Mineral identification is easiest in unweathered, or fresh, rock. When geologists are outside doing fieldwork, they carry rock hammers and frequently smack off pieces of rock to examine the fresh surfaces with a magnifying hand lens. While hiking along the Inca trail to Machu Picchu, I thought how enticing it would be to break off corners of stone blocks on stairways and temple walls just to inspect the minerals in a fresh rock face. I resisted this urge, of course; I would never harm ancient landmarks. But I also must admit that it helped that I wasn't carrying my hammer. That's how powerfully alluring the geology of the Andes is to a "rock person." Let me explain more.

How to Build a Rock

We classify rocks according to the geologic processes by which they form. Hot magma creates igneous rocks that are spewed from volcanoes or cool slowly deep underground; sedimentary rocks are cemented together from small fragments of other rocks or organic material; and metamorphic rocks start as any type of rock that is then altered by extreme heat and pressure. Which rocks can we find in the Andes, and how did these influence the ancient cultures? We'll have a look, starting by considering the qualities of the three main types of rocks or organic material: igneous, sedimentary, and metamorphic.

Igneous Rocks

Magma, the molten material that originates from deep within the earth, is the raw material that creates igneous rocks. The name appropriately comes from the Latin term *ignis* for fire. When hot magma boils out onto the earth's surface to form lava in volcanic eruptions and then cools, *extrusive* igneous rocks form. The chemistry and temperature of the molten lava play important roles in determining the specific type of rock that is created. Whether an eruption oozes out quietly or explodes violently relates to magma chemistry and the location of the eruption. These qualities also influence the safety, and even the life expectancy, of the volcanologists who study volcanoes. As you might suspect, volcanology is a dangerous profession.

Crystallization occurs as the magma cools, organizing molecules into discrete minerals. Rapid cooling and solidification give most volcanic rocks grain sizes too small to be seen without a microscope, resulting in a smooth and uniform appearance. Extremely rapid cooling prevents even the smallest crystals from forming and results in volcanic glass, known as obsidian. Volcanic rocks can also incorporate large crystals or fragments of different rock types that were torn from the sides of the underground magma chamber or the vent that molten material traveled through before erupting.

I once had the privilege of witnessing fiery lava pouring into the ocean during an eruption of the Kilauea volcano on the Big Island of Hawaii. As our boat maneuvered ever closer to the glowing fountain, hot blobs of lava were ejected out over the water and toward the boat (an exciting, but also somewhat terrifying experience!). The baseball-sized lumps rained onto the metal roof of our vessel and hit the surrounding water, where they skated for a distance over the surface accompanied by a peculiar sizzling sound (imagine tossing red-hot charcoal briquettes from your barbecue into a swimming pool, then having the coals float). Gas trapped in bubbles as a volcanic rock solidifies leave many rocks filled with pits or voids, allowing some to even float in water.

Andesite is the principal volcanic rock type found in the Andes.[1] You can probably guess where the name comes from. Dark brown or greenish, andesite typically has crystals that are visible to the unaided eye and inclusions of other rock fragments. Other common volcanic rocks in the Andes are basalt, which has a dark gray, fine-grained look, and dacite, which has medium-grain sizes. Basalt, dacite, and andesite are suitable construction materials that were used by the ancient Andeans.

Intrusive or plutonic igneous rocks develop if a magma pool stays deep below the ground surface and crystallizes slowly. We associate Pluto, the ancient Greek mythical ruler of the underworld, with the term "plutonic." As magma gradually cools, crystals of various minerals form at specific temperature ranges. The minerals that contain metallic elements, including magnesium and iron, form first and sink down to the bottom of the magma pool. As the magma reaches lower temperatures, the less dense and silica-rich minerals, such as quartz and mica, crystalize. Slow cooling times result in larger crystals that we can see without magnification.

The silica-rich minerals form granitic rocks, which are the most common igneous plutonic rocks. Granitic rocks typically contain tightly packed crystals, so they are extremely strong and hard. Many mountain ranges, including the Andes, are underlain by enormous areas of granitic rocks created by large pools of magma that cool into forms known as batholiths, or plutons (Pluto's underworld again). Over millions of years, the vast areas of granitic rocks that developed along the western edge of South America were uplifted and exposed in the Andes Mountains.[2]

Granitic rocks were an important construction material for the ancient Andeans (Figure 2.1). Zones of weakness that develop along thin cracks or fractures, also called joints, are common in granitic rocks. The joints open initially from release of pressure when rock deep underground is uplifted towards the surface and uncovered, as well as from folding and fracturing of the rock. Subsequent exposure to wind and to water that freezes and expands, then thaws, opens the joints further. This process results in "natural quarries" with blocks that are in sizes that are convenient for construction. At Machu Picchu, we can

FIGURE 2.1. Granitic blocks at Machu Picchu. Photograph by author.

see the remains of the granitic quarry that the Inca builders used on the west side of the site, as described in Chapter 19.

Joints and cracks in granitic rocks may also become filled with quartz. When quartz forms under specific geologic conditions, the veins may contain gold. The ancient Andeans revered shiny gold, the color of the sun. From the earliest hunter-gatherers who placed gold jewelry in the burials of important individuals to the sheets of gold covering the walls of Inca temples, gold was a valuable resource in Andean societies. Gold was also the major reason the Spanish conquistadors explored the Andes and subjugated the Incas. It is another reminder of how geology can shape cultures. The same rocks that allowed the Incas to construct sturdy walls capable of withstanding earthquakes and create exquisite gold art objects also led to the destruction of their empire.

Sedimentary Rocks
From exposure to wind and water over time, all types of rocks eventually break apart during weathering and eroded fragments end up in rivers, lakes, and oceans. As these fragments settle and accumulate, increasing weight and

pressure force out water. Some of the dissolved minerals in the water make a cement that binds the fragments together into sandstone, mudstone, and other sedimentary rocks. The skeletons of marine organisms and fragments of coral can collect under shallow seas and solidify into limestones. Some sedimentary rocks originate from other organic materials, such as decaying plant debris from swamps that forms coal. Chemical rocks, such as salt, develop when water evaporates in enclosed coastal basins or lake beds in arid environments.

Over millions of years, mountain-building processes in the Andes pushed sedimentary rocks that had accumulated along the western edge of South America up to high elevations.[3] Along with igneous rocks, the sandstones and limestones found throughout the Central Andes became valuable construction materials for the ancient builders. The ancient Andeans also put both the coal and the salt that are found in sedimentary rocks to good use; today, people in the regions with these natural resources continue to harvest them.

Sedimentary rocks are especially fascinating to me because they can contain fossil shells, bones, and plant remains that provide clues about the environments where the sediments were deposited initially. When we combine this evidence with a small amount of imagination, we can picture the surface of the earth as it existed many millions of years ago.

We find sedimentary rocks with enormous numbers of dinosaur footprints on the Altiplano, the 13,000 ft (3,962 m) high plateau that spans southern Peru and northern Bolivia.[4] One area in Bolivia has so many tracks in random patterns that people refer to it as a "dinosaur dance floor." While hiking among the tall peaks of the Cordillera Blanca in northern Peru, I admired many marine invertebrate fossils that are now exposed at elevations above 14,000 ft (4,267 m). I would love to know what the ancient Andeans thought when they saw gigantic footprints and the shells of creatures that inhabited ocean waters, all now entombed high on mountainsides.

Metamorphic Rocks

Metamorphic rocks form when the minerals in a parent rock experience intense pressure and/or high heat and then recrystallize. Usually this process happens deep underground, but it can also happen close to the ground surface, such as next to the hot magma of an erupting volcano. In the process of recrystallization, calcite-rich limestones can alter into marble and quartz-rich sandstones into quartzite. The ancient Andeans took advantage of the hard and strong

FIGURE 2.2. Limestone blocks at Sacsayhuaman. Photograph by author.

characteristics of quartzite and other solid metamorphic rocks for tools and other uses.

An Abundance of Rock
The wide variety of igneous, sedimentary, and metamorphic rock types found in the Central Andes provided numerous building material choices for the ancient Andeans. These rocks also provided other valuable materials, such as obsidian for tools, and gold and silver for decorative items and offerings to deities.

The ancient builders used rock ranging from volcanic types only a few thousand years old to metamorphic types that are tens and even hundreds of millions of years old, along with sedimentary rock and granites of all ages in between. They often combined several types of rock in a single complex. For example, overlooking Cuzco, the Incas constructed the massive temple complex of Sacsayhuaman with andesite, basalt, and limestone (Figure 2.2). At Tiwanaku, the capital city near Lake Titicaca, builders used andesite, basalt, sandstone, and quartzite.[5]

Rock characteristics played a key role in the monumental constructions built by ancient societies. Qualities such as color and hardness were important, as was access to natural quarries where workers could collect partially shaped blocks. The ancient builders and artisans selected strong rocks that are resistant to weathering from wind and water for their creations—a major reason that we can appreciate impressive archaeological sites today.

Continents and Oceans on the Rocks
For a greater understanding of where various rocks form, we need to look more closely at the composition of our planet. The thin layer of material that covers the earth, known as the crust, occurs in two distinctive types. Oceanic crust underlies about 65 percent of the surface of the earth, lying beneath the nearly three quarters of the earth's surface that is covered by water. Continental crust makes up the other 35 percent, as continental shelves covered by shallow seas and the adjacent land above sea level.[6]

Most of the lands we inhabit on the continents have elevations within 1,000 ft, or about 300 m, above sea level.[7] When we include mountains in the mix, the average elevation of land on the continents is around 2,600 ft, or 792 m, above sea level. We all know that oceans are deep, but how deep are they on average? The answer may surprise you: ocean floors typically lie about 16,000 ft (4,877 m) below sea level. Impressively deep! The dramatic dissimilarity between continent and ocean elevations is related to the rock types found in these two types of crust[8]—and therefore why understanding the differences between igneous, sedimentary, and metamorphic rock is important.

You might suspect that the elevation difference between continents and oceans has something to do with rock density. This is correct. The most widespread rocks found on the continents are light-colored granitic rocks rich in low-density minerals with abundant silica, aluminum, potassium, and sodium. In contrast, the composition of most oceanic crust is basalt and similar volcanic rocks that are dark colored and have large quantities of heavy iron and magnesium, giving these rocks much greater densities than continental rock.[9] The contrast between oceanic crust and continental crust is a key factor in mountain building.

The Central Andes incorporate some of the youngest rocks on our planet. New volcanic rocks are being deposited on the surface in this geologically active environment, and plutonic igneous rocks and metamorphic rocks are forming deep underground. Weathering and erosion of mountains are washing mineral fragments downslope into accumulations that will gradually consolidate into sedimentary rocks. Geologic processes have been building the edge of the South American continent for millions of years, and they continue.

Rocks provide windows into the forces that sculpt our landscapes. In the following chapters, we will look at some of those forces, starting with the structure of the earth and then examining earthquakes, volcanoes, and other natural processes. All of these have created the spectacular Andes Mountains and helped to shape the cultures that amaze and impress us today.

3

Tectonics

Thousands of years ago, the ancient Andeans controlled many aspects of their natural environment. They straightened and redirected river courses to reclaim useable land and supply water to irrigation canals. Along hillslopes, they constructed terraces to carve out level fields for crops, homes, and civic structures. Over time, they learned the construction techniques that allowed them to build the adobe and stone block structures that can stand for millennia.

Throughout the window of time that people have been living in the Central Andes, large earthquakes and explosive volcanoes have been building the mountains. Millions of years before these dramatic events shaped the region, the landscape was flat and close to sea level. Marine creatures flourished in quiet seas and dinosaurs roamed across swamps in river deltas. The rock record preserves traces of these different lowland environments that existed far back in time. When I first visited the Andes Mountains and understood the tremendous changes that have occurred in this diverse landscape, I wanted to learn more about the geologic history.

Why have the Andes experienced so much geologic activity in the recent past? When was this region that is directly next to the Pacific Ocean uplifted to form high mountains? We can find the answers in plate tectonics—a unifying theory that emerged in the 1960s. The term explains the formation of the enormous tectonic plates that are floating about on the outermost layer of our planet. Tectonics can explain Andean landforms, as well as virtually all other global-scale landforms on earth. The boundaries between two plates are converging, diverging, or have a transform motion, in which they slide past one another along faults, such as the San Andreas fault in California. Understanding plate motions and how they build mountain ranges helps to "set the stage" for us to appreciate the natural environment that shaped Andean cultures.

From Core to Crust

We can divide planet Earth into three approximately concentric shells: core, mantle, and crust. The layers of an egg roughly mimic this arrangement: think of its hard shell on the outside, white as the mantle, and yolk as the core. Core and mantle are both composed of extremely hot material, swirling around in various states ranging from liquid to possibly solid in the inner core.

The structure of our planet, with a diameter of around 8,000 mi (12,875 km), is complex.[1] The earth's crust and the uppermost part of the mantle compose the lithosphere, which is broken up into tectonic, or lithospheric, plates. A relatively cold and hard uppermost layer of crust—the ground we walk on—forms tectonic plate surfaces. The plates float on a hot and viscous uppermost layer of mantle called the asthenosphere. Like the flow patterns we can see in a bubbling pot of thick soup, the asthenosphere moves in thermal currents beneath the crust.

The temperature of the earth increases steadily with depth, reaching extremely high temperatures deep in the core. Decay of radioactive elements is primarily responsible for this heat energy. How are tectonic plates affected and why do the plates move? The plates travel because of thermal currents created by the tremendous amount of internal heat escaping outward toward the surface of the earth.[2]

The western margin of South America is especially effective in releasing internal heat energy. The Central Andes contain both the highest density and tallest concentrations of volcanoes on earth.[3] Volcanic eruptions that can darken the sky for months and coat the landscape with thick layers of ash are a part of life in the Andes. And it's all because this region is in a unique position on the western edge of the continent.

Oceans and Continents Converging

Scientists today count seven large tectonic plates and several smaller plates that are traveling about the earth.[4] The boundaries where these plates join are the site of the most spectacular geologic action on earth. Think about this: the rigid tectonic plates enveloping our planet fit tightly together, and they are also constantly moving. Enormous forces are pushing or pulling the plates, so their positions

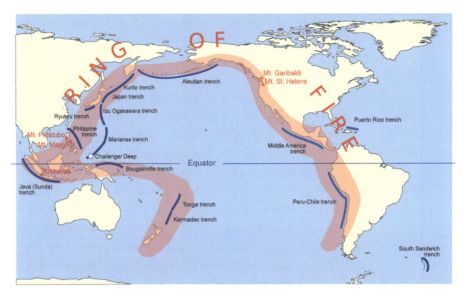

FIGURE 3.1. Map of Pacific Ring of Fire. Map by Gringer, 2009, modified from U.S. Geological Survey/W. Jacquelyne Kious and Robert I. Tilling, *This Dynamic Earth: The Story of Plate Tectonics* (1996).

change at the average rate of as much as a few inches per year (about the same rate of growth as our fingernails). However, like a pair of dancers where each wants to lead the dance and not follow, the plates are traveling in different directions. Wherever plates join, their dissimilar relative movements create concentrated stress that builds in rocks, eventually triggering earthquakes.

An intense band of geologic activity, known as the Pacific Ring of Fire, loops from South America to Alaska, Japan, through the Philippines and on to New Zealand. Wrapping around the edges of the Pacific Ocean are the locations of most of the earth's earthquakes and active volcanoes.[5] This impressive concentration occurs because tectonic plates are colliding all around the Pacific Rim. Specifically, the plates underlying the Pacific Ocean, including the Nazca plate that is next to the western edge of South America, are converging with continental plates along subduction zones (Figure 3.1).

Collisions between oceanic and continental plates destroy oceanic crust and recycle it into the mantle as it sinks, or is subducted, beneath a continental plate. Why does the oceanic crust descend beneath the continental crust and not the opposite? Remember the major difference between the rocks composing oceanic crust and continental crust. The metal-rich oceanic crust is

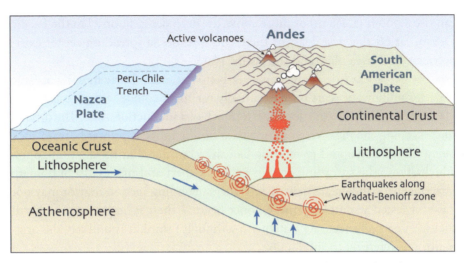

FIGURE 3.2. Schematic of the subduction zone along the Central Andes.

extremely dense and so it sinks beneath the low-density, quartz-rich granitic rocks of continental plates. When two continental plates collide, the crust on both plates buckles upwards, forming exceptionally tall mountains such as in the Himalayas and Tibetan Plateau.[6]

The Andes Mountains are growing in height on the continental South American plate.[7] Located immediately to the west is the oceanic Nazca plate. Earthquakes outline the subduction zone that defines the convergent plate boundary between the two plates.[8] A deep, undersea trench where the descending oceanic plate bends downward and sinks into the mantle, and a line of volcanoes that form on the continental plate above the descending oceanic plate, define subduction zones[9] (Figure 3.2).

Massive Plates on the Move

What specific forces are powerful enough to move the massive tectonic plates? By understanding the inner structure of our planet, we can answer that question. Along extensive lines that encircle the earth, hot magma bubbling up from the mantle reaches the surface and cools to form new oceanic rocks. Rifts, or spreading centers, are the linear features along which these new rocks are created. We find rifts at divergent plate boundaries where two plates are moving apart, typically in the middle of an ocean. When magma oozes out of spreading centers for millions of years, young rocks form exceedingly long ridges that can rise 8,000 ft (2,438 m) or more above the deep ocean floors.[10] In the Pacific Ocean, far off the west coast of the Central Andes, a spreading center exists between the Nazca plate and the Pacific plate.

The new rocks ride along, conveyer-belt-style, on a slowly moving oceanic plate for millions of years until eventually the rocks collide with a continental plate and descend into the deep ocean trench of a subduction zone. The driving force keeping the massive tectonic plates on the move is primarily from rock being drawn down and re-melting beneath continents in subduction zones, which allows the spreading centers to move apart and magma to bubble up into this space and create new rock.[11] The "suctioning" action may or may not have suggested an amusing quote I once heard: "There is no gravity; the Earth sucks." A partially accurate statement, although I think it is unlikely the originator was referring to subduction.

The Dance of the Plates
Like a giant mosaic that slowly morphs into a new scene, oceans on the earth have repeatedly opened and closed, while continents join and then break apart. Supercontinents with colorful names such as Pangaea and Rodinia have assembled, broken apart, and then reformed into different configurations throughout perhaps the past three billion years of earth's history.[12] In the past few decades, scientists have reconstructed the travel paths and locations of ancient continents and oceans using information from plant and animal fossils, and from iron-bearing minerals that record ancient magnetic fields.[13]

For a few hundred million years, the eastern edge of South America joined the western edge of Africa as part of Gondwana, the southern portion of the supercontinent Pangaea. Many assumed that the fit between the two continents was a coincidence until the theory of plate tectonics became accepted. The two continents were separating by around 120 million years ago,[14] when dinosaurs dominated the continents and small mammals hid in the shadows. The split began as a new spreading center developed, and the equatorial section of the Atlantic Ocean opened.[15]

Building Mountains
The process of mountain-building, known as orogeny, happens whenever tectonic plates collide. Around the Pacific Ring of Fire, where slow-motion smash-ups of continental and oceanic plates have been ongoing in repeated episodes of subduction, the crust thickens and mountain chains like the Andes grow.

When giant tectonic plates crash and grind together, one can easily imagine that rocks along the boundaries experience extreme forces of compression and friction. The result is rocks that are essentially squeezed and forced upwards into mountains. Push the edge of a rug and watch wrinkles develop and increase in size. Similar processes of folding and faulting from earthquakes compress and thicken the crust, creating high mountains.

What gives the Andes Mountains such towering heights? There are several "ingredients," most importantly earthquakes and volcanoes, which we will look at in more detail in Chapters 4 and 5. Vast quantities of magma erupt in volcanoes or cool underground in gigantic reservoirs, or batholiths, of granitic rock, and that material thickens the crust above subduction zones. Beneath tall mountain ranges like the Andes, continental crust floating above the hot layer of the asthenosphere can be up to about 45 mi (70 km) or greater in thickness. More commonly the continental crust is 18–25 mi (30–40 km) thick; oceanic crust is relatively thin at only about 3–5 mi (5–8 km) thick.[16]

Thick crust plays a major role in forming two unusual geologic features in the Central Andes: the high and flat Altiplano-Puna plateau that forms the widest part of the entire Andes Mountains chain, and the abrupt bend in the western margin of South America called the Bolivian Orocline. We will examine the geologic history of these structures and how they link to mountain-building processes in Chapter 6.

The process of isostatic uplift, or isostasy, also raises mountain ranges to great heights. During subduction, the plunging oceanic slab pulls the continental plate margin downward. Eventually, deep below the surface, the heavy oceanic rocks in the slab break off and sink downwards into the mantle.[17] This effectively removes a counterweight to the continental crust, which is then buoyed upwards as isostatic uplift commences. The western margin of South America has experienced a significant amount of isostatic uplift, contributing to the towering heights of the Andes peaks.

Another "ingredient" helps to build mountains. New lands have been patched onto the western margin of South America over the past few hundred million years.[18] These crustal pieces have a variety of origins. As tectonic plates move, they can carry large, buoyant blocks of material, such as volcanic islands or fragments of continental blocks, for thousands of miles across an ocean. Segments of oceanic crust that formed as parts of mid-ocean ridges over spreading centers are also commonly moved. When a block of continental crust or a section of hot and relatively light ocean floor collides with the margin of a

FIGURE 3.3. Aconcagua, the tallest mountain in the Americas at 22,838 ft (6,961 m), view of south wall. Photograph by Dmitry A. Mottl, 2020, available under a Creative Commons Attribution-Share Alike 4.0 International License.

continental plate, it is too buoyant to be subducted, so it is plastered or accreted onto the continental plate. These "exotic" accreted terranes have expanded the South American continent westward, essentially forming the expanses of lands inhabited by the ancient Andeans. Scientists have correlated the emplacement times and locations of rich metallic ore deposits in the Peruvian Andes with the subduction of ancient spreading ridges.[19]

Currently, many crustal pieces are floating about the Pacific Ocean that someday may become attached to an adjacent continent as accreted terranes. These include the Hawaiian Islands, part of a vast and mostly undersea mountain chain. Eventually, the islands will weld onto the North American continent after being subducted into the Aleutian Trench along the southern coast of Alaska.

For at least the past 200 million years, the western edge of the South American continent has bordered an oceanic tectonic plate and experienced long intervals of subduction.[20] During this time, abundant volcanic, plutonic, sedimentary, and metamorphic rocks have been produced, numerous crustal fragments riding on the ocean floor have collided with the continent, and ongoing faulting, folding, and mountain uplift has occurred. Earthquakes and volcanoes play a major role in forming the impressive chain of Andes peaks (Figure 3.3). In the next chapters, we will examine these dynamic geologic events in more detail.

4

Earthquakes

Powerful earthquakes have destroyed settlements throughout human history in the Andes Mountains, either by severe shaking or by triggering avalanches, landslides, and tsunamis. The visible effects of these events are widespread in Andean landscapes. The effect on ancient Andean structures is more difficult to distinguish. Archaeologists frequently recognize multiple different ages of construction of ancient architectural monuments in the Central Andes. Were the times of these reconstructions chosen by the builders, or did the structures need to be restored following destruction from earthquakes? In the absence of written records, the answers to these questions are uncertain.

The consequences of large earthquakes can be tragic and catastrophic. Although the historical record of earthquakes in the Central Andes is incomplete, we know that devastation from these events has been a recurring challenge for all who live in this region. How often were towns simply erased from the face of the earth by landslides and avalanches, such as the one that occurred in northern Peru in 1970, described later in this chapter? We will never know.

As a lifelong resident of California, I have experienced many earthquakes. During the shaking, sometimes accompanied by the creaking of a building and the sound of objects crashing to the floor, I always wonder anxiously when it will stop. Earthquake hazard evaluations have been a major part of my career, and I am keenly aware of the destructive power of these events. I often think about earthquakes when I walk below tall office buildings with their hundreds of plate-glass windows. In a large earthquake, glass released from window frames will crash downward to shatter with deadly force. While on holidays in coastal areas around the Pacific Rim, I think about the potential for towering tsunami waves. Great earthquakes and tsunamis are infrequent and perishing in a car accident or being struck down by a fatal disease present far more risk for most of us. Still, the deadly forces of these geologic processes are a genuine threat that will eventually affect the lives of millions of people.

Breaking New Ground
We think of our planet as "rock solid," but it isn't. The tectonic plates enveloping the surface of the earth are essentially floating on hot mantle material, and the plates push and pull against each other continuously. Rocks can change shape, as usually happens under conditions of great pressure and heat that slowly fold and deform rock. Deformation occurs up to a point in hard rock, but after reaching that limit, the built-up stress is violently and instantaneously released in a powerful earthquake. The rock ruptures along a planar fracture, or fault, with rock on one side of the fault displaced with respect to those on the other side. As the stored energy locked in the rock discharges, earthquakes propagate along faults, somewhat like unzipping a zipper or a collapsing line of dominoes.

A tremendous amount of deformational strain is being placed on the western edge of South America today because the oceanic Nazca plate is subducting beneath the continental plate.[1] As the oceanic plate dives downward, it is pulling the leading edge of the continental plate along with it. This enormous strain eventually exceeds the strength of the rocks, which then rupture in an earthquake. Relative to a fixed South American plate, the Nazca plate is moving eastward at a rate of around 3 in (7–8 cm) per year.[2] This makes the Nazca plate among the fastest moving of all the tectonic plates today. Scientists believe that most of this movement is being accommodated by releases of pressure during large earthquakes.[3] The result is that the Andes region is one of the most seismically active areas on earth.[4]

Great Earthquakes—Deep Earthquakes
The Andes Mountains have the dubious distinction of being the location of the most powerful earthquake ever recorded instrumentally. This immense magnitude 9.5 earthquake[5] occurred on May 22, 1960, south of Santiago near the coast of central Chile, and we know it as the Valdivia earthquake after the busy harbor town that was essentially flattened. The stretch of fault that ruptured was roughly 500 mi (800 km) long, and the South American tectonic

plate lurched as much as 78 ft (24 m) towards the west, relative to the underlying Nazca plate.[6]

Great earthquakes—those events having magnitudes greater than 7.5—have occurred repeatedly in the Andes. Written historical records since the 1500s show that dozens of great earthquakes have shaken the Central Andes between northern Peru and northern Chile.[7] Clearly, earthquakes were also a part of life for the ancient Andean people and had an important influence on Andean societies.

Why are subduction zone earthquakes along the Andes Mountains so large? What are some factors that contribute to the widespread destruction that can result from these earthquakes?

In the Pacific Ocean near the coast of South America, the oceanic crust riding along on the Nazca plate begins a downward plunge toward the mantle in a deep offshore trench. Known as the Peru-Chile Trench, this vast feature is the longest trench found in the Pacific Ocean, stretching for approximately 3,660 mi (5,890 km). The trench reaches a maximum depth of about 26,500 ft (8,077 m) below sea level and has an average width of 40 mi (64 km).[8] If it were on land and not hidden by ocean water, this trench would dwarf the majestic Grand Canyon of the Colorado River. The trench parallels the South American coast about 100 mi (160 km) offshore, where it defines the Nazca/South American plate boundary. Earthquakes originate at this trench and increase in frequency eastward towards the continent.[9]

When I first saw a map of the locations of earthquakes along a subduction zone many years ago, it amazed me that the depths of these earthquakes could clearly outline the upper surface of the descending plate. When subducting oceanic crust plunges beneath continental crust at an offshore trench, the cold oceanic lithosphere sinks into the mantle with a low slope. Instrumentally recorded earthquakes in the continental crust delineate the slope of the descending oceanic plate along an inclined plane called a Wadati-Benioff zone, named for the two seismologists who independently discovered them[10] (see Figure 3.2).

Earthquake origin points, called focal depths, can be traced from the Peru-Chile Trench downward along the interface between the Nazca and South American plates as the oceanic crust gradually sinks deep beneath the continent.[11] The earthquakes closest to the trench and coastline are shallow and then become progressively deeper towards the east (Figure 4.1).

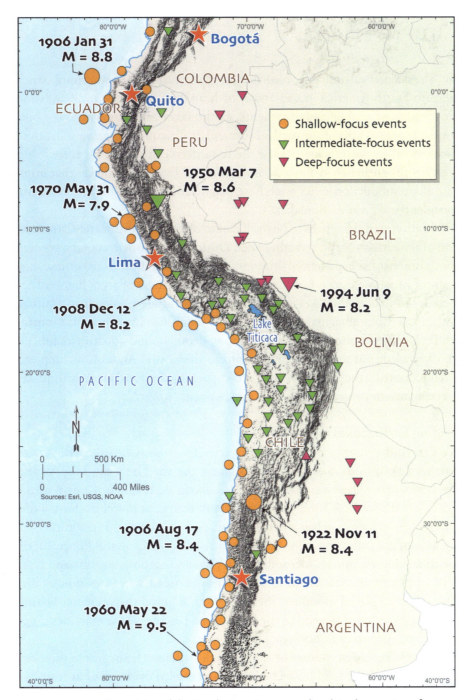

FIGURE 4.1. Seismicity of the South American coastal and Andean regions from 1900–2000. Circles are shallow-focus events, open inverted triangles are intermediate-focus earthquakes, and inverted filled triangles are deep-focus earthquakes. Larger-sized symbols are for events of magnitude (M) greater than 7.8; smaller symbols represent earthquakes in the magnitude range of 7.0–7.7. Modified from Robert L. Kovach, *Early Earthquakes of the Americas* (2004): Figure 2.9.

The deepest earthquakes, recorded far to the east from the offshore trench beneath South America, occur at astonishing depths of about 370 mi (600 km).[12] In most geologic environments, earthquakes originate within the outermost 12 mi (19 km) of the earth's crust and are uncommon below a depth of about 18 mi (29 km). Scientists use the term deep earthquake for events with focal depths greater than about 44 mi (70 km).[13] Deep earthquakes that originate along subduction zones often have magnitudes of 7.5 or higher, so we also consider these great earthquakes.[14]

South America happens to be the location of a disproportionately large fraction of the earth's very deep earthquakes. During the twentieth century, western South America has experienced fifteen intermediate and deep-focus earthquakes, many of which were great earthquakes having magnitudes of 7.5 or higher. They include the great earthquakes in 1994 (Bolivia, magnitude 8.3, depth 400 mi[644 km]), 1970 (Columbia, magnitude 8.1, depth 385 mi[620 km]), and 1922 (northern Peru, location uncertain, magnitude 7.9, depth around 400 mi[644 km]).[15] Our knowledge of the earthquake record in the central Andes is incomplete, but undoubtedly the violent shaking accompanying deep and great earthquakes affected ancient Andean societies, as also happens currently.

Finding Earthquakes in the Andes

We can find evidence of recent fault activity in the Cordillera Blanca of northern Peru in dramatic exposures along the road between Huaraz and the 3,000-year-old archaeological site of Chavín de Huántar. Known as the Cordillera Blanca fault zone, west-facing fault scarps, or low cliffs, form a distinctive line as they march across the landscape for about 75 mi (120 km).[16] On one side of the fault zone are young granitic rocks (Miocene and Pliocene); on the other side are much older sedimentary shales composed of silts and clays deposited from the slow rain of sediment onto an ocean floor (Mesozoic).[17] The fault displaces glacial moraines, the large piles of gravel that were left behind when ice retreated at the end of the Pleistocene Ice Age. These moraines range in age from 11,000 to 14,000 years old (Figure 4.2).

Detailed geologic studies of the Cordillera Blanca fault, where there are exposures along the road near Huaraz, have revealed evidence of at least five and possibly seven surface-faulting earthquakes.[18] Each of these earthquakes displaced the glacial moraines, so we can confidently assume they occurred within the past 14,000 years. Geologic data suggest that roughly 1,500–2,000

FIGURE 4.2. Scarp on the Cordillera Blanca fault east of Huaraz, probably formed in an earthquake that occurred about 2,000 years ago. Photograph by author.

years have elapsed since the last major earthquake. The ground surface appears to have moved vertically by about 6–9 ft (1.8–2.7 m) in each earthquake. These are large breaks in the earth's crust, showing that each event was quite powerful and likely had a magnitude of 7 to 7.5. These earthquakes surely would have affected the ancient Andean inhabitants, and they probably wondered why their earthquake deity was angry. This topic will be discussed more in future chapters, especially in Chapter 17.

38   CHAPTER 4

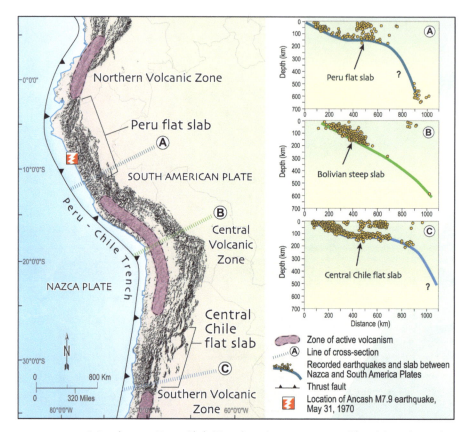

FIGURE 4.3. Map showing Peru-Chile Trench and cross sections of flat slab and steeply dipping subduction zone segments. Modified from Joseph Martinod et al., "Horizontal Subduction Zones, Convergence Velocity and the Building of the Andes" (2010): Figure 2.

The stretch of land encompassing most of modern Peru and northernmost Chile currently has the greatest number of earthquakes, or highest level of seismicity, in all South America.[19] This region includes Cuzco and corresponds with a major portion of the Inca Empire in the late fifteenth century. The reason earthquakes occurred more frequently in the central part of their empire compared to the outlying areas may have puzzled the Incas, but science provides many clues for us today.

Along the subduction zone bordering the western edge of South America, a series of distinct segments display differences in tectonic processes. We can recognize segments by alignments of earthquakes along the plate interface, or slope, where the South America and Nazca plates intersect. These interfaces angle down into the earth with initially steep, around 30°, angles. On shallow sloping or "flat slab" segments, at depths of approximately 95 mi (150 km), the plate interface flattens out to less than 5° and can extend for hundreds of miles beneath the South American continent. In steep slab segments, the slope of the interface is consistently around 25–30°. Most of modern Peru is currently within a zone called the Peruvian flat slab segment (Figure 4.3).[20]

Abrupt transitions can be seen between segments having shallow and more steeply inclined planes. Scientists don't understand why dramatic differences in dip occur between the segments, but the effect on the landscape overlying the different segments is profound.

The frequency of earthquakes is higher above flat slab regions than over adjacent steep slab segments. More frequent earthquakes result in more rugged topography. Scientists studying mega-earthquakes, such as the magnitude 9.6 Valdiva earthquake in Chile in 1960 and the magnitude 9.3 Alaska earthquake in 1964, have found that these large events preferentially occur on flat slab plate interfaces. The cause is likely because of larger expanses of cooler lithosphere that are associated with a shallow interface, and which result in stronger and more homogenous rock that can rupture across a broad area.[21] Not surprisingly, above the shallow-dipping segments of the subduction zone we find the highest mountains in the Americas, including Huascarán in northern Peru and Aconcagua in Argentina.

Along the Andes Mountains, scientists estimate the amount of energy released in earthquakes averages three to five times higher on shallow-dipping segments of the plate, compared to the more steeply dipping segments.[22] Flat slab segments also coincide with volcanic gaps, as volcanic eruptions occur above steeply dipping sections of the subducting plate (described in Chapter 5).

Subduction Zones and Tsunamis

Earthquakes can do much more than violently shake the ground. The large earthquakes that originate along subduction zones also frequently trigger tsunami waves that can travel for thousands of miles across oceans before smashing into locations far from the earthquake origin. An earthquake off the coast of southern Peru in 1868 generated tsunami waves that devastated the populations of coastal

California locations and then rolled across the Pacific Ocean over 7,000 mi (11,265 km) to crash into areas as distant as Japan and New Zealand.[23]

Tsunami waves develop when a large volume of water is displaced. Most occur in the Pacific Ocean, where they frequently originate from subduction zone earthquakes having magnitudes of 7.5 or greater. Along the South American coast, the earthquake record since 1562 shows that a tsunami has accompanied about half of all the great earthquakes. Submarine landslides, volcanic explosions, glacier calving, and other disturbances that displace large amounts of water can also cause tsunamis.

A simple mechanism can create a mound of water that will become a tsunami after a large subduction zone earthquake. Where a slab of seafloor descends into a subduction zone, the leading edge of the overriding continental crust that is being dragged downwards can break free suddenly and spring seaward during an earthquake. This process has the effect of raising the elevation of the seafloor; water then forms a mound above it, since fluids are incompressible.[24] Gravity instantly acts to level the mound of water, in the process setting up an oscillating wave that can travel outward at speeds of 500 mi (805 km) per hour, comparable to commercial jetliners.

In deep water, the distance from crest to crest (or wavelength) in a tsunami can be over 300 mi (483 km), while the wave height above the ocean surface may be only a few feet or lower. For a ship on the open ocean, such a wave may not be noticeable. As the seafloor shallows in an approach to a shoreline, however, the wave speed decreases. Conservation of energy requires the advancing wave front to steepen and so water piles up, creating a towering wave that grows in height until it finally breaks on land. The devastating effects of tsunamis result from both the smashing force of a massive wall of water and the powerful effect of a large volume of water draining back seaward that picks up and carries the debris in its path.

For as long as people have inhabited the coastal regions of the Andes, damaging tsunamis have wreaked havoc on their communities. Within the past century a major tsunami was associated with the enormous 1960 Valdivia earthquake. Waves as high as 80 ft (24 m) pounded the Chilean coast and washed away entire villages. The 2010 Mw 8.8 Maule earthquake[25] also generated a tsunami that battered the coast of Chile. Waves up to 50 ft (15 m) crashed onto the shoreline, with a maximum of 95 ft (29 m) recorded at one locality. Despite the middle-of-the-night timing of the earthquake (local time 3:34 a.m.), many local coastal residents were knowledgeable about tsunami danger and evacuated to higher ground shortly after being roused by the earthquake shaking. Others were not so fortunate. More than one hundred fatalities occurred in coastal campgrounds, where tragically, disoriented visitors died when they were swept out to sea.[26] Although we do not know the timing and extent of the tsunamis that affected the earliest Andeans, we can be confident that they were familiar with the devastating effects.

The incredibly deadly power of tsunamis was demonstrated to the world in the catastrophic subduction zone-generated Sumatra-Andaman earthquake of December 2004. Originating near the northern tip of Sumatra in Indonesia, this magnitude 9.1 earthquake began at a relatively shallow depth of 19 mi (30 km) and ruptured a 1,000-mile-long (1,610 km) section of the boundary between the Indo-Australian and Eurasian tectonic plates.[27] The resulting tsunami overwhelmed coastal communities around the Indian Ocean with wave heights up to 100 ft (30 m). The number of fatalities was staggering, with over 230,000 people perishing. Following this earthquake and tsunami, the potential for similar events worldwide began to be examined much more carefully by scientists assessing geologic hazards.

The May 1970 Disaster in Ancash

One of the worst natural disasters in the Western Hemisphere was associated with a magnitude 7.9 earthquake that shook the Ancash region of northern Peru on May 31, 1970 (location shown in Figure 4.3). Although this earthquake originated about 20 mi (32 km) offshore from the Pacific Coast town of Chimbote, it triggered a massive ice and debris avalanche some 80 mi (130 km) to the east off the slopes of Huascarán, the tallest mountain in Peru (Figure 4.4).[28]

Within seconds after the earthquake shaking began, a debris avalanche broke loose from the sheer west face of the north peak of Huascarán at an elevation of roughly 20,000 ft (6,096 m; Figure 4.5). Preceded by a deafening noise and a blast of turbulent air, a massive amount of ice and rock dropped thousands of feet onto a slick glacier and then raced downslope. The debris flow moved at a speed calculated to range between 175–210 mi (282–338 km) per hour, probably with a cushion of compressed air beneath the material that allowed it to slide with minimal friction.

Devastation was ahead for the valley below. On the floor of the Callejón de Huaylas valley below Huascarán, the avalanche engulfed the villages of

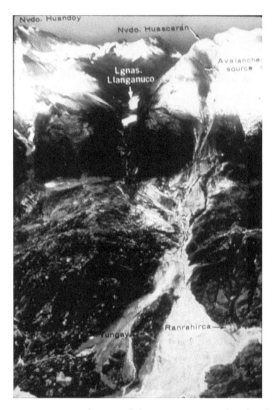

FIGURE 4.4. Aerial view of the Huascarán avalanche that destroyed Yungay, Peru. Photo by George Plafker, National Oceanic and Atmospheric Administration, National Geophysical Data Center, and U.S. Geological Survey, ca. 1970.

Yungay and Ranrahirca.[29] The rubble split into two smaller lobes in Yungay, swept around a hill on which the cemetery was located and buried the town plaza with 16 ft (5 m) of debris. Only the tops of a few palm trees and shattered walls of a cathedral would remain, protruding above the mud. The extremely high velocity of the debris flow hurtled mud, boulders, and blocks of ice high into the air, launching the material as far as a mile across the valley. A deadly rain of thousands of boulders, many weighing several tons, killed and injured people and livestock and literally pulverized adobe homes and vegetation. The blasting force of mud and rocks stripped leaves from vegetation, toppled and crushed trees, and pockmarked agricultural fields with impact craters.

FIGURE 4.5. Huascarán as seen from Yungay. Photograph by ZiaLater, 2018.

And the destruction did not stop there. When the avalanche reached Río Santa near the center of the valley, it blocked the river, and water temporarily backed upstream for a half mile (0.8 km). Below the blockage, Río Santa carried a destructive flood wave of muddy water and debris for 90 mi (145 km) down to the Pacific Ocean. Overflowing the riverbanks, the flood wave caused extensive damage to structures of all types, including roads, bridges, and communication networks. Based on the arrival times clocked in at various locations, the rate of flow was around 22 mi (35 km) per hour. In the town of Huallanca, about 30 mi (48 km) downstream, the river rose to 65 ft (20 m) above its pre-earthquake level for several hours, sweeping away homes and vehicles in its path. Observers of the front of the flow described it as a dark-colored, noisy, turbulent wave choked with blocks of ice. Also carried in that surge of water were hundreds of corpses, many of them deposited along the river edges as the wave raced seaward.

The May 1970 earthquake took a tragic toll. The huge debris avalanche that shook loose from the steep slopes of Huascarán resulted in over 18,000 fatalities, including about 15,000 of the roughly 17,000 inhabitants of Yungay. Estimates of the total number of fatalities associated with this earthquake are as many as 70,000.[30] Although this death toll may have been especially high, similar types of damage have undoubtedly affected Andean inhabitants for millennia.

Contemplating Life, Death, and Earthquake Hazards
Many factors determine the extent of earthquake destruction. We know that damage to rigid buildings is directly associated with earthquake magnitude and proximity to the rupturing fault. Local geologic conditions, including the strength of the underlying soil or rock, and depth to groundwater, may amplify or reduce the propagation of earthquake waves. The length of time that shaking occurs is also significant. In the 1964 Alaskan earthquake, powerful shaking lasted four-and-a-half minutes; in the 2004 Sumatra-Andaman Islands event, an astounding eight to ten minutes of shaking took place.

Earthquake shaking intensity is lowest on strong, hard bedrock and highest in areas underlain by unconsolidated and water-saturated sedimentary units. Structures on soft or partially saturated soils typically perform poorly in earthquakes. This is especially true for unreinforced masonry structures built from brick or adobe and without bracing from steel rebar or other reinforcing materials. During the past century in Peru, earthquakes affecting several cities have destroyed a significant percentage of buildings, including in Chimbote during the May 1970 earthquake.[31] These disasters affected enormous populations.

Many Andeans live in highland communities built on poorly consolidated sediments in mountain valleys that are underlain by relatively shallow water tables. These geologic conditions, combined with buildings constructed of unreinforced adobe or brick, are a set-up for extensive destruction in an earthquake. Sadly, this truth has been tragically demonstrated many times in the Andes and throughout the Pacific Rim. In the May 1970 earthquake that destroyed Yungay, in areas that experienced strong shaking, some 20,000 fatalities can be attributed to the collapse of adobe and masonry structures. Most of the failures were from purely vibratory damage, as this type of construction has little shear resistance to the lateral forces imposed by earthquakes.

Substantial hazards can be associated with landslides and avalanches triggered by earthquakes. Recent great earthquakes in the Central Andes have resulted in thousands, and sometimes tens of thousands, of landslides within the regions experiencing strong shaking. The vast majority involve falls or slides of rock and poorly consolidated soil and rock debris along steep valley walls, stream banks, and road cuts. These slope failures result in extensive loss of life and damage to structures, and they can change river courses and create lakes.

Remarkably, many stone structures constructed by the ancient Andeans have proven to be quite resistant to earthquake shaking and have remained undamaged for centuries. Perhaps the most notable example is the curved Inca wall from the Coricancha in Cuzco, used by the Spanish Dominicans for the foundation of the Church of Santo Domingo. Large earthquakes in both 1650 and 1950 destroyed the colonial church walls but left the strong Inca wall intact, as described in Chapter 1. Machu Picchu, with foundations built on a solid rock ridge of granite, has experienced shaking from many large earthquakes, but the terraces and foundations of the stone block buildings have remained unharmed.

After traveling along the broad valley of the Callejón de Huaylas on one of my trips, with towering snow-covered Huascarán sparkling high above in the bright sunlight, I visited the former town site of Yungay. Many dramatic reminders of the size and extent of the 1970 avalanche and debris flow remained. Most notable were the giant boulders randomly spread across the landscape, many as large as the small dwellings in the region. Optimistic farmers had cleared, plowed, and planted new agricultural fields, and many recently constructed buildings were sprouting up amongst the rocky debris. With a sense of foreboding, knowing that there could be a repeat of the 1970 disaster, I studied the steep and jagged white slopes of Huascarán looming high above the former desolation. The resilience of the Andean people is admirable, but the dynamic landscape they inhabit is certain to wreak future devastation, as surely as it has for thousands of years.

5

Volcanoes

Imagine standing outside your home and seeing steam and volcanic gases rising from the top of a mountain—the ominous first signs that a volcano is stirring to life. Next, the ground might shake beneath you as molten magma rises towards the surface, breaking up rocks along the way. Vast clouds of poisonous gases, surging rivers of molten lava, and ash and fiery rocks propelled into the air become life-threatening menaces. Depending on how far away you are from the eruption, you might observe the drama from a safe distance. But if you are in the wrong place at the wrong time, you will be out of luck.

Few spectacles in nature rival both the sight and the destructive power of an erupting volcano.

I have watched in amazement the fiery lava erupting from volcanoes in Hawaii and Costa Rica. And I've spoken with many volcanologists and heard firsthand stories about their adventures studying active volcanoes. An especially exciting one: A scientist who suddenly found himself jumping from one clump of rock to another as they transformed into "rock islands" moving downhill from hot lava flowing just beneath the surface. Yikes!

Building Volcanoes

Now imagine how the epic spectacle of an exploding volcano must have seemed to the ancient Andeans. The Andes Mountains have one of the largest concentrations of volcanoes on earth. Volcanologists estimate over one hundred volcanoes have been erupting in the past 10,000 years or so, with another one hundred volcanoes considered potentially active because of evidence of unrest, such as earthquake activity or gas discharge.[1] Besides the large number of active volcanoes, the Andes also encompass the tallest volcanoes on land,[2] including the two highest, which stand over 22,000 ft, or about 6,705 m, above sea level. These are Ojos del Salado and Llullaillaco, both active and on the northern border between Argentina and Chile.

Although places where cold oceanic rocks are descending beneath a continent may seem an unlikely location for extensive volcanism, clearly this is not the case. Let's have a look at what causes volcanic activity.

Chains of volcanoes, like the long string found along the 4,000 mi (6,437 km) length of the Andes Mountains, are associated with subduction zones, where dense oceanic crust is plunging below less dense continental crust. These volcanoes occur in a defined band that falls within a predictable series of topographic zones that are associated with subduction.[3]

We begin at the Peru-Chile Trench, about 100 mi (160 km) offshore from the western edge of the South American continent. Here, rocks sink downward toward the mantle where they encounter intense pressure and extremely high temperatures. Some of the rock becomes hot enough to melt and release water vapor, which triggers the melting of the adjacent rock. The molten material and associated water vapor and other gases accumulate in large subsurface reservoirs. Eventually, this hot liquid magma may rise to the surface, as it has a lower density than the surrounding solid rock (see Figure 3.2, which shows a trench and the volcanoes rising above the subduction zone.)

When a subducting oceanic plate sinks to a depth of roughly 60–90 mi (97–145 km) beneath a continent, volcanoes begin to erupt from the pools of magma that have accumulated.[4] A sharp, roiling line of activity, called the volcanic or magmatic front, appears on the ground surface above the magma reservoir. Scientists call the chain of volcanoes that develops a volcanic arc. Arc shapes originate from the shape of our round earth; push your finger into an inflated balloon or a soft snowball and the curve of an arc appears.

In the Central Andes, the volcanic arc begins on land between about 150–185 mi (241–298 km) east of the Peru-Chile Trench.[5] Many of the eruptions in volcanic arcs are violently explosive, ejecting enormous quantities of molten rock and clouds of ash tens of thousands of feet high into the air. The abundant water trapped within the subducted sediments and the high silica content of the magma are major contributors to this high volatility.

Yes, water is a contributor to violent volcanic activity, as it lowers the melting point of the magma (similar to the way that salt lowers the freezing point of water). The water in the magma combines with carbon dioxide to form bubbles that expand rapidly and explosively. We know the greatest amount of accumulated water is directly behind the volcanic front, so this area is where the most violent eruptions occur. As the subducting oceanic slab continues to dive toward the mantle and moves farther away from the volcanic front, volcanic activity decreases. When the slab eventually reaches a depth of about 125–150 mi (193–241 km) below the ground surface, molten material stops forming and volcanism ceases.[6] Quiet returns.

Volcanic eruptions bring devastation, death, and, of course, terror. Today we understand the science of volcanoes. People who live in volcanic regions can usually receive warnings of eruptions in advance. That wasn't the case for ancient Andeans. When a volcano burst into action, decimating communities and lives, people attempted to appease the angry gods they believed were causing these violent disturbances. The Incas built over one hundred shrines on tall mountain peaks,[7] where they left offerings of shells, coca leaves, and even human and animal sacrifices, which are described in Chapter 13. Most of these ceremonial sites are in the southern part of the empire, now in southern Peru, and in Bolivia, Chile, and Argentina.[8] Why are they concentrated in this region? Scientists have discovered a plausible reason.

Volcanic Zones in the Andes

Volcanic activity along the length of the Andes Mountains is occurring in four distinct zones. Named the Northern, Central, Southern, and Austral zones, wide gaps separate the areas with active volcanoes from those with none[9] (Figure 5.1).

The Central Volcanic Zone extends from southern Peru into Bolivia, northern Chile, and Argentina. This region is the same area where mountaineers have found Inca shrines on mountaintops. Many ancient Andean societies inhabited this region, and people were surely familiar with the dramatic releases of volcanic gases and lava erupting from these active volcanoes. While we cannot know for sure why the Incas selected specific peaks for their shrines and sacrifices, the correlation of these sites with this volcanically active zone strikes me as not simply a coincidence.

Within the Central Volcanic Zone are forty-four major and eighteen minor active volcanic centers,[10] all of them within a region approximately 1,200 mi (1,930 km) long and 100 mi (160 km) wide. Presently, the level of activity within

FIGURE 5.1. Map of four volcanic zones along the west coast of South America. Modified from Victor Ramos and A. Aleman, *Tectonic Evolution of South America* (2000): Figure 26.

this zone is low, but since these volcanic centers have been active within the past 10,000 years, scientists consider them capable of erupting in the future.

The tectonic setting of this region, and specifically the geometry of the colliding South American and Nazca plates, controls the distribution of volcanoes. The Central Volcanic Zone overlies a segment of the subducting Nazca plate that is sloping down toward the mantle with an approximately 25–30° dip.[11] To the north is the Peruvian flat slab segment of the subduction zone, where active volcanoes are currently absent. Instead, earthquakes predominate over flat-dipping segments, as described in Chapter 4. Volcanic activity occurred across the region of the modern Peruvian flat slab segment prior to around 10 million years ago, but gradually decreased and ceased by about 2.7 million years ago.[12] The angle of descent of subduction zone segments changes over millions of years; segments that are flatter now may have been steeper in the past and thus volcanically active.

Steep-sided volcanic cones are a characteristic shape for volcanoes throughout the Andes, including the spectacular Misti volcano near Arequipa in southern Peru. The chemical composition of the erupted magma influences the shape of a developing volcano and the type of igneous rock that forms. Andesite, the principal volcanic rock found in the Andes, contains a high percentage of silica, which results in a thick, sludgy lava that cools into the distinctive cone shapes of Andean volcanoes.[13]

Gifts of Glass

At the astonishingly remote elevations of around 14,500 ft (4,420 km), cliffs of volcanic andesite contain alcoves that form ancient rock shelters. This elevation is equivalent to the height of Mount Whitney, the tallest mountain in the United States outside of Alaska. In these rock alcoves, now above the Pucuncho Basin in southern Peru, archaeologists have found some of the most accurately dated and highest altitude Pleistocene settlement sites on earth. Ceilings covered with soot from fires, walls with rock art, and floor sediments with charred plant and animal materials reveal a long history of human occupation. Multiple radiocarbon age dates from the remains show people were using these shelters from as far back as about 12,300 to 11,100 years ago.[14]

What could have been the motivation to occupy such a cold, treeless, and hostile environment? One answer: obsidian. The ancient people who used these rock shelters collected and worked pieces of this shiny glass-like substance

FIGURE 5.2. Volcanic rocks showing areas where gas-filled bubbles formed and obsidian, Panum Dome, California. Photograph by author.

eroding from volcanic rocks on the mountain slopes. Among the artifacts they left behind, the most impressive are hundreds of projectile points, scrapers, and other tools made from obsidian and fine-grained andesite. Numerous bones found along with these objects show the early inhabitants were hunting deer and wild camelids, the ancestors of domesticated llamas and alpacas.[15]

Roaming hunter-gatherers were the earliest people to visit these high mountain shelters. At certain times of the year, howling winds, hail, and snow could batter the landscape, so people visited the camps seasonally, dropping to lower elevations to avoid storms and collect edible plants. Living at such a high elevation throughout the year would require adaptations the earliest visitors had not yet achieved. The annual average temperature in these mountains today is 37°F (2.8°C). It was probably a few degrees cooler 12,000 years ago, so this environment was very cold and damp.

Why was obsidian so important to these ancient people? The answer lies in the properties of this material. Obsidian develops when lava high in silica cools extremely rapidly and forms volcanic glass. Individual atoms "freeze" in place instead of combining with other minerals and forming crystals (Figure 5.2). With no crystals present, the naturally formed glass is hard, brittle, and can produce shell-shaped, or conchoidal, fractures when struck. These properties make this material optimal for precision chipping and also mean that obsidian produces the sharpest edge of all stone artifacts. Today, some surgeons use thin blades of obsidian in scalpels for precise surgery such as in eyes, as these blades have a cutting edge many times sharper than high-quality steel surgical scalpels.

The ancient people prized obsidian and used it primarily for cutting and piercing tools, including knives and scrapers for animal hides. The Andeans also used obsidian for decorative objects and even polished it to create early mirrors.[16] This volcanic rock had an important place in ritual contexts and, over time, gained social and religious significance.

Tracing the Trading of Obsidian
The conditions that create high-quality obsidian are rare; nonetheless, the early Andeans located those few sources within their vast and rugged landscape. They needed superior glass, free of gas bubbles or small crystals, for their tools. The material also needs to be relatively young in age, as the glass becomes unstable over time and loses its favorable fracturing properties, especially in the presence of water. Because of these constraints, high-quality obsidian became an important trade item over long distances in the Andes, perhaps as far back as 12,000 to 11,000 years ago.[17] Obsidian nodules were probably the major trade item, as the edges of sharp tools can fracture during travel.[18]

The ongoing volcanic activity in the southern part of the Central Andes created at least eight sources of obsidian used by the ancient Andeans.[19] Based on trace element composition, distinctive geochemical "fingerprints" allow scientists to match obsidian from archaeological sites to the volcanic source.[20] I find it fascinating to know that researchers can trace shiny shards of obsidian

Volcanoes 53

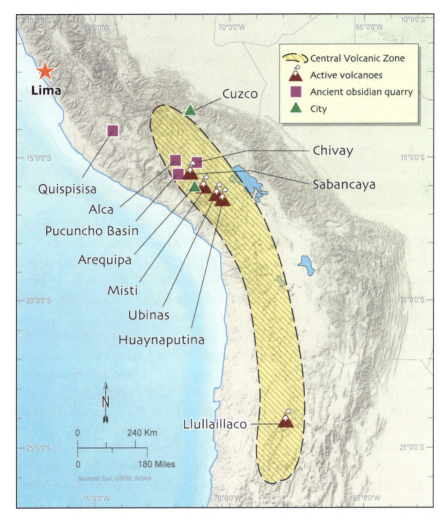

FIGURE 5.3. Map showing ancient obsidian quarries and active volcanoes mentioned in text. Modified from Nicholas Tripcevich and Daniel A. Contreras, "Quarrying Evidence at the Quispisisa Obsidian Source, Ayacucho, Peru" (2011): Figure 1.

across hundreds of miles back to the individual volcanoes where the material originated; it is as if that volcano had autographed each precious piece.

By analyzing the origin locations of hundreds of obsidian fragments, archaeologists have gained valuable information about Andean cultural groups over thousands of years. Specifically, found obsidian types show interactions between different groups within a geographic area, or in contrast, the isolation of a particular group.[21] The Andeans transported high-quality obsidian for hundreds of miles, eventually using llamas as pack animals.

Researchers have traced most obsidian used by the ancient Andeans to three principal sources: the Alca, the Chivay, and the Quispisisa. The earliest visitors who occupied the rock shelters above the Pucuncho Basin worked Alca obsidian. Archaeologists have found Alca obsidian at a site called Quebrada Jaguay on the coast of southern Peru, about 80 mi (130 km) south of the source.[22] Age dates show people were using the Alca obsidian around the same time as the earliest occupation of the rock shelters above the Pucuncho Basin, approximately 12,000 years ago. Since no geologic mechanism could have transported the Alca obsidian to the Quebrada Jaguay site, archaeologists believe the coastal Andeans may have made specific procurement trips or acquired it in exchanges or trades. Alca obsidian has been found at archaeological sites as far away as northern Peru, about 600 mi (965 km) from the source volcano. This obsidian was also the major type used in the Cuzco region[23] (Figure 5.3).

Most of the obsidian artifacts found in northern and central Peru are from the Quispisisa source.[24] Here, as early as 4,000 years ago but possibly much earlier, the Andeans undertook intensive mining efforts to find high-quality obsidian. Laborers excavated dozens of quarry pits, ranging from 30–150 ft (9–46 m) across and up to 10 ft (3 m) deep. Researchers estimate that one particularly large pit originally reached a depth of over 20 ft (6 m). Small nodules and flake debris from the initial stages of trimming form dark carpets of discarded obsidian in rings around the pits—the residue of ancient human labor.

The Chivay source supplied much of the obsidian found today in artifacts at archaeological sites in southern Peru and Bolivia.[25] This source is at a lofty elevation of about 16,000 ft (4,900 m) and was first exploited around 9,400 years ago, after exposure when melting finally removed the remnants of Pleistocene glaciers. Like the natural distribution of obsidian at the Alca site, Chivay obsidian occurs in large nodules up to several inches in diameter; the ancient people could easily collect these pieces from the ground surface.

Researchers have found many Chivay obsidian objects in the Lake Titicaca Basin, about 100 mi (160 km) to the east of this obsidian source. During Hiram Bingham's 1912 investigations of Machu Picchu, his team found small Chivay obsidian nodules buried in a cache near the entrance to the city.[26] Long ago, someone carried these naturally rounded and unworked pebbles for many miles and apparently left them as an offering. Perhaps this individual intended the obsidian nodules as a link between the Machu Picchu estate and the volcanic powers of the Chivay region, far to the south? We will never know.

Fertile Soils

Volcanic eruptions destroy, but they can also provide. The formidable Andean volcanoes helped feed large populations of people and enormous herds of llamas and alpacas. What is the connection between volcanoes and food? In the aftermath of an eruption, volcanic deposits contribute to building fertile soils that support abundant plant growth.[27] Mountain soils are typically thin and rocky, since gravity keeps soil particles and water moving downhill. The frequent volcanic activity in the southern part of the Central Andes continuously improved the soil. In these mountains plant growth has many limitations, including cool temperatures, high winds, and low moisture levels, but the richness of some soils provided beneficial advantages to the ancient farmers and herders.

Volcanic eruptions produce enormous amounts of fresh lava that cool rapidly and harden to form rough, solid rock. After the fire and fury has ceased, rainfall slowly breaks down the rock, vegetation grows, and fertile soils gradually build up. Seeds that are blown into rock cracks and crevices sprout. The growing plants form roots that mechanically break apart the rock, and chemical weathering from the organic acids in decaying vegetation disassembles minerals. Each of these processes contribute to soil formation. The volcanic soils that develop are rich in many key nutrients essential for plant growth. Iron, calcium, magnesium, potassium, phosphorus, sodium, sulfur, silicon, and many other elements help to create a rich mix. Minerals in volcanic soils also contribute to helpful properties, such as high retention rates for water and nutrients.[28]

Fertile soil can develop many miles from an active volcano. Ash clouds that form above an eruption frequently create plumes that extend high into the atmosphere. The ash plume from the May 1980 Mount Saint Helens eruption in Washington State extended to a height of 18 mi (29 km), so we can assume that the eruptions observed by the ancient Andeans produced similarly spectacular plumes. Wind currents will move this ash for long distances and eventually distribute thick layers hundreds and even thousands of miles away.

A deep and dense layer of ash chokes all life in the area where it falls, creating a gray wasteland, but this is temporary. Over time, as rain falls and plants grow, the underlying soil incorporates the fine particles of ash and becomes rich in nutrients, making it productive,[29] like the soils that develop from hardened lava. Regular ash falls can also be beneficial, as they replenish the soil by replacing nutrients. A similar phenomenon happens in floodplains, where rivers deposit sediments that periodically refresh the nutrient stores of soil. Mineral-rich volcanic soils, together with fertilizers from seabirds and domesticated llamas and alpacas, helped to produce crops that could feed expanding Andean populations.

Life in Volcano Country

The largest volcanic eruption in South America in recorded history took place in 1600 CE at Huaynaputina, about 50 mi (80 km) southeast of the modern city of Arequipa in southern Peru.[30]. Huaynaputina, or Waynaputina, means "young volcano" in Quechua, the language of the Incas. The Huaynaputina explosion blanketed a vast region in volcanic ash up to 6 ft (1.8 m) deep, destroying entire villages and causing widespread destruction of settlements and crops. The ash combined with soil and water to create menacing volcanic mud flows called lahars that have the consistency of wet cement. The Huaynaputina lahars flowed downhill as far as 75 mi (120 km) to the Pacific Ocean, engulfing several villages within a broad swath along the route.[31] Winds in the upper atmosphere transported volcanic ash around the earth, contributing to severe climatic cooling that resulted in devastating crop failures worldwide.

The current greatest threat of an eruption in the Andes Mountains may be in an area in the Southern Volcanic Zone, east of the center of Chile and partially overlying the boundary with Argentina. The Laguna del Maule volcanic field contains at least twenty-five separate volcanoes that have erupted within the past 20,000 years. The volcanoes are arranged around a large, icy blue lake in an area almost 200 mi^2 (322 km^2) in size. During the decade beginning in 2007, the ground surface encompassing the lake and the surrounding hills rose ominously at an exceedingly fast rate of almost 8 in (20 cm) per year.[32] Scientists attribute this uplift to a growing body of magma at a relatively shallow depth in the earth's crust. Combined with geophysical imaging of the current magma body and the geologic history of a single gigantic eruption that created the field 765,000 years ago, the extent of the ground elevation growth suggests that a major eruption is likely to occur in the future.[33] Will this happen in ten or one hundred or 1,000 years? No one knows.

FIGURE 5.4. Misti volcano and the city of Arequipa in 2009; the gray urban area is bordered by green agricultural fields. Photograph by NASA Earth Observatory.

Active volcanoes currently are near Arequipa, which has a population of around one million people. Ubinas volcano, about 45 mi (72 km) east of Arequipa, has erupted twenty-three times at low-to-moderate magnitudes in the past 500 years.[34] From April 2006 through September 2007, volcanic explosions at Ubinas ejected boulders of more than a foot in diameter, launching them for distances of over a mile. Sabancaya volcano, about 40 mi (64 km) northwest of Arequipa, has been erupting throughout the past 10,000 years and had increased activity in 1986 that led to an explosive eruption in 1990.[35] Ash associated with both Ubinas and Sabancaya explosions contaminated water supplies and suppressed crop production, causing major disruptions to the lives of people and livestock within a large area around the volcanoes.

Perhaps the most potentially catastrophic volcano is Misti, a spectacular circular cone that soars to more than 19,000 ft (5,791 m) only 10 mi (16 km) from Arequipa's densely populated urban center[36] (Figure 5.4). Vents releasing steam and volcanic gases have been active near the summit of the mountain within the past century. The last major eruption of Misti took place between about 2300 BCE and 2050 BCE. A low-intensity eruption occurred during Inca times, in the mid-1400s. The proximity of Arequipa citizens to Misti lava flows has resulted in city structures constructed on volcanic rocks that formed after an eruption only 2,000 years ago.

When will the next significant eruption of Misti volcano occur? It could be anytime, as scientists estimate that the recurrence period for Misti eruptions during the past 5,000 years has been 500 to 1,500 years, and we are currently within that time window. Whenever Misti stirs to life again, potential is high for widespread devastation to the populations living below.[37]

The ancient Andeans lived with the menace of volcanic eruptions. Yet they also valued precious obsidian and took sustenance from the fertile land created by those eruptions. The double-edged sword relationship between residents of this dynamic region and powerful volcanoes is a hallmark of life in the Andes.

6

Landforms

A bird's-eye view of the landscape prompts many geologists to choose airplane window seats routinely. I'm not an exception, and so the views glued me to my window during a flight over the Andes, heading from Lima northwest to Huaraz above the mountains of northern Peru. After leaving the Pacific coast, we rapidly ascended across an array of steep snow-covered peaks, deep and broad valleys scraped by glaciers, and hundreds of sparkling blue lakes. As the small plane labored to skim over the mountain tops, I could almost ignore the strong air turbulence rocking us in our seats. I was on my way to join a ten-day trekking tour through the Cordillera Blanca, and eagerly expecting the adventures ahead. After arrival in the Huaraz airport, I ended up stranded for several hours, waiting for a ride into the city. And during those hours I felt absolutely content to relax and simply breathe the thin air, while I soaked up the views of majestic Huascarán soaring above the region, slopes blanketed with snow sparkling in the bright sunlight.

The Andes Mountains can be divided into a series of mountain ranges separated by deep valleys and high plateaus. In the Central Andes, we recognize two major ranges, the Western Cordillera and the Eastern Cordillera. Between the two major mountain ranges in the south is the Altiplano-Puna plateau, a unique high elevation region of vast flat expanses and low rolling hills extending from southern Peru into Bolivia and Chile (Figures 6.1 and 6.2).

The geologic processes that uplifted and shaped the Central Andes over tens of millions of years set the stage for the Indigenous cultures to flourish. Cold temperatures, erratic weather patterns, earthquakes and volcanoes, and many other challenges had to be faced by the early Andeans. The environment also

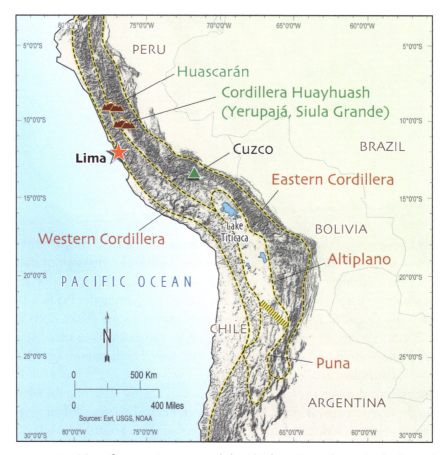

FIGURE 6.1. Map of mountain ranges and the Altiplano-Puna plateau in the Central Andes. Approximate boundary between the Altiplano and Puna sections is indicated by the crosshatch symbol. Modified from Onno Oncken at al., "Deformation of the Central Andean Upper Plate System—Facts, Fiction, and Constraints for Plateau Models," (2006): Figure 1.1.

had advantages. A variety of foods are available, from the rich marine resources of the Pacific Ocean to the fertile river valleys where many types of plants can grow. On the high plateau, vast grasslands provide pasturage for grazing animals and abundant lake resources offer useful aquatic plants, fish, and edible waterfowl. The rocks of the region hide extensive deposits of valuable metals. These rich natural resources provided the foundation for complex cultures to develop.

FIGURE 6.2. Alpacas grazing near Ausangate southeast of Cuzco, Peru. Photograph by Marturius, 2008, available under a Creative Commons Attribution-Share Alike 3.0 Unported License.

Majestic Mountains

A series of high and snow-covered mountain ranges compose the Eastern Cordillera in the Central Andes.[1] On the north, the Cordillera Blanca is a major range, named "white mountains" in Spanish. This towering mountain chain extends for about 125 mi (200 km) along a northwesterly trend and is one of the most extensive of the ice-covered tropical mountain ranges on earth.[2] On the eastern slopes of the Cordillera Blanca, to the east of the modern city of Huaraz, the Chavín culture developed and rose to prominence 3,000 years ago, as described in Chapter 17.

Summit elevations in the Cordillera Blanca are well above the mean elevation of most other ranges within the Andes Mountains. Numerous peaks rise upwards of 10,000 ft (3,048 m) above the surrounding valleys. The imposing Huascarán soars to a height of 22,205 ft (6,768 m). Other spectacular tall peaks include Alpamayo at 19,511 ft (5,947 m), a steep (60°) ice-covered pyramid that was chosen as the world's most beautiful mountain in an international survey of mountaineers and photographers conducted in 1966.

A southern extension of the Cordillera Blanca, known as the Cordillera Huayhuash, is a compact and distinctive cluster of lofty peaks about 18 mi (29 km) in length. This mountain range includes Yerupajá, the second highest peak in Peru at 21,709 ft (6,617 m). The peaks within these two ranges straddle the crest of the Andes and define the drainage divide between the headwaters of the Amazon River that flow eastward to the Atlantic Ocean and the rivers that drain west to the Pacific Ocean. Both Huascarán National Park in the Cordillera Blanca and the Huayhuash regions are renowned for trekking and mountaineering. The latter is the location of Siula Grande, made famous by the 1985 near-death experience of climber Joe Simpson and Simpson's autobiographical book and film *Touching the Void*.[3]

Within the Western Cordillera is the Cordillera Negra. This range has no glaciers or snowfields, hence the Spanish name, "black mountains." The western side is steep and rugged, while the eastern topography is gentler and more subdued. Valleys are V-shaped, indicating downcutting by streams and not glaciers (which typically carve U-shaped valleys), although near the crest of the range evidence can be seen of glacial action in the distant past. The Callejón de Huaylas, a fertile river valley holding Río Santa, separates the Cordillera Blanca and the Cordillera Negra.

Rocks underlying these mountains record a history of repeated episodes of colliding tectonic plates and subduction over hundreds of millions of years. The oldest and most widely distributed sedimentary rocks formed beginning about 200 million years ago when an ocean covered the region.[4] Sediments eroded from the continent washed into an ancient sea, and as sea level rose and fell over time, thick layers of sediment accumulated. Tens of millions of years later, folding and faulting uplifted these sedimentary layers into mountains.[5]

A major period of volcanic activity began about 60 million years ago[6] (early Paleogene), a few million years after the demise of the dinosaurs. Massive volcanic eruptions produced lava and pyroclastic flows that buried the older sedimentary rocks. Deep underground, large magma pools formed and then cooled, creating granitic batholiths that were eventually uplifted to underlie the Cordillera Blanca and Cordillera Negra. Another period of major volcanism and the cooling of large granitic batholiths began about 15 to 10 million years ago.[7] As the mountains rose, folded sedimentary and granitic rocks became exposed at the surface and volcanoes erupted.[8]

The climate worldwide changed dramatically beginning about 2.5 million years ago, during the Pleistocene glaciation period of the Quaternary. Glaciers carved the jagged high peaks and bulldozed broad U-shaped valleys in the Cordillera Blanca. The Callejón de Huaylas, between the Cordillera Negra and the Cordillera Blanca, filled with a thick blanket of poorly consolidated sediments, shed from the steep mountain slopes in landslides, debris flows, and ice-rock avalanches.

Why does the Cordillera Blanca contain so many tall peaks? Immense quantities of volcanic and granitic rocks thickened the South American plate margin during tens of millions of years of subduction. Compressive forces folded and faulted these relatively warm and weakened rocks. The thick continental crust is being buoyed upwards through the process of isostatic uplift (described in Chapter 3). The combination of all these powerful processes builds mountain ranges.

A High and Cold Plateau

In the southern part of the Central Andes, between the mountains composing the Western Cordillera and Eastern Cordillera, is the high and wide Altiplano-Puna plateau. Extending for roughly 500 mi (805 km) from southern Peru, through Bolivia and into northern Chile and Argentina, it is the largest and highest plateau found in the Andes Mountains. At an average elevation of close to 13,000 ft (3,962 m), the Altiplano-Puna plateau is the second highest plateau on earth, behind only the Tibetan Plateau, which has an average elevation of 16,000 ft (4,877 m).

The Altiplano-Puna plateau forms the widest part of the 4,000 mi long (6,437 km) Andes Mountains and ranges from about 200–250 mi (322–402 km) in width. Exceedingly tall mountains rising to 20,000 ft (6,096 m) and higher border the plateau on the west and east. Rivers originating in these mountains drain into the plateau interior. These rivers once created vast lakes that covered large sections of this region within the past few million years. Today, Lake Titicaca, the largest lake in South America, is a remnant of one of those ancient water expanses.

I have seen many enormous lakes in my lifetime. Nonetheless, I was astonished when I first saw Lake Titicaca. The blue water seems to stretch into infinity and merge with the distant sky. The sight is breathtaking, both literally and figuratively, given the high elevation on the plateau and the expanse of water that appears to be as endless as an ocean.

Fifteen hundred years ago, the magnificent city of Tiwanaku grew near the southern shores of Lake Titicaca. The Tiwanaku culture built monumental architecture, crafted fine textiles and objects of gold and silver, and developed highly productive agricultural methods that produced food for tens of thousands of people, described in Chapter 18. Despite the challenges of their environment, the impact of this culture spread and influenced an extensive region of the Andes.

The rich cultural history of the Tiwanaku civilization is a match for the complicated geology of the region. The two distinctive segments of the Altiplano-Puna plateau have different elevations and geologic histories.[9] On the north, the Altiplano segment has an average height of around 12,500 ft (3,810 m) and is mostly flat. The Puna plateau to the south is much higher, with an average elevation of about 14,500 ft (4,420 m) and more gently rolling terrain than the Altiplano segment.

Unusual Landforms

In all the tens of thousands of miles around the earth where oceanic plates are being subducted beneath continental plates, two topographic features in the Central Andes stand out as highly unusual. These distinctive landforms are the high and wide Altiplano-Puna plateau and a prominent bend in the high peaks of the Andes, paralleling a similar bend along the western coastline of the South American continent. The close geographic proximity of the two unusual landforms suggests a common geologic history. We can take a deeper look to better understand how these landforms developed and came to foster the growth of ancient Andean civilizations.

A glance at a map of the South American continent clearly shows a bending and widening of the Central Andes mountain chain with the coastline pushed sharply to the east. This seaward concave bend in an actively subducting plate margin is one of only a few found on our planet.[10] It looks as if some powerful force on the east shoved the northern part of the mountain chain so that it curves toward the northwest, interrupting the generally north–south mountain trend. And that is basically what happened. Geologists call this type of bend in a mountain chain an orocline and name the Central Andes feature the "Bolivian Orocline." The abrupt turn in the coastline is called the Arica Bend or Arica Elbow (Figure 6.3).

Landforms 65

FIGURE 6.3. Topography of Bolivian Orocline, Arica Bend, and Altiplano-Puna plateau with Lake Titicaca (center of image) showing at the northern end. Digital elevation model by NASA, 2005.

Rocks of the high mountain ranges bordering the western side of the Altiplano-Puna plateau have a different geologic history than the rocks in the mountains on the eastern side.[11] In much of the Western Cordillera, volcanic rock younger than a few million years old obscures older geologic units. In contrast, the Eastern Cordillera has exposed outcrops of thick sequences of much older folded and faulted sedimentary rock. The youngest are sandstone and shale originating from sediments deposited in lakes, deltas, and nearshore marine environments. Scientists have found thousands of dinosaur footprints in these rocks, with some tracks in groups that suggest animals moved together in packs.[12] Along with marine fossil assemblages that are exposed in the high mountains today, the footprints show this eastern region was at sea level until around 66 million years ago, when dinosaurs became extinct at the close of the Cretaceous period.[13]

The unique landforms of the Central Andes prompt questions about their origin. Given the extensive length of the South American continent, why is there a high plateau for only about 500 miles (805 km) and only in the central area of the Andes? Researchers have found that the Altiplano-Puna plateau developed within the past few tens of millions of years.[14] Since active subduction along the western margin of South America has occurred for hundreds of millions of years, why did the plateau grow in height only relatively recently? What forces acted on the mountains surrounding the plateau and the continental coastline to dramatically change the trend of the peaks and form the Bolivian Orocline?

Geoscientists have reasonable explanations to answer these questions. From study areas ranging from as small as tens of square miles to as large as thousands, researchers are developing datasets that reveal the deep architecture and geologic history of the Central Andes.

Thick Crust and Drifting Plates
Most scientists agree that multiple phases of uplift began building the Altiplano-Puna Plateau within the past 45 to 30 million years.[15] They also accept that only within the past 10 million years did the plateau reach most of the 13,000 ft (4,000 m) high topography.[16] Paleo-elevation histories are based on detailed geologic studies of the sedimentary rocks in the region. These include identifying the place of origin, or provenance, of specific rock minerals, and analyzing plant pollen and other data that can show the temperature decreases that accompany elevation increases as mountains rise.

The anomalously thick crust beneath the ground surface is a major contributor to the unusually high elevations of the plateau and the bordering mountain ranges. Typical continental crust is about 20 mi (32 km) thick. The crust beneath the Puna segment is around 25–43 miles (40–70 km) thick; the central and eastern Altiplano is as much as 50 mi (80 km) thick.[17] There are multiple explanations for the origin of the extreme crustal thicknesses beneath the plateau, as well as for the differences in topography and elevation between the Altiplano and Puna segments. Most scientists favor a combination of contributing processes.

A few tens of millions of years ago, an episode of compression affected this region. These compressive forces squeezed the crust upwards and thickened it vertically beneath the high plateau, causing the extremely thick crust to develop. Picture, once again, pushing the edge of a rug and watching the wrinkles increase in height. In the Central Andes, the greatest amount of thickening occurred in the Altiplano segment of the high plateau. In the Puna section, tectonic shortening and thickening started later and was less intense, roughly half the amount estimated for the Altiplano segment.[18] As you might expect, the compression that results in thick continental crust also makes it hot, weak, and more susceptible to shortening. And shortening is still active and continuing today.[19]

Magma rose above the subduction zone, causing volcanic eruptions on the surface and emplacement of batholiths deep underground, and that process thickened the crust. About 10 million years ago, a violent interval of volcanism resulted in vast expanses of volcanic rocks deposited over the central section of the Altiplano-Puna Plateau. Following this episode, rocks record additional distinct pulses of volcanic activity every 2 million years until about 4 million years ago, with a decrease in activity since that time.[20] Scientists recognize the volcanic rocks produced as silicic ignimbrites, which originate from extremely explosive eruptions. The heat from such eruptions weakens the crust, making it more susceptible to deformation, including crustal shortening.

Researchers believe that an increase in the westward drift rate of the South American plate had an important role in the crustal shortening of the Central Andes.[21] Roughly 30 million years ago, far to the east in the Atlantic Ocean, the Mid-Atlantic Ridge raised the output of new magma. Why this happened is a mystery, but the impacts are clear. The rate of westward movement of South America increased, and this extra "push" on the plate increased the compressive forces along the subduction zone between the continental and oceanic plates. A boost in folding and faulting—which builds mountains—resulted. Around this same time, mountain-building was enhanced from other changes in the subduction zone, including a shallower angle of the dipping oceanic slab[22] and an older age of the oceanic crust being subducted.[23]

Climate also contributed. In the arid regional climate of the Central Andes, a much smaller amount of sediment washes down into the offshore subduction zone trench, relative to other segments of the Peru-Chile Trench. Sand and silt along the oceanic-continental plate interface essentially lubricate this contact. When sediment input is reduced, the frictional strength of the coupling increases between the two plates. The higher friction effectively harnesses the forces that create higher earthquake magnitudes, accompanied by larger surface displacements and associated folding, shortening, and uplift of the continental plate margin.[24]

In a region with ongoing active subduction, the parameters that can trigger the formation of a high plateau and bend a mountain range are extremely specific and have only rarely persisted during earth history. And these confluent forces happened to occur only in the Central Andes and within the past few tens of millions of years.[25] Multiple processes have contributed to crustal shortening in the high plateau and Bolivian Orocline regions,[26] including the strength and age of rock units, the movement of molten material deep underground, the arid climate, the westward drift rate of South America, and the rock age and dip angle of the oceanic slab subducting beneath the continent.[27]

Configuring the Continent
The action-packed geologic history of the Central Andes isn't focused only on the uplift of the Altiplano-Puna plateau. The curved and concave seaward edge of the continent was being shaped into its current configuration around the same time the plateau was forming. And once again, rocks play a major role in this drama.

We can see on maps of the Andes that the central section of this otherwise north-to-south trending mountain range is rotated to form the Bolivian Orocline. A variety of data show that in the curve region, a suite of faults displaced the upper crust beginning around 35 million years ago.[28] Near modern southern Peru and northern Bolivia, faulting resulted in a counterclockwise rotation to the north of the Arica Bend, and south of the bend a clockwise rotation in southern Bolivia, Chile, and Argentina.[29] Rocks younger than 25 million years do not show evidence of rotations, indicating the bending that forms the Bolivian Orocline essentially stopped 25 million years ago.

What do we know about what was happening on the geologic stage in this region around 35 to 25 million years ago? The westward drift of the South American plate acclerated—the same velocity growth described above that increased the rate of subduction.[30] The result: this confluence of forces pushed the mountains of the Central Andes to the west. The shortening rate along the mountain chain to the south was lower, which had the effect of bending the plate boundary, leading to the development of the Bolivian Orocline.

The thick crust in the high plateau region was warm and relatively soft around the time that the orocline formed. In contrast, a portion of the ancient and tectonically stable South American plate interior, called the Brazilian shield or Amazonian craton, consists of extremely old, cold, and stiff rock. The acceleration in the westward drift of the South American plate shoved the cold and stiff rock from the continent's interior into the warm and soft rock of the Central Andes, contributing to the indent developed around the continental rocks that form the Bolivian Orocline.[31]

As Albert Einstein reportedly said: "nothing happens until something moves." And the movements of tectonic plates shape mountain ranges and continents. Marvelous!

The Next Act—Explorers Arriving on the Scene
Now that we have seen how the high mountains and plateau of the Central Andes came into existence, we have set the stage to examine the human cultures that occupied this dynamic landscape. How the earliest explorers lived when they first reached South America, and the many skills developed by subsequent societies that allowed them to flourish in this environment, are the subjects of chapters in Part Two.

Part II

Culture Comes to the Andes

7

Migrations

The story of when and how the first people reached South America has many twists and turns. Traveling from Eurasia, the earliest migrants initially explored North America. As the small bands of hunter-gatherers moved southward, they left few traces on the landscape. Over the millennia, geologic processes and rising sea levels from climate change have erased evidence of cooking fire rings, dwelling sites, and artifacts that might have been preserved. Nonetheless, the puzzle pieces of the migration story are falling into place as archaeologists, geologists, and other researchers make fascinating new discoveries.

Thousands of years ago, the first people to reach the Central Andes initially lived along the Pacific Coast, where they harvested the bounty of both sea and land. Over time, adventurers harvesting resources seasonally ventured into ever higher mountain environments. They eventually established permanent settlements in the thin air of the highlands.

Cold and erratic weather patterns make it difficult to carve out a lifestyle in high mountains. People needed to make many adaptations to adjust to limited resources, such as fuel for fires, and to have adequate protection against freezing temperatures. While camping in the high Andes, I have had opportunities to ponder the heartiness of the earliest Andeans in their animal-skin garb. Despite my silk long underwear, fleece pants, down jacket, wool hat and socks, and leather boots, I shivered frequently during frosty mornings and evenings. These mountains are not a simple place to live.

Mega-Ice Sheets and Miles of Land Bridges

About 2.6 million years ago at the beginning of the Pleistocene Epoch, global climates began to cool, resulting in a large volume of ice that periodically covered large portions of North America, Europe, and Asia.[1] Snow and ice also blanketed the high Andes Mountains. The major continental plates were in essentially the same position as at present, but the earth looked quite different. Continental ice sheets many thousands of feet thick covered tens of thousands of square miles, along with widespread smaller glaciers at high elevations, and extended over much of the northern hemisphere, as well as parts of the southern hemisphere. Scientists recognize multiple glacial advances and retreats during this epoch, corresponding with cyclical climatic variations. The final glacial period finished about 11,700 years ago, marking the end of the Pleistocene. The warmer climate that followed, known as the Holocene, continues into the present.

The large expanses of ice trapped tremendous amounts of water during the coldest periods of the Pleistocene. Sea level fell dramatically, sinking 300 ft (90 m) or more.[2] This drop exposed extensive areas of continental shelf in some regions, creating bridges between land masses previously separated by water. During the time these land bridges existed, they created important migration routes for people and the herds of grazing animals they were hunting.

The Bering Strait, a 50 mi (80 km) stretch of land between the northwestern edge of North America and the Asian continent, has a seawater cover today that extends to depths of about 150 ft (53 m).[3] During the Pleistocene as sea level rose and fell, this region was alternately inundated by a shallow seaway and then exposed as a land bridge, known as Beringia. From reconstructions of Pleistocene sea-level history, scientists know the Beringia land bridge was most recently exposed from about 30,000 to 11,000 years ago.[4] While it existed, the bridge provided an important migration route. With the onset of the warmer climate of the Holocene, sea level rose again, the land bridge flooded, and the area reestablished as watery straits.

Although it might be difficult to picture today, vast ice sheets covered much of the North American continent near the end of the Pleistocene. The Cordilleran and Laurentide ice sheets stretched continuously across the width of Canada and a large area of the northern United States[5] during the last glacial maximum period ending about 19,000 years ago. Devoid of any vegetation and interrupted by deep cracks, this expanse of ice created an effective barrier to any humans or animals attempting to cross.

As the climate gradually warmed, the ice retreated. This transition occurred first along the Pacific Coast, where glaciers that extended into the ocean melted and withdrew eastward towards the mountains. Later, an ice-free corridor opened along the east side of the north-south trending Rocky Mountains. The warming of the climate and retreat of glacial ice set the stage for human migrations into the Americas.

The First Americans

Who were the first Americans? Multiple lines of evidence show that people migrated from Asia into the Americas at least 15,000 and possibly as early as 21,000 or more years ago. In recent decades, archaeologists have uncovered evidence that the earliest southward migrations from Siberia took place when Asian explorers in small boats skirted the Pacific Coast.[6] Beginning roughly 17,000 years ago, melting glaciers along this coastline opened a convenient marine route for migration, while ice continued to block overland routes.

The Kelp Highway is the name used for the marine route. This name recognizes the vast and productive kelp forests that extended almost continuously from modern Alaska to Baja California, and then sporadically through Central America and south along the coast of the Central Andes. Home to numerous fish, shellfish, and marine mammals, the kelp beds could provide ample and dependable resources for the people traveling south. These earliest explorers would have relied primarily on the bounty of the sea, essentially making a living as marine hunter-gatherers, while also foraging for food on land.[7]

Until a few decades ago, a widely accepted migration theory held that northeastern Siberian people used only the Beringia land bridge to travel on foot into what is now Alaska before heading south into the Americas. Moving southward and following herds of animals as they traveled overland, they fanned out into the vast woodlands, grasslands, and forests of the Americas.[8] These people shaped distinctive stone tools known as Clovis projectile points, and researchers recognize many Clovis-age archaeological sites throughout North America, with a few found along the Pacific Coast into South America.[9] The sites date to roughly 13,000 years ago, and possibly a few centuries earlier.[10]

As scientists examined more archaeological sites and developed better dating methods, however, the puzzle pieces of this "Clovis-first" model gradually fell apart. Foremost among the new findings: accurately dated occupation sites

FIGURE 7.1. Map of the oldest archaeological sites mentioned in text.

several thousand years older than the Clovis sites. And some of these extremely old settlement sites are near the southern tip of the South America continent.

Researchers have found evidence for early migrations most convincingly at the Monte Verde archaeological site in southern Chile, which contains a treasure trove of remarkably well-preserved ancient artifacts.[11] Recovered artifacts included wooden corner posts that supported huts, scraps of animal hides used for clothing and bedding, many wood and stone tools, and hearths with scattered berries and seeds.

Fortuitously, a swampy bog developed over this ancient settlement site shortly after abandonment by the inhabitants, and the anaerobic conditions inhibited organic matter decay, creating optimal preservation conditions. Multiple lines of evidence show occupation by hunter-gatherer people at least 18,500 to 14,500 years ago, and possibly even earlier[12] (Figure 7.1).

The first archaeological excavations at Monte Verde began in 1977 under the direction of anthropologist Tom Dillehay. When radiocarbon age dating indicated the great antiquity of the site, many archaeologists and anthropologists reacted with disbelief and outrage. Surely, they argued, the Clovis culture that is securely and consistently dated at numerous sites represented the earliest migrations into the Americans.[13] And surely, the early dates from Monte Verde must be erroneous. Forty years, and multiple age-dating analyses later, the great antiquity of the Monte Verde site is confirmed.[14] Clovis culture people appeared on the scene relatively late in the migration story.

The lifestyles of the hunter-gatherers who inhabited the Monte Verde site have been pieced together from the artifacts they left behind. Solid evidence shows that these hunter-gatherers roamed across a wide range of environments, collecting food from the coast into the mountains and trading with other people living in the region. Most notably, ample evidence supports their extensive knowledge of marine resources, including the remains of nine species of seaweed found at the archaeological site.[15] In an amazing case of detective work, researchers discovered that certain species of seaweed and other edible plants appear to have been harvested throughout different seasons. Based on this finding, archaeologists suggest year-round occupation of the settlement, which is unusual for a hunter-gatherer society. The Monte Verde region must have been a comfortable place to live.

Along the Pacific coast of North and South America archaeologists continue to search for more evidence of early migrations on the Kelp Highway. They have found pre-Clovis occupation sites from Vancouver Island in Canada to northern California, offshore from southern California in the Channel Islands, in Baja California, and coastal Peru and Chile. Many more sites have surely disappeared because of sea level rise when glaciers and ice fields melted at the end of the Pleistocene.[16] Landscape changes from tsunamis, earthquakes, and coastal erosion have also obscured ancient habitation sites.

As to the question of the first Americans and their time of arrival, the Monte Verde site shows people were in South America by at least 14,500 years ago and probably much earlier. In a supporting line of evidence, studies of genetic data from ancient skeletons suggest that the ancestors of Native Americans diverged from Siberian populations roughly 25,000 to 18,000 years ago.[17]

New discoveries at archaeological sites are also producing extremely ancient age ranges. Archaeologists have found indications of small groups using stone tools at campsites or quarries in central Brazil, with possible ages of 20,000 years ago or even older.[18] A remarkable series of human footprints carefully dated to between 23,000 and 21,000 years ago were discovered in what was formerly soft mud near the ancient shoreline of a now-dry lake in White Sands National Park in southern New Mexico.[19] Three independent age-dating techniques of the stratigraphic layers containing the footprints all produced similar results, with two based on plant material (radiocarbon dating of ditch grass [*Ruppia cirrhosa*] seeds and also of fir, spruce, and pine pollen) and a third on optically stimulated luminescence data (an age-dating technique that shows the last time quartz grains were exposed to sunlight),[20] powerfully supporting the extremely ancient age of the footprints.

Assuming archaeologists find additional sites with evidence consistent with the 23,000-to-21,000-year age range of the human footprints at White Sands, these data will indicate that the first Americans arrived thousands of years earlier than current estimates. Fascinating!

Although controversy still rages, and questions about details remain, multiple lines of evidence indicate that groups of people migrated from Asia into the Americas possibly as early as 23,000 or more years ago. New archaeological discoveries and fiery debate will probably continue for many more years.

Moving into the Mountains
Throughout human history, fundamental needs for food and security have encouraged people to migrate to gain access to new opportunities. For ancient

societies in the Andes, the search for new lands to colonize and exploit became important as populations grew, as trade developed in valuable natural resources such as gold and obsidian, and as increased social complexity promoted the establishment of collective identities and group boundaries.

Dozens of fertile river valleys suitable for agricultural production were available along the narrow and arid coastline of the Central Andes.[21] Once people settled in these lands and populations grew, some seeking more space began migrating eastward and upwards into the highlands. There, they could find improved conditions for growing crops during milder climatic periods. Moving into the highlands also became more attractive when either droughts or floods plagued lower-elevation lands.

The ancient Andeans likely ventured into the highlands within a few thousand years of the first migrations to the region. Late Pleistocene archaeological sites in the high Andes are rare, however, the roughly 12,000-year-old rock alcove sites used by obsidian hunters above the Pucuncho Basin[22] (described in Chapter 5) clearly indicate that people were exploring these areas soon after arrival in South America. The many lowland river valleys draining into the Pacific Ocean provided convenient travel routes into higher elevations.[23] Exploring ever farther, the ancient hunter-gatherers initially sought plants, animals, and mineral resources seasonally. As these early adventurers learned to cope with the environmental challenges of the high mountains, they established permanent settlements.

Adaptations were necessary. Environments above about 8,000 ft (2,438 m) in elevation are challenging for all forms of life. With increasing altitude, oxygen concentration decreases. Low oxygen availability, or anoxia, makes rest as well as work more strenuous and energy-demanding due to increased respiratory and circulatory requirements. Limited oxygen also produces a strong negative stress on reproduction for plants and animals, including people. Scientists recognize physiological changes, including enlarged lung volumes and blood modifications, as characteristics that allow highland populations to flourish.[24]

Living and working in a treeless landscape above 10,000 ft (3,048 m) is particularly difficult. Oxygen decreases to only about 60 to 70 percent relative to sea level conditions and physiological adaptations such as larger lungs have developed in highlanders over many generations.[25] Cold air also requires additional energy input to maintain metabolic rates. The area surrounding the Pucuncho Basin rock shelters—where people were collecting obsidian 12,000 years ago— was probably a few degrees cooler than the annual mean temperature of 37°F (2.8°C) recorded today. Very chilly—especially when mountain breezes (or gale-force winds) are blowing.

Another notable archaeological site, also dating back to about 12,000 years ago, is Guitarrero Cave. At an elevation of 8,465 ft (2,580 m), this cave has a commanding view over the western floodplain of Río Santa in the Callejón de Huaylas valley of northern Peru. Beginning in the 1960s, archaeologists discovered that the unusually dry conditions of the cave preserved a wide range of perishable artifacts that record several thousand years of occupation. Among the finds are remarkably well-preserved plant fibers, leather, wood and bone tools, and stone scrapers, blades, and projectile points.[26] Groups of people who were hunting and collecting plants for food and fiber probably used this site seasonally as a base camp.

The fiber work from Guitarrero Cave marks the beginning of the longest continuous textile record on earth.[27] Artists created the uniformly twisted, looped, and knotted plant fibers with a variety of structural techniques. Age dates indicate some were made between 12,000 and 11,000 years ago, making them the oldest examples of those technologies found in South America.[28]

Textiles became highly valued in many later ancient Andean cultures as indicators of wealth and ethnic identity. Lightweight and portable, textiles were used to spread religious iconography, as political gifts, as burial goods, in offerings to deities, and in utilitarian applications from fishnets to clothing (more on textiles in Chapter 16). Remarkably, and in contrast to early cultures on other continents, textiles predated fired ceramics in the Andes by thousands of years.

Starting Out on the Long Road to Domestication
A major turning point in human history was underway when plants and animals began to be domesticated worldwide near the end of the Pleistocene approximately 13,000 to 12,000 years ago. The earliest domesticated species were likely dogs (*Canis familiaris*), the companions of early hunter-gatherers migrating from Eurasia into the Americas.[29] The earliest domesticated plant was probably the bottle gourd (*Lagenaria siceraria*), also known as a calabash gourd.[30] Because people valued both dogs and bottle gourds mostly for uses other than as a source of food, we consider them "utilitarian" species. Both became valuable long before people domesticated any plants for food or tamed and bred other animals.

New World bottle gourds are most closely related to African gourds, based on detailed DNA studies. Ocean-current drift modeling suggests that the ancestors of New World bottle gourds could have floated across the Atlantic Ocean to the coast of Brazil in the Late Pleistocene. The modeling implies transatlantic crossings can take place in the tropical latitudes in less than 12 months.[31] Seeds within the fruits of domesticated bottle gourds can be completely viable after nearly a year floating in seawater. Once the African bottle gourd seeds arrived on the eastern shores of South America, they were likely dispersed by animals. Eventually a wild population of this plant became established, and then the Indigenous people subsequently domesticated and widely distributed the plants. Archaeologists have identified bottle gourds in the Americas as early as around 10,000 years ago.

Bottle gourds are a "container crop," with strong and hard-shelled fruits that people can use as a bottle or utensil. Gourds were helpful for transporting and storing water, the equivalent of the ubiquitous water bottles that we carry with us today. They also provided convenient food containers for people who had not yet discovered pottery, and the hard shells could be used for decorated objects and musical instruments. Along the Pacific Coast of the Central Andes, gourds had an important use in ancient fishing practices, where they served as floats for nets woven from cotton, another plant species that was domesticated early in Andean history.

Researchers believe dogs accompanied the earliest explorers to reach South America from Eurasia. Detailed genetic studies suggest that all ancient and modern domesticated dogs worldwide share a common origin from Old World gray wolves. Genetic data suggest that the long road to domestication for Arctic wolves began by about 26,000 to 20,000 years ago. Dogs in the Americas are from at least five founding dog lineages, suggesting a substantial amount of divergence occurred in lineages prior to dogs accompanying their human companions to the New World.[32]

Rich Resources

The Kelp Highway provided an efficient route for the earliest Americans to colonize South America. Ranging from Pacific Ocean waters to arid coastal deserts and soaring mountain peaks, diverse environments provided valuable resources that played a major role in the development of Andean cultures. From the kelp, fish, and marine mammals of the Pacific coast to the herds of deer, guanacos, and vicuñas roaming the grasslands of the Altiplano, food was available for harvest in abundance. Metals, obsidian, and many types of rock were available for construction materials, as well as to make tools and other needed items. The record of success of the ancient Andean societies remains in the impressive art and monumental architecture that they left for us to see today.

With small populations and an abundance of resources, little or no conflict among neighboring groups is typical. As populations grow and occupy the richest resource locations, these changes can gradually push people into less favorable zones. In bad years, such as when too much or too little rain causes widespread crop failures, these marginal areas may not meet the needs of the resident population and unrest may erupt. Social arrangements that can limit conflict include cross-group ties of kinship and cooperation in food sharing, and many Andean societies practiced these traditions.

A combination of population pressure and environmental factors, such as prolonged droughts, can set the stage for violent conflict. At the largest and most ancient of the Andean archaeological sites, no evidence of warfare has been found.[33] Eventually, however, many Andean cultures became highly competitive and warlike.[34] This trend culminated in the prominently celebrated militarism of the Incas, who were engaged in wars almost continuously to expand the frontiers of their empire and suppress rebellions, as well as in sporadic civil conflicts over who would lead as the Inca emperor.[35] Controlling access to valuable resources, from food crops to luxury items for elites, was frequently a major motivation for expansion efforts—and losing control of resources ultimately a contributor to the downfall of societies.

In the next chapters we will look in greater detail at the natural resources and climate of the Andes, as these had a major role in helping to shape the amazing Andean cultures.

8

Animals

Llamas are the furry animal icons of the Andes Mountains. During my first visit to Peru, one highlight of the trip was visiting a llama and alpaca reserve. With their expressive eyes, long eyelashes, and thick coats, these graceful creatures are inquisitive and intelligent. They are interested in their surroundings and check out human visitors with more than simple "are you going to feed me?" curiosity. In my teenage years, llamas enchanted me, although now I can't recall what prompted this fascination. In looking back, perhaps it was an early and unrecognized hint of the decades-later fascination I would develop for the Andes and the ancient cultures that are so closely linked with these animals. Along with their distant wild camelid relatives, the guanacos and vicuñas, llamas and alpacas have an interesting history. All these animals became extremely valuable to the ancient Andeans.

Long before the earliest explorers wandered through the high Andes and discovered the wild camelids, they were likely in awe of the giant ground sloths, bears, saber-toothed cats, and other large animals roaming the landscape. The Pleistocene mammals of South America are especially notable for their enormous sizes. They are now extinct, but we know about them because we have found many fossils of their bones and teeth, sometimes along with remains from the cooking hearths and trash heaps of ancient settlement sites. To begin this chapter, we look at the Pleistocene animals that the earliest Andean people encountered.

Stalking Massive Mammals with Spindly Spears

The Pleistocene Epoch (lasting from about 2,580,000 to 11,700 years ago) is renowned for exceedingly large mammals, birds, and reptiles.[1] We know these as megafauna, a term commonly used for animals such as elephants, rhinoceroses, and other creatures larger than humans. The evolution of an enormous body gives animals advantages in regulating their body temperature and an improved ability to cope with changes in seasonal food supplies. We correlate large body size with environmental conditions of a cold climate. Perhaps the most notable of the Pleistocene megafauna were wooly mammoths, shaggy icons that have been the subject of artistic renderings from rock art thousands of years old to modern animated movies.

The South American continent had a rich collection of Pleistocene megafauna. Unique animal forms evolved during the over 100 million years that this tectonic plate was isolated, floating in a vast ocean like a giant island. The Isthmus of Panama connected the North and South American continents only around 3 million years ago, prompting animal migrations and increased faunal diversity on both continents.[2] These exchanges included the southward-moving ancestors of bears, cats, dogs, horses, and camels and northward-trekking ground sloths, armadillos, porcupines, and opossums.

Further exchanges of animals took place between the Americas and Asia beginning about 70,000 years ago and continuing during the thousands of years that the Bering land bridge existed. Animals that evolved in Asia, including the ancestors of modern elephants and large cats moved south, while the ancestors of horses and camels migrated from North America into Asia.[3]

The Pleistocene mammals of South America are especially notable for their enormous sizes and distinctive characteristics.[4] Short-faced bears (genus *Arctotheirum*) achieved the distinction of being the largest-known carnivore and mammalian land predator of all time. The large males could stand 11 ft (3.3 m) tall when they reared up on their hind legs and likely weighed around 3,500 lb (1,587 kg; about the weight of the average car today). Another top carnivore was the powerfully built *Smilodon*, commonly known as a saber-toothed tiger, although not closely related to modern cats or tigers. This meat-eating hunter had exceptionally long and curved upper canine teeth and could probably make terrifying snarling noises. Both predators would have been highly intimidating to the early explorers. Possibly, eliminating them from human neighborhoods became a top priority?

FIGURE 8.1. Reconstruction of animals around a lagoon in central Chile during the late Pleistocene. From left to right, two ground sloths with long claws (*Glossotherium robustum*, *Megatherium* [*Pseudomegatherium*] *medinae*), gomphothere (*Notiomastodon platensis*), horse (*Hippidion saldiasi*), camelid (*Palaeolama* [cf. *P. weddelli*]), jaguar (*Panthera onca*), and camel-like odd-toed ungulate (*Macrauchenia patachonica*). Illustration by Jorge González, 2015, available under a Creative Commons Attribution-Share Alike 4.0 International License.

Other large Pleistocene animals were docile herbivores that were likely threatening to humans only when cornered or injured. One of the largest known of these mammals was the giant ground sloth, *Megatherium*. These enormous creatures were up to 20 ft (6 m) in length from head to tail and weighed as much as 8,000 lb (3,628 kg). Slow-moving browsers that fed on leaves, they likely ignored the puny humans that appeared in their territory—at least for as long as they could. Another large mammal armored with bony plates and related to modern armadillos was *Glyptodon*. We know this creature had a tortoise-like shape, but it was roughly the same size and weight as a Volkswagen Bug. Elephant-like mastodons and gomphotheres, distant relatives of mammoths and elephants (all in the order *Proboscidea*), also roamed South America, living in social herds, and browsing on grasses and coarse vegetation (Figure 8.1).

Pleistocene archaeological sites in South America contain evidence that people hunted all these large herbivorous mammals. At one ancient settlement site, stone tools are mixed with the bones and scales of *Glossotherium*, a giant ground sloth.[5] Plate-like scales composed of bone covered this sloth, called osteoderms. Although most common in reptiles, notably dinosaurs, osteoderms can also be found in a few mammals, including modern armadillos. Archaeologists found thousands of osteoderms, some modified into ornaments with perforations and beveling from abrasive tools or covered with red pigment. The possible use of these items for adornment may show the importance of the relationship between the hunters and their prey.

Archaeologists have found mastodon bones near hearths at the ancient Monte Verde site in Chile.[6] These gigantic creatures, as well as other large mammals, must have been a formidable prey for fur-clad people using only spears and bolas (leather cords with weights on the ends, thrown to entangle the legs of an animal). With only stone knives and scrapers, butchering such enormous animals would also have been quite challenging. During studies of a North American mammoth butchery site in the state of Wyoming, archaeologists found evidence of campfire rings and scattered household artifacts.[7] These items suggest that to process a massive quantity of meat and hide, several families would temporarily move to the site of a large kill for a week or more. This same practice likely was followed whenever the earliest Andeans butchered a large animal.

The days of hunting large South American animals ended rapidly. Along with global extinctions on other continents, South American megafauna began to disappear at the end of the Pleistocene and into the early Holocene, roughly 12,000 to 10,000 years ago. The most severely affected were large mammals, followed by large birds and reptiles; most marine creatures were not affected. The South American continent had an extremely high extinction rate, with over 80 percent of the large-bodied genera lost.[8] Only wooly-coated camelids, the guanaco and the vicuña, along with deer, survived to become the largest mammals that are native to South America. On the North American continent, the extinction rate was about 70 percent. On both continents, entire groups of large mammals disappeared, including mastodons, mammoths, and horses.

Widespread debate continues over the reasons for the dramatic extinction rate at the end of the Pleistocene. Overhunting by expanding populations of humans was likely a major contributor,[9] along with a warming climate that

FIGURE 8.2. The four types of camelids in the Andes. Drawing courtesy of Natalie Lazo, in Michael A. Malpass, *Ancient People of the Andes* (2016): Figure 3.4.

changed many habitats.[10] In the Americas, as human populations increased, people prevented animals adapted to open environments from moving freely between food and water sources, which also likely contributed to extinctions.[11]

Taming and Domestication

Megafauna loss in South America left only a few large animals that the ancient people could potentially domesticate. At lower elevations they could hunt deer and wild guanacos. At higher elevations in the mountains, they added vicuñas to the hunt list. All these animals provided valuable meat, fat, and hides for the earliest hunters. Spear points used for hunting are common artifacts found in rock shelters and caves high in the Central Andes, including at the sites above the Pucuncho Basin where obsidian was being collected some 12,000 years ago[12] (as described in Chapter 5).

Hunters likely followed herds of animals and gradually learned to encourage them to congregate in specific areas by improving pasture conditions. Burning grasslands was one important method that early hunters could use to promote growth of young plants.[13] By initially managing food supplies and then eventually by separating and selectively breeding the animals, ancient Andeans domesticated species that became different from their wild ancestors. The wild guanacos and vicuñas, and domesticated llamas and alpacas, are separate species; however, these closely related animals can interbreed and produce fertile offspring[14] (Figure 8.2).

Both guanacos and vicuñas are well-suited to cold and harsh mountain environments.[15] Their camel heritage gives them a complex plumbing system that allows them to survive on much less water than other animals. Instead of hooves, they have two-toed feet with toenails and soft, moveable foot pads that help them maintain a solid grip on steep and rocky terrain. Vicuñas are small and graceful creatures. Weighing about 100 lb (45 kg), they have extremely soft and thick coats. Vicuñas inhabit high-altitude grasslands, from roughly 10,000 to 15,000 ft (3,048 to 4,572 m). Wild guanacos are larger than vicuñas and weigh about 200 to 310 lb (90 to 140 kg). They live in mountainous terrain at elevations up to about 13,000 ft (3,962 m).

Alpacas may have been the first of the camelids to be domesticated, possibly as early as about 6,000 years ago.[16] Once thought to be descended from guanacos, recent genetic studies show that the ancestors of alpacas are actually wild vicuñas. Alpacas are larger than vicuñas, reaching weights of around 150 lb (68 kg). Initially, they were most likely bred primarily for food. Eventually, people developed rigorous breeding selection practices to provide specific color and fiber characteristics in the soft and lustrous alpaca fleeces. Alpaca fiber became an essential component of the fabulous textile tradition that arose in the Andes.

The ancient Andeans selectively bred llamas from wild guanacos and domesticated them by about 4,000 to 5,000 years ago.[17] Llama coats have coarse guard hairs useful for ropes and rugs, with a fine undercoat that is suitable for garments. Llamas are larger than guanacos and reared to serve as sturdy pack animals; they are the only beast of burden native to the Americas. They are not strong enough to carry people, and they have limitations in load weight and the distance they can travel. Males can carry loads of up to around 75 lb (34 kg) and will walk about 10 mi (16 km) per day. Llamas are more independent and opinionated than many domesticated animals; they can refuse to move when tired and display other uncooperative behaviors to their human handlers.

Both llamas and alpacas are extremely intelligent and very curious and observant of what is going on around them. While on my 10-day trek in the Cordillera Blanca of northern Peru, I watched the llamas working as pack animals with great amusement. Instead of walking behind one another along the trail like the docile horses and mules, they frequently set off on excursions to investigate plants and other interesting objects. The herder spent hours each day shouting and running after them.

Like their wild ancestors, both llamas and alpacas are hardy animals that live in social groups and could adapt to being herded.[18] Although initially domesticated at the high elevations where their wild ancestors roam, over millennia

FIGURE 8.3. Llama residents of Machu Picchu. Photograph by author.

the ancient Andeans deliberately bred alpacas and llamas at increasingly lower elevations, and eventually these species adjusted to mating and giving birth at sea level.[19]

Camelids played prominent roles in Andean cultures and artists depicted them frequently in sculptures and on pottery.[20] They appear in origin myths and were sacrificed, sometimes by the hundreds, as part of religious rituals of the Moche, Incas, and other Andean societies. People mummified some of these sacrificed animals and placed them in the tombs of important dignitaries. Camelids provided meat, fiber, tallow, and bones that were made into useable products. Their dung provided a valuable crop fertilizer and fuel for fires.

Beginning at least 1,500 years ago, from Tiwanaku through Inca times, enormous herds of llamas and alpacas that could number in the tens of thousands became a source of significant wealth on the Altiplano. Besides providing meat and wool, the llamas had an essential role in carrying trade items in caravans.[21] Inca armies on the move used pack trains with enormous numbers of llamas to carry supplies. When the animals were no longer needed as beasts of burden, they became a convenient source of food (Figure 8.3).

Squeaky guinea pigs, known as *cuys*, are also native to the Andes Mountains. People domesticated these small rodents as a supplemental meat source, and they had important roles in the religious and social practices of the ancient Andeans.[22] The Andeans prepared cuys for consumption at special meals; they played a role in traditional healing rituals, and they were given as gifts and used as sacrificial offerings in rituals.[23] Archaeological evidence of the early penning of guinea pigs shows domestication as far back as around 7,000 years ago.

Guinea pigs have many advantages as a domesticated animal. They can readily live in a free-range style alongside people in their homes, eating vegetable scraps and reproducing quickly. These traits contribute to their being a small, but otherwise ideal, livestock alternative.

I learned about the cultural importance of these small creatures firsthand, and unusually, when I first visited Cuzco and saw a unique 1753 painting that is displayed in the Cathedral Basilica. Painted by an Indigenous (Quechua) Peruvian artist, Marcos Zapata, it is a scene of the Last Supper with a guinea pig, lying on its back with all four feet in the air, elegantly served to Jesus Christ and his disciples. In this striking painting, glasses of chicha, the fermented maize beverage that also has a long history of cultural importance in the Andes, accompany the guinea pig. Forgoing the traditional wine and bread, as shown in Leonardo da Vinci's classic painting, Zapata wanted to show the ceremonial foods of his homeland. I was surprised that the Catholic elders tolerated this painting and that it still survives today. Marcos Zapata was a prolific painter of religious subjects, so perhaps his pious reputation played a role—or possibly, the church leaders also enjoyed chicha?

Today, guinea pigs continue to be an important part of Andean culture. They are a source of income and add protein to the diets of many in Peru and Bolivia, particularly in the Andean highlands. Guinea pigs are also on the menu of restaurants in Cuzco, where I felt compelled to taste a small sample (unremarkable; tasted like chicken).

The Muscovy duck is another native South American domesticate. These tropical birds adapt well to cooler climates. As large ducks, they were likely kept for their meat and eggs, although little information has been found about their early domestication.[24] The ancient Andeans, including the Moche and Inca, depicted them on pottery and feather work, and artists incorporated their plumage into textiles. Wild flocks of these birds range from Mexico to Argentina today.

Animals in the Americas

When the earliest explorers reached the Americas, some twenty-four large herbivores or omnivorous mammals were potential candidates for domestication[25] (large carnivores don't consistently cooperate with different—and edible—species). The Andeans domesticated only the llama and the alpaca, and llamas became the sole beasts of burden. In contrast, from a pool of about seventy-two candidates in Eurasia, people domesticated twelve large mammals.[26] These Old World animals provided food and fiber, as well as pulled carts and plows, and some carried riders—developments that had profound effects on the trajectory of human societies.

Although the absence of large, domesticated animals created limitations in the lives of the ancient Andeans, people took full advantage of other available fauna. Andean environments provided bountiful fish and marine mammals in the Pacific Ocean, and allowed thousands of llamas and alpacas to flourish in high elevation pastures. Together with soil and water resources suitable for growing crops, a wide variety of environmental zones to produce food, and metallic ores for tools and art objects, the lands that the earliest Andeans inhabited offered many riches.

9

Water

In my wanderings through wildlands, I've spent long days experiencing oven-like temperatures in arid deserts and below-freezing temperatures in high mountains. In both extremes, accomplishing productive tasks—even walking a significant distance—becomes difficult. Certainly, humans are highly adaptable and adjust to their environments; nonetheless, climate plays an important role in shaping human cultures.

The weather we experience each day—hot or cold, windy or calm, cloudy or clear, wet or dry—collectively create our climate, which is typically defined for a specific area over intervals of dozens of years. Scientists have compiled information from a variety of sources about Andean climates, providing a look back extending for many thousands of years. Ice cores drilled from Andean glaciers are a valuable source of climate data because they show changes in precipitation over time.[1] The layers of dust and pollen embedded in the ice offer information about past agricultural and grazing activities. Pollen from local plants collected from cores drilled into lake sediments can show shifts in plant communities as these respond to changing weather patterns.[2]

The availability of water shaped ancient Andean cultures. Irregular episodes of high rainfall alternate with times of low rainfall throughout the Central Andes. These climatic conditions control the distribution and abundance of many types of plants—and especially, the yields of crops planted by the ancient people. Using water efficiently to produce food became a major concern for ancient Andean societies, and it continues to be in the changing climatic conditions of the twenty-first century (more on this in Chapter 21).

FIGURE 9.1. Overview of the Central Andes near Cuzco in 2021 (13° 42'S, 70° 06'W). Photograph by NASA.

By combining our knowledge of regional climatic conditions with other types of geographic and archaeological information, we can recognize how the availability of water shaped ancient Andean cultures. First, let's look at how climates have varied across their homelands.

Arid Deserts and Snow-Covered Mountains

Water is distributed extremely unevenly in the Central Andes. Snow and ice blanket high mountains. Steep valleys echo with the sound of water in streams racing down to meet the sea. In stark contrast, the windblown strip of land along the Pacific coast is one of the driest places on earth. Year after year, no measurable rain falls on this desert landscape. The complex cultures that prospered from the coastlands to the highlands learned to control water supplies to maximum advantage (Figure 9.1).

Most of the precipitation falling in the Andes is swept westward across the South American continent from the distant Atlantic Ocean. The Eastern Cordillera above the Amazon Basin captures most of this moisture. The steep slopes force the warm air upwards, and the air loses the ability to hold water.

This water then falls as rain that nourishes the tropical forests and as snow that blankets high elevations. By the time clouds reach the Western Cordillera, they have already released virtually all the moisture in the air, creating a "rain shadow" over this range. This "shadow" of dryness contributes to the aridity of the western side of the Andes, from the mountains rising above the coastal strip down to the Pacific Ocean.[3]

About 90 percent of the Central Andes precipitation drains east from the mountains into rivers that eventually reach the mighty Amazon River.[4] This river has a larger drainage basin and carries more water than any other river on earth. Winding across the vast South American continent, this and other eastward-flowing rivers may exceed 4,000 mi (6,437 km) or more in length before reaching the Atlantic Ocean. In contrast, the westward-flowing rivers that originate in the Andes Mountains are relatively short, with the longest extending only about 185 mi (298 km) before emptying into the Pacific Ocean.

Mountainous areas of the Andes have two seasons: wet and dry. The rainy season extends approximately from December to March and the dry season from June to September. Rainfall amounts are higher in the northern part of the Central Andes, with increasingly drier conditions toward the south. The quantity of rainfall typically increases as temperatures decrease along with a rise in altitude. The result is distinctive ecological zones or tiers within a narrow vertical band of land that extends from the coast into the highlands.

On the high Altiplano plateau, Lake Titicaca sediments and high-resolution seismic reflection data reveal dramatic fluctuations in rainfall and lake levels over the past several thousand years[5] (Figure 9.2). Small fluctuations in rainfall substantially affect water levels in Lake Titicaca because the lakeshores are shallow. A drop in lake level of even 3 ft (0.9 m) can cause the lake shoreline to constrict laterally for 3 mi (4.8 km).[6] Imagine having waterfront property—and then not. These extraordinary shifts severely affected local settlement patterns and livelihoods.

On the arid coastal strip south of the equator, the warmest months are from December through March. Wide expanses of sand dunes periodically interrupt the narrow ribbons of green that surround rivers flowing to the Pacific Ocean. These rivers are important to our story, as the earliest Andean societies settled down and thrived in these fertile oases.

The extreme dryness of the coastal strip along the Pacific has been a boon for archaeologists. Perishable materials such as cloth, wood, shell, and bone that

FIGURE 9.2. Lake Titicaca. Photograph by Sasha India, 2014.

readily disintegrate in wetter environments of the highlands can be preserved superbly along the coast. Well-preserved human remains from arid areas even allow investigations of ancient injuries and diseases.[7]

The tectonic history that built the Andes Mountains strongly influenced the development of the strikingly different climatic regimes along the length and width of the mountain chain. In the Central Andes, as the mountains rose over millions of years, they blocked the moisture-laden easterly winds. This "wall of rock" resulted in a moist climate developing along the Eastern Cordillera, while effectively starving the Altiplano-Puna and Western Cordillera regions of moisture.[8] On the western side of the Central Andes, atmospheric circulation over the Pacific Ocean also changed, causing increased aridity along the coastal strip.[9] Across this wide range of environments, Andean societies developed and flourished, as people learned to control water supplies to maximum advantage.

Cold Current Controls

Offshore ocean currents are the source of another significant influence on the climate of the Central Andes. The cold Humboldt Current, or Peru Current, plays a major role. Originating near the Antarctic, this deep, cold current flows north along the west coast of South America in a wide band that extends outward for several hundred miles from the shoreline.[10]

Surface winds strongly influence the Humboldt Current. Offshore, in the southeastern Pacific Ocean, winds move counterclockwise around the South Pacific High, an area of high atmospheric pressure, and blow from the southwest toward the Central Andes. The massive topographic barrier of the Andes deflects the winds away from the continent as they blow northward toward the equator.[11] When the wind moves the warmer and saltier tropical water away from the land, upwelling brings cold Humboldt Current water up toward the surface. (In contrast, the Gulf Stream is a warm Atlantic Ocean current that flows from the Gulf of Mexico northward along the eastern coastline of the United States.)

The Humbolt Current water thus has a strong cooling influence on the coastal climates of Ecuador, Peru, and Chile. Water temperatures where this current flows offshore from northern Peru are around 61°F (16°C), while typical tropical water temperatures at these latitudes are warmer by almost 16°F (9°C).[12] Low evaporation rates and water vapor transport result in minimal precipitation, contributing to the coastal aridity.[13]

The humid marine air above the cold current also creates thick clouds and fog (known by the Spanish word for mists, *garúas*), trapped in an inversion by the warmer air above. From about April to November, the cool air and fog blow eastward over the coastal regions. The moisture condenses on steep coastal slopes, where the water supports plant communities known as *lomas* (Spanish for "small hills"). The lomas are established at elevations between about 650 ft (200 m) and 3,280 ft (1,000 m) and have been important to the coastal societies for fields for planting crops and grazing areas for camelids.[14]

The Humboldt Current has played a major role in the rise and fall of ancient Andean societies. This current generates one of the most productive ecosystems found on earth. The cold water contains a nutrient-rich soup of nitrogen, phosphorous, potassium, and other elements. Phytoplankton, the tiny organisms that use these nutrients, form a broad base for a prolific food chain ranging from microorganisms to birds and large sea mammals. The nearshore bounty includes vast numbers of anchovies and sardines that people can net by the thousands, plus many types of larger fish.[15] This abundance was all available to people using traditional fishing techniques with simple nets and reed boats. The enormous richness of this highly productive ecosystem has allowed Andean societies to prosper for millennia. When disruptions replace the normally cold water with warm water, however, the results can be devastating.

Changing Climates and Cultures

When the earliest fisher-hunter-gatherers first settled along the north coast of the Central Andes, rainfall levels were higher and ocean waters were much warmer than they are today. Fish and mollusk remains collected from early archaeological sites are predominantly tropical species.[16] Then, roughly 5,800 years ago, a climate transition established cooler and drier conditions on the northern coast. Researchers attribute this change to upwelling, which brought cold Pacific Ocean water up to the ocean surface. They believe an extension of the Humboldt Current, stretching to the northern border of modern Peru as it does today, is responsible for this climate change.[17]

Once cold ocean water flowed consistently along the northern coast, it set the stage for significant cultural change. Small and mobile groups of fisher-hunter-gatherers gradually became replaced by groups who settled in one place. Coastal societies harvested the bountiful marine resources and began exchanges with communities growing cotton and food crops in the fertile inland river valleys.[18] Farming lifestyles allow birth intervals to be shorter, so populations expanded.[19]

The high productivity of the nutrient-rich cold currents played an important role in these developments, but other factors also brought change. By around 5,800 years ago, sea levels stabilized after rising for thousands of years following the end of the Pleistocene glaciations. While sea level was gradually rising, the coastal strips narrowed and effectively pushed populations together that had formerly been widely separated. A robust mixed valley–marine economic system developed and flourished. The abundance of high-quality food could sustain larger populations living in high-density settlements. These conditions also promoted the development of political complexity and social stratification that separates elites from commoners.[20]

The productivity of the Humboldt Current and settlement patterns has a clear connection. Around 5,000 years ago, people established the large Norte Chico settlements along the northern section of the Central Andean coast. We recognize this region today as having the highest marine productivity, associated with the greatest amount of cold-water upwelling to the ocean surface.[21]

The Norte Chico people constructed impressive monumental architecture in archaeological sites about 100 mi (160 km) north of the modern city of Lima (described in Chapter 12). The ocean current and climatic changes that resulted in a more productive marine ecosystem are key pieces in the puzzle of why monumental construction began then and in those coastal areas.

Warm Current Catastrophes
Centuries ago, the coastal fishers of Peru gave the warm ocean current that periodically arrives around the time of Christmas the name El Niño, as a reference to "the boy," or Christ child. El Niño is the warm water phase of the phenomenon and La Niña, or "the girl," is the cooling phase. This combined ocean and atmosphere weather phenomenon, known as the El Niño-Southern Oscillation, or ENSO, presents significant challenges for Andean societies. Much of the region bordering the Pacific Ocean, especially in tropical latitudes, experiences dramatic changes in the weather because of the ENSO, in patterns that continue today.

In the Central Andes, the warm El Niño water transforms the normal conditions dominated by the cold Humboldt Current. When an El Niño weather pattern is underway, the northeasterly trade winds weaken, decreasing upwelling in equatorial regions so that the temperature of surface waters increases. Warm water accumulates in the western and central parts of the Pacific Ocean and then flows east along the equator, turning south and pouring over the top of the cold current after reaching the South American coast. The resulting warm and humid air produces dense rain clouds, and thunderstorms develop. Torrential rains batter the lowlands during El Niño weather, while severe droughts can affect the highlands.[22]

The unusually warm El Niño water also severely disrupts the normal marine ecosystem. Fish populations move away from their typical habitats or perish, resulting in birds and marine mammals being deprived of food and facing starvation. Some warm-adapted tropical fish move southward along the coast to replace the fish species that have died or migrated further south, but overall, marine life is significantly reduced.[23]

During very strong El Niño events, flooding can be catastrophic in coastal areas. The severity varies depending on river valley topography, orientation with respect to storms, plant cover, and other geographic and geologic characteristics.[24] In some areas, the normally arid climate is associated with sparse plant cover, and so the soil is only weakly stabilized, resulting in massive mudflows. In the event of recently occurring earthquakes, landslides at higher elevations can also produce large amounts of sediment that wash down to the coast to form temporary deltas at river mouths.[25] Ocean waves redistribute the influx of fine material into long ridges of sand and silt along beaches, covering intertidal zones and smothering all life forms. Onshore winds then blow the fine sediment onto field systems, reducing crop productivity.[26]

The frequency of the El Niño phenomenon has varied throughout the thousands of years that people have lived in the Central Andes. Direct geologic evidence of early El Niño events is scarce, as early occurring flood and landslide deposits typically disappear when they become reworked in subsequent severe events.[27]

Nevertheless, clever scientific and archaeological sleuthing has revealed details of recurrence and variability of these climate-related fluctuations. One notable approach involves analysis of the water temperature preferences of mollusks found in the refuse piles of ancient Andean settlements. An abundance of warm water species shows that the near-shore ocean temperatures were warm, and an El Niño pattern dominated.[28] In the highlands of Ecuador, scientists have correlated El Niño events with thin layers of inorganic material that washed into Lago Palcacocha during storm events. They obtained radiocarbon-age dates on clastic layers that span the past approximately 15,000 years. These data show that the layers have close correlations with historic records of all the severe and most of the moderate El Niño events during the past 200 years, indicating a progressive increase in frequency to modern periodicity beginning around 5,000 years before present.[29]

El Niño effects vary significantly in geographic extent and intensity, and their frequency has changed over the past millennia. Paleoclimate data show that El Niño events in the Central Andes were absent or extremely rare from about 8,800 to 5,800 years ago. Between approximately 5,800 years to roughly 3,000 years ago, they probably occurred every fifty to one hundred years. Beginning around 3,000 years ago, researchers believe El Niño occurrences increased to the higher frequency levels of moderate-to-severe events that have been recorded approximately every ten years.[30] Within the past century, severe events have occurred beginning in 1925, 1982, 1997, and 2014.

Historically, frequent but mild El Niño occurrences have limited consequences, while severe events can have devastating effects. During El Niño in

January 1998, the temperature of ocean water offshore in Peru increased as much as 40°F (5°C) above the typical temperatures.[31] Unsurprisingly, this shift had a significant negative impact on wildlife and people who depended on the affected species. During the same 1997–1998 El Niño, the Tumbes region on the northwest corner of Peru received a disastrous 130 in (330 cm) of rain, when less than 8 in (20 cm) is normal.[32] These modern observations illustrate the harshness of the El Niño events that ancient Andean cultures must have experienced throughout the past 3,000 years.

Coping with Floods and Famines

A severe El Niño can destroy decades of human toil in hours. Torrential rains and floods from rivers that overtop banks wash away agricultural fields, roads, and even entire communities. Homes and civic structures built from sun-dried adobe bricks collapse into a muddy mass, and water sweeps them away. Fields become stripped of fertile topsoil and refilled with either silt or gravel and boulders. Irrigation canals are destroyed, and erosion reshapes the surrounding slopes. Riverbed gradients are modified. And in the warm El Niño-affected oceans, the fish and other marine species that provided essential sustenance for so many vanish.

After an El Niño, large numbers of disease-carrying insects, such as mosquitoes, breed in standing water and bring sicknesses, including malaria and dengue fever, to the local populations. Sandfly populations may also multiply, carrying a dreadful Andean disease known as bartonellosis. The bacterium that causes bartonellosis results in a fever and severe skin rash, similar to smallpox. The Moche, Nazca, and Chimú societies all made pottery showing the nodular skin lesions that are a symptom of chronic bartonellosis.[33]

After the rain stops, locusts and mice and other rodents can proliferate and consume crops that either escaped the flooding or that people planted shortly after the floodwaters receded. The prevailing onshore winds blow silt and sand off the river deltas and sediment ridges that develop on beaches during the flooding, and the fine particles blanket settlements and agricultural fields with thick sediment layers. The destruction of farmland leads to starvation, and landless farmers seek refuge in other areas. Soaring demand for arable land leads to conflicts.

El Niño effects are especially severe along the northern coast of modern Peru.[34] In an unfortunate twist of fate, the Norte Chico people took advantage of the richest marine resources, courtesy of the Humboldt Current, but they also happened to reside where El Niño effects are most devastating. Leaders may have persuaded local populations to build monumental temples along the coast with claims that by honoring the supernatural forces believed responsible for rain, then the negative impacts of adverse weather would be reduced. This belief could convince people for a while, since many El Niño events had only mild effects and occurred infrequently throughout much of the history of the Norte Chico cultures.

Impacts intensified when warm waters began appearing off the coast more regularly, beginning around 3,000 years ago.[35] A frequency of dramatic El Niño events occurring less than once a generation differs greatly from the occurrence of one or more each decade.[36] The coastal populations faced serious trouble. When they encountered the erratic nature of El Niño, authorities attempting to maintain social order and their own political positions most likely found themselves and their followers in a drastic decline.

Ancient Andeans could not have understood that El Niño conditions originated in the Pacific Ocean far to the west. From their perspective, the flash floods in the rivers that descended from the mountains, as well as the dark clouds and heavy rains over the coast, appeared to be beginning over the highlands to the east. In an intriguing correlation, around the time that El Niño occurrences significantly increased in frequency along the northern coast, construction of monumental temples began in mountainous settings located high above the hardest-hit coastal sites.[37] Perhaps self-confident leaders in the mountains believed they could influence this weather phenomenon and convinced the coastal people of their power?

The most prominent of these highland sites, built beginning around 3,000 years ago, was Chavín de Huántar, the center of a religious cult visited by large numbers of pilgrims over hundreds of years (described in Chapter 17). Archaeologists have found artifacts suggesting connections between Chavín and the coastal communities that were suffering from the effects of El Niños.[38] The most notable artifacts are large painted cloth banners, preserved for three millennia in the dry air of the arid coastal sites. These textiles show the religious iconography of the Chavín culture and hint of strong ties with the authority and prestige of this highland center.

Following the decline of the Norte Chico societies, the coastal plain beneath the high mountains continued to be inhabited periodically by Andean cultures.

Many of these groups experienced devastating floods associated with an El Niño. They made attempts to intervene with the deities they believed controlled the rain, including rituals with human and animal sacrifices (described in Chapter 13).

Evidence also suggests that El Niño events helped to trigger some of the societal upheavals occurring throughout ancient Andean history. Although many social and economic factors can play a role in such disruptions, the destructive flooding, droughts, and subsequent disturbances in food production and livelihoods surely played a role. We can interpret the fragmented archaeological record of the ancient Andeans in multiple ways, and new information will undoubtedly provide additional insights.

From what we have learned to date, environmentally induced social stress associated with the erratic climate of the Andes clearly had significant consequences. Nonetheless, despite these challenges, for thousands of years the ancient Andeans exhibited substantial resiliency and cultural continuity.

10

Agriculture

On my first visit to Peru, our group spent a few nights in the Sacred Valley town of Yucay to acclimate to the high thin air before starting our days of hiking and camping. One afternoon we set out on a walk, wandering along the dirt roads that meandered into the hills above the hotel. When we finally turned around and were heading back toward the hotel on a different route, at one point I realized to my surprise that we were walking along stone walls that were once part of ancient agricultural terraces. Although the terraces had been abandoned for centuries and were now overgrown with vegetation, the solidity of the walls amazed me, and so did casually finding them near our hotel. Clearly, the traces of the Incas and their ancestors who had once inhabited these mountains were all around us.

Ancient Andean cultures were based on an agricultural foundation that involved the domestication of robust plants and useful animals and the arduous transformation of rugged terrain into arable farmland. Over time, societies developed innovative and effective methods to grow food in a wide variety of environments, from arid coastal deserts to the high and cold mountain slopes. People reclaimed, cultivated, and then deserted lands at various times and rates, reflecting the precariousness of the farming way of life.

The earliest Andeans who migrated from Asia reaped the wealth of the ocean. When people eventually established permanent villages along the coast, these were based on the availability of maritime resources. The move into the mountains most likely occurred over centuries.[1] In trips to hunt and to collect valuable resources such as obsidian for tools, people ventured upwards initially in seasonal forays and then dropped back down to lower elevations during times of inclement weather. After learning how to provide enough food, fuel, and warmth to accommodate the challenges of life at high elevations, people lived permanently in the highlands. Andeans devised foraging, farming, and herding strategies that allowed them to take maximum advantage of the diverse environments and natural abundance available.

The Farming Way of Life

From dependence on wild foods in a hunter-gatherer lifestyle to reliance on cultivation and eventually to the farming way of life, the transition was a gradual process. The ancient Andeans domesticated cotton and bottle gourds and grew them early in their history.[2] These items were important innovations for fishing, as they made fishing lines and nets with cotton, as well as used dried gourds as floats for nets. Hunting was eventually reduced as an economic activity when farmers and herders learned how to raise llamas, alpacas, and guinea pigs (cuys). Effectively, these animals composed the livestock species of the Andes, although quite different from those of the Old World. Agricultural production became increasingly important as domesticated plant yields and human populations grew larger.

The diverse Andean topography presents valuable opportunities. Within distances as short as 30 mi (48 km), the topography of the Central Andes can range from sea-level beaches to towering snow-covered mountains. By walking either uphill or downhill for only an hour or two, a person can travel through multiple distinctive ecological zones. In recognizing the distinctive features of these stacked geographic zones, or tiers, and developing crops that were optimal for specific local conditions, the ancient Andeans became highly successful at producing food.

As shown in Chapter 9, challenges presented by the environment, especially erratic weather, are a constant in the Andes. With such conditions, productivity at a specific elevation zone can fluctuate widely from year to year. Gaining access to the resources of multiple ecological zones and storing food for lean times became important survival mechanisms. Families or communities would take advantage of growing conditions at several elevation levels.[3] Farming could take place in multiple ecological zones along a vertical transect, with llamas and alpacas pastured at the highest elevations and cultivation of tubers, grains, and other vegetables at successively lower elevations.

Mutual exchanges of food, raw materials, and labor became the foundation of ancient Andean social relationships, as trade or barter was essential to obtain resources not readily available locally. From the fish, shellfish, and salt harvested along the coast to the fruits and vegetables of the mid-level elevations and the llamas and alpacas in high pasturelands, farmers could produce a rich and wide variety of plant and animal resources.

With increased social complexity, societies collected and stockpiled food for the good of the community. Storing food for lean years was crucial given the high failure rate of crops because of inclement weather. In the mountains, one good crop harvest could be followed by several years of meager production.[4] Over time, people increasingly emphasized quinoa, maize, and other grains that they could store for a relatively long time.[5] They dehydrated potatoes, meat, fish, and many other foods in the dry air and then stored them for later use. A major advantage of dehydrated food was that it is light and relatively easy to transport.

The storehouses of the Inca Empire were legendary, as thousands of these were scattered across the empire.[6] The frequent feasts the Inca authorities held for local populations required large quantities of stored food. Also, in a mountainous region where the transportation of goods happened only on the backs of humans and llamas, moving food and supplies for long distances was impractical. A remarkable achievement of this empire was maintaining sufficient levels of production and distribution to meet the food, clothing, and shelter needs of every citizen in the realm.[7]

Harnessing Water to Grow Food
Controlling water to produce food was a constant concern once Andean societies with substantial populations relied on agriculture. Water management techniques practiced by the ancient people worked well under normal conditions. Adverse climatic conditions, however, brought challenges from the coastal regions into the highlands. Powerful Andean leaders built their formidable reputations via efforts to control water—either in the spiritual world by intervening with supernatural forces believed to command weather, or in the material world by directing the construction of water collection and distribution systems.

Along the coast of the Central Andes, dozens of short and steep rivers descend from the western mountains. Spaced about every 25 mi (40 km), these perennial rivers drain summer rainfall from the highlands and meltwater from seasonal snow and long-lived glaciers. Slicing through shifting sand dunes on the coastal plain, many rivers typically flow year-round to the Pacific Ocean. The regions surrounding the rivers were probably the earliest areas used for crop cultivation,[8] as the availability of water and fertile floodplain soil provides advantages for plant growth.

The erratic weather of the Andes, however, means the amount of water available in even perennial rivers is unpredictable and the flow rates of the westward draining rivers can vary significantly. Mountain soils act like sponges that must reach a high level of saturation before runoff can reach rivers. Evaporation and seepage can consume a large volume of water. Drought in the highlands strongly affects river volumes, and diminished flows could cause significant crop losses for coastal farmers.

Surface Water and Irrigation Systems
In the mountains, farmers can grow crops by taking advantage of rainfall. At elevations of around 7,500–11,500 ft (2,300–3,500 m) they could rely primarily on precipitation.[9] At lower elevations, irrigation systems became valuable as insurance for erratic rainfall, with the added advantages of shortened crop-growing times and increased yields. The ancient Andeans constructed gravity canals that directed water from lowland rivers into coastal irrigation systems by around 5,000 to 6,000 years ago in the foothills of the northern Central Andes.[10] Showing the importance of irrigation agriculture for the Norte Chico culture approximately 4,000 to 5,000 years ago, the rich mix of domestic plant food remains found at these archaeological sites includes cotton, gourds, squash, peanuts, potatoes, avocados, and beans of many types.[11]

The first irrigation systems were likely modest works built by a single family or a small group of families. Over time, these developed into highly elaborate systems that covered entire inland valleys, with water and land usage tightly controlled by authorities.[12] In the relatively flat coastal valleys, major irrigation canals could be several miles long (e.g., near Inca Cuzco, the Chinchero canal had a length of about 11 mi/18 km).[13] System design needed to take into account the slope and length of canals, the use of stone paving or a clay lining, and the types and distribution of crops grown. Problems developed when earthquakes uplifted or dropped sections of the landscape, and when riverbeds sank through downcutting, stranding the canal intakes above the water level. Keeping irrigation systems operating properly required constant maintenance.

Subsurface Water Systems
Ancient Andean societies grew in extremely arid areas along the Pacific coast and in the Atacama Desert, now in modern southern Peru and northern Chile, where rivers are completely absent or flow for only a short time each year. Rainfall amounts are about 0.6 in (1.5 cm) per year on average, which translates to multiple years of no measurable rain, punctuated by an occasional downpour in a severe storm. Fortunately for the creative people who lived in these hyperarid areas, rivers can flow underground toward the sea, so groundwater can be located close to the surface. Also, in some places along the coast, people laboriously excavated agricultural fields down to depths where plant roots could reach groundwater, known as sunken gardens.[14]

Ancient cultures could flourish because people developed an ingenious system to tap into water flowing in the subsurface. Around 400 to 500 CE, the Nazca culture built an extensive system of subsurface filtration galleries and aqueducts called *puquios*. They constructed these by excavating a series of vertical shafts along a gentle slope until reaching groundwater and then digging a horizontal tunnel or channel to direct the water into a reservoir for domestic and irrigation water use. Large circular structures with stone walls defining a corkscrewing funnel-shape let wind flow into the underground channels, where changes in atmospheric pressure forced water along the system.[15]

Dozens of puquio water collection systems are recognized along the south coast of Peru. Many are still functioning and used in the Nazca region today[16] (Figure 10.1). Although the availability of water became more dependable with puquios, diminished water supplies in times of drought were surely a source of significant stress to the local populations.

Innovative Farming Techniques

Andean farmers transformed their environment through innovative farming techniques that effectively tapped the productive potential of the landscape. The agricultural practices of the ancient Andeans became among the most sophisticated on earth, with large-scale landscape modifications requiring substantial labor for construction and maintenance. People performed all farming work. Although llamas could carry loads as pack animals, they are delicate creatures and not capable of pulling plows, as described in Chapter 8.

The terraces built by the ancient people still sculpt the Central Andes today. With the appearance of giant stair-steps covering hillslopes, terraces increase

FIGURE 10.1. Puquios built by the ancient Nazca culture near the city of Nazca, Peru. Top photograph by PsamatheM, 2019. Bottom photograph by Diego Delso, 2015. Both available under a Creative Commons Attribution-Share Alike 4.0 International License.

the amount of arable land and create flat surfaces suitable for crops. In the Lake Titicaca region and other areas with groundwater close to the surface, people built raised fields and ponds for fish and aquatic plants. They added soil amendments such as fertilizer from animal dung and ash from burned vegetation to agricultural fields over many centuries, leaving mineral element traces that are still recognizable today.[17]

Terraces

Terraces have many advantages for cultivated crops. They reduce erosion and increase water retention, and deep soil allows plants to have better root development.[18] Modifying slope aspect to improve sun exposure creates microclimates that are helpful for plant growth. Frost damage to plants can be minimized because a series of terraces creates turbulence in the cold air that flows downslope. Effectively, terraces lower the ecological altitude for farmers—a major advantage in the high and steep terrain of the Central Andes.

FIGURE 10.2. Terraces built by the Incas in the Sacred Valley, Peru. Photograph by author.

People constructed terraces for crops in the Titicaca Basin as early as 3,000 years ago.[19] The ancient Andeans gradually developed optimal locations and construction techniques in different regions. Terraces typically followed the contours of the landscape and were deeper and narrower on steep slopes, with walls sometimes reaching heights of 6 ft (1.8 m) and only slightly wider. On gentle slopes, such as valley floors, retaining walls needed to be built only at wide intervals (Figure 10.2).

Terrace construction required a significant investment of labor. Workers built retaining walls that typically had large rocks at the base and smaller ones near the top. They added sand and gravel at terrace bases to improve drainage, and layered soil on top.[20] Terrace-fill material could be brought in from elsewhere. At Machu Picchu, for example, most of the soil for the extensive terraces had to be carried up to the ridge top from the valley below. In basket-load after basket-load, the Inca laborers collected the rich topsoil from the Río Urubamba floodplain and packed it 1,600 ft (4,877 m) uphill to the ridge top.

As the Inca Empire expanded, thousands of workers toiled to construct these expansive terraces and massive irrigation systems. Crop harvests improved, and surplus food was available for local communities, as well as the state and religious elites. Food surpluses provisioned frequent community feasts and supported members of the society who were too old or ill to provide for their own needs. The rapid expansion of the Inca Empire was possible not only because of the highly efficient organizational capabilities of the Inca elites, but also because of effective technologies related to agricultural production developed by their ancestors.

Raised Fields and Aquaculture
In marshy areas with high water tables, such as around Lake Titicaca, people employed other highly effective farming practices. The most widespread were raised beds on large, elevated planting platforms that kept plant roots above saturated zones.[21] Platforms could be low or as high as 12 ft (3.6 m) above the surrounding ground surface. Workers excavated canals or ditches on one to four sides around the raised beds, and elaborate systems regulated the water flow to the fields. The platforms improved the microclimate for plants, as well as the production and recycling of soil nutrients. Beginning around 500 CE when the Tiwanaku culture was flourishing, farmers transformed the landscape by building raised fields on a massive scale.

Similar to the case for terrace farming, growing crops in raised field systems provided advantages.[22] These benefits included protection from frost damage as the water-filled canals effectively absorb and conserve the heat of the sun and then slowly release it at night. Constant water availability shortened crop cycles, making it possible to harvest more than one crop during the growing season. An added asset was aquaculture in the canals, which supported fish and waterfowl, as well as growing aquatic plants to be skimmed out for use as fertilizer. In recent years, agricultural specialists have reintroduced raised field cultivation to farming communities in the Lake Titicaca region, in recognition of the enhanced productivity of this method.[23]

The Tiwanaku people took the expansion of aquaculture further by constructing artificial ponds or reservoirs to store rainfall, called *qochas*.[24] These water bodies were habitats for various types of fish and birds during annual migrations. They could support crops growing on their sloping sides, and when drained and left fallow, the ponds became grazing areas for llamas and alpacas. Qochas were especially beneficial in the dry and high elevation areas of the Altiplano, and they continue to be used today.

Gifts of Guano

Along the Pacific Coast of the Central Andes, the millions of cormorants, pelicans, gulls, and other seabirds feasting on fish produce an abundance of guano, a resource of high value to humans. Bird excrement is rich in nitrogen, phosphate, and potash, and is an excellent fertilizer. Seabirds roosting and nesting on offshore islands deposit an enormous amount of guano that is preserved in the dry climate, accumulating to depths of as much as 100 ft (30 m) or more.[25]

The ancient Andeans recognized the value of guano for fertilizer far back in history, perhaps as long ago as 5,000 years. Along the coastal river valleys, this fertilizer enhanced the early production of domesticated cotton and, later, the widespread cultivation of maize. Flourishing on the northern coast of Peru from about 100 to 700 CE, the Moche culture is renowned for explicit ceramic artwork that depicted aspects of their society. Moche line drawings show the reed boats used when they visited the offshore islands, presumably to transport the guano back to coastal agricultural fields, and archaeologists have found Moche artifacts in guano deposits.[26]

In the arid Atacama Desert of modern northern Chile, large quantities of desiccated crops show successful agricultural production beginning about 1,000 years ago.[27] Researchers analyzed the plants, as well as bone and teeth from human remains, and found extremely high nitrogen values. They attributed these levels to the use of bird guano as fertilizer for crops, which provided high crop yields in a challenging environment. Thus, water was not the only factor in successful crop production in the Central Andes.

The Mystery of Moray

Moray is a sculpted landscape masterpiece, comprising of a set of four large bowl-shaped circles lined with concentric rings of terraces.[28] The Incas built these structures around depressions that are natural sinkholes called *muyus* (Quechua for circles). Extensive limestone deposits that are locally overlain by younger volcanic rock underlie the Moray region. The calcium carbonate and calcium sulfate in the limestone is subject to chemical dissolution that opens solution cavities and sinkholes in what geologists call karst topography. Constructed during the peak of the Inca Empire, Moray is on a high plain about 20 mi (32 km) northwest of Cuzco.

Aerial photographs taken in 1931 introduced Moray to the outside world. Speculation on how and why the Incas built Moray has been ongoing in the decades since. Inca religious and ceremonial purposes, and/or some type of agricultural experiment station, are the primary theories proposed by researchers (landing pads for extraterrestrials are among "other" more dubious explanations). What is clear is that the Incas created features that are admired today, nearly five centuries later, for their precision, complexity, and beauty.

Building the muyus was a monumental task. Site preparation required filling and compacting a massive amount of soil to grade the area; in some places, imported soil fill is as deep as 16 ft (5 m). Hundreds of tons of rock had to be hauled to construct the terrace walls. The largest muyu has circular terraces that decrease in size with depth, then extend out onto a large flat plaza and a series of oval-shaped terraces—a total length of about 720 ft (219 m), equal to two American football fields. The diameter of the circular section is 390 ft (119 m), and the depth is 120 ft (37 m), with terrace walls that are 8–13 ft (2.4–4 m) high[29] (Figure 10.3).

Volcanic rocks overlying the limestone contain springs that the Incas incorporated into the design of the muyus. Durable volcanic andesite from a nearby quarry was the source for stone blocks that were shaped and used to build the

FIGURE 10.3. Muyu terraces at Moray, Peru. Photograph by Gertrudis, 2011, available under a Creative Commons Attribution-Share Alike 3.0 Unported License.

terrace walls and structures at the site. (If builders had used the softer limestone in construction, it would have largely disintegrated over the past centuries.) The smallest muyu is unfinished, and partially-shaped stone blocks and tools scattered about this site suggest rapid abandonment, possibly when the workers learned of the arrival and advance of the Spanish conquistadors.

Water management at Moray—collecting, transporting, and delivering water—shows the exceptional hydraulic engineering skills of the Incas.[30] The water that originally formed the muyus could have caused rapid destruction, so the Incas had to control the natural springs carefully and account for an annual rainfall of around 20 in (50 cm). They also built reservoirs with stone linings to store water from the springs. With a capacity of about 90,000 gal (340,687 l), these water bodies were adequate to provide a consistent supply of water needed during the dry season. Stone-lined canals directed the water to the reservoirs and then downhill to the muyus, where the Incas could use the water as needed.

A significant engineering challenge was how to drain the water that flowed downward into the large and deep depressions. Even after centuries of disuse, signs of subsidence at the bottom of these features are absent, showing that precipitation and drainage from higher terraces can infiltrate in a controlled manner. Although no subsurface explorations have occurred at Moray, engineers believe the Incas installed drains beneath each muyu. They probably constructed these in deep excavations with large andesite blocks at the lowest level, followed by layers of rock and gravel in decreasing sizes upwards, and capped by sand and then topsoil.[31] Since the depressions have not reverted to their rough sinkhole heritage after several centuries, we can infer that the construction of these drains was impeccable.

Why did the Incas undertake such a difficult construction project? Using the terraced circles and adjoining large plazas for religious ceremonies and community gatherings is consistent with what we know about Inca practices, but the tremendous effort suggests the builders had additional objectives. Specifically, several lines of evidence suggest some type of agricultural investigation.

Researchers have found that on certain dates and times throughout the year, distinctive patterns of sun and shade occur on the terraces, which influence soil temperature and plant growth rates.[32] The Incas might have conducted side-by-side crop testing of different plant varieties to determine those types that would grow most successfully in specific locations. Importantly, on a small scale, Moray environments simulated the microclimates of the much larger terrace systems under intensive cultivation in the surrounding region. Predictions of the climatic conditions for important actions, such as when farmers should begin planting or add more water at certain times for optimal plant growth, could then be disbursed more widely to farmers in surrounding locations.

Two additional pieces of information support the idea of an agricultural experiment station.[33] First, many wild plant species were growing on some terraces before restoration efforts began. Many of those were apparently quite rare outside the site, and evidence suggests the Incas could have used these plants as sensitive ecological indicators to reflect the diversity of regional growing conditions. Second, researchers have found other archaeological sites with concentric terraces in Peru. Constructed in different ecoclimatic conditions, the Andeans may have built some of these circles with the same objectives as for Moray.

Mysteries remain! What is crystal clear: Moray and the many other monumental constructions of the Incas and their ancestors provide evidence of the extraordinary sophistication and skill of these ancient Andeans.

Expanding Surpluses and Societies

Successful food production and food surpluses led to increased populations and social changes. Occupational specializations could develop, along with social stratification into higher-status and lower-status individuals.[34] Powerful leaders rose who could direct the distribution of resources, including water in irrigation systems, and who could claim to have access to the deities controlling the weather. An elite class of priests and shamans could keep track of planting and harvesting times, as well as important ritual events, by observing the paths of celestial bodies during the passing of seasons. Artisans could specialize in textile, pottery, and metalwork production. Where rich agricultural lands needed to be protected from outsiders, a warrior class arose.

The success of Andean agricultural production is undeniable. We recognize it from the large populations that ancient societies could successfully feed and clothe over thousands of years. Ancient puquios, qochas, and many of the terracing systems built by the ancient people are still in use in the Central Andes today. This continuity is a true measure of success.

11

Plants

Whenever I have visited the Andes, seeing snow-covered mountains soaring within view of Pacific Ocean waves is always a surprise. The juxtaposition of these two landscapes is unusual and impressive. And other widely differing Andean environments are in proximity, as the arid coastal plain rises to high cold mountains, which transition downslope into humid and thickly vegetated Amazon jungles. Unsurprisingly, this range of landscapes produces a tremendous variety of plants and animals. Weather patterns and landforms—the geography of the region—create this vast and unique environmental diversity.

The ancient Andeans took advantage of the natural abundance of their lands, and their population centers developed in areas of high biodiversity.[1] By domesticating many fruit and vegetable species, and combining these plant foods with protein from fish, marine mammals, deer, camelids, and other sources, the ancient people consumed a nutritious diet and could build surpluses of food for times of need. The wide assortment of plants that could flourish in their diverse environments was an important factor that helped to shape ancient Andean cultures.

Domesticating Plants

Plants were gradually modified from their wild ancestors in a domestication process like that for animals. As foraging people crisscrossed Andean landscapes, they selectively harvested the wild plants with the most desirable qualities. Among these are larger size, fleshy or seedless fruits, oily seeds, and tastiness. In cotton, they favored the long fibers used for cording early in Andean history and later spun into yarn.

As people moved about, often visiting the same sites seasonally, they dispersed seeds of their preferred plants. This process happened along trails and at campsites, both accidentally from seeds left in trash heaps and deliberately once people realized they could influence plant growth. When selected seeds germinated and began growing, plants effectively were starting on the road to domestication.

Encouraging plants to grow in harsher and more marginal environments took place continuously as people moved upwards into the Andean highlands and transported plants from favorable to less favorable settings. Domestication probably took place at many geographic sites and origin times.[2]

By 8,000 to 10,000 years ago, researchers recognize domesticated plants that were being cultivated in the highlands, suggesting that the path of domestication must extend much farther back in time.[3] The ancient beans and chili peppers found in Guitarrero Cave in northern Peru are among the oldest cultivated plant remains recovered in *either* the Old World or the New World.

Archaeologists recognize fully domesticated chili peppers from sediment layers in Guitarrero Cave dated between about 12,000 and 8,000 years ago, and maize (corn)[4] and beans at levels dating to about 8,000 years ago. The ancient Andeans may have tended these plants in small plots along the nearby river, as they were hardy types that they could sow and then leave alone while pursuing seasonal hunting and gathering in other areas.

How are the dates and locations of ancient domestication and farming practices known? Fragments of foods found at dwelling sites and genetic data used to trace plant origins provide this information. One surprising food fragment source is in the teeth of long-deceased individuals. Trace amounts of plant material such as starch grains can indicate domestic plants when researchers identify the distinctive silica bodies called phytoliths that form cell walls.[5] Such detailed studies frequently offer illuminating results.

An Andean Buffet

A bountiful buffet was available to the ancient Andeans when they combined the foods from many diverse ecological zones. In the Central Andes, these zones extend over a broad range of elevations with distinctive environmental tiers, or stair steps. From the coastal desert valleys near sea level to 13,000 feet (3,962 m) or even higher in the mountains, farmers could grow a wide variety of fruit and vegetable crops. Below is a look at an Andean "menu," including the principal foods specific to different geographic areas.[6]

Coastal Desert and Lowlands
The coastal river valleys that benefit from water drainage from the mountains are ideal for agricultural crops. In these lowland areas, the richer soils, higher moisture levels, and warmer temperatures create favorable conditions for plant growth.

Where the valleys are wide and irrigation is practicable, cotton and gourds may have been the first cultivated crops.[7] Over time, the Andeans added carbohydrate-rich vegetables and fruits, including beans, squash, chiles, tomatoes, avocados, peanuts, maize, guava, jicama, and the tuber cassava (also known as *manioc*, and as tapioca when dried). Without the availability of water, production of these crops would have been extremely limited, if even possible.

The region between about 1,000 to 7,500 ft (305 to 2,286 m) above sea level, called the *yunga* zone, is a warm and arid area favoring thorny plants, including cactus. Various types of fruits, including guava, cherimoya, and avocado—as well as coca, maize, peppers and other warm-weather crops—grow well in this zone, especially with irrigation.

The yunga zone is found on both the western and eastern sides of the Andes. On the eastern slopes, the sparsely vegetated mountains merge at lower elevations with the lush tropical forests of the Amazon Basin. Known as the "eyebrow of the jungle" (in Spanish, *ceja de selva*), luxurious yunga vegetation includes fruits and medicinal plants, such as coca. Many ancient Andean cultures traded with jungle societies to gain ritual drugs, gold, hardwoods, and the brilliant feathers of jungle birds.

Mountains
In mountainous regions, vast tracts of tempting open lands beckoned, but they also brought the disadvantages of steep slopes, rugged terrain, and thin and rocky soils. Low temperatures, sparse moisture levels, and frequent winds at high elevations created significant challenges for plant cultivation. Weather patterns exhibited impressive seasonal and annual variations and affected the length of already-short growing seasons. Productivity fluctuated dramatically from year to year, even between fields that are closely spaced, and crops that produced well in one area might fail in fields nearby.

The growing season in the mountains shortened as elevation increased. Each 30-ft (9 m) gain in elevation could reduce the growing season by one day, which means crop viability became more precarious as farming moved higher and higher in the mountains. Irrigation sped up the growing cycles of plants, allowing harvests to move forward to outrace killing frosts. Early or late storms could cause crop failure in one zone, but perhaps not in others.

In the *quechua* zone, between elevations of about 7,500 to 10,000–11,500 ft (2,286 to 3,505 m), dry farming could produce maize, beans, *quinoa* and the closely related *canihua*, a lupine bean (legume) called *tarwi*, and many kinds of tubers, including potato, sweet potato, *oca*, and *ulluco*. Irrigation was also used to provide water to plants when rainfall was irregular or insufficient, as well as to speed up their growth cycles during the short growing season. Above about 10,000 ft (3,048 m) in elevation, freezing temperatures can occur throughout the year.

The *puna* zone extends above the quechua zone up to about 13,000 ft (3,962 m). This region is cold, damp, and a marginal location for most agriculture. Potatoes and quinoa can grow successfully here, as well as tarwi, the lupine bean. Herding llamas and alpacas in this highland zone became an important puna activity, as the coarse grasses that grow at these high elevations provide suitable feed for these animals.

Altiplano
The high Altiplano region, with elevations of 12,000 ft (3,658 m) and higher, is cold, windswept, and subject to frosts and hailstorms throughout the growing season. Although agriculture has severe constraints at these high elevations, Andeans grew hardy tubers here like potatoes and cold-adapted quinoa.

For the societies that lived on the Altiplano, dietary staples included maize, beans, and fruits. These foods and nonfood items, such as coca and psychotropic drugs, had to be grown at lower altitude regions and then carried to the highland communities. Vast herds of llamas and alpacas became the source of wealth for many Altiplano people.

Notable Andean Plants

The Incas and their ancestors built their societies on a foundation of potatoes and maize. Potatoes grow successfully high in the cold mountains, and they became a staple food for millions of people. Maize produces the greatest yields in the more temperate weather of lower elevations.

Potatoes

Species of wild potatoes (genus *Solanum*) can be found throughout the Americas, where they need cool and moist growing conditions to produce starchy tubers. Archaeologists found scraps of wild potato dating back to 13,000 years ago at the Monte Verde site, showing the importance of this food early in Andean history. The potato findings at Monte Verde also suggest that potatoes may have been domesticated in the more humid lowlands of southern Chile, as well as in the high and cold Andes where they flourish.[8] Now a staple foodstuff around the globe, the Spanish introduced potatoes to Europe in the sixteenth century, and from there, people spread the plants to other continents.

Exploring the potato selections of a well-stocked produce market will make it obvious that potatoes are highly diverse in shape, skin, and color. Potatoes readily hybridize and adapt to numerous microclimates, most notably at high elevations in the Andes Mountains where they are resistant to frost. The ancient Andeans developed many potato types over thousands of years. An impressive 6,000 varieties, give or take a few dozen, are grown by Indigenous farmers in Andean countries today.[9]

People domesticated potatoes in the Andes as far back as 7,000 to 10,000 years ago.[10] They are a vitamin-, carbohydrate-and fiber-packed food that became an important part of traditional diets. One disadvantage was that potatoes are naturally quite vulnerable to molds. The ancient Andeans, however, found a solution. They developed a freeze-drying method they could use in the high mountains that is still practiced in the Andes today.[11] The *chuño* (Quechua word meaning frozen potato) that is produced from this process can be stored for months and even several years (Figure 11.1). Chuño became an important item for highland people to trade for products from lower elevation regions. It was a staple food for a majority of the Inca population, including the many thousands of soldiers in Inca armies.[12] Cooks typically combined chuño with other vegetables and meat in stews and ground it for use as flour, traditions that continue today.

To make chuño, Andeans spread small potatoes out on flat ground, where they freeze during the frigid nights. During the day, the potatoes dehydrate in the intense sunlight. After a few days, people walk back and forth on the potatoes to break open the skins and manually force out the water held in the plant cells.[13] The potatoes then continue to dry and shrink in size. This

FIGURE 11.1. Chuño from a market near Cuzco. Photograph by Eric in SF, 2006, available under a Creative Commons Attribution-Share Alike 3.0 Unported License.

technique also has the advantage of breaking down toxic glycoalkaloids that are poisonous and give the tubers a bitter taste. Clever adaptations!

Maize

The staple crop maize has a long and important history for ancient Andeans, both as a food and an offering in religious rituals. Similar to potatoes, many varieties of maize have adapted to different environmental conditions. The plants exhibit a variety of textures, sizes, and colors that range from white to red or black[14] (Figure 11.2).

Ancient people domesticated and cultivated maize in western Mexico roughly 9,000 years ago[15] and then dispersed it southward and into the Andes over the next few thousand years. Archaeologists have found domesticated maize at sites as old as about 6,000 years in the Andes, although it appears at first to have been a minor part of the diet until becoming a dietary staple around 3,000 years ago.[16] Maize has high water requirements, so increased consumption of maize may have been related to a period of increased rainfall or to an

FIGURE 11.2. Maize from Latin America, used in the Germplasm Enhancement for Maize (GEM) project to combine germplasm from unusual maize with domestic corn lines. Photograph by Agricultural Research Service, United States Department of Agriculture, 2005.

expansion of irrigation, which is usually required for this crop. Establishing a practice of fertilizing plants with camelid manure or bird guano also may have promoted the increase in maize cultivation.

Maize became valuable for trading and gift exchanges because it is a nutritious food that can be stored for long periods of time. The Incas held maize in especially high esteem, with evidence supporting its importance in their diet. When they brought new territories into their empire, Incas set up state farms rapidly to cultivate vast fields of maize.[17] Inti, the Inca god of the Sun, was closely linked to the growth of maize. In a shrine to Inti in the Coricancha in Cuzco, the Incas adorned a small garden with life-sized, gold-covered sculptures of maize plants[18] that were displayed in the annual festivals that marked the sowing and harvest times for maize.

Beginning over 2,000 years ago, the Andeans fermented maize to make an important ceremonial and ritual beverage called *chicha*. From the Tiwanaku culture[19] through Inca times, archaeologists have found ceramic vessels used for chicha brewing and serving in ceremonial contexts, indicating the important role of the beverage in religious rituals. This alcoholic drink was used frequently as an offering to the gods and given in quantity to people who were about to become sacrifice victims.

Preparing chicha took several weeks. People, usually women, produced the beverage by placing dried ground corn in the mouth and chewing to mix it with saliva, beginning the process of breaking down starches into sugar.[20] The corn and saliva balls were then spit into ceramic jars where they fermented. The Incas selected "chosen women" at a young age, whose major task was to make the vast quantities of chicha used in large social and ceremonial gatherings.[21]

People consumed chicha in enormous amounts at public festivals and feasts,[22] which sometimes could last for days and even weeks. The Incas believed that drinking copious amounts of chicha honored the Andean deities and its consumption was a ritualized form of worship. Spanish observers of multiday Inca festivals held during early colonial times were reportedly aghast at the public drunkenness with chicha, not understanding its ties to religious practices.

Chicha continues to be available in many Andean countries today. During my first trip to Peru, one man in our hiking group bravely sampled the local version. He promptly became unpleasantly ill and did not recover for several days, although most likely the water was the culprit in the mix and not the fermented corn. Bottled beer was a safer bet, so most in our group made that choice.

Bags, Boats, and Bridges
Plants played important roles beyond food, as robust types of grasses, reeds, vines, and other plant fibers had practical uses, including in many types of construction projects. In the coastal deserts of the Central Andes, 5,000 years ago or more, people made mesh bags called *shicra*, woven from grass or reed to enclose rounded river cobbles.[23] Builders of the Norte Chico step pyramids packed shicras into the foundations of their structures (described in Chapter 12). Archaeologists have found many of these durable fiber bags preserved at arid coastal sites today, and they are valuable for obtaining age dates. I was amazed to see photographs of these bags and picture the efforts of the long-ago builders who filled and placed them (Figure 11.3).

Many Andean cultures used thatched vegetable fibers to construct the roofs of buildings. The most useful material was coarse *ichu* grass (*Jarava ichu*, also known as Peruvian feather grass; ichu is Quechua for straw). The major

FIGURE 11.3. Shicra bags at Caral archaeological site, Peru. Photograph by Håkan Svensson, 2004, available under a Creative Commons Attribution-Share Alike 3.0 Unported License.

disadvantage of this practice was the flammability of the material. Archaeologists have found evidence of large fires in ancient Andean settlements, some of which likely were tied to times of civil upheavals, violence, and abandonment of settlements.[24]

Communities along the coast and near Lake Titicaca used plant fibers to build boats. For construction material, builders used lightweight balsa wood and bundles of naturally buoyant totora reeds.[25] Wood and reed boats built by Tiwanaku people were used to transport enormous stone blocks across Lake Titicaca (described in Chapter 18). Moche artists depicted distinctive reed boats on ceramics. Fishing people still use similar boats along the Central Andes coast and at Lake Titicaca today.

Built by the Incas as part of their extensive road network, rope bridges represent impressive engineering feats.[26] These bridges significantly improved travel in rugged mountainous areas, where rivers have carved deep canyons. They wove the ropes used for the swinging bridges from saplings, vines, and grasses that were twisted, plaited, and knotted into strong cables and then securely attached to stone abutments or anchors. Constructing bridges to link lands separated by deep canyons played a strategic role in Inca expansion,

FIGURE 11.4. Inca rope bridge across Río Apurimac, Peru. Drawing by archaeologist E. G. Squier, 1845.

allowing Inca armies to conquer new territories and to connect trade routes and the agricultural fields of previously separated communities. During conflicts, destroying bridges provided an effective way to slow a pursuing army. In stable periods, the bridges were valuable control points for monitoring travelers and collecting taxes.

Many bridges had remarkably large spans, sometimes extending to 150 ft (46 m; about the width of an American football field).[27] Stone bridge foundations, built from blocks expertly cut and fit to match exactly the contours of the underlying bedrock, anchored the heavy ropes. The suspended design of the longest bridges required substantial strength. To achieve this, bridge builders used three main cables. Each of these cables needed to support at least 20,000 lb (9,072 kg). With a margin of safety, the breaking strength of the largest cables may have been as high as 50,000 lb (22,680 kg).[28] The cables could be quite large: Garcilaso de la Vega, one sixteenth century chronicler, stated some were as thick as or thicker than a man's body.[29] Creating cables of this size and strength, and successfully spanning rivers and anchoring the cables, demonstrated significant engineering expertise (Figure 11.4).

A 100 ft (30 m) fiber suspension bridge connects two communities in the Andes today. Known as the last remaining Inca suspension bridge, the local people rebuild the *Q'eswachaka* across Río Apruímac periodically.[30] Working together, they collect the grass, intertwine the fibers to construct thick ropes, and then pull them across the river. The bridge is a remarkable acknowledgement of the engineering skill of the Incas, and the impressive extent to which the Indigenous people adapted to the challenges of life in the Andes Mountains.

Building Societies and Increasing Risk
In the vertically stacked ecosystems of the Andes, from the coastal valleys to the high plateaus, the variety of wild plants gave the ancient people opportunities to domesticate and grow many fresh foods. They could optimize crop production through their farming methods. As reliance on cultivation increased, flexibility and mobility became more limited. Foraging societies could adapt most easily to changing climates and resource availability, as they had committed little time and energy to building substantial structures. Once people settled down and invested in their lands with tilled and sown fields, irrigation, durable housing, and stored food, moving became more difficult. Andeans came to rely increasingly on domesticated animals, vegetables, and grains for food, as well as on associated social, political, and economic systems.

In the Central Andes, producing food posed many challenges, including erratic climate patterns, short growing seasons, and disruptions from geologic hazards. Nonetheless, Andean societies effectively adapted to their range of environments, and successfully fed their populations, generation after generation.

12

Monuments

The iconic symbol of the Inca Empire, Machu Picchu, is a spectacular place. An ancient checkpoint high above the city, known as the Gate of the Sun, holds the first memorable views for those who walk for several days to reach the city. Many of these hikers stumble toward the Gate of the Sun in the predawn darkness, hoping to see the first rays of sunlight illuminate the ruins. Most are disappointed because morning clouds and mists frequently obscure the sun. Also, since the last official camping site is a couple of hours distant from the gate, these hikers miss seeing the sights along the trail in the darkness. Fortunately, when I hiked this route, my group walked the last section in daylight. Many types of orchids and other lush tropical vegetation lined the superbly crafted paving stones and stairways along our path, and expansive views of distant peaks surrounded us. Our several-days-long hiking and camping trip was about to have a grand finale.

After admiring bird's-eye views of Machu Picchu from the Gate of the Sun and hiking for about a half hour down to the site entrance, our group of tired and rumpled hikers waited to see the destination we so eagerly anticipated. I felt somewhat out of place in the crowd of other tourists, most of them recently showered and wearing clean clothing.

Finally, we entered the site to an awe-inspiring view. A single doorway allows access into the city, and the ancient builders carefully placed that entry point to frame a view of Huayna Picchu, a towering mountain. Below, the intricate arrangement of stone structures, terraces, stairways, and a large grass-covered plaza revealed the meticulous order and beauty of the site. The next several hours spent wandering through Machu Picchu and exploring its multifaceted beauty will always rank among the most memorable times of my life. This monumental site is without equal.

Tremendous efforts were required to transform landscapes and build ancient Andean monuments. From the 5,000-year-old Norte Chico structures on the northern coast of modern Peru to the highland estates of the Incas throughout the Central Andes, these edifices have continued to impress people long after the societies that created them passed into the dust and ashes of history.

Ancient Andeans were building enduring monumental structures long before they could rely on intensive agriculture, and even before fired pottery was in use. These ancient people built the earliest Andean monuments over 1,000 years earlier than the massive structures of the Olmec, Maya, and Aztecs in southern Mexico and northern Central America. Monumental architecture along the coast of the Central Andes also predated the Great Pyramids of Giza in Egypt by several hundred years.[1]

How are monumental constructions distinguished? They generally have an unusual form and a scale that significantly exceeds what people need for practical function. Size counts, but more important is the tremendous amount of human labor required.[2] These structures can involve thousands of workers, toiling over years, decades, and even centuries. The engineering requirements, enormous size, and fine craftsmanship of many ancient Andean buildings are characteristics that define them as monumental. Such constructions in the Andes also include the hundreds of enormous geometric patterns and animal-shaped geoglyphs known as the Nazca Lines in southern Peru, as well as the vast road system the Incas built across thousands of miles of mountainous Andean terrain, the Qhapaq Ñan (variously translated from Quechua as "Royal Road" or "Road of Power"). Each of these monuments are enduring evidence of the notable and historically significant achievements of the ancient Andeans.

Why Build a Monument?
What was the motivation for building enormous adobe or stone-block pyramid temple structures along the Pacific coast, or the highland temples at Chavín de Huántar, or the massive Inca walls of Sacsayhuaman above Cuzco? Since monumental architecture first appeared on the earth's stage some 5,000 to 6,000 years ago, very few societies have invested the enormous expenditures of human labor and other resources for such constructions.[3] Why were some ancient leaders motivated to direct such ambitious projects, and why did the followers of

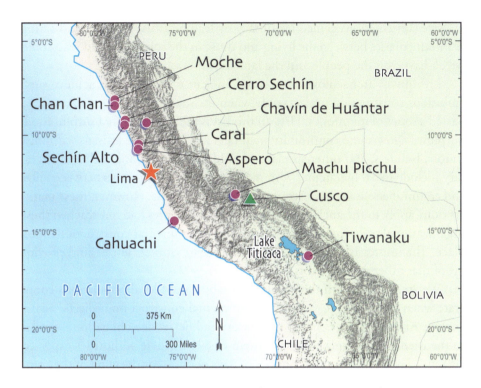

FIGURE 12.1. Map showing locations of monuments mentioned in text.

these leaders cooperate? The reasons vary over time, so the topic inspires ongoing fascination and scholarly debate. One thing that is clear, however, is that the environmental setting played a major role in monumental constructions in the Central Andes.

In a place where erratic weather patterns brought floods and droughts, and where natural disasters of earthquakes, volcanoes, landslides, and avalanches were frequent occurrences, logic suggests that the ancient Andeans would attempt to influence these hazards. By honoring the deities that controlled the natural phenomena, the ancient people hoped that their appeals *not* to have disasters happen would be heard.[4] Andean cultures were polytheistic, so they worshiped several gods that they believed could command events in the natural world. Building large and complex temples was a way of honoring their gods. Towering structures brought people closer to those gods who lived in the sky and to whom they paid homage. Authorities who rose to direct these massive constructions gained legitimacy by leading ritual practices and acting as intermediaries between the living and those in the spiritual world who could wreak havoc on the people and the landscape.[5]

Previously, archaeologists accepted ancient cultures could achieve such ambitious construction projects only when the social organization of a society passed a series of milestones. First on this list is the production of surplus food. Surpluses allow some community members to be full-time artisans, administrators, builders, and other specialists.[6] Additional milestones believed necessary include social hierarchies with marked differences in status between elites and commoners, as well as a strong central government. However, these markers don't apply to the ancient Andeans, as their societies had not reached these organizational milestones when the earliest monumental constructions took place. The impressive structures that the ancient workers left behind provide proof that other causal factors were in effect.

We are still left with the question of why would local populations cooperate when directed to take part in monumental construction projects? Many ancient Andean cultures had a mandatory public service obligation,[7] similar to the Medieval European corvée system of labor, where authorities expected citizens to work for a certain number of days per year for the good of the community. In the Inca Empire, they knew this obligation as *mit'a*. Also, strong and charismatic leaders could control religious ideology to gain cooperation. By contributing to these construction projects, workers would enjoy the blessings of religious leaders and, by extension, the deities who controlled so many important aspects of the natural world.[8]

Another key factor encouraging local populations to take part in constructing monumental architecture was access to food and useful plants. Some Central Andean environments had limited plant resources, especially in arid coastal deserts and high in the cold mountains. Archaeological evidence shows that food storage and distribution became centralized at an early date in many Andean cultures. Such integration of critical resources would have provided leaders with tremendous leverage to gain the cooperation of local populations and to organize work forces. By supplying laborers with an assortment of foods available in the different environmental tiers surrounding the monument sites, leaders could recruit them to take part in the economic system.[9]

People received other rewards for participating. Andean cultures have a long history of sharing food and drink to cement social bonds, as well as the exchange of goods and services based on reciprocity between and among individuals and groups. Hosting celebratory feasts as a gift to a community became widespread practices. The anticipation of participating in feasts, plus the opportunity to share a rich variety of foods, provided convincing reasons to cooperate in community activities, monumental construction projects included.[10]

Over time, motivations to build and occupy monumental structures changed. The earliest Andean complexes were civic and ceremonial centers that served as the social and religious focus for the surrounding communities. Many were pilgrimage destinations. Leaders planned the size and grandeur of the structures both as demonstrations of their power and to attract followers to a community.[11] These earliest sites showed no evidence of household refuse, hearths, or other indications that people used them as dwellings, or that leaders were exploiting their power to accumulate wealth by building palaces.[12]

Thousands of years later, the emphasis shifted and ego clearly played a part, as monumental structures explicitly began to display the wealth and power of the elite members of a society. When a leader can direct the expenditure of immense amounts of energy and resources for nonutilitarian purposes, that action is a universally understood and convincing expression of authority.[13] From the distinctive architecture used for temples and palaces to the vast agricultural terraces, irrigation systems, and extensive road network, monumental constructions served as frequent reminders of the supremacy of the Inca rulers. These displays of power produced Machu Picchu, Sacsayhuaman, Ollantaytambo, and the many other impressive monuments we can see at archaeological sites today.

The Earliest Monuments

The thin strip of Pacific coast beneath the high Andes peaks is among the most barren places on earth. With mile after mile of monotonous blowing sand, this flat landscape doesn't appear to be an inviting place (definitely *not* a land of milk and honey). Yet tucked into this landscape are fertile river valleys, where the brown colors of the sand and rock abruptly change to shades of green, and life-giving water supports vibrant plant life. Over 5,000 years ago, sophisticated cultures emerged among a cluster of these river valleys, in a region known as the Norte Chico.[14] Monumental architecture played a central role here, as archaeologists find remnants at more than thirty sites. Each of these ancient locations contains as many as seven massive, terraced platform mounds, an exceptional amount of monumental architecture.[15]

Associated with these impressive structures are dozens of urban centers. Stretched along the Supe, Fortaleza, Pativilca, and Huaura river valleys, the sites cover a north-to-south span of approximately 50 mi (80 km), with some areas constructed as far as about 15 mi (24 km) from the coast (Figure 12.1).

The Norte Chico people followed similar site designs for most of their monumental structures.[16] Typical shapes involved constructing a series of flat terraces, decreasing in size upwards, to produce enormous mounds (Figure 12.2). Many of the complexes were in a U-shaped design, with a large and terraced flat-topped mound flanked on both sides by longer terraced platforms. Often, the U-shape opened to the east and towards a water source, such as a river or snow-covered mountain peaks. Sunken circular plazas adjoined the mounds, with stairways leading upwards to provide access to the summit. The builders typically placed an open atrium and a series of small rooms on the mound tops. One impressive platform mound at the Caral site in the Supe valley measures about 520 by 490 ft (160 by 150 m) and rises to 59 ft (8 m), or about the height of a six-story building.

Substantial investments of labor were required to move the millions of cubic feet of fill material and rock to assemble the Norte Chico pyramid mounds. Some Norte Chico sites have natural hills incorporated into the pyramids, enhancing the mound size with an additional benefit of reducing the amount of construction labor required.

This monumental architecture reveals aspects of ancient Andean life. People designed the early pyramid mounds and plazas for prominent display and for community functions, where large numbers of people could assemble to observe activities conducted at the tops of the mounds. Archaeologists believe the large plazas, an integral component of many of the large mounds, show the importance of community participation in public events.[17] Although no one knows for certain what went on in these open areas, they likely provided space for feasts and parades. Entry into rooms on the mound summits was likely restricted to a chosen few. These rooms were hidden from view, and access was controlled with narrow passageways, suggesting an atmosphere of mystery and exclusivity.[18]

For over 1,000 years, near continuous refurbishing and remodeling enlarged and transformed many large pyramid mounds in the Norte Chico region.[19]

FIGURE 12.2. Terraced Pyramid at Caral in the Supe Valley. Photograph by Håkan Svensson Xauxa, 2004, available under a GNU Free Documentation License.

These cultures could support large regional populations with irrigation systems for growing a variety of food crops, combined with the rich abundance of marine resources. Centralized political systems developed, including leaders who had the power to direct people to build more monumental architecture.[20]

Moving Inland

Around 4,000 years ago, change came to the coastal areas of the Central Andes. The Norte Chico settlements were abandoned, and people established large new centers in the river valleys farther inland. The reasons for these shifts are uncertain but may have resulted from flooding and other adverse effects from El Niño events. The move inland also corresponded with an increase in irrigation agriculture, the foundation for the growth of subsequent Andean cultures.[21]

Many of the new settlements included monumental architecture. Structure designers continued the U-shaped configuration with pyramid complexes, adjoining sunken courts or plazas, and stairways leading to the top of a terraced central mound. They oriented the configurations consistently with the open face angled northeast towards the mountains, the source of essential water.[22]

Along the central to northern coast of modern Peru, at least forty-four of these complexes display strong design similarities. Together with other elements such as iconography, pottery styles, and settlement patterns, these repetitions suggest communication between distinct groups in the region.[23]

The groups built an especially impressive set of monumental structures of enormous size and uniformity at six major sites along the Sechín branch of Río Casma. One massive flat-topped mound constructed in the political center of the valley we know as Sechín Alto. This mound measured 985 by 820 ft (300 by 250 m) in area and was 115 ft (35 m) tall; it contains about 2,000,000 m² of construction material[24]. The builders used stone blocks in about 50 percent of the structure, some weighing over 4.5 tons (4,082 kg). Most of the remaining building material is of mud bricks (adobe), mortar and plaster from silty clay. The pyramid mound was part of a U-shaped temple complex with a total length of over 0.5 mi (1 km).

At Cerro Sechín just west of Sechín Alto, friezes carved along an outer wall of a small temple show a gruesome display of figures of warriors interspersed with dismembered human bodies. The specific message of this wall is unclear, with plausible explanations ranging from commemoration of a mythical battle to that of an actual battle, but the explicit violence is striking.

The leaders who controlled the Casma Valley cultures had considerable social control over their societies, enabling them to direct the construction of monumental architecture. A succession of leaders apparently ruled for some four centuries, an impressive display of political and social development.[25] These elites likely derived their authority by controlling rituals to protect the population, including efforts to appease the weather gods and promote the success of agricultural production.

By approximately 3,000 years ago, change was underway again in the northern part of the Central Andes. Societies abandoned many of the major coastal valley settlements with monumental architecture over a period of about 200 years.[26] At some sites, evidence implies that construction work on monumental structures stopped abruptly. People moved their settlements from the river valley floors to higher elevations, and into fortified sites built in defensible positions. Archaeologists suggest this change provides evidence for an increase in conflicts.

The environmental record reveals no strong indications of damaging El Niño events, but a different climatic regime in the mountains apparently developed. Cores drilled from ice in the Quelccaya Ice Cap glacier and from Lake Titicaca sediments provide data indicating low water levels in the lake starting around 1000 BCE and persisting for about 200 years because of decreased rainfall.[27] The rivers draining the highlands would have had reduced flows, which would have severely limited the amount of water available for irrigation downstream in the coastal valleys. Direct evidence for a decrease in irrigation water would be difficult to identify, however, the apparent collapse of coastal societies over a wide geographic area suggests this process as the cause. Climatic changes can strongly influence the trajectory of human societies.

Monuments in Mountains and Deserts

By around 3,000 years ago, the ancient Andeans continued to build some monumental structures along the Pacific coast, but they were building many more in the high mountains of the Central Andes. Societies had constructed platform mounds in the highlands before that time, but they were of relatively small size, probably reflecting the smaller populations then living in that challenging terrain.

Chavín Culture

The Chavín culture began land modifications and construction around 1200 BCE at a center named Chavín de Huántar, high in a valley in the Cordillera Blanca of northern Peru,[28] A dramatic set of monumental structures are arranged in a U-shape and include platform mounds, sunken plazas, staircases, and terraces. In the interior of the complex, builders incorporated a series of narrow passageways, small rooms, and water channels in a mysterious labyrinth. The Chavín people built and remodeled these structures over several centuries, expanding their construction as the center increasingly attracted pilgrims from great distances in the Andes. More details are provided on the Chavín culture in Chapter 17.

Nazca Culture

The Nazca culture dominated the southern coast of modern Peru from approximately 100 BCE to 700 CE. This society is famous for the enormous geoglyphs they created, known as Nazca Lines. Drawn on the broad and flat plateaus of the

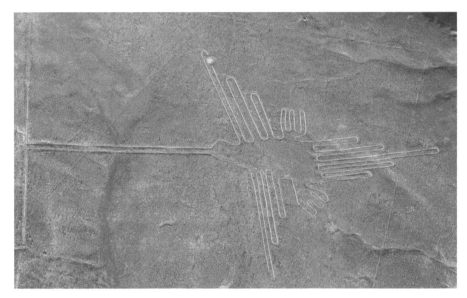

FIGURE 12.3. Hummingbird geoglyph by Nazca artists. Photograph by Diego Delso, 2015, available under a Creative Commons Attribution-Share Alike 4.0 International License.

coastal region, designs range from simple geometric shapes to plant and animal shapes, including a monkey, hummingbird, llama, whale, dog, cat, and other creatures (Figure 12.3). To create these line drawings, people moved the darker, reddish-brown stones that cover the ground surface to the side and scraped the sharply contrasting light-colored soil down to a depth of a few inches.

Theories on the cultural meaning and function of the geoglyphs range from the ritualistic to the practical. These explanations include worship of the mountain gods that controlled water, to astrological information representing constellations, to maps of groundwater flow and locations of wells.[29] People drew the Nazca Line geoglyphs over many centuries, so they may have had different purposes at different times.

The Nazca people also built a massive adobe ceremonial center at Cahuachi, which overlooks some of the Nazca Line designs. This center has over forty platform mounds[30] and three enormous pyramids, the grandest of them about 65 ft (20 m) high. Many of the platform mounds encase natural hills with walls of adobe bricks surrounding fill material of rock, soil, plant remains, and domestic trash. Archaeologists have found rich offerings in the adobe structures built on the tops of many of the mounds, including jewelry made of precious metals and ornamental stones such as blue green chrysocolla, painted textiles, ceramics, basketry, and even painted gourds.[31] Two of the monumental complexes at Cahuachi had U-shaped temples with the courtyards facing north towards two large geoglyphs and Río Nazca.

Multiple construction stages to enlarge and reshape the monumental structures at Cahuachi took place over several centuries. Eventually, the Nazca people abandoned the city around 300 to 400 CE. Archaeologists attribute this decline to crises that include an extended drought and possibly a destructive earthquake that damaged the complex. Evidence shows extensive ceremonial activity around this time, including numerous human sacrifices, possibly conducted to appease the anger of the gods and end the natural disasters. After they deserted the temples, the Nazca continued to use Cahuachi as a burial site. Geoglyph construction in the region apparently increased, perhaps as a ritual effort to increase water delivery during a long period of drought.

Moche Culture
While the Nazca people were tracing geoglyphs on the southern coast of modern Peru, people of the Moche culture were building monumental structures of adobe bricks in the lowlands on the northern coast. The Moche, flourishing from about 100 CE to 700 CE, built their principal city near the volcanic peak of Cerro Blanco in the Moche Valley, now adjacent to the modern city of Trujillo. At this location, they constructed two enormous platform mound complexes as sacred ceremonial structures. Viewed from a distance today, these complexes appear to be large natural hills.

The Temple of the Sun, named by the Spanish, may have been the largest mound erected in the Americas. In multiple stages of intensive construction, about 143 million sun-dried adobe bricks[32] were used to build a vast cross-shaped platform that measured approximately 1,100 by 525 ft (335 by 160 m) and stands over 130 ft (40 m) tall. Distinctive markings on the bricks suggest more than one hundred different groups shaped and then put them into place. The groups probably represent builders drawn from communities throughout the geographic area of Moche influence.

Archaeologists have found evidence of a royal residence, high-status burials in tombs, and the remains of ceremonial activities including feasting in structures on the summit of the massive mound.[33] The Moche people also constructed a nearby and smaller Temple of the Moon that incorporates a natural hill. A platform built over a steep rock outcrop is part of this structure.

The Moche spread a once-splendid city between the two major platform mounds. These structures, and over two-thirds of the Temple of the Sun, however, were destroyed in an appalling act. Early in the seventeenth century, searching for the hidden treasure they believed to hide in rich tombs in the pyramid, Spanish looters diverted the waters of Río Moche to "hydraulically mine" the pyramid.[34] Colonial period documentation shows that they discovered treasures,[35] but in the process they washed away much of the priceless heritage of the Moche culture.

Tiwanaku Culture
The Tiwanaku culture was a major power on the Altiplano between about 500 and 1000 CE. This society built an extensive ceremonial center with magnificent monumental structures in their capital city, Tiwanaku, near the southern edge of Lake Titicaca and now in modern Bolivia. The ceremonial core, surrounded by a shallow moat, contained massive stone gateways, platform pyramids, and sunken courts. Artists carved stone sculptures that were placed in the sunken courts, some over 15 ft (4.5 m) tall and decorated with human and mythical animal figures. This center was rebuilt and transformed almost continuously over several hundred years and attracted pilgrims from a wide region.[36] More details on the Tiwanaku culture appear in Chapter 18.

Chimú Culture
The royal city of the Chimú culture, Chan Chan, is one of the largest adobe architecture settlements in the world. Located on the arid coast of modern northern Peru, it is about 3 mi (5 km) west of the modern city of Trujillo. Prospering from 900 CE until conquered by the Incas in 1470, this culture built twelve monumental structures to house Chimú kings sequentially over hundreds of years. Each palace served as an administrative center and residence for a single king, and after the king died, caretakers maintained it as a royal mausoleum.

Adobe walls as high as 50 to 60 ft (15 to 18 m) surrounded much of the city, and some of the monumental structures had exterior walls that extended to heights of 18 ft (5.5 m). On the smooth faces of the adobe bricks, Chan Chan artists carved intricate designs of fish, birds, turtles, crabs, and other creatures, as well as geometric designs. Besides the monumental enclosures, dozens of intermediate-sized building complexes housed lesser elites, along with a minimum of 25,000 small, irregular-shaped individual rooms that were the residences and workshops of the commoners who served the royalty.[37]

Inca Culture
Last, there are the legendary monumental structures of the Incas. Most were built during the height of this powerful empire, in the decades following 1438. The Inca state carefully controlled architectural design and construction techniques, resulting in distinctive architecture throughout the realm. Core elements include stone block masonry styles and unique design details, including trapezoidal doors, niches, and windows; inward sloping walls; gabled or hipped roofs; and rectangular buildings.[38] For more on the Inca culture, see Chapter 19.

From the impressive imperial architecture in the capital city of Inca Cuzco to the palatial estates built for high-ranking elites in the far-flung corners of the empire, Inca monumental structures are prominent and spectacular symbols of the power of the Inca Empire.

Buildings of Adobe Bricks, Stone Blocks, and Shicra Bags

The ancient Andeans efficiently used local materials for their monumental constructions. Adobe bricks, or mud bricks, were commonly employed in coastal areas, while abundant outcrops of strong rock provided primary components in the highlands. Builders also combined stone and adobe in many structures. Built around 5,100 years ago, the earliest Andean monumental architecture is made of adobe bricks[39].

The optimum compositions and shapes for adobe bricks were likely established after a long period of experimentation. The ancient builders cut the first bricks from natural silt and clay deposits left by El Niño floods.[40] Later, people made more durable bricks by mixing soil components to achieve desired proportions.[41] Typically, these contain sand as one-half or more of the composition. Since sand consists primarily of tiny fragments of strong quartz, it provides strength and structure for the bricks. Silt and clay particles in smaller amounts than sand are necessary. Clay provides cohesion to bind the sand and silt and hold the mixture together, but too much results in uneven drying and cracking. Organic matter—such as straw, manure, or animal hair—can be added to form a reinforcing meshwork for the mix. These additions also help to make drying more even and produce a stronger brick. Workers shaped the bricks by hand or pressed the soil mixture into molds to achieve uniform sizes.

Similar soil mixtures were used to make paste-like mortar for filling gaps and sealing the bricks together, as well as to make mud plaster. Ancient builders frequently applied plaster to both interior and exterior walls to protect them from water damage and to provide a smooth surface for painted decoration. In the Norte Chico platform mounds, builders placed trimmed stone blocks on the outside walls of the structures and then covered these with plaster decorated in shades of yellow, red, beige, or white.[42] For descriptions of the pigments and paints used by the ancient Andeans, see Chapter 16.

Stone walls in Andean monumental constructions range from the finest trimmed masonry to rough work with unshaped field stones. The walls of the most important Inca structures contain blocks shaped into uniform rectangular shapes that fit closely together with little or no mortar, known as ashlar. Other walls incorporated polygonal shapes with multiple irregular faces and fit together like a puzzle. As one example, archaeologists have identified eighteen different stone-wall types at Machu Picchu (Figure 12.4) alone.[43]

Workers frequently quarried rock from local sources, although many societies transported stones for tens and even hundreds of miles. Naturally jointed outcrops of rocks are widely distributed in the Central Andes from tectonic folding and faulting, and these sources provided convenient "quarries" for the ancient builders. Chapters 17, 18, and 19 feature more details about the selection of rocks for monumental architecture.

Buildings That Last

At archaeological sites we can see today, monumental structures built by the ancient Andeans have survived hundreds and even thousands of years. Since frequent earthquakes are a characteristic of the entire Central Andes region, the resilience of this monumental architecture is impressive. What factors contribute to the earthquake resistance of these structures?

The curved wall of the Coricancha (described in Chapter 1), buildings in the citadel of Machu Picchu, and many other Inca structures have survived because of the dry-stone masonry techniques used by the builders. Workers carefully cut and trimmed stone blocks to fit together tightly without mortar. During

FIGURE 12.4. Terraces at Machu Picchu. Photograph by author.

earthquakes, these blocks move slightly, effectively dissipating the earthquake wave energy, but then resettle into the original positions.

Other characteristics of ancient Andean construction also contributed to earthquake resistance. Builders used strong igneous rock for many monumental structures, such as granite at Machu Picchu and the andesite of the curved Coricancha wall. Used for both adobe and stone block structures, solid foundations of blocks of rock and compact, box-like designs are stiff and strong architectural forms that are resistant to the deformation of earthquake-shaking.[44] Andeans also inclined thick walls a few degrees inward in a process called "battering" which further contributes to earthquake resistance. Builders constructed battered temple walls at Chavín de Huántar over 3,000 years ago, and the practice possibly began even earlier.[45]

Thousands of years before the Chavín culture appeared, builders used a unique method to limit earthquake vibrations in monumental structures at Norte Chico and other Pacific coast locations. These coastal societies placed *shicra* bags in the foundations of their step pyramids. These mesh bags were woven to encompass river cobbles and piled behind retaining walls or layered into the bases of the temple terraces (See Figure 11.3). Archaeologists at one ancient site found that the standardized weights of the bags ranged from about 50 to 60 lb (23 to 28 kg)—a weight that one or two workers could carry.[46] Bagging rocks sounds like a lot of extra work, but the Andeans knew what they were doing.

A group of engineers in Japan recently investigated the earthquake response properties of shicra foundations.[47] Using replicas of the rock-filled shicra bags as the substructure and large steel plates to represent the pyramid buildings, shaking table experiments produced accelerations that revealed the stability of the shicra foundations. Researchers found that, effectively, the woven bags with river cobbles displayed behavior similar to the base-isolation technology used for seismic resistance in important buildings today. When—and how—did the ancient Andeans discover this method of strengthening their ceremonial structures? We will probably never know, but the 5,000-year examples of the use of this method are extremely impressive.

Qhapaq Ñan—The Great Inca Road

Known as Qhapaq Ñan in Quechua, the vast road network that tied the Inca Empire together is also a monumental construction. We can trace the ancient roads along the western edge of central South America for some 3,500 mi (5,632 km), and they once extended across much of modern Ecuador, Peru, and Bolivia, as well as into northern Chile and northwestern Argentina. Today, this road system comprises the largest archaeological monument in the Americas.[48]

Archaeologists estimate the linear extent of the major thoroughfares in the Inca Road network add up to an incredible 25,000 mi (40,233 km) or more.[49] One north–south trunk line extends through the arid coastal plain close to the

Pacific Ocean, where dense fog hangs for months at a time and sand dunes shift continuously. A second major road parallels the coastal route along the spine of the Andes Mountains, rolling up and down through steep mountain passes, some with elevations as high as 16,000 ft (4,877 m). Extending from the Pacific Ocean to the tropical forests of the Amazon Basin, many east–west lateral roads once crossed the mountains to connect the two north–south roads. Radiating outwards from the Inca heartland in Cuzco, the road system unified the empire physically and conceptually, tying together this highly diverse geographic region. A map of the road system appears as Figure 19.1.

For comparison, the monumental road network of the Roman Empire that encircled the Mediterranean Sea and extended throughout Europe may have covered an astounding 250,000 mi (402,366 km) in the time of Emperor Hadrian, who ruled from 117 to 138 CE. The network of trade routes composing the Silk Road extended for about 4,000 mi (6,437 km) from China into southern Europe, and travelers used these roads from around 100 BCE into the middle of the fifteenth century.

Complex engineering was required to construct the roads of the Inca Empire over rugged terrain.[50] Skillfully designed drains and culverts redirected torrential rains alongside or under the roadways, walls of stone blocks protected coastal sections from blowing sand, and causeways spanned swampy wetlands. In steep and rocky areas, the builders carved paths, stairways, and tunnels directly from the underlying rock. Carefully fit together to smooth rough surfaces, flat paving stones covered even remote sections of the road network. Many precipitous canyons occupied by raging rivers had to be crossed. Wood was used to construct some bridges, but more frequently, the Andeans built swinging suspension bridges with thick ropes anchored to stone block foundations, as described in Chapter 11.

An essential function of the road network was to redistribute resources throughout the extensive empire.[51] Caravans of thousands of llamas carried agricultural products and domestic goods from the provinces as items of tribute that poured into the Inca heartland. Armies could move rapidly to wherever required, quelling local rebellions or expanding imperial boundaries. Trails led to shrines used for religious rituals, with some routes to high mountaintops where priests would conduct human sacrifices to appease deities. Carrying verbal messages and lightweight goods, relay runners provided an effective means for communication between distant parts of the empire.

Covering distances as far as 155 mi (250 km) in a day,[52] a series of these couriers would quickly transport fine fabrics, tropical fruit, and even fresh fish from the Pacific Ocean to the Inca emperor and other elites in lofty highland estates.

Throughout the road network at regular intervals, state-operated storehouses and rest stops (*tambos*) supplied food, gear, and resting places for travelers. The scale of these facilities is impressive—perhaps as many as 2,000 tambos throughout the empire[53] and tens of thousands of storehouses. The Incas stockpiled material of all types, including weapons, sandals, quilted armor, and blankets for the army; fine objects of gold, silver, textiles, and ceramics for the local elites; and wool, leather, rope, maize, quinoa, freeze-dried foods such as potatoes and fish, salt, and charcoal. The Inca leaders could distribute these items when needed, including for the frequent state-organized feasts for the local populations.

Inca law strictly controlled the road system, and only travelers having official permission and journeying on state business could use the major routes.[54] The mere presence of the extensive network served as both a physical and conceptual link that unified the Cuzco heartland with the most remote corners of the empire. The elaborate design of many of the roads went far beyond what was necessary for practical travel, including some sections with widths of up to 60 ft (18 m), about the size of five-lane highways, with lanes typically 12 ft (3.6 m) wide. Accordingly, the symbolic nature of the road system was likely very important; the roads were intended to amaze all citizens with the power of the empire and to highlight spaces where royal permission was required. In utilizing sections of these roads and trails today, the accomplishments of the Incas surely impress modern hikers.

Enduring Spiritual Power

Over millennia, many of the oldest monumental structures, especially those along the Pacific coast, have been modified by landslides, dust storms, and flood deposits. With those transformations, many monuments have taken on the appearance of natural hills. Despite these changes, and from the flat-topped pyramids along the Pacific coast to the Tiwanaku temple complexes on the Isla del Sol (Island of the Sun) in Lake Titicaca, evidence supports that many monumental centers had sporadic use long after being abandoned by the societies responsible for the original construction.

People most likely believed these sites embodied a focus of sacred power, where appropriate offerings and rituals could help to bring good health, crops, and fortune to worshipers.[55] Ritual offerings of shells, metals, and jewelry left by later cultures—including the Incas—have been found on many of these once majestic structures. This practice continues today, with offerings of coca leaves, coins, cigarettes, and trinkets left by those who hope that power emanating from these ancient monuments will enhance their own lives and those of the surrounding community. These traditions have deep roots in Andean history.

13

Ritual Drugs and Sacrifices

A distinctive plant with bright green leaves and red berries grows wild on steep slopes midway between the lofty peaks of the Andes Mountains and the tropical lowlands of the Amazon Basin. This plant is coca (genus *Erythroxylum*), and its role in Andean culture—not to mention its impact throughout the rest of the world—has been enormous.

The leaves of the coca plant contain several alkaloids, including a small amount of cocaine, which are released when chewed along with a source of calcium carbonate such as lime. Ancient Andeans considered this plant to be sacred, and they recognized its usefulness for suppressing hunger, pain, and fatigue.

Coca leaves continue to be used widely today in the Andes for a variety of traditional purposes. In the mountains of Peru, people commonly serve coca leaf tea, believing that the leaves are beneficial to health and capable of alleviating altitude sickness. When I drank coca leaf teas on airline flights within Peru and at hotels in Cuzco and Huaraz, or I chewed coca leaves, my mouth felt numb, but I had no other noticeable effects. Coca is also used to flavor foods and beverages in Peru, including hard candy. While perusing local consumables at a Lima airport gift shop, I thought about bringing coca candy back to California, until I considered the drug-sniffing dogs likely to be on patrol in the airport.

Neither the coca plant, nor its derivative, cocaine, are considered sacred in the United States—at least not by law enforcement.

It's a different story in the Andes, where plant-based narcotics, along with hallucinogens, have a long history. Chavín, Moche, Tiwanaku, Inca, and many

FIGURE 13.1. Chavín carved stone sculpture of an anthropomorphic jaguar bearing a San Pedro cactus in the right hand. Photograph by Aristóteles_Barcelos Neto, 2008, available under a Free Art License.

other Indigenous Andean cultures offered coca and other sacred plants to their deities, and they consumed them in their religious rituals. These ceremonial practices were as rich and diverse as the spectacular surrounding landscapes.

Offerings of many other types of precious items, from exotic tropical seashells to animal and human sacrifices, were made to inspire the gods' favor. When natural catastrophes occurred, such as violent volcanic eruptions or the devastating floods of El Niño weather, people attributed the events to gods who were angry or dissatisfied with humankind. Sacrifices were entreaties made seeking the support of supernatural powers to restore balance and normalcy in the world. While some of these practices appall many of us today, the ancient Andeans were clearly attempting to interpret and control the mysteries of the landscapes they inhabited.

Ritual Uses of Drugs

When the ancient Andeans ingested what they considered divine plants, they accessed a separate realm, a supernatural domain. Consumption of special plants induced altered states of consciousness and views of other worlds. Priests provided guidance for the altered states, presumably out of concerns for the physical effects of the drugs and religious consequences of the spirit journeys.

In the Americas, an impressive number of psychoactive plants, estimated at between eighty and one hundred different species, were available to ancient people.[1] By comparison, only eight or ten wild species of plants with these traits are native to the Old World, where ancient societies emphasized sharing the milder euphoric characteristics of alcohol, often in large groups.[2] In the New World, small numbers of ritual specialists used the intense properties of hallucinogens, shaping religious views that were strongly rooted in other realms of consciousness.

Two principal psychoactive plants, San Pedro cactus and the pods of the Andean tree called *vilca* (genus *Anadenanthera*), were consumed as a part of religious practices over millennia by the Andeans. Together with the stimulant coca, these prized plants played important roles in ancient cultures.

San Pedro Cactus
This cactus grows at high altitudes in the Andes Mountains and contains the naturally occurring psychedelic compound mescaline. It is a fast-growing columnar cactus (*Echinopsis pachanoi*) and flourishes naturally at elevations of about 6,600–9,800 feet (2,011–2,987 m) in the Central Andes. The plants are tolerant of low temperatures and can withstand high levels of rainfall. We know San Pedro cactus and other types of cacti, such as peyote, for their hallucinogenic effects.

Ancient Andean artists have prominently depicted the San Pedro cactus on pottery, textiles, and rock sculptures for at least the past 3,500 years. In the temples of Chavín de Huántar, artists associated San Pedro cactus with jaguars.[3] Some archaeologists suggest that the Chavín shamans believed this hallucinogen transformed them into these creatures when they used it. In the elaborate carved sculptures of the Chavín culture, artists illustrated San Pedro cactus as a staff held by anthropomorphic beasts (Figure 13.1). Depictions of San Pedro cactus on the decorative pottery of the Moche, Nazca, and other ancient Andean cultures provide evidence of ritual uses to achieve contact with supernatural realms.[4]

Colonial Spanish officials tried to suppress the use of the San Pedro cactus in their quest to convert their subjects to Catholicism. They failed in this effort, but perhaps they found some consolation in successfully assigning a Christian name to the plant. In what was a likely recognition of the plant's powers, the Spanish named this cactus after the apostle San Pedro (Saint Peter), who is the guardian of the gates to worlds that are unseen.[5] Traditional healers continue to use it in purification rituals to diagnose and cure "magical" ailments,[6] somewhat comparable to the psychosomatic disorders recognized in Western medicine.

Vilca

Many Andean cultures used the pods of the Andean tree *vilca* or *wilca* (from the Quechua word meaning "sacred") as a hallucinogen. The plant grows in tropical forests on the eastern slopes of the Andes and local people traded it to others in the highlands and on the coast.[7] Enclosed by pods, the seeds contain psychoactive substances. Ritual specialists pulverized these seeds to be inhaled as snuff, smoked, or ingested. Archaeologists have found evidence of use from the times of the Chavín culture through the Incas including wood and bone inhaling tubes, small spoons, pipes, and elaborately carved mortars and pestles.[8] Imagine the surprise of the early archaeologists who first encountered millennia-old drug paraphernalia! The Spanish Jesuits waged a sustained attack to suppress the use of *vilca* by equating it with devil worship. This campaign was successful, and by the time the Spanish colonial period ended, most public knowledge of this drug had disappeared.

Coca Leaf

Archaeological evidence extending back for about 5,000 years shows the widespread use of coca in the Andes.[9] To release the cocaine alkaloid, leaves are chewed with a small amount of calcium carbonate lime that can be obtained by burning seashells or certain plants to make an ash.[10] Researchers have found traces of both substances at ancient Andean settlement sites, including in the mouths of mummies, either as particles lodged in the teeth or as a lump in one cheek. In elite burials, the Andeans left small vessels of coca and lime along with other burial goods and placed these items in the mouth of the deceased, most likely to help the person in the afterlife.[11]

Coca held an important role in religious practices, and it was an offering to deities and venerated ancestors in many ancient Andean cultures. People favored it as a gift in social exchanges and widely shared it during public festivals and feasts. Medicinal uses include treatment for gastrointestinal problems and high-altitude sickness, although people also credit the leaves with easing an array of other problems, including headaches, constipation, asthma, and even healing open wounds. When people consume coca leaves in a natural form, they induce no physiological dependency.[12]

The colonial Spanish discouraged the use of coca in Inca religious practices, but they quickly learned the grim value of the plant for increasing productivity. Coca plantations became an important industry. Cultivation of coca leaf actually increased under Spanish rule, as it was used to pay native Andeans forced to work in the harsh conditions of silver and mercury mines.[13]

Growing, selling, and possessing coca for traditional uses is legal today in Peru and a few other Andean countries. The dark side of cocaine, or "white silver," has become a dreadful problem, as discussed in Chapter 21.

Exotic Seashell Offerings

Along with the exquisite gold and silver art objects that the Andeans used as offerings, they highly prized marine seashells from the warm tropical waters to the north. How and why this practice began is lost in the mists of time, but archaeologists have found beads made from these tropical shells in Norte Chico sites that date back to around 5,000 years ago.[14] The most important of the tropical shells was a spine-covered orange bivalve *Spondylus* sp., often called a spiny oyster, although more closely related to scallops than to oysters. The Incas and their ancestors believed these unusual sea creatures were a favorite food of the gods. They thought the shells brought rain and thus fertility and fresh growth, and that they represented the power of the sea[15] (Figure 13.2).

The *Spondylus* that Andeans collected in tropical waters were important items of the long-distance trades that were underway for centuries before extensive agriculture, social stratification, and ceramics appear in Andean cultural records. Over millennia of Andean cultural history, officiants placed these shells in the graves of prestigious individuals and used them as ceremonial offerings. Artisans carved the shells into beads and small figurines, and they incorporated pieces in jewelry and textiles. Controlling trade in these items motivated territorial expansion by many Andean cultures, most notably the Incas.

Archaeologists have found *Spondylus* shells at numerous sites in the Central Andes. The ancient people placed them in burial mounds at the 5,000-year-old sites of the Norte Chico. In the temples of Chavín de Huántar, the shells are a part of collections that include exotic pottery, and artists depicted them in

FIGURE 13.2. Pacific thorny oyster (*Spondylus crassisquama*), which lives in equatorial regions off the coast from Ecuador. Photograph by Kevin Walsh, 2005, available under a Creative Commons 2.0 Generic License.

stone carvings.[16] Moche artists portrayed *Spondylus* in the fine-line drawings on their ceramics. The importance of these shells is apparent for many other Andean cultures, culminating in the greatest and last of these, the Incas. *Spondylus* shells carved into small figurines were offerings at sacred locations, and archaeologists have found them recently in mountaintop shrines[17] and beneath the waters of Lake Titicaca, where Inca religious leaders placed them carefully centuries ago.

Sacrificial Rituals

Sacrifices of animals and humans were an important part of religious rituals practiced by many ancient Andean cultures. And they were not the only cultures in the New World to develop these rituals. From modern Mexico south into South America, for thousands of years ancient people widely practiced various forms of ritualized bloodletting, including human sacrifice, brutal games that ended in the deaths of the participants (winners and/or losers), and self-mutilation.[18] Given the limited cultural exchange between Mesoamerican and Andean cultures, archaeologists believe these practices arose independently in different regions.[19]

For the ancient people, the infliction of pain and sacrificial killing had different meanings than in our modern times. Researchers attribute the practices to an environment where natural disasters occur frequently. In some of these disasters, people disappeared when avalanches buried them, or they were swept out to sea by tsunamis, but in many others, blood was spilled. In what likely seemed a logical leap, people concluded the gods needed human blood, or bodies,[20] and so human sacrifice became accepted New World ceremonial practices.[21] The Aztecs carried this ritual to an extreme, as they believed that the Sun god had to be sustained by nourishment from the human hearts of war captives; they waged battles primarily to gain the thousands of captives they required for sacrifices.[22]

During periods of environmental challenges, religious practices assumed great importance, and ancient people employed elaborate rituals in efforts to appease deities and decrease risks. In our secular and highly technological societies today, it is easy to underestimate the powerful level of belief held by Indigenous Andeans that natural disasters could be related to human interactions with the supernatural world.

Andean ceremonies involving human and animal sacrifices followed important political events such as a victory in battle or the coronation or death of an emperor.[23] Ritual specialists used them for ensuring good harvests, during eclipses of the sun or moon, or in response to a volcanic eruption, earthquake, drought, flood, or other natural catastrophe. Many ancient Andean cultures performed sacrifices as temples were under construction, incorporating the victims within the building foundations. When an important person died, selected individuals were sacrificed and placed in the same tomb to accompany him or her into the afterlife. Ritual specialists held sacrifices at many sacred features of the landscape, including caves, springs, and mountain peaks and passes.[24]

For sacrifice, the Incas selected children and young women from throughout the empire based on their beauty, as only the best could be worthy to be sent to join the gods. Prior to sacrifice, the individuals ate special meals, dressed in elaborate clothing, and were fortified with alcoholic chicha. Throughout ancient Andean history, young llamas and guinea pigs also were frequent sacrificial offerings. In some ceremonies, priests cut these animals open and examined their entrails for omens.

Other Andean cultures sacrificed warriors, recognizable from the scars of past injuries that had healed such as skull fractures and broken limb bones.

Genetic testing indicates some victims were from local communities, but others were from more distant Andean locations, suggesting they may have been prisoners of war.[25]

Archaeologists have found evidence of notable mass sacrifices by the Moche culture, circa 600 CE, and about 800 years later by the Chimú culture, around 1400 to 1450 CE. Made under the duress of what appeared to be El Niño-induced flooding disasters, these ceremonial events involve unusually large numbers of victims. For both the Moche and Chimú, the sacrifices took place close to the crashing waves of the Pacific Ocean at the mouth of the Moche Valley, near the modern city of Trujillo.

The Chimú sacrifice site is in an area of sand dunes within a quarter mile, or a half kilometer, from the Pacific shoreline and a few miles north of the Chimú capital city of Chan Chan, at a site named Huanchaquito-Las Llamas.[26] During what was likely a dark and stormy time, religious leaders sacrificed three adults and more than 140 boys and girls chosen from the multiple ethnic groups in the Chimú state, along with over 200 young camelids. These were probably llamas, based on dental characteristics, but possibly also alpacas; distinguishing the two species based on bones is difficult. Most of the children appear to have been between the ages of eight and twelve years old, and the camelids around the age of only one year. Sacrifices all appear to have happened at about the same time, with most of the victims arranged in large pits dug through the mud and down into the clean sand. The ancient people left a few of the sacrificial animal and human victims out in the elements on the muddy ground surface.

The Moche leaders conducted sacrificial ceremonies in a plaza of their Pyramid of the Moon, a formal place of ritual and power.[27] In one group, they sacrificed at least 75 male warriors within a time slice of probably days or weeks.[28] Archaeologists found the bodies in a vertical sequence separated by five separate layers of the mud that was washing down from the adobe brick walls of the pyramid. Initially, the sacrificial victims were all left uncovered on the surface of the plaza, where the shapes of their corpses became imprinted into the thick mud.[29]

Shocking as they may be to us, these elaborate rituals appear to be a sign of the desperation the authorities faced as they made appeals to their deities to stop the devastating rains.

Mountaineers have found dozens of Inca shrines on mountaintops higher than about 17,000 ft (5,182 m) in southern Peru and northern Chile and Argentina.[30] The artifacts discovered provide hints about the ceremonies, including human sacrifices, which took place at these sites. Interestingly, the locations of these shrines overlap the Central Volcanic Zone of the Andes, where active volcanoes have been releasing steam, ash, or molten lava for thousands of years. Those who selected the ritual sites[31] may have been worshipping mountaintops as a source of water and fertility. Astronomical phenomena, such as the track of the sun at the solstice, may also have been motivations. The ancient Andeans, along with many other societies worldwide, believed that angry gods controlled volcanic eruptions and that placating these deities was crucial.

I understand the draw of mountain peaks. I have had the extraordinary experience of standing on the summits of many high mountains reached by technical rock climbing or hiking, and I have experienced the exhilaration of completing an arduous ascent and then being captivated by a spectacular view. The top-of-the-world locations, and perhaps evidence a volcano was stirring to life, surely provided powerful incentives for the ancient ones to undertake challenging climbs to honor their deities.

Most notable among the offerings found in Inca mountaintop shrines are the frozen bodies of children and young women, sacrificed on the mountain peaks as part of important religious rituals.[32] Many were the children of elites and dignitaries. Having a child chosen for these important ceremonies reportedly brought great honor to a family, although it also must have brought great sadness. Pilgrimages were sometimes taken to reach a sacred site, with groups walking for months while accompanying the individuals to be sacrificed.[33]

Many mountaintop shrines have suffered damage after centuries of weathering from wind and water, lightning strikes, and looting by devious mountaineers. Nonetheless, researchers have recovered a variety of intriguing artifacts in the past few decades. On small stone platforms and in stone block enclosures, they have found an assortment of common objects such as llama bones, feathers, coca leaf, maize, pottery, and fiber cords. In some undisturbed shrines, archaeologists have found high status goods of fine ceramics, exquisite textiles, *Spondylus* shells, feathered items, and elaborate gold and silver artifacts. Some objects likely honored the male Sun and female Moon, such as small, paired male and female figurines fashioned from precious metals and decorated with fabrics and feather ornaments, while items carved from spiny *Spondylus* seashells paid homage to the Mother Sea.[34]

FIGURE 13.3. Inca shrine at the top of Llullaillaco (22,110 ft/6,739 m), border of Argentina and Chile. Photograph by Christian Vitri, 2012, available under a Creative Commons Attribution-Share Alike 3.0 Unported License.

Ritual sacrifices took place on the slopes of the highest volcanic peaks in the Andes, involving strenuous climbs for anyone, but especially for children.[35] On Aconcagua, the tallest peak outside of Asia with a summit elevation of 22,837 ft (6,960), mountaineers found a mummy of a young boy buried inside a stone structure at 17,400 ft (5,303 m). A ceremonial complex with offerings, including the remains of three children, stood at an elevation of 22,110 ft (6,739 m) on the summit of the second highest active volcano on earth, Mount Llullaillaco (Figure 13.3). Archaeologists also excavated six Inca mummies and other artifacts from the inner crater of active Misti volcano, near the modern city of Arequipa, Peru. The mountaineering skill, as well as the faith of the Incas, was formidable.

The ancient Andeans who built shrines, left offerings, and conducted sacrifices cast themselves as mediators between human society and deities. The traditions they developed over millennia were a profound response to the dynamic environments of the world surrounding them.

14

Metals

Gold and silver beads in the shapes of spiders, peanut shells, and owls. Nose ornaments decorated with intertwined serpents and birds in gold and silver. A tall gold crown etched with the fanged face of a supernatural creature erupting into a swirl of snakes, and a small silver figurine of a llama. A death mask of gold with the features of a vampire bat, originally painted with bright red, blue, and green pigments. Clothing appliqued with thousands of tiny squares of shimmering gold. Small male and female figures shaped in gold and silver and dressed in tiny feather headdresses and mantles of woven wool. Ceremonial bronze knives, decorated with ornamental sculptures of animals and humans, sharpened for ceremonies involving sacrifices. These items—and thousands more recovered from ancient shrines, temples, and burials—represent millennia of metal art from the Central Andes.[1] They provide a glimpse into the profound role of metallic ores in Andean cultures.

Since far back in time, people around the earth have used seven principal metals. These "metals of antiquity" are gold, silver, copper, tin, lead, iron, and mercury.[2] We can find rich deposits of all seven in the Central Andes. The dynamic geologic environment that built the rugged Andes Mountains created some of the largest deposits of these metals found worldwide, and they became intertwined with Andean cultures.

Andean metallurgy used the same metals and alloys, or combinations of metals, that were valued elsewhere in the ancient world. Many of the objects produced by the Andeans, however, were quite different. In the Old World, from Africa through Europe and Asia, metallurgies emphasized the mechanical properties of metals—strength, hardness, and sharpness—for use as tools and weapons. In contrast, the ancient Andeans created metal products primarily for aesthetic uses and for religious items to honor deities,[3] and their material choices displayed a special appreciation for brilliance and a spiritual attitude toward light.[4]

I felt the attraction to sparkling gold at an early age while growing up near the Sierra Nevada foothills in California. Throughout my childhood, I heard many stories about the California Gold Rush, which began in 1848 with the discovery of gold in the sands and gravels of Sierra streams and rivers. Gold seekers from around the world raced to the region by the thousands, with high hopes of finding fortunes.

Although miners collected the most easily retrieved Sierra Nevada gold during the Gold Rush, this metal continues to erode from bedrock and wash into the rivers that drain these mountains. Panning for gold was a memorable summer activity when I was a young camper at the fittingly named Camp Gold Hollow. Standing in California's Eel River, I swirled multicolored sand and water around in a heavy pan. I carefully washed out the lighter mineral fragments, all the while imagining the gold nuggets that would appear if I could be patient. A small amount of black sand on the bottom of the pan rewarded my efforts. Poured into a small metal film roll canister, the black sand became a prized possession. Treasure to a child, but did this black sand really contain gold?

Metal Deposits from a Dynamic Environment
Concentrations of metals are irregularly distributed over our planet. Accumulations sufficiently large to make metal extraction practical, known as metallic ores, typically develop from the high temperatures, pressures, and shearing forces that deform rock when tectonic plates collide. The rows of volcanoes in the Andes Mountains contain especially high accumulations of gold, copper, silver, lead, tin, and other metal ores. Some of these metals, such as copper and silver, disseminate throughout a large area of rock. Others localize, such as gold accumulations in quartz veins within granitic rocks high in the mountains. Metallic ores concentrate along the major fault zones in the Andes, and the contacts where different types of rocks join.[5]

As magma bodies cool deep underground, different chemical elements and minerals crystalize at distinct and characteristic temperatures. Dense crystals form, settle downwards, and accumulate at the bottom of hot magma pools. After underground temperatures have cooled sufficiently to form rocks, folding and faulting associated with colliding tectonic plates can eventually push them

FIGURE 14.1. Map showing extent of principal metals found in the Central Andes. Modified from Jorge Oyarzún, "Andean Metallogenesis: A Synoptical Review and Interpretation (2000): Figure 11.

upwards to the ground surface. There, the rocks are exposed to highly erosive forces of wind and water. As the rocks gradually weather and disintegrate, they release the constituent minerals. Washed down into streams, heavier elements such as gold accumulate into placer deposits.

Geologists recognize repeated earthquakes as an important mechanism that concentrates gold. When water flows along faults and fractures in granitic rocks over millions of years, silica-rich veins of quartz gradually develop. During an earthquake, these fluid-filled cracks deep underground can grow, and fluid pressure will plummet. Trapped fluid instantly expands to form a low-density vapor that subsequently hardens along the cavity walls, depositing a thin layer of silica and trace elements, including gold. Over time, the cracks again fill with water, multiple earthquakes occur, and gold accumulates repeatedly during this "flash vaporization" process.[6]

In the Central Andes, concentrations of specific metals occur in elongated zones or belts that parallel the mountain ranges and major faults. These belts range in width from about 30 mi to nearly 200 mi (48–322 km).[7] The quantity of metal in each zone can be rich to scarce, and most contain a variety of metals besides the type(s) that dominate in the zone. The iron and/or copper belt occurs along the western edge of the Andes, with gold found where copper dominates. Next, a polymetallic belt contains copper, lead, zinc, and silver. Farther to the east is a tin belt, with tungsten, silver, and bismuth (Figure 14.1).

The linear metallic zones also correspond to segments with different geologic conditions along the mountain chain. These segments result from diverse geologic histories over tens of millions of years, arising from different compositions of bedrock units, areas of seismic and volcanic activity, thickness of the continental crust, and ages and composition of accreted terrains plastered or subducted beneath the South American continent (described in Chapters 3, 4, and 5). Erosion extent is also a factor in some regions, as deeper erosion levels into older rocks expose certain types of ore deposits. The geologic history of the Andes Mountains makes this mountainous region one of the most metal-rich regions on earth.

The Seven Metals of Antiquity

The seven metals of antiquity—gold, silver, copper, tin, lead, iron, and mercury—have relatively low melting points and are easy to process, except for iron. Most have the favorable properties of being soft and malleable, which allow the metal to be hammered into thin sheets and then shaped. Finely ground metals yield colorful pigments that the ancient ones used as cosmetics for elite women, body decorations for warriors, and on corpses in burials.

Metal use in the Central Andes developed early and became highly sophisticated, but before reviewing that history, let's look at each of these metals and their properties.

Gold
Most of us are familiar with the many uses of gold but might not be aware of where we can find it. In the Andes, it commonly occurs in nuggets and flakes of native gold, known as elemental or pure gold. We also find gold in naturally occurring alloys mixed with silver, copper, and other metals. Grains of gold can be completely enclosed within other minerals or can coat the outsides of minerals as rimes. The characteristic yellow color varies in brightness, depending on impurities.

Quartz veins disseminated throughout igneous rocks in the Andes contain considerable quantities of gold.[8] The erosive forces of wind, water, and scouring glacial ice eventually break down these rocks, freeing fragments of the shiny metal. In sizes ranging from fine powder to large nuggets, heavy gold washes downward into streams and rivers, accumulating with hard and resistant quartz sand. Glaciers break particles of gold out of rocks and transport them downhill, eventually depositing this metal along with rocky rubble in moraines left behind by retreating ice. The ancient Andeans could handpick nuggets and flakes of gold in the cold water of rivers and streams, and in glacial gravels. People continue this practice today in the high Andes.

Metalworkers can use native metals directly, extracting them from an ore is unnecessary, and the soft and malleable properties of native gold allow the metal to be shaped easily into objects. On the cold and windy high plateau near Lake Titicaca, archaeologists uncovered a gold necklace approximately 4,000 years old during the excavation of the Jiskairumoko burial site.[9] Nine beads hammered from gold nuggets and interspersed with greenstone beads, possibly sodalite or turquoise, were found near the skull of an elderly individual. Distinctive hammer marks on the beads suggest an artisan flattened gold nuggets with a stone hammer and then curled the pieces to create a tubular shape. The high social status of the owner is highlighted by that individual's apparent wealth.

Archaeologists also have found ancient evidence of goldwork from the burial site of a young man, dating back at least 3,000 years and possibly older. At the Waywaca site near the modern town of Andahuaylas in central Peru, this burial produced tiny pieces of hammered gold foil.[10] Also found near the burial site was a toolkit for a metal worker, comprising an anvil and three small stone hammers.

Ancient Andean cultures revered shiny, glittering gold, with color as the property that was most important. Gold had special ritual and political significance and became equated with status and power.[11] This conviction culminated in the immense respect that the Incas held for this metal. The vast mineral wealth of the empire belonged to the Sapa Inca, the supreme Inca ruler, as the society believed he was the son of the Sun, and gold was the essence of Inti, the Sun god who was their principal deity.[12]

Silver

In the Central Andes, silver is rare as a pure, native metal and miners must extract it from silver-bearing metallic ore. Silver occurs in natural alloys with copper, gold, lead, and zinc, particularly in sulfide ores found in areas of rock altered to a distinctive bright yellow-to-red color, called "iron hat."[13] These zones form when water reacts with sulfides associated with silver in exposed veins, producing sulfuric acid that oxidizes and creates the bright colors of the ore. The brilliant white luster of polished silver reacts easily with sulfur, and silver loses its shine when a black tarnish of silver sulfide appears.

Archaeologists can trace silver processing back for almost 2,000 years to around the first century CE. On the northern shores of Lake Titicaca, in an area rich in silver ore, archaeologists have found debris that shows complex silver production technologies.[14]

Silver combined with copper was likely the first alloy produced in the Central Andes.[15] This mix of metals has physical properties that are helpful for shaping objects, and artisans also could use the alloy as a solder for joining thin hammered sheets of gold or copper.

Ancient Andean societies revered silver along with gold. The shiny reflectivity of silver led the Incas to consider the metal sacred and as representing the tears of the moon.[16]

Copper

Copper typically associates with combinations of gold, silver, tin, and other metals, and occurs widely in the Central Andes. Native copper is rare in rock outcrops, as water reaching exposed or shallowly buried native copper alters this metal to various types of secondary minerals. Strikingly colored green malachite (hydrous copper carbonate), blue chrysocolla (hydrous copper silicate), and other copper minerals are readily visible and frequently found in the oxidation zones of Andean copper deposits.[17]

The Atacama Desert region of northern Chile is rich in copper-containing ores. Ancient miners from pre-Inca and Inca societies excavated turquoise, chrysocolla, and other copper minerals to make tools and artistic creations, particularly those used for ritual offerings.[18]

Andean artisans produced decorative copper beads as early as around 5,500 years ago from copper ore mined in the Atacama Desert.[19] Artisans frequently combined copper with gold and silver, using techniques that conferred rich gold or silver colors to art objects. They used copper to make small tools such as needles, tweezers, whorls for spinning yarn, chisels, and axes.

Mercury

Native mercury, also known as quicksilver, is rare. This shiny silver-to-gray metal is unique in occurring in liquid form at normal temperatures and pressures. Mercury can occur in a native state as tiny droplets, or occasionally filling a geode, a hollow, rounded rock.[20]

We find this metal most commonly in a scarlet red mineral called cinnabar (mercury sulfide), which typically occurs as thin vein-fillings in volcanic rocks associated with hot springs. When heated, cinnabar ore volatilizes, and drops of pure mercury collect on nearby cold surfaces. Inhalation of mercury fumes, or other direct contact with the mineral, is highly toxic to humans. The Incas, and possibly earlier Andean metalworkers, recognized mercury as a poisonous substance.[21]

Grinding cinnabar produces a bright red pigment called vermillion. Archaeologists have found this pigment in the burials of high-status individuals from Chavín to Inca times. The ancient people used it also in cosmetics and to decorate textiles and a wide variety of metal and wood objects.[22]

The ancient Andeans found several cinnabar sources in the Central Andes, with the richest of these in the Huancavelica region, now in modern central Peru. Researchers have measured the mercury isotopes from ancient artifacts left as grave offerings and identified most of the cinnabar as originating from the Huancavelica ore. The sampled artifacts came from the coast to the mountains and from archaeological sites that are nearly 3,000 years old, suggesting that people actively traded this metal across hundreds of miles.[23]

I have a special fondness for this metal. Mercury-in-glass medical thermometers were a part of my childhood experience in the 1950s; now, digital electronic types are safer. When my siblings and I were running fevers and a parent waved a thermometer in front of us, they would caution us not to bite down on it, which could shatter the glass and release the toxic mercury. But occasionally a thermometer would break, and we could empty the mercury into a glass—or into small hands, if an adult was distracted. Shaking the mercury would break it up into tiny silver beads that then roll back together to recombine, providing a fascinating toy. The name quicksilver is fitting.

Tin
Silvery white-to-gray tin occurs naturally primarily as tin oxide known as cassiterite, a heavy and dark-colored mineral. Ancient miners could recognize and collect the cassiterite mixed into placer deposit gravels. This mineral occurs in igneous and sedimentary rock, and it frequently associates with copper, gold, and silver ores in the Andes.[24] Extensive cassiterite fields in the highlands of modern Bolivia constitute one of the richest sources of tin on earth.

When metalworkers melt a small amount of tin or arsenic with copper, the result is bronze, a hard and durable metal alloy. The earliest bronze objects may have had either tin or arsenic introduced as a trace metal component of copper ore. This natural, unintentional alloying led to experimentation and the eventual adoption of bronze production. The ancient Andeans used bronze for ritual items and for tools such as axes, chisels, and knives. The Tiwanaku builders sometimes poured molten bronze into carved forms, or clamps, that held massive stone blocks together in their monumental architecture.[25]

Lead
Most lead ores are obtained from galena, a common lead sulfide mineral. Lead has a low melting point and can be extracted relatively simply from galena. Silver and galena often occur together, and so metalworkers probably discovered lead as a by-product of silver production.[26]

Archaeologists recognize many types of lead objects crafted by the ancient Andeans, including spoons, discs that may have served as jar lids, club heads likely carried by hunters or warriors, and in spindles that were employed for spinning llama and alpaca yarn. They have also found small, spherical lead artifacts at an Inca site in southern Peru that resemble the lead sling ammunition used by ancient Roman and Celtic groups, and likely had a similar function for warfare.[27]

Iron

Iron readily reacts with the oxygen in air to form oxide minerals, including hematite and magnetite, and rarely occurs on the surface of the earth in a native form. Many subsurface iron ore occurrences can be found throughout the Central Andes. The ancient Andeans valued this ore for preparing pigments such as ochre, the yellow brown to dark red colorings made from finely ground iron oxide mixed with clay.[28] They used ochre in body paint for warriors and in elite burials, for decorations on ceramics and walls of buildings, to preserve food and wood, for medicinal uses, to cure animal hides, and as adhesives. Iron artifacts are absent from the archaeological record of the Incas and their ancestors, as Andean metallurgy did not achieve the high temperatures required to work iron.[29]

Traces of the Past

How do we really know the history of the human use of metals in the Andes, especially those metals that were exploited thousands of years ago? We find an extremely helpful phenomenon in a "natural archive." Metalworkers release tiny particles of metals into the atmosphere during metal ore processing.[30] Eventually, wind or rain carries some of this material into lakes, where it becomes incorporated into accumulating sediments. Scientists today can retrieve sediment cores of thick layers of silt and clay drilled from beneath Andean lakes. They can analyze the metal content of the ancient sediments and find corresponding age dates from the sediment organic materials.

As one example, researchers have found the earliest recorded increases in lead concentrations over background levels beginning about 400 CE on the Altiplano. These increases are indicators of metallurgical activity involving lead by the Tiwanaku and Wari cultures in the surrounding region.[31]

Metal concentrations from specific time periods provide valuable records for reconstructing the history and intensity of metallurgical activity in a region. Combined with metal artifacts from archaeological sites, lake sediment studies provide clear evidence that the ancient Andeans used all of the seven metals of antiquity. More details on the sophisticated metalworking practices that the ancient Andeans developed are provided in the next chapter.

And what about the black sand that I carefully collected at Camp Gold Hollow? My imagination conjured up the wealth it must surely contain, perhaps allowing me to travel someday to the exotic locales I admired in the photographs of *National Geographic* magazines. Returning home from my time at camp, I would proudly show this treasure to my father, a chemist. He gently expressed his doubt that it contained gold. Decades later, I learned that black sand is a typical component of placer deposits. The black fragments I found in the sparkling river were heavy metals, probably the iron ore magnetite, left behind after softer minerals weathered away. Despite not finding gold, my childhood interest in minerals endured, and my professional work as a geologist fortuitously provided opportunities for visits to remote and fascinating places worldwide.

15

Mining and Metallurgy

Carving out a living in the Andes isn't easy. Meeting basic survival needs for food and warmth in the cold and thin air of high mountains and in arid coastal deserts requires great effort. Nonetheless, ancient Andeans did much more than devote themselves to tasks required for survival. From the earliest times, artisans invested significant labor in creating impressive works of art. Their art reflects concerns about the unpredictability of the natural world and human attempts to influence weather patterns, as well as destructive natural phenomena such as earthquakes and volcanoes.[1]

The ancient Andeans developed the most sophisticated metallurgical techniques in the precolumbian Americas.[2] For thousands of years, they crafted exquisite gold and silver metalwork items as prestige objects for religious rituals and for the elite members of society, conveying social status and political power. Innovations made by many earlier cultures paved the way for the fabulous Inca metallurgy.

An Inca myth gives insight into the cultural significance of metals. In this story, Earth lacked people and so the Sun, who needed worshipers, sent three metal eggs to Earth—one gold, one silver, and one copper. The gold egg produced noblemen, the silver egg produced noblewomen for their wives, and the copper egg produced common people.[3] As in the myth, the Incas favored sparkling gold and silver metals, but they also recognized the importance of copper. In metallurgy, copper provides strength and support in combinations with gold and silver in alloys. Similarly, the service of commoners is essential to sustain the lifestyles of society elites.

Mining and Metallurgy   167

FIGURE 15.1. A mythical condor or eagle from a hammered gold sheet by a Chavín artist, 2.5 in (6.4 cm) height and 2.8 in (7.1 cm) width (Ebnöther Archaeological Collection, Museum zu Allerheiligen, Schaffhausen, Switzerland). Photograph by Helvetiker, 2008.

The Andean people took advantage of the many metal resources found in their homeland. With a few exceptions, such as the gold nuggets people could pluck from icy streams, these metals needed to be mined. When we think about mining and quarrying operations today, we usually picture heavy construction equipment belching diesel fuel. It's difficult to imagine that the ancient Andeans made all their excavations only with simple hand tools, plus a tremendous number of hours of human labor.

Geologists today use steel hammers to break off fresh, unweathered samples of rock to identify the mineral components. Early in my geology fieldwork days, I learned that repeatedly hammering hard rocks is strenuous work, and so I especially appreciate the efforts of the ancient miners. Using only heavy rocks to crush and remove another type of hard solid rock seems like an attempt to carry water in a sieve. Quartz veins with hidden gold have an especially strong crystalline structure that makes them difficult to break. Whether angled into a slope or straight down into the earth, such veins would have been exceedingly difficult to follow.

Archaeological evidence of mining and processing of metals provides insights into the importance of metal resources in Andean societies. Widespread tunnel and trench excavations, piles of waste rock, and simple stone tools left behind are among the many indications of ancient mining activity throughout the Central Andes. Evidence also supports the sacredness of mines, from offerings left in shrines to musical instruments hidden away. We can visualize ancient rituals taking place, and perhaps imagine we can hear the soft echoes of flute music.

Andean Metallurgy through Time

With its intriguing heaviness and luminous yellow color that reflects the sun, gold was probably the first of the metals to be worked extensively by the early Andeans. Among the earliest Andean art objects found are gold beads, created by ancient artists who cold-hammered native gold into paper-thin sheets and then rolled small pieces into bead shapes.[4]

The physical properties of metals change when metalsmiths hammer or heat-treat them.[5] Workers seek a balance between the properties necessary for a material to be deformed and shaped, including strength, hardness, malleability, and melting temperature. In the simplest form of cold hammering, using a stone to crush fragments of metal against a rock anvil, hammering changes the internal structure to make metal pieces brittle and hard. Careful heating and cooling in a tempering process can reduce these unfavorable characteristics. Although this method may sound simple, the required knowledge and skill likely took a significant amount of time to perfect.

Archaeologists have found abundant evidence for a close association between religious ceremonies and metalworking that dates back thousands of years in the Andes. On the top of a monumental U-shaped, flat-topped, terraced pyramid at the Mina Perdida archaeological site about 25 mi (40 km) south of Lima, archaeologists have found gold and copper artifacts, along with ceramic and textile fragments, in refuse piles dated to roughly 3,000 years ago.[6] Small pieces of copper and gold foil appear to have been hammered from native metals, and the foils attached with some type of adhesive. Folds on pieces of foil suggest heating of metals in an annealing process that

FIGURE 15.2. Reconstruction of the tomb of the Lord of Sipán in Huaca Rajada, Peru. Photograph by Bernard Gagon, 2014, available under a GNU Free Documentation License.

the artisans used to increase the ductility, or flexibility, of the metal while it was being worked.

A few hundred years later the Chavín culture made significant advances in metallurgical technology. Working around 3,000 to 2,500 years ago, Chavín metalsmiths specialized in gold sheet metal technology by hammering gold into thin sheets and then embossing the back to create a raised relief design on the front of the sheet. They converted these sheets into three-dimensional objects by soldering different parts together, techniques that required an understanding of different melting points necessary to join the pieces.[7] Complex Chavín-style motifs of bizarre animal-human composites with the fangs and claws of predatory creatures decorated many of these objects (Figure 15.1).

Chavín metalsmiths also may have been the first to recognize that they could enhance the properties for working gold by intentionally adding silver to form alloys.[8] The addition of impurities—other metals that either occur naturally or are added deliberately—changes the properties of pure metals. By using alloys with varying concentrations of different metal minerals, metalworkers could make great leaps in achieving desirable qualities.

Almost all the Chavín artifacts archaeologists have found were items for adornment, including decorative crowns, face masks and other headgear, and small pieces of metal sewn onto garments in appliques. The trails connecting the extensive sphere of influence of the Chavín culture facilitated the sharing of both the exquisite metal objects crafted by Chavín artisans and the metallurgical technologies required to make them.

The Moche culture on the north coast of Peru produced highly sophisticated artisans and master metalworkers.[9] Following Chavín cultural traditions, Moche metalsmiths hammered metals into thin sheets and embossed the backs, then shaped the sheets into three-dimensional ornamental objects.[10] They worked different combinations of gold, silver, and copper in metal alloys as well.

Composite gold and silver was frequently used within a single ornament, plus pairs of objects created in gold and silver, and these combinations clearly were of special importance.[11] Archaeologists believe the Moche and other Andean cultures had a profound belief in the dualistic nature of the universe, in which two elements emphasize and improve the qualities of each other. From this relationship perspective, gold and silver are a natural pair, as well as male and female, and the sun and the moon.

Numerous elaborate gold and silver funerary artifacts recovered in recent decades from Moche tombs provide abundant evidence of the outstanding artistry of Moche metalworkers. The richest and most important burial site, known as the Royal Tombs of Sipán, are in the Lambayeque Valley on the north coast of modern Peru (Figure 15.2).[12] Although some tombs had been looted, archaeologists have recovered hundreds of stunning gold-copper and silver-copper alloy objects from other tombs, including a necklace with beads displaying peanuts (an important source of food for the Moche) and images of animals. One spectacular three-dimensional piece is in the shape of spiders clinging to webs, with human faces on their backs; artists applied over 100 solder points on each of ten gold beads.[13]

The richly appointed tombs of both Moche noblemen and noblewomen have revealed many treasures. In 2006, archaeologists excavated a magnificent tomb with a rich and diverse funerary assemblage north of the modern city of Trujillo. A mummied body was accompanied by extravagant gold and silver jewelry,[14] painted and embroidered textiles, gilt war clubs, spear throwers, and other weapons. Since similar grave goods had been found at other elite Moche complexes, such as Sipán, investigators initially believed the body was of a male ruler. Subsequent analysis indicated that it was a female, now known as the "Lady of Cao." Clearly, this woman was an important priestess or ruler of high status in Moche society. Her relationship to men of high rank, as well as the role of women in the power structure of Moche society, are mysteries.

The Moche excelled at creating objects that appeared to be made of pure gold or silver but were actually the result of sophisticated surface-gilding techniques.[15] Beginning around 300 CE, the Moche crafted a gold alloy called *tumbaga*, composed of gold-copper-silver in various amounts. Metalsmiths could work this alloy more easily, as it has a lower melting point and an increased hardness. To achieve the desired shininess on tumbaga, the Moche workers developed a process called depletion gilding. They combined copper with gold, and sometimes silver, and then applied the mixture to the outside of an object. The object was then either burned or treated with an acid to form a copper oxide on the surface that was rubbed away, leaving only a sparkling gold finish.[16]

After Moche societies disintegrated around 700 CE, traces of this sophisticated culture rose again a few centuries later in the coastal Chimú Empire. Also known as the Kingdom of Chimor, this society occupied an extensive territory along the north coast of Peru from about 900 CE until conquest by the Incas around 1450. Chimú artisans excelled at metalwork, and metallurgical production was a major industry in their capital city of Chan Chan, west of the modern city of Trujillo. Appliqued gold garments—in which they attached thousands of tiny gold squares to tunics, bags, and even shoes—were crafted for the elite members of society, along with many other decorative items including large ear spools in gold and silver.[17]

The Chimú and Inca metalworkers also produced tumbaga and practiced depletion gilding. Writing in the sixteenth century, a Spanish chronicler described how workers would apply a special concoction of crushed plants and manure to a piece and then dry it in a fire. When they removed the oxidized layer, a rich and shiny golden finish appeared, even when gold content was low.[18]

FIGURE 15.3. Ancient Andeans used these types of hammerstones, found at Machu Picchu, for mining, quarrying, and shaping stone blocks for construction. Photographs by J. P. Torres of San Francisco, 2006.

Metalworkers also practiced gilding by mixing gold flakes with either lead or mercury in a paste or resin and painting it onto a copper object. When heated, the lead or mercury would volatilize, and the gold would adhere to the copper, forming a gold sheet as thin as fine silk and producing coveted shiny surfaces. Many items, ranging from figurines to vases to jewelry, were gilded in this process. Records show that when the conquistadors carried their gold and silver loot back to Spain and assayed the metals, they found that the actual precious metal content varied considerably and typically was not as high as they expected.[19]

Metalwork reached a peak during the Inca Empire. A major focus was controlling territory with valuable resources, and the Incas expanded their empire to include distant regions with rich metallic ore deposits. To exploit the existing copper production and distribution systems in the Atacama Desert, they extended roads, expanded mines, and established new settlements with Inca-style architecture.[20] When they conquered the Kingdom of Chimor, the ruling Incas also recognized the exceptional work of the Chimú metalsmiths. To ensure that these artists would produce splendid objects for the benefit of the Inca elite, they forced Chimú artisans to move to the Inca capital of Cuzco.[21]

Precious metals conveyed rank and power and were important components of Inca gifts given to political leaders to integrate them into the political structure of the empire and as rewards for their services. The variety and abundance of gold and silver articles the Incas produced is legendary and a hallmark of this brilliant culture.

Tunnels and Trenches—Mines and Quarries

The ancient Andeans excavated the earliest mine recognized in the Americas, beginning roughly 12,000 years ago in modern northern Chile. At the ancient San Ramón 15 mine, miners dug a deep trench down into iron oxide-rich veins to collect the minerals hematite and goethite for red and yellow ochre.[22] We know the tools that were used to open this mine: hammerstones (Figure 15.3).

By using heavy hammerstones of hard rock to shatter the iron vein and extract the pigments, the ancient miners extended the San Ramón 15 mine trench for about 130 ft (40 m) with widths and depths of up to 20 ft (6 m).[23] How long this took by pounding hard rocks upon other hard rocks, we will never know. Around the mine, archaeologists have found hundreds of complete and broken hammerstones, some of them weighing up to 35 lb (15.8 kg) and composed of andesite, granite, basalt, quartzite, and other locally available rock. Debris found in the trench vicinity includes charcoal and food remains of mollusk shells, as well as fish and mammal bones. Radiocarbon age-dating of these materials indicates mining activity between about 12,000 and 10,500 years ago and then again for about 400 years beginning 4,300 years ago.[24]

Dozens of quarry pits provide evidence for ancient mines near the modern city of Puno, next to Lake Titicaca. Some of these quarry pits are up to about 32 ft (9.8 m) across and over 20 ft (6 m) deep. Large piles of mine tailings, or waste rock that was discarded, are still in place next to the pits.[25] The ancient miners completely excavated the ore bodies that were originally present, leaving archaeologists unable to verify which minerals were being mined. The former miners, however, likely focused on lead-containing galena with silver. On the northern shores of Lake Titicaca, at a U-shaped pyramid at a site named Huajje, archaeologists have documented a continuous 16 ft (5 m) deep sequence of silver metalworking remains, extending back for almost 2,000 years.[26]

In the Atacama Desert region of northern Chile, many open pits and trenches remain from Inca mining complexes.[27] The largest of these excavations are more than 65 by 85 ft (20 by 26 m) and 30 ft (9 m) or deeper. Archaeologists have found hundreds of stone hammers around the mines, along with heaps of rock refuse. Many of the hammers show evidence of a natural or pecked groove that once held a handle, most likely of wood that decomposed.

Ancient people recognized gold-bearing quartz veins in granitic rocks high in the Andes early in time. In this chilly, windswept terrain, the early miners followed the quartz veins by excavating tunnels that were only large enough to fit a single person. The miners relied on sunlight to illuminate their excavations, digging tunnels that typically extended only short distances of up to about 10 ft (3 m). Archaeologists have found numerous ancient small gold mines at altitudes clustering around an impressively high 16,000 ft (4,877 m) and higher.[28]

Sunlight, the availability of glacial meltwater, and the hardiness of the miners all controlled mining activity at these intensely cold high elevations. The miners collected flakes of fine-grained gold through gravity separation in water, known as placer mining. In canals or sluice boxes lined with animal skins or coarse gravel, the heavy gold settles out and can be separated from lighter minerals. For only a few months each year, and a few hours each day, enough warmth and sunlight were available to provide the meltwater needed to wash and separate the ore. During other times of the year, when storms rolled in and snow blanketed these regions, miners would retreat to settlements at lower elevations.[29]

Archaeologists recognize persistent hammering as the most important ancient mining practice in the Central Andes. An early technique practiced in other parts of the world, known as fire setting, may have been used to open tunnels into bedrock. In this process, miners would build a fire against a rock face, and when the rock was extremely hot, douse it with cold water, causing the rock to shatter. In my research, I found no reports of the use of this technique in the Andes, although some archaeologists have looked for evidence.[30]

The Andeans employed simple mining techniques, and mines stayed small in scale for thousands of years.[31] During this expanse of time, however, they developed an impressive understanding of the complexities involved in mining. Archaeologists have found evidence that they could identify optimal areas to excavate and to find suitable tools from their environments. They could also determine how to prevent a mine from collapsing, to cope with water seepage, and to minimize the potential for accidents. The tremendous efforts directed at mining, and the benefits of obtaining metallic ores, were a consequence of the rich natural deposits of metals found in the Andes.

Mineral Separation Steps

Excavating valuable ore-bearing rocks from mines and quarries is only the first step in mining, as most metals need to be separated from surrounding waste rock. Metallic minerals typically combine with other elements, including oxygen in oxides, sulfur in sulfides, and oxygen and carbon in carbonates. Crushing or grinding ore is necessary to begin separation and concentration processes.

Most of our information about Andean metal separation techniques comes from the Incas, as recorded in firsthand reports from Spanish chroniclers. The Incas, of course, used many technologies that people had been handing down for centuries.

Researchers have found evidence of crushing and separating activities near ancient mines throughout the Central Andes.[32] Discoveries include heavy grinding stones of granitic or metamorphic rocks, some weighing as much as several thousand pounds. Inca miners built grinding mills in two parts: a lower stationary base and a larger movable piece above that they could rock back and forth to crush the ore. To operate the upper part of the mill, workers pulled on poles, or walked back and forth along a plank across the top like a seesaw. Evidence of ancient canals, reservoirs, and drainage areas near some metal processing areas reveal that they also harnessed waterpower to grind ore. Fragile llamas were not capable of pulling grinding stones, so only human muscle or waterpower was needed and available.

High Temperature Smelting

The ancient Andeans could separate silver, copper, and other useful metals from impurities by high temperature smelting. Workers typically placed the metal ore in shallow stone or ceramic crucibles. They added chemical purifying agents during the melting process to drive off the oxidized slag, or waste material. After separating the pure metals and heating them into a molten form, the metalworkers cast them into solid ingots in stone or ceramic molds.

Smelting took place in furnaces composed of large ceramic vessels with ventholes along the sides. To increase fire temperatures, the Andeans placed these furnaces in areas of reliably high night winds, usually along hill slopes. Charcoal, llama dung, and the local coarse ichu grass were used to fuel the furnaces, and they also may have used the low-grade coal found in parts of the Central Andes. Visiting the silver-rich Potosí region in 1549, a Spanish chronicler, Pedro Cieza de León, noted that during dark nights, the thousands of glowing furnaces visible around the mines looked like decorative lights (luminarias).[33]

Ancient artifacts show that ore reduction techniques requiring temperatures greater than 1,800° F (982° C) were in use by the ancient Andeans roughly 2,000 years ago in the Lake Titicaca Basin. The remains of these processes include small bits of silver and copper ore, together with smelting debris of

FIGURE 15.4. Ceremonial tumi knife of gold, silver, and turquoise, height 14.25 in (36.2 cm), used by Lambayeque (Sicán) culture ca. 900–1100 CE (Metropolitan Museum of Art, New York).

chunks of glassy slag by-products and slag-encrusted crucibles.[34] Native silver with lead contaminants, or lead-containing galena with silver sulfide impurities, was probably being processed.

Vestiges of ancient practices coincide with the rise and fall of cultures. In the Lake Titicaca Basin, lead particles entombed in lake sediment cores corroborate the extent and duration of silver smelting.[35] Beginning around 400 CE and corresponding with the rise of the Tiwanaku empire, lake sediments on the high plateau record an increase in lead levels over naturally occurring background levels. About 600 years later, around 1000 CE, lead pollution levels fell dramatically, paralleling the decline of this imperial power. For the next few hundred years, the measured concentrations of lead in the Lake Titicaca region remained low but still exceeded natural background levels, suggesting limited but continued smelting activity. Following the Inca conquest of Lake Titicaca region societies around 1450 CE, high levels of lead pollution reappear in sediment records.

Cores drilled from sediments beneath other lakes in the Central Andes record similar patterns of lead pollution. One small lake named Llamacocha is located close to the rich silver-bearing ore deposits of Cerro de Pasco in the highlands of modern central Peru. Sediment analysis shows lead level increases correspond with silver smelting during the expansion of the Wari Empire, and then again throughout the time of the Inca Empire.[36] The Cerro de Pasco region eventually became one of the world's foremost producers of silver in the 1600s when the Spanish exploited the ore deposits.

Cinnabar and Mercury
Mercury, the only metal that is a liquid at normal temperatures and pressures, is abundant in the cinnabar found in the Andes. The ancient Andeans learned to separate mercury from cinnabar ore using a retorting process. When cinnabar is heated, the mercury turns into a gas that condenses on cool surfaces, allowing collection of the liquid metal. Archaeologists have identified cinnabar residues in ancient retorting vessels found in the Huancavelica area, now in modern central Peru.[37]

The ancient Andeans used mercury produced from cinnabar to purify Andean gold. Combining mercury with crushed gold-bearing ore produces a heavy gray mass called amalgam. Heating this amalgam volatilizes the mercury into the atmosphere, leaving behind pure gold. Analytical data on the composition of Andean gold artifacts shows levels of mercury consistent with amalgamation and subsequent burning to volatilize mercury.[38]

Metalsmiths can produce extremely bright and reflective gold by directing a focused and very high-temperature flame onto a gold-mercury amalgam in a crucible.[39] By blowing into long, narrow, copper or ceramic tubes, or blowpipes, metalworkers could volatilize residual mercury. The Incas used blowpipes up to a few feet long. Archaeologists have found these at archaeological sites dating back to the Tiwanaku culture, and artists depicted them on Moche ceramics more than 1,500 years ago.

Cores from Andean lake sediments reveal additional valuable historical information. As early as 1400 BCE, sediment cores show that the extensive cinnabar deposits at Huancavelica were being mined, probably initially to collect the red pigment called vermillion. Markers in the sediment records reveal a peak in this mining at about 500 BCE and then again at 1450 CE, dates that correspond with the timing of Chavín and Inca domination in the Andes.[40]

Bronze and Iron

Metalworkers produce the hard and durable metal alloy bronze by melting a small amount of either tin or arsenic with copper. In the Andes, copper-tin bronze artifacts appeared around 1,000 years ago, following copper-arsenic bronze that was in use roughly 150 years earlier (circa 850 CE).[41] The northern part of the Central Andes contains rich deposits of arsenic-bearing copper ores, and these were used to make arsenic bronze. In the southern part, people had access to cassiterite and made tin bronze. Andean workers typically cast molten bronze into ceramic molds for shaping. For centuries, geologic controls determined the type of bronze produced, since metalworkers used the local ores.

The Incas controlled the cassiterite mines in the southern part of their empire, and tin bronze became an imperial alloy. They sent cassiterite to northern settlements so metalworkers could manufacture tin bronze alongside the arsenic alloy.[42] Distinctive bronze tumi knives with cylindrical handles and semicircular flaring blades became symbols of Inca power, adopted from earlier Andean cultures including the Chimú and Sicán,[43] or Lambayeque (Figure 15.4). Sharp and highly decorated tumi were used in ceremonies involving sacrifices of llamas or humans. The Incas also used this alloy to make bronze maceheads and small ax-heads, with all considered markers of royal presence as they were crafted from an imperial alloy.

Andean technology did not develop beyond the use of copper-bronze.[44] The smelting technologies of the ancient Andeans were incapable of producing the sufficiently high temperatures required to reduce iron minerals into metal durable enough for weaponry. Given the long history and sophisticated metallurgical technologies of the Andeans, the absence of iron metallurgy remains curious. Perhaps this skill would have developed if the Spanish conquest had not halted cultural progress so abruptly. Alternatively, maybe Central Andeans simply had no need for iron, as bronze provided adequate hardness for common tools and ceremonial items. Creating ritual objects of precious metals to honor the gods and high-ranking members of society may simply have been enough.

The Sacred Nature of Mines

The ancient Andeans recognized metallic ores as a product of the earth, similar in value to agricultural crops and other valuable natural resources. Shrines and offerings found at mines and quarries—and evidence of ritual practices within mines—reflect their sacred nature and religious significance.[45] From the desert lowlands to the highlands, the Andeans built rock platforms for ceremonial activities on summits of local mountains overlooking quarries and mines. People made offerings to seek the favor of the mountain and mine deities, and in exchange for the minerals that were extracted. Artifacts found at shrines include *Spondylus* shells, which have had a ritual significance in many Andean cultures. Inca religious leaders left offerings that included small figurines of people and animals crafted from precious metals. Reports of human bones found at some of these shrines support the idea that these ceremonies incorporated human sacrifices.

We gain a glimpse of the sacredness of mines from an ancient hematite mine excavated into a cliff at Mina Primavera, now in southern Peru. Intriguingly, musical instruments are among the artifacts found alongside fragments of ceramics, woven cotton bags, and a collection of tools—bedrock mortars used to grind the ore, hammerstones, and other stone and wood-mining tools.[46] Carefully hidden in a small alcove over 1,000 years ago, and apparently undisturbed since then, archaeologists found two intact cane panpipes. Each panpipe comprised seven cane tubes of diminishing size, bound with cotton cording. Discs made from bottle gourds plugged the bases of several of the pipes, demonstrating that people could play these instruments. On the dusty cave floor, archaeologists found more gourd plugs, along with fragments of a flute carved from bone, suggesting that people had brought other panpipes and flutes inside to play in the mine's darkness. Researchers suspect people collected iron oxides from the mine and used this material to prepare ochre over many centuries. The ritual use of the mine may have continued even after hematite removal had slowed or stopped.

In the Andes today, people still consider mines sacred places. Sometimes, after work finishes, candles flicker and soft flute music may be heard in the shadowy underground darkness. Coca leaves, cigarettes, liquor, and other small items are left as offerings—and traditions established over thousands of years endure.

16

Decorative Arts

Ancient Andean artists created some of the finest textiles ever produced. Museum collections and photographs of these ancient textiles captivate me. A prized possession from a trip to Peru is a traditional weaving that I bought in the courtyard of the Museo Inka, near the Plaza de Armas in Cuzco. After viewing the fabulous collection of Inca artifacts housed within the museum, I admired the wares of the weavers displaying their woven textiles on the courtyard grounds. The piece I finally purchased has intricate geometric patterns in subtle shapes of olive and sage green, burgundy, and blue, and it now hangs in my home. I think about Andean weavers often when I see this beautiful piece.

Artistic endeavors were important in ancient Andean cultures, ranging from the earliest simple bone and shell jewelry to the exquisite textiles and ceramics produced by Inca artists. Materials from a wide range of environments were available for these creations. For thousands of years, the Andeans delivered cotton fibers grown in coastal valleys eastward to the high mountains and sent soft wools from camelids westward to the coast. They traded luxury items of woven textiles and decorated ceramics. They exchanged exotic items ranging from tropical seashells found offshore from modern Ecuador to the colorful feathers of jungle birds from the Amazon Basin. Trade networks played an important role in sharing technical information about weaving, ceramics, and other artistic developments.

Stylistic motifs on prestige art objects established cultural affiliation and could communicate social information across distances. Artists incorporated the symbols and icons of the dominant cultures of the time into textile designs and added them as decorations on pottery. Design elements rendered by the ancient artists include both the abstract—such as stripes, diamonds, and chevrons—and the representational—people, birds, fish, and plants. Older cultures, such as the Chavín, typically used a distinctive mix of part animal and part human designs. Later cultures moved towards more abstract and geometric patterns, culminating in distinctive and standardized Inca designs. Today, archaeologists use design elements as useful tools to understand the range of influence of a particular culture.

The tremendous contrasts in their environment—coastal beaches to rugged high mountains to Amazon rainforests—shaped the art and cultures of the ancient Andeans. They were surrounded by these distinctive landscapes, and subject to a wide range of unpredictable natural hazards. In response, the ancient Andeans built their societies around diversification, exchange, reciprocity, and control. Their artistic achievements reflect these fundamental practices.[1]

Fabulous Fiber Arts—Cotton, Wool, and Beyond
An exceptionally rich and extensive tradition of fiber arts developed in the Andes; possibly the longest continuous history of fiber use found anywhere on earth.[2] Specialists widely acknowledge Andean textiles as among the finest made by hand found in any culture, and industrial methods can never duplicate some of their techniques and patterns. As a highly valued craft, textiles could convey important social, ceremonial, and religious meanings.[3] They also had vital roles in economic and military realms. Many Andean cultures gave elegant cloth as gifts and grants in diplomatic exchanges and to cement political allegiances. Textiles had significant uses in rituals, including in offerings where religious leaders burned large quantities of the most exquisite materials. They are relatively light and easy to carry, making widespread distribution possible.

The earliest archaeological evidence of Andean textile traditions can be traced back to Guitarrero Cave in northern Peru. Archaeologists have found ancient artifacts of uniformly twisted and looped plant fiber that were made between 12,000 and 11,000 years ago.[4] The fiber products found at Guitarrero Cave are simple, but uniform and well-executed, supporting they are not the earliest attempts at fiber work.[5] These ancient ones constructed textiles and cordage from the leaf fibers of agave or bromeliad (*Agavaceae* or *Bromeliaceae*), and both plant families grow near the cave today.

People of the Chinchorro culture used artificial mummification early in Andean history. This culture flourished along the Pacific coast in the Atacama

Desert of northern Chile, where the climate is extremely arid. Artists produced handwoven textiles for mummification practices beginning around 7,000 years ago and continuing for nearly 3,000 years.[6] After a body decomposed in the dry climate, the bones were reassembled and held together with cords and canes, and a wig of human hair was placed on the skull. The Chinchorros then covered bodies in fabric shrouds skillfully woven by hand from vegetal fibers (looms were not yet in use). People apparently kept many of these mummies above ground and revered them as members of the family. This practice continued into Inca times, when the mummies of long-dead rulers were displayed and treated as if they were still alive.

The weavers of the Chavín culture, which flourished from about 1200 BCE to 500 BCE, made many technical innovations in textile production. These included extensive incorporation of camelid fleece into textiles and among the earliest recognized use of dyes for this wool. The Chavín were also innovators in creating textile paints and using textiles as a surface for painted designs, and their woven creations were used to circulate Chavín-style religious iconography.[7] Artists combined cultivated cotton and wool from alpacas and llamas in embroidered tapestries and weavings of many types.

In the highland climate of Chavín de Huántar, dampness has prevented ancient fabrics from remaining intact. In other areas, however, archaeologists have found many well-preserved Chavín textiles, revealing valuable information about the cultural life of this society. Archaeologists recovered hundreds of Chavín-style textile fragments from a burial site on the arid Paracas Peninsula, located approximately 300 mi (482 km) to the southeast of Chavín de Huántar. Many of these fabric pieces contain paintings of colorful Chavín plant and animal motifs in shades of brown and rose dye. Painted cotton fabric panels sewn together into large pieces were likely used as banners or decorative wall hangings.[8] Distinctive hangings, altar covers, and clothing constituted a portable form of ritual items that likely were incorporated in the religious ceremonies of Chavín sects.

On the southern coast of modern Peru, the Paracas culture (circa 700 to 100 BCE) used fabulous intricately embroidered cotton and alpaca wool textiles to wrap their high-status dead in mummy bundles (Figure 16.1). To make these bundles, many yards of colorful fabric covered with tiny embroidery stitches were wrapped around and around the body,[9] similar to how thread winds onto a sewing machine bobbin. Artists created some of these embroidered cloths on

FIGURE 16.1. Mantle for the mummy of a man, Paracas culture, fabric of camelid hair, 250–100 BCE (Textile Museum, George Washington University, Washington, DC). Photograph by Daderot, 2015.

a massive scale. One impressive piece measured 11 ft by 85 ft (3.3 by 26 m) and must have taken thousands of hours to make. Archaeologists have also found a mummy bundle of a prominent person that is approximately 7 ft (2 m) high, with the enormous lengths of fabric wrapped around the body after it was folded into a fetal position.[10]

The arid air of the region has preserved hundreds of Paracas mummies, and the cemeteries of this culture are likely the richest burial grounds ever found for preserved ancient textiles.[11] Inside the bundles, or nearby in these burial sites, Paracas people left offerings of prestige items of gold and shell jewelry and food items including maize, peanuts, and deer meat, suggesting that they believed the body needed sustenance in the afterlife.

Many Andean cultures also wove cloth for items of warfare. Slings were important weapons used to throw projectiles, made by weaving and braiding animal and plant fibers. The Andeans used woven cloth to make blankets and tents for soldiers, as well as packaging such as sacks for carrying supplies. They made helmets and armor of quilted cloth, or wound layers of cloth around

FIGURE 16.2. Quipu of cotton string, Inca, 1400–1600; cords are about 8.5 in (21.6 cm) long (Yale University Art Gallery, New Haven, Connecticut).

the arms and bodies of soldiers. Soldiers in Inca armies wore a uniform of a tunic with a black and white checkerboard pattern and a red yoke.[12] The sight of thousands of warriors in these bold checkerboard tunics surely conveyed a powerful message of imperial power.

The decorative schemes, weaving techniques, and garment forms signified ethnic identity and social rank.[13] The Incas produced vast amounts of fine textiles for use by the elites, some fabrics so soft that the Spanish chroniclers described them as silks. Commoners used coarser cloth. The designs woven into cloth were mostly geometric patterns of simple forms for lower status textiles and extremely complex patterns for royalty. Religious leaders burned the finest cloth in ritual offerings to deities, as they offered only the best to spiritual powers.[14]

For millennia, the ancient Andeans made knotted string devices that served a completely different purpose than other domestic items. Called *quipus*, from the Quechua word meaning "knot," these pieces could contain from a few to more than a thousand fiber cords of cotton and wool, with different knots arranged in clusters.[15] Although no Andean culture developed a writing system that we recognize, people could record a vast amount of information on *quipus*. They used these for basic arithmetic and to record numerical information pertaining to calendar events, tribute and tax collections, and census data. Non-numeric information, possibly representing syllables or words in a type of writing system, may also be encoded in features such as cord length, color, type of knot, and hierarchical position (Figure 16.2).

Archaeologists have found quipus at ancient Andean sites stretching back to the Norte Chico settlement of Caral, where one dates to between 4,500 and 4,000 years ago.[16] As these fiber strings typically deteriorate quickly, they are rare in the archaeological record. They are best known from their usage by the Incas, especially due to the written records of the Spanish during early colonial times. Sadly, as part of Spanish efforts to obliterate the Inca culture, the conquerors destroyed many quipus. Deciphering the information in the small number of quipus remaining in museums and private collections worldwide—perhaps only around 900—is an ongoing effort.[17]

Cotton and Wool

Cotton was one of the first crops domesticated in the Andes. The ancient people would have gradually modified the plant from its wild ancestors by selective harvesting from wild plants that had desirable characteristics such as long fibers. Cultivated in the fertile river valleys along the coastal plain, the first major use of cotton was for fishnets.[18]

At a few ancient Andean coastal archaeological sites dating back to around 5,000 years ago, researchers have found fragments of cotton cloth that were made without looms in a twining technique somewhat like macramé. Many of the fragments contain extremely complex designs of birds, snakes, crabs, and other creatures, in sophisticated imagery that is matched by the impressive technical achievement.[19]

The Andeans spun threads that are recognized for their extraordinary regularity in diameter and for their fineness, allowing them to create silklike fabrics. They spun raw wool and cotton fibers by hand, using drop spindles that comprised a wooden shaft about 12 in (30 cm) long with a heavy spindle whorl made of wood, stone, ceramic, or metal. One hand would hold the raw fibers to stretch and feed them into the hand holding the spindle, which was dropped while spinning rapidly, producing a thinly spun thread. The spinner could also twist two or three threads together using a drop spindle.

Over thousands of years of experimentation, the Andeans used virtually every weaving method known around the world today. The weavers employed three different looms to make cloth.[20] We know these looms primarily from depictions on pottery, but also from preserved artifacts. The most ancient and widely used is a backstrap loom, where the weaver leans backward or forward to apply pressure on the long warp threads while passing the weft through the warp. The Incas also used vertical/upright and horizontal looms that have fixed tension.

Feathers and Fur

The ancient Andeans highly prized the brightly colored feathers of birds, especially those from the Amazon jungles. Feathers were important items of long-distance trade. They placed them in elite burials and structures at archaeological sites in the Norte Chico, where they date back to approximately 5,000 years ago.[21]

Artists incorporated colorful and brilliant bird feathers of many types in headdresses and sewed them onto clothing.[22] They used feathers of local birds, including pink flamingos, which are native to both the highlands and the coast in the Andes, plus ostriches, rheas, ducks, hawks, and eagles. The most prized bird feathers were from hummingbird, macaw, and other colorful species found in the tropical Amazon rainforest.

Among the most prestigious creations of the Andeans were the complex designs they created by sewing feathers of various colors onto cloth. Thousands of artists were required to create such exquisite items. A tunic that belonged to a Chimú nobleman (circa 1400 CE) is completely covered in feathers, with a decoration of large blue pelicans being carried on red litters by smaller blue pelicans and all the birds surrounded by a field of yellow feathers.[23]

Feathers played other esteemed roles for the Incas.[24] The Inca emperor had a crown and wooden staff decorated with feathers. His attendants carried him on a litter covered with gold, silver, and feathers. Feather-covered cloth was given to soldiers. Feathers were used to clothe human sacrifices with headdresses, tunics, bags and other adornments, and archaeologists have found these items with children sacrificed on mountaintop shrines. An important Inca shrine on the Island of the Sun in Lake Titicaca reportedly had gateways to the sanctuary covered with feathers from tropical hummingbirds and trogons (or quetzals).[25] The Spanish chroniclers marveled at the large quantities of bird feathers stored in warehouses in Cuzco. Their reports noted that many of the feathers were quite tiny, likely from hummingbirds, and featured iridescent colors, shimmering in shades of green and gold.

A Spanish conquistador recorded seeing an especially unusual item of Inca clothing in 1533.[26] It was a fine cloak, worn by the Inca emperor Atahualpa while he was being held as a hostage. Dark brown and extremely soft, the origin of the material was a puzzle to the conquistador. Then the Inca explained: the cloak was of small pelts from bats. Artists had stitched thousands of bat pelts together. The Incas made the most of the vast abundance of resources available to them.

Colors of the Rainbow
Color was deliberately added to Andean creations in many contexts. For millennia, the ancient Andeans produced brightly painted ceramics, wooden vessels, textiles, and wall decorations. They extended the use of color to cosmetics for elite women and body decorations for warriors, and applied colorants to corpses in burials.

Artists made many pigments from powdered minerals that contain iron, copper, manganese, and other elements as oxides, hydroxides, sulfites, and carbonates. Organic materials used to create colors included roots, flowers, bark, and insects. Pigments do not chemically bond to the object they color. Paints are water-based or oil-based and convert to a solid film on an object. The Andeans made paints from powdered pigments suspended in a binder that could include animal fat, egg, plant juices, or blood. Dyes that use pigments are bound into fibers and are usually water soluble, requiring them to be "fixed" with a mordant such as urine and various chemicals, including metals.

The most frequently used minerals for pigments and the colors they produce are:[27]

- Blue and green from copper-rich minerals, including azurite, atacamite, chrysocolla, malachite, and sodalite
- White from gypsum (hydrated calcium sulfate) and calcite (calcium carbonate)
- Yellow-brown from goethite (iron oxide)
- Purplish-red from hematite (iron oxide)
- Orange-red from lead or cinnabar (mercury sulfide)

Fiber properties vary in the extent to which they can hold colors. In the earliest textiles, the artists rubbed colorants into fibers or painted them onto the surface of the fabric. Chavín artists painted banners that have been preserved for 3,000 years in dry coastal environments.[28] Proteinaceous camelid wool holds color more tightly than the cellulose of cotton fibers. Tiwanaku tapestries woven by artists more than 1,500 years ago still display colors as vibrant as if they were made only yesterday.[29]

Artists also incorporated colorful gemstones into artistic creations, such as jewelry and other decorative items. They used amethyst, emerald, garnet, jadeite, lapis lazuli, malachite, opal, turquoise, and other gems—plus iridescent nacre, or mother-of-pearl, from the interior of clam and snail shells.[30]

A Perfect Red

The ancient Andeans especially revered the color red, as did many other ancient societies. Red ochre from iron oxides, vermillion from cinnabar, or red plant-derived colorants have been dusted over corpses for hundreds of thousands of years.[31] As the practice of dyeing fabrics became an important cultural tradition, red colors became especially highly valued. Andean artists eventually happened upon an extremely vivid red dye called "cochineal," sometimes called "a perfect red."

I learned about this dye when I worked on a volunteer service project in Capitol Reef National Park in Utah. Midway through our tour of the remains of ancient Native American residence sites, the park archaeologist pulled a tiny insect off a prickly pear pad, placed it on her palm, and smashed it with her fingernail. A surprisingly large quantity of a bright red liquid appeared on her hand—*cochineal*.[32]

A tiny scale insect (*Dactylopius coccus*), closely related to aphids, produces cochineal, a carminic acid that is a deterrent to predators. These scale insects grow and feed on American cactus belonging to the genus *Opuntia*, or prickly pear. Cochineal most likely originated in the Oaxaca region of Mexico, and the timing of when the insect appeared in the Andes is unknown.[33]

To make cochineal dye, the bodies of the scale insects are brushed or plucked from the cactus pads, boiled briefly, then dried and ground into powder. People learned to extract the dye using various heat treatments, including by boiling the insects in water along with additions of alkali chemicals such as ammonia or calcium carbonate. Controlling these chemical additions, as well as temperature and exposure to sunlight, produces an extremely wide range of colors, from a deep crimson red to a bluish purple to a bright pink.[34]

Researchers have identified cochineal as the primary source of red dye for Andean textiles beginning around the third century CE, although people may have used it much earlier.[35] The major cultures of this time, from the Nazca and Moche through the Incas, used cochineal as their primary red dye. Artists could produce various shades depending on the white, gray, brown, or even black colors of the camelid wool yarn, as well as the preferences of the different cultures. The Incas produced cochineal-dyed garments with both red and purplish-blue that required special knowledge and skill. They considered the red and blue combination an important pairing, or duality, and used it during ceremonial activities.[36]

Spanish conquistadors recognized the value of cochineal when they first found cakes of the material in Aztec markets. They reported these cakes to the King of Spain in 1523 as a potentially important dye for European textile manufacturers.[37] After cochineal arrived in Europe, people received it with great enthusiasm. Vivid, fire-red scarlet was a color prized by painters and the wealthy members of society. The dazzling hues and colorfast characteristics of cochineal far surpassed any other red dyes available.

Cochineal usage fell when chemists developed synthetic red pigments in the mid-nineteenth century. In recent years, however, natural dyes have gained favor as part of a trend to reduce the use of artificial ingredients. Manufacturers add cochineal to many food products today,[38] including juice, yogurt, and candy, as well as cosmetic products such as lipstick and shampoo, providing appealing pink to red colors.

Crafted from Clay—Ceramics

Fire-hardened clay ceramics, or pottery, appear fairly late in Andean cultural history. Although the earliest pottery items may have crumbled into the dusts of time or have not been found yet, fired clay apparently became an important material only as recently as around 1800 BCE.[39] Andean cultures were making complex textiles, metallic art pieces, and monumental architecture for almost 2,000 years before they used ceramics—a time formally referred to in Andean chronology sequences as the "Preceramic period."

Ceramics appeared around the time that societies in the Central Andes began relying increasingly on agricultural production and becoming more sedentary. People may have discovered the path that led to pottery accidentally when fires burned above clay deposits, developing an intriguingly hardened surface beneath the fire. Also, items made of unfired clay might have fallen into fires, and they could admire the improved qualities.

Foragers used containers that are lightweight and were easy to carry, such as leather bags and dried gourds. Once people were living in permanent settlements, the durability of pottery became an asset and weight was no longer a concern. When agricultural crops began to be consumed widely, pottery vessels were especially valuable for boiling food.

The types of clays essential for pottery making are available throughout the Central Andes. Clay contains fine-grained particles that have a high percentage of silicate minerals, including quartz, with sheetlike chemical structures that trap water. The small particle size and a high-water content mean that clay can be shaped when wet and can keep that shape when dried, while also becoming hard and brittle. When clay is fired at high temperatures in simple pits with wood fires or in sophisticated kilns, the clay particles meld and bind and the material becomes especially strong and stiff.

Since the composition of clay is variable, people made additions called temper, comprising various minerals and organic materials to change the clay characteristics. The tendency to shrink during firing, for example, could be minimized when the ancient artists added charcoal, sand, wood ash, powdered bones, shell, or other fine-grained substances to the clay. Before or after firing, colored pigments, known as slips, were added to many types of ceramics. These decorative additions provided important opportunities for cultural and artistic expression.

The earliest method used to shape pottery was to form long rolls of clay that were coiled on top of each other and then smoothed out to build a shape. At least as early as the Moche culture, artists began to use molds, which allowed certain types of vessels to be mass-produced.

I developed an early appreciation for coiled ceramic works, although I was ignorant of the long history of this method until recently. As a child, under the watchful eye of my mother, for hours I practiced using coils of clay to build cups and bowls. My mother was an artist and made lovely ceramic pieces. I still use items she made many decades ago (my designs, however, quickly hit the local landfill).

Ceramic artifacts are exceptionally valuable to archaeologists. The durability of pottery means that ceramic items can survive for thousands of years after those made of plant fibers have disintegrated. Also, characteristic chemical compositions allow clays to be traced to the area of origin, and different cultures developed distinctive pottery shapes and decoration styles. In the Andes, the geographic areas occupied by isolated societies, the cultures that influenced them, and the time periods of their initial development through eventual decline are reconstructed largely from pottery artifacts.

Ceramic Creations

Beginning about 3,000 years ago, pottery from the Chavín cult was the first to be distributed along the Pacific coast and in the Andean highlands. These thin-walled ceramics are of high quality from a technical perspective, and they have an elegant and powerful aesthetic.[40] Chavín cult images are in the bold forms of fanged snakes, jaguars, and half-human/half-animal figures, and they show shamans metamorphosing from humans to animals to supernatural beings. The artwork depicts transformations from one plane of existence into another, reflecting beliefs that became common to many Andean cultures.

Distinctive stirrup-spout pottery vessels are characteristic of the Chavín-influenced cultures of this period.[41] This style has a cylindrical upright spout that splits into two curved ones that join a rounded vessel, effectively combining handle and spout (Figure 16.3). Artists incised the Chavín images into the moist clay and then selectively burnished with a smooth tool, resulting in a glassy sheen on the images so they became distinct from the background matte or textured portions of clay. Red and black colors were used to emphasize the figures.

The Nazca culture were not only the creators of enormous geoglyphs on the south coast of Peru about 2,000 years ago, but also the first Andeans to introduce vibrant colors to decorate pottery.[42] These artists created up to thirteen different slip colors to apply to clay vessels before firing, using a variety of mineral pigments. The colors included rare blue-gray, maroon, and light purple, along with red, black, white, and other colors. Nazca artists applied patterns to ceramics like those they used in weaving textiles. Turntables were used to revolve the pots so that the artist could make decorations evenly on all sides.[43]

Along the north coast of Peru, the Moche culture created a ceramic art that is arguably the pinnacle of Andean aesthetics. Moche artists created many pieces in three-dimensional forms depicting animals such as birds and monkeys, and the faces of men in "portrait heads" with the defining features of specific individuals.[44] They also decorated their ceramic vessels with exquisite fine-line drawings of intricate narratives.[45] The meticulous scenes cover a wide range of

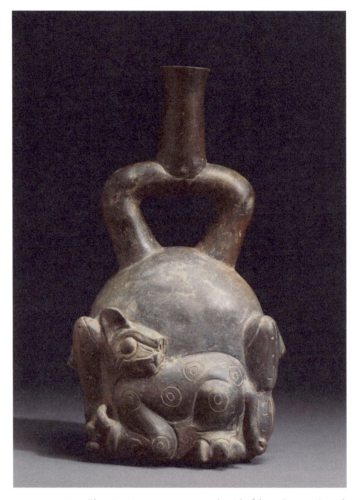

FIGURE 16.3. Chavín stirrup-spout vessel with feline (jaguar?) and San Pedro cactus, 11.7 in (29.8 cm) height and 6.7 in (17.1 cm) width (Walters Art Museum, Baltimore, Maryland).

political, mythical, erotic, and supernatural subjects with rich imagery. These range from including marine activities with reed boats and sea creatures—some animated by attaching human arms and legs to the images—to burial scenes, to a shaman becoming an owl. The artists frequently depicted the ritual violence that was part of this culture, including human sacrifice, in scenes such as a high lord receiving the blood of prisoners having their throats cut.

FIGURE 16.4. Moche stirrup-spout vessel with portrait head, 7.25 in (18.42 cm) height and 7.12 in (18.08 cm) width (Metropolitan Museum of Art, New York).

The Moche ceramic vessels of portrait heads for high-status men are especially notable. Believed to be realistic portraits, these ceramic images convey personality besides the careful depiction of nose shapes, chins, and other distinctive details of appearance (Figure 16.4). Extraordinary series of portrait vessels exist, including one of over forty-five portraits created throughout much of the life of an individual with a distinctive scar on his lip. Other chilling sequences depict important men who later are shown as captives with ropes around their necks, likely prior to sacrifice, providing a window into the shifting and volatile political powers of the Moche world.

For many years, archaeologists considered the narratives presented on Moche pottery as myths. Then, beginning in the 1980s, they found undisturbed burials of lavishly ornamented individuals dressed in finery that was the same as that shown in drawings on ceramics—extraordinary evidence the pottery depictions were true to life.[46] These remarkable Moche burials, the

Royal Tombs of Sipán, also contained exquisite gold and silver art objects, as described in Chapter 15.

The Inca Empire introduced a standardized artistic style that was widely applied for ceramics and other aesthetic items.[47] Based on simple geometric patterns and motifs that artists could reproduce throughout the kingdom, the Incas designed their styles to be readily recognizable as symbols of imperial presence. This approach extended to specific identifiable shapes, including long-necked jars with low-set handles and pointed ends that could sit on the ground for easier pouring. They standardized the internal volumes of many of these vessels so that someone could easily identify the amounts of maize kernels or maize beer. Enormous numbers of chicha-brewing vessels, serving dishes and other pottery dishes were produced for the large-scale feasts that were frequently held. These ceramics were decorated with geometric designs, ranging from straight to curved and wavy lines and flame-shaped images, and these symbols were used to spread the power and prestige of the Inca Empire.

***

From nutritious foods to useful materials for construction projects and artistic endeavors, the tremendous variety of natural resources available in the central Andes provided a foundation for the development of sophisticated cultures. In the chapters that follow in Part III, I describe the accomplishments of three major cultures with influence over extensive areas of the Andes—the Chavín, Tiwanaku, and Inca.

Part III

Three Monumental and Unifying Cultures

17

Water and Power

A spectacular mountain valley high on the rugged eastern flank of the Cordillera Blanca was once the home of a sophisticated culture with refined art and monumental architecture. Beginning about 3,000 years ago, ancient builders constructed a ceremonial center in this narrow, steep-walled valley where two rivers tumble down from the surrounding mountains and join. To the ancient Andeans, these waters were a source of sacred power. The waters became the centerpiece of a monumental complex called Chavín de Huántar, built by a society that thrived for hundreds of years beginning as early as about 1200 BCE.

This is the Andes, so along with the beauty of the surrounding landscape, rumblings are afoot. The picturesque scenery of the Chavín site masks the dynamic geologic setting of the area. Frequent earthquakes and a large seasonal variation in rain and snowfall combine to make these mountains renowned for their instability. Catastrophic landslides and avalanches periodically sweep down from the peaks, bringing devastation to people living below.

Traveling from Huaraz east to the Chavín region on one of my trips to Peru, my geologist friends and I saw the signs of large earthquakes as we examined prominent fault scarps we could trace for miles along the western edge of the mountain front. After crossing the highlands, and as we followed a winding road in our descent into the mountain valley, many scars left by landslides were clearly visible on the slopes surrounding the archaeological site. Seeing this evidence of geologic hazards that could have been devastating for the ancient people made a powerful impression. Despite these challenges, the Chavín culture thrived for hundreds of years.

Archaeologists believe that Chavín de Huántar was the principal seat of an important religious power and that the monumental structures built by this society provided a gathering place for pilgrims.[1] An exceptional style of art represents a set of sacred beliefs and an essential part of Chavín culture—a Chavín cult. No one knows for sure, but this cult may have worshipped weather gods associated with rainfall, hail, and frost, or possibly an earthquake god. Guided by what were likely charismatic priests or shaman, this cult had phenomenal longevity.

For the first time in Andean history, Chavín leaders could develop a common influence across many distinctive societies throughout a wide geographic region. Visiting pilgrims brought offerings from coastal and highland areas at great distances. Archaeologists have discovered Chavín iconography in settlements of roughly the same age along the north and central coasts and in the highlands of the Central Andes. Portable art objects of exquisite textiles, ceramics, and precious metals decorated with distinctive Chavín artwork, allow researchers to trace the far-reaching influence of this culture.[2]

What factors contributed to the rise and eventual demise of the society that accomplished so much at Chavín de Huántar? Many difficulties came with living in their mountain valley. And why did the ancient builders choose a site subject to frequent floods and landslides even though areas less vulnerable to these hazards are located nearby in the valley, including the site of the modern town of Chavín?[3]

By understanding the natural setting of the active landscape where the Chavín people prospered, we can better appreciate the unique features of that valley, as well as the challenges the inhabitants faced.

A Dynamic Setting

The ancient Andeans nestled Chavín de Huántar into a small valley at a chilly elevation of about 10,400 ft (3,170 m) approximately 25 mi (40 km) directly east of the modern city of Huaraz. Located roughly midway between the Amazon jungles and the Pacific coast, and near two mountain passes that permitted east–west travel, the valley is in a favorable position for collecting and disseminating ideas and material goods.[4] The dramatic mountain setting, as well as the dynamism apparent in the earthquakes and floods that frequently occur in the area, suggests that the site is of special importance as well. The power and unpredictability of the location would have strongly impressed Chavín residents and visitors, and likely played an important part in its selection for the monumental constructions of a religious center.

Throughout the Central Andes, the ancient people recognized landscape features—including mountains, rocks, rivers, and streams—as having important religious and ceremonial significance. At Chavín de Huántar, where two rivers join, running water became significant in the ceremonial importance of the monumental complex.[5] Río Wacheqsa extends down the small valley and meets Río Mosna, a larger river and major tributary to the Amazon, which flows along the lower edge of the archaeological site. Both rivers are glacier-fed with headwaters originating in the ring of tall peaks bordering the valley.

The surrounding glaciated peaks of the Cordillera Blanca, the highest and steepest mountain range in the entire Andes cordillera, have slopes that typically range from 45° to 90°. These high angles are extremely unstable. Rapidly alternating cycles of snowfall and melt, characteristic of high-altitude mountains near the equator, contribute to even more instability. As a result, slight earthquake tremors can trigger landslides and rock falls, and glaciers and ice fields are susceptible to frequent avalanches of ice and rock.

Great earthquakes have been shaking the region for millennia. The evidence is visible in the prominent fault scarps that form low cliffs slicing for miles across young geologic units, including through glacial moraines and alluvial deposits. These long and linear scarps are especially prominent where the Cordillera Blanca fault crosses the road between Huaraz and Chavín, as described in Chapter 4 (see Figure 4.2). In recent geologic history, volcanoes have played a prominent role here, too. Although volcanic activity has been absent for several thousand years, the region has many hot springs, indicating this earlier volcanism.

Today prominent scars left by recent landslides descend along the valley slopes, particularly in areas of agricultural terraces on the eastern hillslopes. Floods also are regular occurrences in the valley surrounding the Chavín site. These hazards likely affected human settlement throughout the centuries that the Andeans built and occupied monumental structures. When heavy rainfall saturates the thin soil and rock on steep mountain slopes, landslides and rockfalls are especially common. The seasonal rainfall in the region is high, at 31–35 in (78–89 cm) per year. Regional paleoclimate records suggest similar precipitation amounts during the past 3,000 years in the Central Andes.[6] In the millennia since people abandoned Chavín, geologic processes have continued to alter the landscape.

Subsurface imaging techniques show landslide deposits cover extensive areas of the archaeological site. In 1945, a large debris flow, also known as a channelized debris avalanche (locally, it's referred to as an *aluvión*), swept down the valley in the Río Wacheqsa channel and spread out to bury portions of the archaeological site and part of the adjacent modern town. In that destructive event, mud and debris reached thicknesses as deep as 13 ft (4 m).[7] The base of the temple complex is still mostly buried in mud from the 1945 disaster. During the hundreds of years that Chavín people occupied the valley, similar landslides and floods undoubtedly took place.

Flowing Waters and Monumental Structures

Much more than immediately meets the eye is present at Chavín de Huántar, and this intrigue has inspired archaeological research for decades. The monumental complex has multiple levels of masonry structures, and it once contained splendid stone art (Figure 17.1). The construction details and engineering design are exceptionally sophisticated. The ceremonial ruins at Chavín have been a focus of investigations for over a century. These began with the work of Julio C. Tello, who first visited the site in 1919,[8] and continued by the Peruvian archaeologist Luis Lumbreras and Yale University archaeologist Richard L. Burger, along with many others. In recent years an active and ongoing archaeological research program has been led by John W. Rick and colleagues at Stanford University, and the interpretations of Rick and associates are primarily what I describe in this chapter.

The builders of Chavín de Huántar began landscape modifications to level the future sites of their temples as early as around 1,400 BCE. Detailed detective work by archaeologists has led to the identification of five major construction stages, with at least fifteen separate phases of work.[9] The major period of monumental construction spanned about 400 years, beginning at approximately 1200 BCE.[10] The most massive and intensive construction took place from roughly 1000 to 800 BCE. Over the centuries, and as the fame of Chavín grew, the community expanded temples and plaza spaces to accommodate more visitors. Architectural renovations continued until about 500 BCE. After this time, evidence suggests disuse and physical collapse at Chavín.

FIGURE 17.1. Overview of Chavín de Huántar. Photograph by author.

Visitors to Chavín de Huántar today see ruins that include an elaborate series of stone platform mounds and monumental buildings, staircases, terraces, and sunken plazas, as well as striking and enigmatic stone art. The first structure built, informally known as the "Old Temple," began as a U-shaped structure with a circular sunken court where people could congregate. The open end of the U-shape faces east toward Río Mosna and the rising sun, an auspicious orientation for ancient worshipers.

Later, builders constructed a "New Temple" by enlarging the south wing of the Old Temple and incorporating additional interior connecting spaces between the two buildings. The New Temple has an imposing doorway with massive stone blocks constructed with white granite on one side and black limestone on the other, representing duality in a favorable pairing. The adjacent stairway extends from the temple down into a large plaza and smaller sunken court. Together, the outdoor plaza and court would have provided space for hundreds of worshipers who could view rituals performed on the temple summit. Inside the temple, staircases led to openings on the flat roof. Through these openings, priests could mysteriously appear and disappear, to the astonishment of worshipers gathered below.

The aboveground ruins of the monumental center are impressive, but even more stunning is an interior labyrinth. Within these hidden spaces is a complex, interconnected system of subsurface chambers and passageways called galleries and constructed from stone blocks. Ventilation shafts provided light, and evidence supports that the ancient builders placed mirrors of polished anthracite (highly metamorphosed coal) strategically along corridors to direct sunlight.[11] Some galleries have smooth, evenly cut rock surfaces; the builders left others lined with rough and irregular rock. When I wandered through this underground warren, the damp chill and my claustrophobic feelings were quite disconcerting. At least one visitor has described having the unpleasant sensation of entering the body cavity of a large and rocky beast, which also fits my impressions.

Beneath the monumental structures are mysterious water-draining features. A complex system of channels, canals and drains runs a total linear extent of over 3,300 ft (1,006 m).[12] These range in size from small to very large. In some of the enclosed drains, a person could walk standing upright.

And there is a mystery here. The Chavín region is subject to high seasonal variations in rainfall with heavy rains needing to be drained away from structures, so some of the water-bearing features clearly served this purpose. However, the water management system far exceeds what would have been necessary to simply drain rainwater.[13] Why were such significant efforts taken to construct this drainage system?

Archaeologists believe the ancient builders designed the channel system beneath the temple complex so that it could amplify the sounds emanating from this rush of water into the central plaza.[14] For people observing ceremonies, the roar of swirling waters hidden deep underground must have been highly dramatic. The worshipers placed their faith in the religious leaders' ability to intervene with the deities who controlled weather and caused the ground to tremble. Witnessing the bizarre acoustic effects of water during rituals to honor these deities was undoubtedly a potent display of power.

Exotic Art and Shamanic Rituals

Art forms created by Chavín artists distinguish this culture. Their art was exotic, somewhat sinister, and recognized as the beginning of a creative revolution with a uniquely Andean style.[15] Carved into stone, crafted from precious metals, and woven into textiles, images depicted stylized jaguars, caimans, snakes, eagles, fish, and other animals from jungle, coastal, and high mountain environments. They combined mythical creatures with sharp fangs and claws in half-human and half-animal composite images. Widely recognized as mescaline-containing hallucinogens, San Pedro cacti also were prominent in decorative imaging[16] (see Figure 13.1). Trumpets made from conch shells of marine snails *Strombus* sp., found in tropical waters far to the north, are also depicted in artwork.[17]

Textiles were important for spreading Chavín-style art to the surrounding region. Although the damp climate of the high mountains did not allow fabrics to be preserved, archaeologists recovered hundreds of Chavín-style textile fragments from burial sites on the arid Paracas Peninsula.[18] The weavings and embroidered tapestries showed the use of cultivated cotton and wool from domesticated alpacas and llamas that lived in the highlands.

Splendid stone artwork ornamented the walls of the Chavín temples and courtyards during the long reign of this society. Walls of the New Temple complex were at one time embellished with rows of fearsome carved heads that projected outward from the walls. Called tenon heads, or pegged heads, more than forty of these larger-than-life-sized heads were installed[19] (Figure 17.2). Today, sadly, only traces remain. Just one tenon head remains in its original position high on the temple wall; others are in museums locally and in Lima. Most are lost.

Archaeologists believe the otherworldly creatures portrayed in Chavín iconography express the interrelationship of the natural and supernatural worlds,

FIGURE 17.2. Temple architecture and sculpted tenon heads at Chavín de Huántar, ca. 1901. Julian H. Steward, *Handbook of South American Indians* (1946): Plate 17.

a theme that appears repeatedly in Andean history. Reconstructions indicate the original placement of the tenon heads was in a sequence representative of a shamanic transformation under the influence of hallucinogenic drugs such as San Pedro cactus or the powerful snuff vilca. The Chavín builders arranged the heads in a series beginning with a human face with almond-shaped eyes, giving way to faces with round and bulging eyes plus grimaces that depict the nausea that accompanies transformation[20]; near the end of the sequence there is a gradual transition into heads with prominent fangs and snakes for hair. To follow this progression, viewers would have to encircle the temple completely.[21]

The ancient Chavín creators set up artistic statements of other dramatic scenes of hidden realms and transformations. In the large circular court within the arms of the U-shape forming the Old Temple, carved panels show processions of walking figures that archaeologists interpret as shamans transformed into jaguars in hallucinogenic rituals.

Most impressive of all is a 15 ft (4.5 m) high granite sculpture called El Lanzón, named for its shape as a slender dagger. Besides its massive size, El Lanzón captivates with its exotic features. It has a human body with animal characteristics that include two giant fangs, claws for fingers and toes, and eyebrows and hair formed by writhing snakes. The right arm gestures upwards and the left arm gestures down, suggesting that El Lanzón is a deity whose powers encompass all realms.[22] In a tall chamber deep within the bowels of the Old Temple complex, this fearsome cult image still stands in its original position. The sculpture was most likely placed first, and then builders assembled the stone block walls of the surrounding temple.

And the story of El Lanzón doesn't end there. Above the elaborate tall sculpture is a single large floor stone that someone could remove from the gallery overhead, allowing a person to speak unseen for the sculptured figure below. This unique feature has led archaeologists to interpret El Lanzón as an oracle who would communicate with privileged supplicants.[23]

Shaping the Landscape

The Chavín de Huántar site has a complex geologic history, and reconstructing this record provides important information to supplement archaeological material. Geologists have found evidence that for thousands of years landslides have periodically caused the local river channels to shift their locations, and river flows have become dammed up behind landslides.[24]

The ceremonial complex at Chavín is on the relatively flat floor of a small valley, and this level area is an unusual feature in these rugged mountains. Long before the Chavín builders appeared, sediments gradually filled the valley floor when a large landslide blocked Río Mosna a few miles north of the modern town. Eventually, the river carved down through the landslide deposits, and a

FIGURE 17.3. View of Chavín de Huántar and near-vertical bedrock fins in Chimú Formation. Photograph by author.

new river channel formed. The ponded floodplain area gradually drained and dried out, creating the level area that the ancient builders selected as an advantageous location for their constructions.[25]

Bedrock characteristics in the region provided benefits for the building of Chavín de Huántar. Sedimentary rocks that are roughly 125 million to 45 million years old surround the site.[26] These rocks are composed of sediments originally deposited in river delta and coastal wetland environments, and rock properties vary significantly in the region. Interbedded siltstones, sandstones, and in some places, thin beds of coal (anthracite) underlay the lower and middle portions of the valley. Geologists recognize these rocks as the Oyon Formation.

On the higher slopes of the valley directly to the west of the Chavín site, prominent white bedrock fins are part of the Chimú Formation. This formation consists predominantly of white sandstone, some of which metamorphosed to quartzite, a strong and hard type of rock (Figure 17.3). Other rocks on valley slopes are of blue-gray marine limestone known as the Santa Formation.

Why are there so many landslides in this area? We associate the low stability of the slopes in the region with soft and weak rock, primarily interbedded coal and clay, alternating with units of hard and strong sandstone and quartzite.[27] All these rocks are strongly folded and fractured, particularly where the beds are steeply inclined—as shown by the prominent fins of Chimú rocks—and they are highly susceptible to sliding.

In profound ways, the Chavín builders deliberately altered the natural landscape around their ceremonial center. To construct the large platforms for their building sites near the rivers, they placed massive amounts of leveling soil and rock as fill. The original ground surface lies as much as 60 ft (18 m) below the engineered surface in some places. The volume of fill incorporated in landscape features is estimated to be enormous, roughly twice the amount of the architectural components in the monumental core area.[28]

The amount of labor invested—millions of baskets of soil and stone that were transported by human workers—represents a truly monumental effort. Although some of the flat platform areas were likely used for agricultural fields, archaeologists believe they also were arenas for ritual activity and built to demonstrate symbolic power over the landscape.[29]

To construct the temples, large blocks of sandstone and quartzite had to be moved, along with lesser amounts of granite, limestone, and volcanic tuff blocks. In the immediate vicinity of the temple site, sandstone and quartzite from the Chimú Formation provided a convenient construction material, and these rocks were used in the earliest phases of monumental construction. Massive 3–9 ft (1–2.7 m) thick beds of these rocks fracture into rectilinear blocks along prominent bedding planes, conveniently forming partially shaped building stones. In later construction phases, workers transported limestone and granite from greater distances and incorporated this rock into focal points in plazas and on stairways.[30]

How were these enormous rocks moved? Human labor transported the stone blocks to the construction site. The nearest source for the massive limestone blocks was about 2 mi (3 km) distant to the west, and the Andeans sourced the granite blocks approximately 10 mi (16 km) away from the site.[31] With no beasts of burden available, the builders of Chavín had to drag the blocks for what must have seemed like very long distances.

The people who worked on the construction and landscape engineering of the Chavín temple complex clearly had sophisticated knowledge of their environment. Their work, possibly unknowingly, also contributed to the instability of the surrounding hill slopes. They excavated on the slopes, manipulated river channels, and removed material from the base of active landslides. These actions decreased slope stability and significantly increased the susceptibility of the site to landslides. Other human activities also weakened slopes, such as vegetation removal from the pasturing of animals, firewood collection, and agricultural production.[32]

Earthquakes of even moderate size, or originating at a distance, also may have triggered massive landslides. Soils saturated by rainfall would have heightened this danger. Since the Chavín cult flourished for hundreds of years, meeting these challenges must have been an acceptable trade-off for what was clearly a powerful location.

The Allure of Running Water

Archaeologists recognize controlling water as a statement of ritual authority by the ancient Andeans, with elaborate manipulation of water considered a significant religious act.[33] The extensive underground system of channels that produced the sound of rushing water in the temple complex was surely a unique display of power by those who presided over the Chavín temples.

Incorporating running water into the ceremonial structures was an impressive engineering achievement. The Chavín engineers undertook massive efforts to control the positions of both Río Wacheqsa and Río Mosna by erecting walls to constrict the river channels.[34] They directed water from Río Wacheqsa specifically into their intricate system of channels and canals within and adjacent to the temple complex core. How the builders accomplished this undertaking remained a mystery for many years, since today both rivers have water levels well below what would have been needed to move water into the ceremonial complex.[35]

The modern course of Río Wacheqsa would require diversion of a canal at least a quarter of a mile (0.4 km) upstream of the temple core to reach the elevation of the highest recognized water-bearing features that were constructed.

This task would have required a substantial engineering feat, but no evidence indicates such a canal.[36] So how did the ancient engineers direct the river water into the water-bearing channels within the Chavín temples?

Detailed geologic investigations at the site have shed some light. It turns out that providing water to the core of the temple complex some 3,000 years ago would have been much simpler than it appears today. Researchers believe that where the steep bedrock fins to the west of the temple pinched the course of Río Wacheqsa, a landslide dammed the river sometime shortly before construction began at Chavín.[37] A lake filled up behind the dam, and an outlet for the water created an impressive waterfall up to 26 ft (8 m) high.[38]

Geomorphic and archaeological evidence show that during Chavín time, Río Wacheqsa flowed above the site at an elevation 20–26 ft (6–8 m) higher than at present.[39] Given this increased river level, with a canal only about 655 ft (200 m) long, Chavín builders could have drawn an abundant and year-round supply of water into the ceremonial core from Río Wacheqsa. This easy access to flowing water most likely was an important consideration for temple siting. And having a waterfall near the ceremonial center must have been another impressive site asset.

The landscape in the rugged Cordillera Blanca is continuously changing. The arrangement of the river channels today differs from what it was only a few thousand years ago. After the collapse of the Chavín culture, Río Wacheqsa cut through the landslide dam, and over time, the streambed eroded downward to grade smoothly into Río Mosna.

The Rise and Fall of a Remarkable Culture

During the height of the Chavín culture, as many as 3,000 residents may have lived in the high mountain settlement.[40] Besides the individuals who lived at Chavín de Huántar, many pilgrims traveled to the site to observe and take part in religious rituals or perhaps to consult an oracle. Some walked great distances, carrying gifts and offerings, sometimes using llamas as pack animals. Evidence of these travels to Chavín and its importance as a ceremonial center is clear from the artifacts brought from distant locations. Exotic materials that archaeologists have found at the site include Quispisisa obsidian,[41] that originated from volcanic rocks several hundred miles away, and *Spondylus* and *Strombus* seashells from tropical waters far to the north. In a storeroom in the temple complex, archaeologists found hundreds of ceramic vessels shaped from clay originating in distant coastal or highland areas and decorated in the different styles of distinctive and remote cultures. Many vessels have the preserved remains of ancient foodstuffs, with traces of camelid, deer, guinea pig, and fish among them. Feasts and festivals were clearly a part of Chavín rituals.

Chavín de Huántar flourished for centuries. Archaeologists have determined that this community prospered at approximately the same time as other complex cultures along the Pacific coast and in the northern Central Andean highlands, where monument building was also taking place. Then, in the hundred years after about 500 BCE, following a period of extensive renovations of the temple complex, social instability ensued at Chavín, and the culture collapsed. What events could have led to the demise of this culture that had prospered for centuries?

Intriguingly, the fall of Chavín de Huántar appears to parallel a similar decline in other coastal and highland centers.[42] Specifically, these other settlements were along the coast and in the mountains directly above them. And these sites coincide with the region that is most subject to disruption from the heavy rains and flooding of the El Niño weather pattern.[43]

Today, we know that the El Niño phenomenon results from warm ocean currents that develop in the western Pacific Ocean. To the ancient Andeans, however, the dark clouds that could bring heavy rain and flooding would seem to originate in the highlands. This opinion might have provided an exceptional opportunity for clever entrepreneurs in the mountains to link the coastal disasters to claims of religious control. Also, mild El Niño events typically occur in intervals between powerful events, adding to the appearance that the divine intervention of religious leaders was effective.

Scientists have found evidence of a major climatic transition when El Niño cycles increased in frequency beginning around 3,000 years ago, as described in Chapter 9. This climate change could have stimulated the development of the new and compelling religion at Chavín de Huántar—especially one based in a dramatic setting and enhanced by abundant water. However, the powers that the Chavín officials might have claimed could not last indefinitely.

Transitions in climate patterns and natural disasters are likely contributing factors to the widespread declines of these ancient societies. Along the Pacific Coast, intensification of El Niño events, accompanied by severe flooding, could have turned the local populations against those who claimed the ability to intercede with supernatural deities. Chaos also could have resulted from a major earthquake, or landslides that followed an earthquake, or a massive avalanche after heavy snows, or perhaps a series of severe floods or years of drought. These events may have occurred locally, causing havoc in the immediate vicinity of Chavín de Huántar. Alternatively, they might have been more widely spread and distant events that affected many other communities as well.

Although no solid evidence supports any of these scenarios, all are plausible, and the historical record holds tantalizing hints of these possibilities. An earthquake on the active Cordillera Blanca fault, located close to Chavín de Huántar on the west, could have caused major damage and many fatalities. Geologic investigations suggest that roughly 1,500 to 2,000 years have elapsed since the last major earthquake on this fault zone, described in Chapter 4. Accurate timing of medium to large earthquakes holds large uncertainties, but possibly sometime around 500 BCE, an earthquake on the Cordillera Blanca fault zone shook the region severely. Indications of potential earthquake damage can even be seen on a section of temple where builders had recently completed construction, and shortly afterwards, people abandoned this ceremonial center.[44] In both local and more regional disasters, if an oracle who was an important part of the religious establishment at Chavín de Huántar did not predict major flooding or a large earthquake, and didn't warn of the deaths and destruction that may have followed, then perhaps people turned away from Chavín leaders?

On a broader scale, by damaging crops, destroying residences, and scattering populations, natural disasters can cause people to abandon the leaders and beliefs that once sustained them. These disruptions also effectively prevent religious and political leaders from mobilizing enough labor for monument construction and repair. We probably will never know the events that brought the Chavín culture to an end. However, changing climate patterns and other natural disasters are certainly high on the list of potential causes.

And what came after the Chavín culture? In the first centuries after the demise of Chavín de Huántar, a succession of small groups of wanderers occupied the monumental temple complex.[45] These settlers salvaged elaborate carved panels and meticulously shaped building stones from the abandoned temples, and they erected temporary structures over the formerly sacred spaces. All that had once sustained the power and prestige of the Chavín culture, drawing thousands of pilgrims to visit the impressive monuments of Chavín de Huántar, had passed.

18

The Top of the World

During one of my trips to Peru, I traveled by bus from Cuzco southward to Puno, a city on the western shoreline of Lake Titicaca. With my eyes glued to the passing scenery, the journey of several hours transported us to another world. As bustling Cuzco disappeared behind us, we first passed valleys blanketed with bright green crops that gradually gave way to sparse and grayish vegetation as the road wound up to higher and higher elevations. Along the sides of mountain valleys, towering piles of gravel tens of feet tall were arranged in long lines that extended outwards toward the roadway. They were so enormous that it took time for me to recognize them finally as lateral moraines from long-melted glaciers, which formed when the ice ground to a halt and dropped an accumulated load of rocky debris.

The bus labored upwards in the thin air, finally crossing a high pass at just under 14,200 ft (4,328 m) elevation midway between Cuzco and Puno. As our vehicle crept slowly down the far side of the pass, the vast and flat Altiplano gradually came into view. The sight was mesmerizing. Muted browns and tans of the grassland vegetation cover the high and wide plateau, merging with the vast expanse of the blue-gray waters of the lake, and with all surrounded by the dark silhouettes of high mountains on the horizon. In my explorations of empty expanses over the next few days, the silence, broken only by the sound of the wind, stands out most strongly in my memory.

At first sight, the landscapes surrounding Lake Titicaca appear to be in a natural state, but that is not the case. People have lived in this region for thousands of years, and they completely transformed the vegetation and the topography. The ancient Andeans who once flourished on the high and cold Altiplano successfully adapted to their harsh environment, but this task took great effort, and their landscape underwent significant modifications.

Life Near the Lake
Southeast of Lake Titicaca, and at the lofty elevation of about 12,660 ft (3,860 m), is one of the greatest archaeological sites in the Americas. Now in Bolivia, Tiwanaku was the capital city of a culture known by the same name that dominated the Altiplano and the southern section of the Central Andes for over 600 years beginning around 400 or 500 CE.[1] The Tiwanaku people built monumental architecture and created exquisite textiles and art objects of precious metals. The growth, persistence, and eventual collapse of this civilization confirm the exceptional creativity and adaptability of the Indigenous people, but also the limitations inherent in a harsh environment.

Fragmentary evidence—including hearths, rock shelters, and projectile points—shows that people occupied the Altiplano region surrounding and to the south of Lake Titicaca at least as far back in time as 8,000 or more years ago.[2] Drawn to the rich resources of aquatic and wetland plants, fish, and waterfowl in the lake and surrounding wetlands, and the grazing deer and wild camelids on the extensive grasslands, these early hunter-gatherers found favorable living conditions.

Over time, and with the bounty provided by the lake, the hunter-gatherers adopted more sedentary lifestyles. They harvested fish and a variety of birds from the lake, as well as plants grown in the rich soils of adjoining river valleys and near the lake shorelines. After people domesticated llamas and alpacas around 6,000 years ago, they pastured large herds of these grazing animals.

As the human populations expanded, people permanently altered the fragile landscape. Initially, the foragers burned grasslands to encourage the growth of new young vegetation favored by the grazing animals. To access the lake more easily, the ancient Andeans also burned widespread wetland vegetation. They harvested gnarled *Polylepis* trees[3] and shrubs in the region—sparsely distributed at such high elevations—for building material and fuel until they gradually deforested the region. Pollen from a variety of plants and charcoal found in lake sediment cores reveals human-induced landscape changes. The pollen record from about 3,000 years ago also shows substantial deforestation of the basin.[4]

Many scattered settlements were distributed around the Lake Titicaca Basin by 3,000 years ago.[5] People built small ceremonial centers as gathering spaces for the surrounding community. These typically had sunken courts placed at the top of raised platforms, a pattern that was adopted by many subsequent Andean cultures. Ancient people may have inhabited the future site of Tiwanaku by 800 BCE or earlier, but later developments in what became a large urban center covered virtually all traces of the former occupation. Why Tiwanaku ultimately gained such prominence is unclear, as the site doesn't have any obvious advantages.[6] Perhaps a charismatic and ambitious leader, or group of leaders, gained power and promoted expansion? In the absence of any written records, we will probably never know.

Archaeologists have determined that Tiwanaku began to emerge as a major ritual and political center around 250 CE. By approximately 500 CE, the city was substantially expanded.[7] Many pilgrims visited for religious rituals and feasts, and the city had become an important trade center. Llama caravans carried highland goods of dehydrated potatoes, quinoa, fish, birds, and camelid wool outward along trading routes in all directions. The caravans returned with maize, salt, coca, peppers, obsidian, copper, hallucinogenic plants, and other items not available on the Altiplano. As more people from throughout the Titicaca Basin and beyond visited the city, the Tiwanaku sphere incorporated a large geographic area. Ceramics, textiles, and other artifacts with elements of Tiwanaku religious iconography are widely spread throughout this region, indicating the scope of cultural influence.

Comprehensive centralized planning with monumental ritual complexes in the central core distinguished Tiwanaku. A major building program began around 500 to 600 CE, in which existing buildings were razed or substantially renovated and large new ones erected. The city flourished for centuries until, by about 1000 CE, it began to decline. Within another hundred years or so, only wind and silt were blowing through the abandoned spaces.

Making a Living in a Challenging Environment
Enormous Lake Titicaca dominates the northern part of the Altiplano. At an elevation of about 12,507 ft (3,812 m), the lake has an expanse of some 3,000 m² (4,828 km²), straddling the border between Peru and Bolivia. When I stood on the shoreline, all I could see was water stretching out to the horizon, reminding me of the vastness of an ocean.

Today, Lake Titicaca is only a remnant of the immense lakes that expanded and contracted on the Puna-Altiplano plateau during the glacial and interglacial periods of the Pleistocene. In the southern part of the plateau, lakes that evaporated completely have left extensive salt flats, including the Salar de Uyuni in southwest Bolivia.

Surrounding Lake Titicaca is a large drainage basin created by faults rupturing over millions of years. Five major rivers and more than twenty smaller streams empty into the lake. Two lakes actually are present, composed of two subbasins containing Lago Grande and Lago Wiñaymarka (also called Lago Pequeño). Lake Titicaca forms a nearly closed basin system, where 90 percent of the water remains in the lake, with additions from precipitation balanced by high rates of evapotranspiration from strong winds and intense sunlight. Less than 10 percent of the water typically flows out of the lake, via a single outlet at Río Desaguadero. This outlet can operate only at high water levels and empties into Lago Poopó in Bolivia.

Lake Titicaca is a sensitive indicator of climate change, with a complex history of major cycles of rising and falling water levels recorded in lake sediments. In the years of low precipitation in the Altiplano, especially during strong El Niño years, the lake level drops rapidly. During the twentieth century, lake level reportedly fluctuated by 20 ft (6 m), representing a volume change of about six percent. A 3 ft (0.9 m) drop in lake level can constrict the shoreline inward by about 3 mi (4.8 km).[8] These dramatic shifts in lake level strongly affected settlement patterns, agricultural production, and regional trade routes. Watching the lake waters either recede far into the distance or creep upwards toward homes and fields must have been quite disconcerting for the Indigenous people.

As populations increased, the ancient Andeans needed to rely increasingly on cultivated crops. They found the best farmland and pasturage in the flat and low-lying areas subject to flooding immediately above the lake, known as the pampa. Richer soils and warmer temperatures in the pampa zone provide advantages, but growing food in this environment has other challenges. The high plateau location is typically chilly and windswept. Intense sunlight during the days is followed by plummeting nighttime temperatures that reach freezing throughout much of the year. A nighttime drop in temperature of 40°F (4.4°C) or more in some months is typical. The rainy season, from December through March, brings about 25 in (64 cm) of rainfall, but this precipitation tends to fall in thunderstorms that can bring extremely heavy downpours. Hailstorms and frosts can occur sporadically throughout the growing season and result in extensive crop damage.

At high elevations, the pronounced temperature differences between day and night pose a major limitation for plant growth. Near the lake, however, the great volume of deep water moderates temperatures, since water absorbs heat from solar radiation during the day and gradually releases it at night. To increase this benefit, and to cultivate crops in areas naturally prone to waterlogged soils or annual flooding, the Tiwanaku people built raised fields over tens of thousands of acres in the Titicaca Basin.[9]

Raised fields brought extensive areas that were marginal for agriculture into production, although this modification required substantial alteration of the land surface and considerable amounts of labor. Separated by water-filled canals, fields could be up to about 30 ft wide by 300 ft (9 m by 91 m) or more in length. The laborers organized the fields into regular patterns that are clearly visible on the Altiplano landscape today. Raised field agriculture significantly expanded the capacity of the region to support concentrated human populations, as this system is highly productive.

The lower slopes of the Titicaca Basin within a few hundred feet above the lake are also valuable for agricultural crops. The Andeans constructed terraces on these slopes, following the contours of the landscape. At up to around 13,000 ft (3,962 m), farmers could cultivate hardy tubers such as potato, along with similar carbohydrate-rich root vegetables with the unfamiliar names of oca, olluco, and mashwa, as well as the cold-adapted grain, quinoa. Near the raised fields, artificial ponds called *qochas* were used to raise fish and other aquaculture, with tubers and grains also grown on the sloping sides. When left fallow, the ponds provided convenient grazing areas for llamas and alpacas.

A useful food and fiber plant from the wetlands known as totora (*Schoenoplectus californicus tatora*) was cultivated extensively.[10] Growing in waterlogged soils and in shallow water along the edge of Lake Titicaca and other wetlands, totora can reach 18–20 ft (5.5–6 m) in height. Roots and the lower stem are edible and are a nutritious feed for animals. Totora provided valuable fiber for thatched roofing, baskets, and mats, and people exploited the natural buoyancy of the reeds by binding bundles together to fashion boats. Boats (*balsas*) and floating islands of the modern Uru people are iconic symbols of the Lake Titicaca region today. The origins of these traditions trace back to the accomplishments of their ancient predecessors.

An abundance of *chicha* brewing and serving vessels show that fermented maize had an important use in the Tiwanaku culture.[11] Since the high-altitude chill of the Altiplano is not suitable for growing maize, satellite settlements at lower elevations became dedicated maize production regions. People produced this beverage in massive quantities and served it in frequent elite-sponsored feasts for the population, as well as using it in religious rituals. Paraphernalia for snuffing hallucinogens—including spoons, tubes, and snuff tablets, some elaborately carved from wood—are common artifacts and indicate that psychotropic drug use was also a prominent aspect of the religion.[12] Many sculpted statues depict both the ceremonial cups, called *keros*, used for chicha and the San Pedro cactus that is the source of mescaline.

From fish, ducks, and geese to large herds of llamas and alpacas, as well as intensive farming with raised field systems, exploitation of the lake resources were key in allowing the Tiwanaku people to prosper. Agricultural surpluses permitted occupational specialization and a stratified society that included priests, engineers, architects, and artisans. An elite class organized economic production and distribution and coordinated the construction of the monumental architecture in major public works programs. The Tiwanaku culture prospered for over 500 years—a remarkably long time for any society.

The Monumental City of Tiwanaku

On the arid, open, windswept Altiplano landscape today, two groups of monuments dominate the ruins of the former city of Tiwanaku.[13] On the southwest is a massive, raised platform with a sunken court and plaza called the Pumapunku. About 0.5 mi (0.8 km) to the northeast is a cluster of monumental buildings that include the Sunken Temple, Kalasasaya, and Akapana. All the important buildings follow a similar model of a large platform with a sunken interior court and a terraced form, with the sizes of the terraces decreasing as elevation increased. Archaeologists suggest these forms may have symbolized the surrounding mountains that were the source of life-giving water. Water-display features built into some of the platform mounds similarly evoke the importance of water.

Tiwanaku monumental constructions emphasized permanence and solidity. The designers intended for them evoke awe in all who set eyes on them. Over the centuries since the city was abandoned, Tiwanaku has suffered extensive damage and defacement, so the historical record of the construction process in the city is incomplete. Nonetheless, what remains provides abundant evidence of the sophisticated culture that thrived on the high plateau.

Construction of each of the monumental structures began at different times during the long history of Tiwanaku, and evidence suggests almost continuous rebuilding or refurbishing over hundreds of years. Monument improvements likely began whenever a new ruling lineage ascended, as the renewed construction efforts helped to legitimize the latest rulers who sought more power and glory. Builders used massive blocks of reddish sandstone in the earliest monumental structures. Centuries later, they incorporated blue-green volcanic andesite extensively, particularly in especially visible and evocative places.[14] Using stone tools to shape stone blocks of hard and strong andesite, and sculpting intricate decorations on the monolithic sculptures, must have been extraordinarily difficult.

The most sacred of the shrines built at Tiwanaku may have been the Akapana pyramid, which probably was developed over many generations.[15] From a distance today, the Akapana appears to be a large natural hill, but investigations have shown that it is a completely artificial construction (Figure 18.1). Many archaeologists believe the builders originally composed a pyramid of seven terraces,[16] decreasing in size upwards to culminate in the smallest platform that reached a height of about 60 ft (18 m). The carefully trimmed stone blocks at the base include some that are more than 6 ft (2 m) long, with smaller blocks on the higher walls. The terraces encompass an enormous amount of fill material, which the builders acquired by excavating a moat around the civic-ceremonial core. Within the Akapana are small walled rooms, some with evidence of feasting and offerings of fine art objects, as well as dozens of human sacrifices. Other spaces contain burials of prestigious individuals and include hundreds of what appear to be deliberately broken ceramic vessels. Remnants of food and drink still line many of the vessels, suggesting people used them in a feast, then smashed and poured them onto the wrapped body in the grave.[17]

Archaeologists have found evidence of a sunken court on the highest terrace of the Akapana. During the rainy season, the court directed rainwater that collected through a complex drainage system, with channels alternately focusing the water over the terrace surfaces or inside the interior of the mound.[18] Researchers suggest these effects produced a dazzling imitation of the Kimsachata range to the south, where rainfall on the mountain summits runs into underground channels, reappears as springs on the mountainsides, then reenters another underground water collection system until finally resurfacing and draining out onto the valley floor. The Kimsachata range provided an

FIGURE 18.1. Akapana pyramid at Tiwanaku. Photograph by Pavel Špindler, 2008, available under a Creative Commons Attribution-Share Alike 3.0 Unported License.

important source of drinking and irrigation water for the city, and mimicking the extraordinary flow of water must have had important ritual significance.

Another unique characteristic of the Akapana are layers of water-rounded blueish-green pebbles placed in lenses within the fill and completely covering the surface of the uppermost terrace.[19] People painstakingly collected these pebbles from the streams of the Kimsachata range, providing further evidence of a sacred connection to this important source of city water.

The Sunken Temple and Kalasasaya were the first two monumental structures built at the Tiwanaku site, with construction starting sometime between 300 and 500 CE. The designers used a north–south orientation for the Sunken Temple, also called the Semi-Subterranean Temple, while all subsequent monumental structures had an east–west alignment[20] (Figure 18.2). A single south-facing stairway built with massive, rectangular sandstone blocks led to the Sunken Temple, and faces the Southern Cross constellation of stars and Mount Kimsachata.

FIGURE 18.2. Sunken temple at Tiwanaku. Photograph by Pavel Špindler, 2012, available under a Creative Commons Attribution-Share Alike 3.0 Unported License.

Tiwanaku workers began construction of the monumental Kalasasaya platform around the same time as the Sunken Temple. A platform 6 ft (2 m) high formed the base of this structure, and a drainage system inside this core draws water off the platform during periods of heavy rain. Massive sandstone blocks were set along three sides of the platform, and on the fourth builders placed eleven andesite columns, added in a later construction stage.[21] Each of these monoliths is 13 ft (3.9 m) tall and carved from a single piece of strong stone. The designers arranged them so that at the time of the austral summer solstice (December 21) the sun sets over the southernmost pillar, as seen from a central platform between the monoliths and the central staircase. On the austral winter solstice (June 21), the sun sets over the northernmost pillar and the peak of Mount Khapia, the source of the andesite used in the construction. The central column in the series marks the equinoxes. Other columns could track a complex cycle of lunar observations, essential for marking the changing seasons and major ritual events.

The residences of priests and other ruling elites were in large compounds located adjacent to the Akapana, Sunken Temple, and Kalasasaya complexes. Substantial walls of cut-stone surrounded the residences, overlain by adobe bricks and covered by thatched roofs. A water-filled moat surrounded the monumental ritual structures and residences physically and symbolically, separating the activities that took place and the individuals who conducted them. Archaeologists suggest the Tiwanaku people constructed this moat to symbolize Lake Titicaca, with the monumental structures representing sacred islands in Lake Titicaca.[22]

Tiwanaku engineers directed the waters of Río Tiwanaku into the city center with a series of canals and drains built with carefully fitted stone blocks and sealed with clay. They channeled some of the water into the moat that surrounded the Akapana, Sunken Temple, and Kalasasaya complexes in the ceremonial core. A sophisticated system of underground canals and drains supplied the center of the city with fresh water and also removed waste.[23] The extensive water collection and distribution system at the site definitely had a functional use, but like Chavín de Huántar, the system far exceeded what was needed for practical purposes. Clearly, ritual manipulation of water was also important.

A monumental complex called the Pumapunku is on the southwest. This platform mound appears to have been the main entryway for pilgrims into the city and provided striking views of the ceremonial core, dominated by the imposing Akapana. The Pumapunku builders incorporated a natural hill into a series of terraces, which contributed to the imposing size of the platform. They superimposed a new terrace level over older ones in three or more construction phases, so that the final platform is about 16 ft (4.8 m) tall.

Carved Stone Sculptures and Gateways
The Tiwanaku culture joined many ancient Andean societies in carving stone sculptures with cultural and religious significance. Artists produced numerous stone sculptures in a wide range of sizes, styles, and different rock materials, carved with important elements of religious iconography. Designers placed most of the sculptures in the ritual spaces of the sunken courtyards of monumental architectural complexes.

The earliest monolithic sculptures at Tiwanaku were carved from sandstone and have a blocky, four-sided form with a distinctive composition on each side. One side typically shows an anthropomorphic image, with distinctive facial

FIGURE 18.3. Gateway of the Sun at Tiwanaku. Photography by Dennis Jarvis, 2010, available under a Creative Commons Attribution-Share Alike 2.0 Generic License, and Georges B. Von Grumbkow, 1877, Colección Museo de Arte de Lima, Peru.

ornaments such as lightning bolts near the eyes, folded arms, and open hands. Clothing of sashes, skirts, and headgear is minimal and decorated with sinuous creatures such as catfish or felines. Often these creatures are slithering or climbing up and down the rock.[24]

Artists carved later monoliths in hard andesite as well as sandstone, and archaeologists interpret these stone figures as elite community ancestors.[25] Carved in the round so that they are three-dimensional, they have impassive faces and wear elaborately decorated garments with flowering plants, llamas, condor faces, and fish. The hand gestures differ from those shown on the earlier statues. Many are offering kero cups of fermented chicha in the left hand and a snuff tablet for hallucinogenic materials in the right hand. Archaeologists consider these gestures as invitational, casting the personages as ancestral "hosts" who are emphasizing consumption of mind-altering substances, perhaps as a way of contacting ancestral beings.[26]

A distinctive aspect of Tiwanaku architecture was the prominence of large gateways and other portals. Clearly, the builders intended to impress the people channeled through these openings with the massive size, elaborate decorations and significant effort required to produce the monumental structures.

The grandest of these portals is the Gateway of the Sun, or Sun Portal. Carved from a single giant slab of andesite approximately 9.8 by 13 ft (3 by 4 m), it has a narrow doorway cut precisely through its center.[27] When European explorers found it in the mid-nineteenth century, the structure was lying horizontally and not in its original position; it was subsequently lifted into an upright position. Across the upper section is a carved composition of a large central staff-bearing figure with a mask-covered face, surrounded by raylike projections ending in circles or puma heads, and smaller faces with rays emanating from them in a lower band. Thirty winged and crowned staff-bearing attendants surround this figure. The carvings most likely hold astronomical significance, and some archaeologists believe the portal may have once stood on the western side of the Kalasasaya, where people could view celestial events on the distant horizon. During its glory, the Gateway of the Sun was likely painted in bright colors and inlaid with gold (Figure 18.3).

Sources of Stone

When I first visited archaeological sites in Peru, the stonework fascinated me. I was curious about the quarries that produced the enormous stone blocks and how the ancient builders could move them to a site and then fit them into place. Fortunately, archaeologists have also been asking these questions, and I've found intriguing information to share (see also Chapter 19).

Researchers have traced the reddish sandstone used in many of the Tiwanaku monuments to the Kimsachata range.[28] Red colors held significance in the Tiwanaku religion. Artists used it frequently on ceremonial vessels and wove it into textiles. Red was also the color of the blood that flowed freely in religious rituals. At a quarry roughly 10 mi (16 km) south of the Tiwanaku site, workers used the naturally occurring joints in the sandstone to simplify carving out large blocks. Ancient laborers moved thousands of blocks from their original locations in this quarry and sorted them into those deemed useable and those that were rejected. These efforts are still visible in the quarry today. Ground surfaces littered with sandstone flakes indicate they trimmed blocks into desired rectangular shapes at the quarry site before transporting them.

Moving multi-ton blocks of stone had to be extremely difficult. Along the road heading toward Tiwanaku from the quarry, abandoned sandstone blocks have two or four depressions carved into the edges—clues as to how laborers moved them.[29] Located about 4–6 in (10–15 cm) below the top of a block on opposing edges, and about 3–4 in (7.5 to 10 cm) long, the depressions are called "rope holds." These indentations suggest that the ancient people used strong ropes to move each block laboriously from the quarry across the miles to the Tiwanaku destination.

Wheels were not in use, as these were not practical on rough terrain and because powerful draft animals were not available. Some blocks show substantial scraping, further indicating they were dragged across the ground. Laborers may have pulled the blocks along on beds of wooden logs, with the logs at the back of the block picked up in sequence and moved forward. Mud might have been used to lubricate this track and reduce the amount of friction. Smaller blocks might have been carried on litters.

Sometime around 500 to 600 CE, when the power and influence of Tiwanaku's realm was expanding, the hard volcanic rock andesite became important in architectural and sculptural elements. Andesite is much denser and harder to shape and carve than sandstone, so the value of this type of rock must have been substantial. Archaeologists interpret the distinctive bluish gray of the andesite to signal the newly incorporated landscapes, communities, and sacred places that came under the influence of Tiwanaku.[30]

At the time of the transition to the use of andesite, the massive Akapana and Pumapunku complexes were under construction, and important additions were being made to the monumental Kalasasaya.[31] New construction had andesite incorporated for important architectural elements, particularly in visible public facades and communal public spaces. The designers interspersed massive andesite blocks with sandstone blocks throughout the Akapana, including a huge portal stone that was placed over the top of the central stairway. They also incorporated architectural elements of andesite into the Pumapunku complex, where a central sunken patio was paved with both sandstone and andesite. Designers placed some of the largest carved andesite blocks into extensions to the Kalasasaya. At some structures, evidence suggests that builders switched out sandstone blocks for carved andesite blocks.

Identifying the location of the andesite quarry mystified researchers for decades, as many outcrops of this volcanic rock are present in the region. Also, the mineralogical and chemical compositions of volcanic rocks can vary during an eruption, making clear "signatures" of origin difficult. One valuable clue, however, was available: abandoned large and roughly trimmed rectangular andesite blocks to the north of the Tiwanaku site on the shoreline of Lago Wiñaymarka. More "sofa-sized" blocks are located across the lake in the foothills of the aforementioned prominent volcanic peak Mount Khapia.

Combined with samples of architectural stones and carved monoliths at Tiwanaku, recent chemical analysis of possible volcanic rock sources confirms the principal source of the andesite as the slopes of Mount Khapia.[32] As the puzzle pieces fell into place, it became clear that laborers quarried and roughly shaped the andesite blocks, loaded them onto rafts made from locally harvested totora reeds, and transported the blocks about 14 mi (22 km) across the lake. Located where Río Tiwanaku enters Lake Titicaca, a town named Iwawe was the port for the andesite blocks. Workers then hauled the blocks overland, using thick ropes and human muscle power, for another 14 mi (22 km) or so towards Tiwanaku. Clearly, the choice of andesite as a construction material involved an enormous amount of labor. Moving multiton blocks on reed rafts was also an ambitious undertaking that required substantial engineering skill. Details of how the Tiwanaku people accomplished this impressive task remain unclear.

Getting Along with the Neighbors

The powerful political and religious leaders of Tiwanaku expanded their influence well beyond the capital city and over a substantial region of the southern part of the Central Andes. Eventually, the entire southern Titicaca Basin in Bolivia and adjacent areas now in modern northern Chile and Argentina were within the Tiwanaku sphere of influence. This relationship also extended to San Pedro de Atacama, Chile, about 500 mi (805 km) to the south, and an important partner in the long-distance trade network.[33]

Artifacts provide valuable information. Tiwanaku-style items compose grave offerings throughout the region of influence, with some artifacts preserved exceptionally well in the dry conditions of modern southern Peru and northern Chile. Archaeologists have uncovered fine textiles in a rainbow of colors, distinctive four-corner hats, carved baskets of wood and fiber, ceramics, and items made of precious metals. No compelling evidence suggests that the region of influence spread through military action; instead, communities simply were drawn into the religious, economic, and social spheres of the culture.[34]

North of the Lake Titicaca basin was the realm of the Wari culture, another powerful Andean political and religious entity that flourished at approximately the same time as the Tiwanaku culture. The Wari had their capital city, called Huari, in the highlands near the modern city of Ayacucho, Peru. A militaristic society, the Wari expanded the territory they controlled until they ruled over much of the highland area of the Central Andes and many coastal river valleys. The Wari people shared a similar religious foundation with Tiwanaku, reflected in a closely related iconography, but the nature of the cultural and political relationship between the two societies remains unclear.[35]

Around 600 CE, both Tiwanaku and Wari established colonies in the warm Moquegua Valley of modern southern Peru, and in this valuable resource zone, both cultures coexisted for about 400 years. The valley, approximately 200 mi (320 km) by road, or a ten to twelve day walk from Tiwanaku, has an elevation substantially lower than the Titicaca Basin, allowing lowland crop production on a grand scale. Importantly, the Moquegua outpost became the source of vast quantities of maize. This crop was vital for the ceremonial chicha used in the frequent public feasts that played a significant role in the Tiwanaku economy. The Wari controlled a portion of the upper part of the valley and built a settlement with a ceremonial center on a high mesa called Cerro Baúl that towers above the valley. Irrigation agriculture predominated in this region, and water from rain and snow high in the mountains had to pass through Wari canals before reaching many Tiwanaku fields. Eventually, this arrangement may have been a source of conflict that contributed to the eventual fall of both cultures in the Moquegua Valley,[36] although some scholars have different interpretations.

Disintegration
The dominance of Tiwanaku waned sometime after about 1000 CE. Some researchers believe a lengthy drought caused this decline, but others have shown that the onset of this climate change began significantly after the societal collapse was underway. Problems may have developed initially in the Moquegua Valley, where the combination of Tiwanaku and Wari demands for irrigation water might have disrupted the region.[37] Control of water resources, as well as production and distribution of agricultural products, may have also promoted an independence movement in the Tiwanaku settlements in this valley. Some evidence indicates significant destruction of these outposts and that local people were rebelling since no signs have been found to suggest an invasion by Wari or other outsiders.

At Tiwanaku, interference in the maize distribution system may have helped to destabilize the authority of the Tiwanaku elites, as it severely restricted the amount of chicha available for the highly anticipated and frequent feasts for commoners and pilgrims. Uprisings by the local people were also apparent, in which elite residences, megalithic monuments, and many of the large doorways in Tiwanaku were defaced and destroyed. Evidence indicates the residential sectors of the city were abandoned in succession. The once-cohesive society appears to have broken down into conflicting factions, perhaps because of both social and ecological factors, especially resource competition. By about 1150 CE, the city was essentially abandoned. The Wari culture had also collapsed by then, although the decline of this culture began somewhat earlier and under circumstances that are even less clearly understood.

What happened immediately after the collapse of the once-powerful Tiwanaku culture? The former city inhabitants seem to have spread out into scattered small communities in the region. Also a major drought, beginning roughly around 1100 CE, likely dealt a final death blow to Tiwanaku. The level of Lake Titicaca dropped significantly, leading to a lowering of groundwater levels around its shores, the abandonment of raised field cultivation, and a major reduction in the food supply. Herding and dry land tuber cultivation became the focus of people remaining in the region. Various chiefdoms arose in which

FIGURE 18.4. Tiwanaku (or Tiahuanaco), ca. 1907. Photograph by Luigi Domenico Gismondi, Diran Sirinian Collection, Buenos Aires, Argentina.

leaders competed for power, and conflict and warfare became a persistent part of life in the Altiplano.

A Lasting Impact
The technological and organizational achievements of Tiwanaku provided a foundation for the Incas when this empire rose hundreds of years later. Recognizing the former glory of Tiwanaku, the Incas attempted to legitimize their rule by claiming the abandoned city as their own place of origin, with their ancestry tied to the ancient rulers of Tiwanaku. Cultural appropriation has a long history.

Seeing Tiwanaku in its prime would have been an amazing experience. Today, only a shadow remains of the once magnificent city. For centuries, visitors have dismantled, buried, defaced, and even blown up the monuments.[38] Beginning during the colonial period, the Spaniards ordered the carved stone blocks of the monumental structures to be carted away as conveniently precut building stone. These were used to construct churches, residences, tombs, and mills in nearby towns, as well as the Bolivian capital of La Paz, about 50 mi (80 km) distant. Military personnel also used monumental structures for target practice. In the early 1900s, workers even broke up stone blocks to provide foundation material for a railroad that was blasted through the ancient city by the Bolivian government. Roads built across a portion of the site for visitor access have caused additional damage. Legends of hidden gold and silver contributed to the site's destruction when looters dug through the ruins seeking treasure (Figure 18.4).

Our understanding of Tiwanaku culture is as fragmentary as the cultural remains that have survived. Archaeologists have studied only a small portion of the over 2 mi^2 (3.2 km^2) area of Tiwanaku. Excavations and reconstructions, conducted in the late nineteenth and early twentieth centuries especially, were amateurish work that increased confusion in the jumble of structural stones and artifacts. Together with the absence of a written Tiwanaku language, the sustained destruction of the site contributes to many mysteries about this highly successful and accomplished ancient society. Nonetheless, remnants provide ample evidence of the former magnificence of this capital city high in the cold and thin air on top of the world.

19

The Inca Builders

Perched high on a steep mountain ridge above dense tropical forests, Machu Picchu is the most famous of all the Inca ruins. It is among the most well-known archaeological sites on earth. The combination of the stunning natural setting and the elegant design and construction of the lofty city make it a magical, mystical place. I have had the privilege of wandering through Machu Picchu on two different trips, and despite absorbing as much as I could in these hours, it was simply not enough. I could return to this mountain city again and again and continue to be enthralled. Machu Picchu distinctly reflects the sophistication and enterprise of a remarkable society and showcases the Inca's exceptional design and construction skills on what is a precipitous ridge.

The Inca Empire is by far the best known of the ancient Andean cultures, attributable largely to the fabulous archaeological remains that we can see today. From imperial complexes in Cuzco to estates in the far-flung corners of the former empire, monumental Inca structures are enduring examples of the accomplishments of the Incas. Engineers and builders constructed a monumental road network, temples and palaces, and enormous agricultural terrace and irrigation canal systems. The society managed food production within ecological zones that extended from the Pacific Ocean up to around 13,000 ft (3,960 m) and higher in elevation and supported millions in their population. An abundance of useful natural resources in an exceptional geographic setting inspired the cultural accomplishments of this empire. Built over thousands of years by their ancestors, a solid foundation of technological achievements and existing infrastructure also permitted the meteoric rise of the Inca Empire.

The Rise and Fall of a Powerful Empire

What are the origins of the Inca culture? There are multiple versions, with the earliest accounts written by Spaniards during the colonial period. Details vary, but the basics usually include the Lake Titicaca region, where the deity Viracocha created all things including the founding ancestors of the Incas. These founders were the son and daughter of the sun, Manco Cápac and his sister-wife Mama Ocllo, who emerged from a cave to the south of Cuzco. After a journey to find suitable fertile land to cultivate, this couple established themselves in the Cuzco Basin. There, they began to raise a new race of children of the sun, as well as to spread their technology and ways of life to the neighbors who they saw as uncivilized.[1]

Archaeological evidence suggests that the Inca state emerged as one of many societies in the region following the collapse of the Wari culture around 1000 CE. Between about 1000 and 1400 CE, the Incas gradually absorbed surrounding sociopolitical groups into their state. These included Killke societies who inhabited the Cuzco region beginning around 1000 CE. With this expansion, the fledgling Inca culture developed strategies eventually practiced so successfully to gain new territories and incorporate diverse ethnic groups.[2]

During the late 1300s or early 1400s, oral histories collected by Spanish chroniclers centuries later show Inca influence began extending far beyond the Cuzco region (in the absence of any written Inca records, specific dates are uncertain). A major period of Inca imperial expansion started in the mid-1400s under the direction of the Supreme Inca, Pachacuti Inca Yupanqui. In recently conquered lands, Pachacuti would order the construction of lavish royal estates, conveying clear messages of his prestige and authority. Focusing on his image at home, Pachacuti is also credited with urban planning in the capital of Cuzco and building magnificent estates at Machu Picchu, Ollantaytambo, and Pisac.[3] We can translate the name Pachacuti from Quechua as "Transformer of the Earth" or "Earth Shaker," and this term is fitting both for what this ruler accomplished during his approximately 40-year reign and for the earthquake-prone realm he ruled.

Pachacuti's expansion efforts were continued by his son, Topa Inca Yupanqui, beginning around 1463. Together, these two leaders brought much of what is now modern Peru, Ecuador, Bolivia, and northern Chile and Argentina under Inca control. Huayna Cápac, who succeeded Topa Inca, expanded the empire even further north into southern Colombia.[4] By about 1500, the Incas had united millions of people and hundreds of ethnic groups under their rule. I suspect that the sweeping range of Inca lands and the diverse populations within this vast territory would have impressed even such celebrated empire-builders as Genghis Khan, Alexander the Great, and Suleiman the Magnificent.

Abundant human and natural resources were clearly available throughout the empire, but how did the Incas mobilize these for the common good? The answer lies in the extremely effective Inca organizational capacity and administrative systems that were aligned with the social values and traditions of those governed.[5] The Inca rulers preferred cooperation, although they readily resorted to force when local resistance arose. The elite employed a variety of practices to win the hearts, minds and stomachs of the populace. These rewards included bestowing generous gifts, supplying stored food in times of scarcity, and providing for elaborate public celebrations.[6]

The labor required to support the nobility and religious institutions and to construct state projects was conscripted from throughout the empire under the *mit'a*, or "turn," labor tax system.[7] Each village or ethnic group was required to contribute a set amount of service to the state through work as soldiers, farmers, masons, miners, weavers, and all other roles necessary to provide economic goods, construction labor, and military conquest and defense. In turn, the state fed, clothed, and housed workers during the time they toiled away from home. At critical periods in the agricultural cycle, workers could return to their home villages to plant and harvest crops.

By the early 1520s, the grim influence of European cultures reached the Central Andes, and the downfall of this thriving civilization began. Initially, changes came in the form of new and lethal diseases. The Indigenous peoples had no resistance to smallpox, which spread south from Mexico after being brought by Spanish explorers. This deadly disease, and possibly others, created turmoil within the empire in 1524 when the reigning Inca emperor, Huayna Cápac, and several of his high-ranking officials died suddenly.[8] Two of Huayna Cápac's sons, Atahualpa and Huascar, ruled the northern and southern halves of the empire for several years, until a power struggle began, and a deadly civil war ensued.

Atahualpa emerged victorious and became the reigning emperor of the empire, but his rule was to be short-lived. A major blow came when the Spanish conquistador, Francisco Pizarro, marched into the city of Cajamarca in northern Peru in 1532, captured Atahualpa, and ultimately ordered his execution.[9]

Valiant Inca resistance efforts continued sporadically for decades, finally ending in 1572 when the last stronghold fell at Vilcabamba,[10] high in remote and rugged terrain above the Amazon Basin. The European influence on Indigenous people and their culture was catastrophic. Between the devastating effects brought about by warfare, disease, and exploitation, the native population plummeted, and many social traditions established over thousands of years collapsed.

Tying the Empire Together
Five hundred years ago, the Inca Empire was the largest state to arise in the Americas, and possibly the largest nation on earth.[11] The Incas called their realm Tawantinsuyu, translated as "Land of the Four Quarters" or "Four Parts Together." From the imperial city of Cuzco, considered the center of the Inca universe, four major roads extended outwards into the geographic quarters of the empire.[12] These roads were part of the incredible 25,000 mi (40,233 km) network of roads and trails that tied together an extremely diverse geographic region and made up one of the largest monumental systems built in the ancient world[13] (Figure 19.1).

Each of the four geographic quarters contained valuable resources. The northeastern quarter, Antisuyu, encompassed Cuzco and the royal estates in the fertile Sacred Valley. Extensive terrace and irrigation systems supported crop production, and valuable tropical resources were available in the Amazon Basin, including coca leaves and the feathers of tropical birds.[14] Proceeding in a clockwise direction, Collasuyu (also Qollasuyu) was the large southern quarter. This coastal desert realm provided valuable minerals, especially copper and tin, and on the eastern side, the Altiplano and the wealth of resources in and around Lake Titicaca.[15] A small southwestern quarter, the Kuntisuyu region, included the dry western cordillera slopes and Pacific coastal strip, with terrace farming along river valleys and the bounty of ocean waters.[16] The northernmost section, Chinchaysuyu, was the most prosperous and had the largest population of the four quarters. Chinchaysuyu provided access to abundant minerals, terraced and irrigated valley slopes, and marine resources, including the revered *Spondylus*.[17]

The ability of the Incas to unite such an enormous geographic region was a major achievement. Throughout the rugged Andes, people were isolated in narrow valleys separated by steep, mountainous terrain. Historically, the result

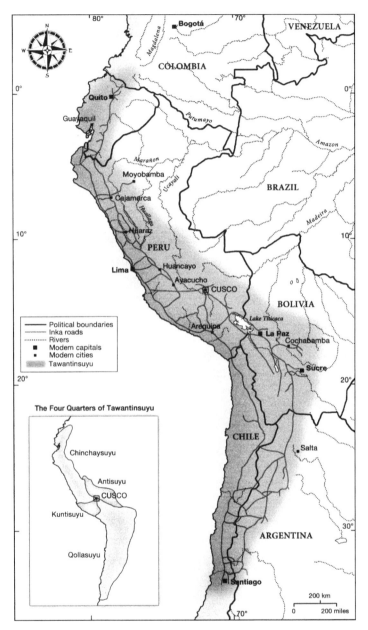

FIGURE 19.1. The Inca Empire showing the four quarters and the road system. Map by Julie Meyerson, in Gary Urton and Adriana von Hagen, eds., *Encyclopedia of the Incas* (2015): 11.

was many autonomous cultures having distinctive languages and social practices, as well as varying degrees of openness to accepting a centralized government. Empires are built when a significant number of distinctly different cultural groups, each with a separate territory, are combined under a single ruling group. Empires also are defined by flexible borders that are expanded by subduing and incorporating additional cultural groups without changing the basic structure or identity of the ruling body.[18] Such a unification process typically involves warfare and oppression, although it can also happen with generous gifts, arranged marriages, and thinly veiled threats. Inca administrators used all these approaches.

At the height of the empire around the year 1500, researchers estimate 12 million people, and possibly millions more, lived under Inca rule.[19] Culturally, the citizens of the empire spoke hundreds of languages and dialects and ranged from city-dwelling artists and accountants to rural farmers and fisherfolk. The genius of the Incas was in their ability to unify these diverse ethnic groups scattered over an enormous territory—a feat never duplicated in any other mountainous terrain on earth.

The Incas built their distinctive architecture throughout their empire, with the greatest number of buildings in the Cuzco Basin heartland where the culture first flourished. Once the empire began expanding, the capital city of Cuzco became the location of the most sacred religious structures and palaces occupied by the living royalty and housing the mummies of deceased rulers.

The Incas filled the entire landscape they inhabited with sacred features. Along with roads radiating outward from the center of Cuzco, they recognized a network of dozens of sightlines to visually link these sacred features. Known as the Cuzco *ceque* system, each of these imaginary lines connected a dozen or more shrines, called *huacas*, which were deeply symbolic to the Incas. Huacas included hills, caves, quarries, temples, fields, springs, ravines, outcrops of rock, mountain summits and passes, and many other natural and constructed features.[20] At these places, they made offerings to deities and performed sacrifices during rituals.

The archaeological site of Sacsayhuaman, with extensive ruins overlooking Cuzco, is renowned for its gigantic stone blocks. These stone blocks once formed immense terrace walls, temples, towers, and storehouses filled with supplies of food, clothing, and art objects from around the empire. To the northwest of the city, in the Río Vilcanota/Río Urubamba drainage, the Inca elite ordered the construction of elegant estates, including Machu Picchu and Ollantaytambo. The engineering feats accomplished at these mountainous archaeological sites demonstrate that the Incas had a reliable measurement system, an understanding of mathematics, knowledge of construction techniques, and a highly sophisticated understanding of their environment.[21]

Imperial Construction
The Incas are renowned for the high-quality stonework found in their most important buildings. This stonework is so impressive that many have found it hard to believe that mere humans, without the help of draft animals and with only rudimentary tools, could be responsible for its construction. The mystery of this accomplishment shows up in local folklore, with the Incas credited with knowing how to make the rocks walk by themselves. Observers have alleged that a race of giants built the structures, while others have attributed monumental construction to satanic assistance or extraterrestrial intervention. Some have suggested stone-softening acids from local plants could have been used either to cut the stone into blocks or so it could be poured or compacted into molds. Still others have proposed lasers that focused sunlight using large parabolic gold mirrors. While some of these "theories" clearly are implausible, scattered information and experiments, using heat or plant-derived acids that can superficially soften rock, contain intriguing information.[22] Unless researchers can replicate these studies scientifically, however, they remain only tantalizing hints of what we might learn from the ancient people.

What we know now, from carefully collected evidence, clarifies that they could have accomplished all construction tasks using only human labor. Archaeologists have recovered ancient stone tools left in quarries and construction sites. They have studied the accounts of sixteenth-century writers who watched the Incas working on Spanish colonial buildings, and they have performed stone-cutting experiments in Inca quarries. While difficult for some people to believe, this research clearly shows that simple tools and highly labor-intensive methods were the construction techniques employed by the Incas.[23]

The Incas are best known for their tightly fitting, shaped dry-stone block masonry assembled without mortar. They used this type of construction for the most important buildings in the empire, building less important structures with adobe brick or uncut stone joined with clay mortar. Builders used several types of fine masonry styles, based on the size and shape of the stone blocks.

At Machu Picchu, archaeologists recognize at least eighteen different stone wall types, ranging from rough stones used in terrace walls to superb smoothed and shaped walls for sacred structures.[24]

Distinctive architectural designs appear throughout Inca lands because the state carefully controlled the major design features and construction techniques. Core elements include stone block masonry styles; trapezoidal doors, niches, and windows; battered, or sloping walls; gabled or hipped roofs; and rectangular buildings.[25]

Rock Quarries

The Incas invested enormous amounts of time and labor in the painstaking work of elite stone block construction. They conscripted tens of thousands of workers from throughout the empire for major projects under the mit'a labor tax system. The principal rocks quarried in the Cuzco region were igneous types, including granite and the volcanic rocks andesite, diorite, and rhyolite, as well as sedimentary types such as limestone. Color was an important characteristic of the selected rock, but also natural fracturing or splitting characteristics.

Selecting, shaping, and moving quarried stone to Inca construction sites required significant effort. The andesite used for the most important buildings in Cuzco was obtained primarily from the Rumicollca quarry, a fractured rock face about 22 mi (35 km) to the east.[26] This quarry still contains blocks abandoned by Inca workers in various stages of production, and the site continues to be worked today. The builders of Sacsayhuaman quarried massive blocks from nearby outcrops for volcanic diorite and limestone, plus they used a dark andesite that was also probably from Rumicollca.

At the royal estate of Ollantaytambo, a reddish volcanic rhyolite (also called red porphyry) was acquired from the Kachiqhata quarries on mountain slopes across Río Urubamba (also known as Río Vilcanota) flowing near the monumental complex.[27] These quarries are about 1,500–2,500 ft (457–762 m) above the valley floor in extensive rockslides beneath an almost vertical cliff face. Transporting the stone down the mountain and across the river, and then dragging it up to the building sites, would have required the labor of thousands of workers.

On one of my trips to Ollantaytambo, I hiked into the Kachiqhata quarry area. On that adventure, a guide led our small group on a steep and rugged climb. As we trudged higher up the mountain slope, a colorful mosaic of the

238 CHAPTER 19

FIGURE 19.2. Kachiqhata quarry above Ollantaytambo. Photograph by author.

modern town and ruins of Ollantaytambo spread out below us, surrounded by agricultural fields and edged by steep mountains and Río Urubamba. When we reached the quarry, we found hundreds of shaped blocks still in place in different stages of preparation (Figure 19.2). Workers clearly had selected blocks that took advantage of the natural fracture planes. They had trimmed many enormous blocks and lined them up above slides for delivery down the steep mountain slope to the edge of the river. From this landing place, the workers probably dragged the blocks across the river during the relatively shallow water levels of the dry season. Although I could hear only the wind, I imagined the quarry area during its prime. The space would have been filled with the ringing sounds of mit'a workers hammering on the rock with their stone tools and supervisors shouting instructions to the laborers working together as they strained to lower the blocks using thick fiber ropes.

Enormous efforts were undertaken to source appropriate rock for important Inca structures. The extremes that the Incas could go to are demonstrated by hundreds of carved andesite building blocks found near an Inca construction site in the town of Saraguro, in the southern highlands of what is now Ecuador. Researchers have determined that this andesite was the same rock as that used to build many of the important structures in Cuzco, and that laborers moved these blocks from the Rumicollca quarry an almost unfathomable 1,000 mi (1,600 km) distant.[28] Archaeologists suggest many motivations for this extraordinary effort, most importantly, a demonstration of the power of the empire and a transfer of sacredness, tying the distant region to the Inca capital in Cuzco.

Shaping and Fitting

Builders used stone tools in all Inca constructions. Most commonly used were hammerstones, extremely hard, rounded cobblestones and boulders weighing up to around 17 lb (8 kg) and found in egg-shaped to football-shaped sizes[29] (see Figure 15.3). Typically collected from riverbeds, hard metamorphic rocks such as quartzite were selected preferentially. Workers trimmed rough stone blocks into final forms at building sites by chipping away at the rock bit by bit, removing flakes by aiming the hammerstones at about 15° to 45° angles to the block, in a process called "nibbling." Virtually all fine Inca masonry displays small pecks or scars near the edges of blocks and larger scars away from the edges. This pattern results from craft workers taking sizeable "bites" of rock with large hammerstones to shape the rock in rough form, followed by progressively smaller "bites" with smaller hammerstones for the final fine trimming.[30] Archaeologists found hundreds of hammerstones in the 1910 excavations of Machu Picchu,[31] as well as at many other Inca sites. Some show the finger indentations the masons used to grip the stones. At Machu Picchu, archaeologists have even found hammerstones left by workers within the centers of walls.

The Incas had an abundance of labor available to assemble the heavy stone blocks in building construction. Unfinished walls show that they shaped the top surface of a row of blocks only roughly before placement, and then they trimmed these top faces to match the precut undersides of the block to be added above. Disassembled walls show that the closely fit joints at the front extend variable distances into the block interior, from only a few inches deep up to the entire thickness of the wall. Multiple adjustments were required for the shaping to achieve close joints, each involving hoisting a block in and out of position to check the fit with adjoining blocks.[32]

Workers used large ramps built with rock rubble as access points to move the stone blocks upwards and into place. Inca workers continued to use this method when constructing the Cathedral of Cuzco under the direction of the Spaniards. When construction was complete, they removed the ramps.[33] While fitting heavy blocks together tightly was clearly time-consuming and labor-intensive, it was not technically difficult.

The Incas built the most important structures in the sacred center of Cuzco using rows of smooth, rectangular blocks of similar sizes. Other foundation and retaining walls were assembled from irregular-shaped polygonal blocks fit together like a jigsaw puzzle. One famously photographed block in a wall in Cuzco has twelve sides, although we know blocks with even more angles.[34]

Many fine stone walls have blocks with a signature rounded or convex "pillowed" shape along the edges and sunken joints. This design creates an artistic effect of light and shadow accentuating the patterns of the walls and drawing attention to the fine seams between the blocks. In some places, these joints have a slightly different color and even a glassy or vitrified appearance compared to the surrounding rock. A plausible explanation is that a thin layer of an acid-rich pyrite mortar superficially dissolved and softened the joints in the rock to a silica gel. The gel would have subsequently hardened, leaving only the glassy traces.[35]

An interesting characteristic of many blocks—especially notable at Ollantaytambo and Sacsayhuaman—is the small protuberances in various shapes seen along the lower edges of stone blocks. These points might have functioned to provide leverage for ropes or poles used in positioning the heavy blocks, or they could be ornamental or even symbolic. Since workers did not remove them during the finishing of the walls, and some even appear to be polished, the small protuberances must have been left deliberately as sculptural wall features.

For a culture without a written language, the Incas had remarkably advanced engineering capabilities. They successfully built impressive structures that have endured for hundreds of years. A characteristic feature of Inca stone walls is an inward slope, or batter, of four to six percent.[36] This slope increased the resistance of the walls to earthquake-shaking and supported a very heavy roof load. In addition, it helped to create a visual effect of an imposing and impenetrable structure. Such adaptations to their environment were key to the success of the Incas and to preserving their legacy for generations to admire.

Inca Cuzco

The Inca capital city showcased the architectural and artistic sophistication and grandeur of this culture. Designed as a religious and political center of authority, the city surely astonished all who visited and impressed these visitors with the prodigious power of the Incas and their gods. When the Spanish conquistadors reached Cuzco in 1533, by all accounts the magnificence overwhelmed them. With its paved streets, channelized rivers, a storm drainage system, extensive manicured gardens, and large temple and palace complexes constructed with superb stone masonry, the imperial city was said to be worthy of appearing even in Spain, a model of cultural sophistication.[37] In addition, the dazzling abundance of gold presented a glorious display of stunning wealth, including a gold fountain, plates attached to temple walls, and a vast number of decorative items including sculptures, vases, and vessels.[38]

The most important religious complex in Inca Cuzco was the Coricancha, considered the center of the empire and the most sacred spot in the universe. The Inca name, translated as "Golden Enclosure," originated from the plates of gold that sheathed the building walls.[39] By reflecting sunlight, the golden walls were visible for great distances. Within the large, walled Coricancha, an extensive series of buildings and courtyards were dedicated to various deities and filled with the finest art pieces. Spanish chroniclers reported a garden area containing life-size silver and gold sculptures of people, llamas, and plants, including cornstalks complete with leaves and ears of corn. Exquisite stonework remains visible today on the curved wall of the Coricancha and on some intact interior walls dividing spaces.[40]

If you happened to visit Inca Cuzco at the height of the empire, you would find a grand plaza dominating the city center, with two large open areas separated by Río Saphy. To the west of the river was an area called Cusipata ("Fortunate Terrace"). To the east of the Saphy was Haucaypata ("Terrace of Repose"). At Haucaypata, thousands of Incas gathered throughout the year to take part in elaborate festivals. Surrounding the plaza you would see important palaces, temples, and shrines with superbly crafted stonework. Substantial walls up to 15 ft (4.5 m) and higher enclosed most of the buildings, creating compounds. Narrow paved streets separated the compounds, many of them with water channels for drainage and stairways on steep sections.[41] Today, we know the Haucaypata as the Plaza de Armas, and it continues to be the heart of Cuzco.

The Haucaypata plaza has an unusual history. During construction, the Incas directed the soil that originally composed the plaza area to be removed carefully. According to a Spanish chronicler who wrote about this process in 1571, the Incas redistributed this soil elsewhere in the empire "because it was greatly esteemed and they covered it over with sand from the seacoast to a depth of two palms and a half, and in some places more,"[42] perhaps about 10 in (25 cm) deep. The combination of sunlight on the expanse of white sand and the polished gold sheets that covered the facades of adjacent buildings surely filled the plaza area with a resplendent light. Buried within the sand were offerings of miniature gold and silver figurines of animals and people. As recently as 1996, during a renovation of the central fountain of the Plaza de Armas, archaeologists recovered small llama figurines that Inca artists fashioned from these precious metals.[43]

Clearly, moving the many tons of sand needed to fill the plaza was an act of great symbolic significance. The ancient Andeans carried sand in basket load after basket load in a tremendous effort, traveling over 250 mi (400 km) up to Cuzco. What was their motivation? Since the Incas recognized an essential and sacred connection between the mountains and the sea, by filling the plaza with sand, it may have become a symbolic "ocean." More about the Haucaypata sand appears in Chapter 20.

Sacsayhuaman
Constructed on a steep hill with an impressive view of Cuzco and the surrounding valley, this grand architectural complex is one of the archaeological wonders of the Americas. What remains today is only a small fraction of the massive monumental compound that existed during the height of the Inca Empire. On the north side of the site are the vestiges of a large circular reservoir and a

network of water channels that once filled the reservoir. Near the middle of the site are a series of extensively carved outcrops of rock. Visitors today popularly refer to one especially large outcrop with several carved tiers as the "Throne of the Inca," overlooking a grand plaza that can hold thousands of people. Numerous foundations of what were once fine stone buildings also are visible, along with the remains of at least two towers. Throughout the site, one can see carefully cut stone drainage channels and conduits for the ritual manipulation of water or other liquids.[44]

The most impressive section of Sacsayhuaman contains three immense terrace walls of gigantic, interlocked stone blocks. The wall heights are approximately 18 ft (5.5 m), and the longest wall extends for about 1,300 ft (396 m), or a quarter of a mile. The workers constructed the walls in a zigzag pattern involving approximately fifty changes in direction.[45] The sizes of the carved blocks are truly tremendous, unmatched anywhere in the Americas. Some blocks reach 13 ft (4 m) in height. Estimates of the weights of the largest blocks range from 100–130 tons (90–120 mt) or more.

Possibly more than at any other Inca archaeological site, the enormous size of these blocks has prompted wild theories that the devil or a race of giants built the walls. In the centuries before the Incas, earlier cultures, including the Killke, built substantial structures at the site. Abundant evidence, however, shows that the Incas expanded the complex immensely during the time of imperial rule.[46] The zigzag terrace walls have been partially dismantled over the passing centuries. Nonetheless, they reflect the Inca genius for design in the shadows cast by the enormous blocks, echoing the shapes of the peaks behind them.

Royal Estates of the Sacred Valley

The Inca elite built spectacular royal estates north of Cuzco, along the Sacred Valley that is traversed by Río Urubamba. Splendid terraces, waterworks, and fine stone masonry structures were all designed meticulously to meld with natural landforms. Royal designers carefully selected estate sites to provide access to a range of resources, including croplands, pastures, forests, water sources, and special features such as salt-producing springs and ponds.

The majestic site of Machu Picchu is the most renowned, but there are other fabulous ruins. At Pisac, a temple complex contains altars and water fountains built around a large carved outcrop of rock on a hilltop with expansive views. A series of ancient terraces still grace the hillslopes, but Spanish conquistadors destroyed the original Inca town in the 1530s. In contrast, the town of Ollantaytambo contains buildings that people have occupied continuously since Inca times.

Some archaeologists believe that each of the estate sites may also have been chosen for its defensive and exclusive elements.[47] The Pisac site could have been used to safeguard the southern entrance to the Sacred Valley and Ollantaytambo to fortify the northern entrance.

To build Ollantaytambo, the Incas channelized the adjacent Río Urubamba to reclaim land for buildings and crops. Archaeologists recognize at least three major construction phases for elite buildings, with stone blocks from earlier structures reworked and/or repositioned. The site displays seven styles of stonework with varying degrees of craftsmanship.[48]

When I visited Ollantaytambo, I was intrigued to see solid stone-block storehouses built on the hillslopes high above the valley. The builders maximized food storage times in these sturdy structures, so they have ventilation systems that capture winds at the higher and cooler elevations above the valley.[49] The visible presence of these storehouses probably reminded the local people of the great wealth of the Inca state and the security of knowing that sufficient food would be available during times of scarcity.

Machu Picchu

Inca builders and artisans created a dazzling aesthetic whole at Machu Picchu by framing and integrating the natural beauty into their constructed features. Perched high atop a steep ridge at an elevation of some 7,970 ft (2,430 m), Machu Picchu is magnificent. The setting is a major part of its grandeur, as the builders nestled the city between two prominent mountain peaks: Machu Picchu and Huayna Picchu. The ridgetop, where numerous stairways connect some 200 buildings, is ringed on three sides by Río Urubamba, flowing a dizzying 1,640 ft (500 m) below. Mists that swirl upwards from the river contribute to an aura of mystery. Towering mountain peaks dominate the views, including Veronica to the east (19,159 ft, 5,850 m) and Salcantay to the south (20,530 ft, 6,257 m).

Although no one knows for certain, Machu Picchu was likely an important religious center and place of retreat for the royal Inca family and high priests. Archaeologists estimate that construction of the city began around the year 1450, or perhaps a few decades earlier,[50] under the direction of the Supreme Inca

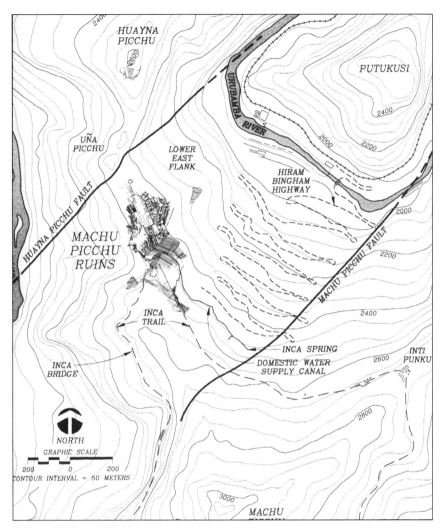

FIGURE 19.3. Faults in Machu Picchu area. Map by Kenneth W. Wright and Alfredo V. Zegarra, *Machu Picchu: A Civil Engineering Marvel* (2000): 5, Figure 1-6.

Pachacuti and took at least fifty years to complete. Its builders likely examined many mountaintops before finding a location suitable for this royal retreat. The Incas occupied the city for only a few decades, as they abandoned it in the mid-sixteenth century after the Spanish began their conquest. The surrounding jungle quickly enveloped and concealed the site for centuries. Although

FIGURE 19.4. Granitic quarry at Machu Picchu. Photograph by author.

the conquistadors explored the surrounding mountains, Machu Picchu fortuitously remained hidden from their view.

Two principal faults border the site: the Huayna Picchu fault and the Machu Picchu fault, named after the adjacent mountain peaks.[51] These two faults form a wedge-shaped structural block, or graben, upon which the Incas built the city (Figure 19.3).

On the north slope of Machu Picchu Mountain, a natural spring that continues to flow today provided a year-round water supply to the city. It is unusual to find a spring at such a high elevation in the mountains, but the Machu Picchu fault controls this perennial water source. The fractured and permeable rock along the fault zone allows precipitation to infiltrate and emanate at the spring site. A stone block collection system of canals enhances the reliable yield of the spring, and this system was so well-engineered it is still operational today.[52]

The availability of water on the ridgetop was surely an important consideration in site selection, but so also was the suitability of the rock for construction. On the western edge of the site, an accumulation of fractured granitic blocks from ancient rockfalls and landslides provided a natural quarry that allowed workers to extract relatively well-formed blocks close to their construction projects (Figure 19.4). This white-to-grayish granitic rock is an extremely strong and durable construction material. Thousands of tons of stone had to be moved and fit into place to build the city. And much of this work is not visible. Engineers estimate 60 percent of the construction effort is hidden underground in an efficient drainage system and deep foundations beneath terrace walls.[53] Heavy rainfall in the region—about 76 in (193 cm) per year during occupation of Machu Picchu[54]—made installation of an adequate drainage system essential.

As a first step in developing the site, the Inca builders stabilized the steep mountain slopes by creating meticulous terraces that opened space for future urban and agricultural uses. The elegant terraces emphasize the natural contours of the mountainside, and their construction had to be started low on the unstable slopes. A sophisticated drainage system includes a lower layer of boulders, a middle layer of gravelly dirt, and a top layer of soil, suitable for cultivating crops and for providing foundation stability.[55] Workers placed all these layers by hand, including the organic-rich topsoil that had to be carried up in baskets from the Río Urubamba floodplain far below or possibly collected from the slopes of the nearby mountains. The terraces provided protection from uncontrolled runoff, erosion, and landslides during the heavy seasonal rains, ensuring that water could percolate through and drain down the mountainside with minimal soil erosion. Without extensive site preparation, deterioration would have occurred rapidly as terraces settled and buildings crumbled.

Fittingly, Machu Picchu was named a UNESCO World Heritage site in 1983 and one of the New Seven Wonders of the World in 2007.

The World Overturning

The Incas believed that history comprises a series of time periods separated by violent upheavals, referred to as a *pachacuti*—an overturning of the world.[56] The imperial expansion that created the Inca Empire began with a pachacuti in 1438, under the Inca ruler who aptly called himself Pachacuti Inca Yupanqui, the Earth Shaker.

By the early 1530s in the Inca Empire, several major building projects were actively under construction, including the temples of Ollantaytambo, rampart walls at Sacsayhuaman, and the circular *muyu* terraces of Moray. Work, however, appears to have stopped abruptly. Evidence found at construction sites includes randomly located stone blocks, abandoned tools, and partially finished additions, revealing a sudden and dramatic interruption. The exact timing of when the Incas suspended these construction activities is uncertain, but one fact is crystal clear. The meeting between the Spanish conquistador Francisco Pizarro and the Supreme Inca Atahualpa on November 16, 1532, ended in disaster for the Incas. On that day, the violent beginning of the end of Tawantinsuyu began. A tragic and historically significant pachacuti was underway—and the world of the Incas changed forever.

Part IV

Pachacuti

An Overturning of the World

20

After the Incas

The streets of Cuzco are alive today with a fascinating and eclectic mix of Inca, Spanish colonial, and modern architecture and culture. In my wanderings through the central part of this city, I've spotted many remnants of the fine stonework walls that once encircled Inca temples and palaces. Today, these form the foundations for modern structures. The most prominent examples are the shop and restaurant facades surrounding the formal Plaza de Armas (formerly the Haucaypata plaza), as well as the ornate Church of Santo Domingo built above the smoothly curving wall of the Coricancha. For me, these blended walls represent an uneasy juxtaposition of two distinctive cultures. They also offer a stark reminder of the brilliance of the ancient people who once ruled the Central Andes.

Visitors marvel at Cuzco's magnificent Inca stonework, yet what we can see are only fragments of the extraordinary city that existed at the height of the empire. Five centuries of wars, demolition, earthquakes, remodeling, and urban growth have taken a tremendous toll. Still, despite those influences and the changes nature and time have brought, the rich Inca history of the city is still apparent. When I was exploring one brisk day, I was fortunate to gain a vivid taste of times past when I happened upon a parade stretching around the Plaza de Armas. Transfixed, I sat on the stone steps of the Cuzco Cathedral, listening to flutes and drums, and watching hundreds of colorfully costumed dancers weaving and twirling in the bright sunlight. On that memorable afternoon, the parade transported me back in time to an Inca festival.

The cultural traditions of the Incas and their ancestors developed independently for millennia. When the Spanish arrived in the year 1532, they found societies entirely different from any they had known. They lost no time in beginning concerted efforts to eliminate Andean customs of which they disapproved, replacing them with European practices. The Spanish promoted their Christian religious beliefs and installed their own political systems and supporting infrastructure.

Economic considerations were of utmost importance to the new arrivals. They pulled valuable metallic resources, especially gold and silver, from mines as expeditiously as possible with little regard for tremendous human costs and environmental destruction. The sharp hooves of introduced horses, cattle, and sheep replaced the soft and broad footpads of camelids, soon followed by widespread overgrazing, erosion, and other environmental degradation. They uprooted and resettled the Indigenous people, forcing them to work in the mines and agricultural fields of colonial powers. Many were ruthlessly exploited. Diseases spread widely, and the social disruption led to failed crops, malnutrition, and starvation. These and many more changes transformed the world of the Incas.

The Dark Side of Gold
The shiny yellow metal revered by so many cultures throughout world history ultimately led to the fall of the Inca Empire. In the sixteenth century, the lust for precious metals lured the Spanish conquistador, Francisco Pizarro, high into the Andes Mountains.[1] Accompanied by a tattered group of 168 soldiers, with sixty-two mounted on horses, the Spaniards were in awe of the riches of these strange new lands. When Pizarro and the reigning Inca, Atahualpa, met in Cajamarca on November 16, 1532, an apparent misunderstanding between the two powerful men erupted into a battle. The prancing horses, steel swords and armor, and guns of the Spanish soldiers rapidly overwhelmed the Inca troops with their padded cotton garments, wood and stone clubs, and slings. While greatly outnumbered, the Spaniards massacred thousands of Inca soldiers, and they captured Atahualpa and held him as a hostage.

Atahualpa quickly realized that the Spanish invaders coveted metals. Attempting to regain his freedom, the Inca emperor promised Pizarro a ransom of gold to fill half the size of the room where he was imprisoned and filled twice with silver.[2] Over the next few months, and to the astonishment of the conquistadors, the Inca emperor's subjects collected this enormous quantity of precious metals from throughout the empire. This ransom was possibly the largest paid for any individual in history. The value of the gold and silver in dollars today is difficult to estimate but was probably roughly $350 million.[3] Pizarro accepted the ransom but continued to imprison Atahualpa for months. Then, in a mock trial, the conquistadors accused Atahualpa of crimes including polygamy, incestuous marriage, and idolatry—accepted Inca cultural practices—and, in August 1533, they executed him.

The Spanish lost no time in plundering the fabulous wealth of Andean gold and silver and dividing up Inca palaces and tracts of land for their own personal property. The furnaces used to melt down nearly all the fabulous gold and silver plates, jewelry, and art objects collected for Atahualpa's ransom reportedly burned for months. Spanish ships carried shipment after shipment of ingots of Inca gold and silver to Spain. These New World metals became an essential component of the Spanish political system and transformed the economy of Europe.[4]

Mines of Death

After plundering all the precious metals they could collect in ready-to-melt form, the Spanish turned their attention to finding the mines that were the source of these metallic ores. Although years went by before the Spaniards could locate the richest ores, exploitation began right away once they were identified. A new phase of colonial mining and mineral processing began, with grim consequences. In their rush to maximize profits, the Spanish conquerors had minimal concern for the health of their labor force and the land. The resulting human and environmental costs devastated the lives of millions of Andeans and created landscapes filled with mercury and other toxins that have never recovered.[5]

In 1545, the Potosí mines, now in Bolivia, were opened to recover enormous deposits of silver-rich ore. A towering cone-shaped mountain of volcanic rock the Spanish named Cerro Rico, or "Rich Mountain", contains the ore (Figure 20.1). One of the most notorious of Spanish mines, Potosí produced approximately half of all the silver from the Americas in the century between 1550 and 1650. During this time, the name "Potosí" became inexorably linked with forced labor and death.[6]

Spanish mine operators initially shipped the mercury required to process Andean silver ore from Europe, especially the Almadén region of Spain. In the mid-1560s, the Spanish colonists recognized the rich deposits of cinnabar near Huancavelica, now in Peru and some 800 mi (1,287 km) to the northeast of

FIGURE 20.1. Cerro Rico del Potosí in the first image shown in Europe. Illustration by Pedro Cieza de León, 1553.

Potosí. Mining these ore deposits for mercury became vital to silver production at Potosí.

For laborers, the "standard occupational hazards" of mining included respiratory diseases, falls from precarious rope ladders, and burial from rock falls and collapses. These risks were intensified for mine workers exposed to the toxic effects of mercury poisoning, recognized at least as early as Inca times and certainly by the colonial powers. Many workers were forced to mix mercury and silver ore with their bare feet, and many more became engulfed in mercury-laden dust that they carried into their homes, exposing wives, children, and other family members to the dangerous element.

During the early years of colonial mining, the Spaniards directed the Incas to use their traditional mining techniques at Potosí. After only two decades, the richest ores were exhausted, costs for labor and fuel rose, and silver production plummeted. This situation created consternation in Spain, where Spanish royalty had become accustomed to relying on Potosí silver to fill their coffers.

To increase output, in 1572 the Spanish viceroy in Peru, Don Francisco de Toledo, introduced two innovations for the mines.[7] The first was a new mercury amalgamation technology developed initially and used successfully in the silver mines of New Spain (now Mexico). This development led to a great leap in production at Potosí, as it permitted lower-grade silver ore to be mined profitably. The second innovation addressed the challenge of providing more workers, as large-scale mining efforts relied on harnessing an abundant and inexpensive labor force. Viceroy Toledo proclaimed a new Potosí *mita* by transforming the Inca *mit'a* labor draft system into one of Spanish forced labor drafts.

The stage was now set for phenomenal wealth for a select group of colonial elites and the Spanish king. Working conditions for miners became even more horrendous, including being forced to stay underground for days at a time, and accidents and disease resulted in the deaths of large numbers of miners. Severe environmental degradation from timber harvesting, livestock overgrazing, and mercury contamination became part of the enterprise.

The combination of the richness of the Potosí silver mines and the Huancavelica mercury mines brought the Andes region into world primacy and became a catalyst for the development of a global economy.[8] Mine operators reached peak extraction levels at Potosí in 1592, and the output in 1715 was essentially the same as had occurred almost one hundred years before. Eventually, miners depleted the silver content of the ores sufficiently so that after about 1800, tin became the principal commercial mineral extracted from the mines.

Today, the cities of Huancavelica, Peru, and Potosí, Bolivia, continue to grapple with the dismal legacy of untold tons of toxic mercury released into the environment.[9] At Cerro Rico, thousands of impoverished miners persist in scratching at the rock with hand tools or picking through spoil piles, seeking elusive fortunes from the silver and tin of the Potosí mines.

A Catastrophic Clash of Cultures
After the death of the once-powerful Inca emperor Atahualpa, sporadic Inca rebellions against the occupying Spanish forces took place for several decades.[10] The Incas centered one significant rebellion in Cuzco for ten long months in 1536 and 1537.

The Inca rebellion that began in 1536 arose in the events of 1533. Shortly after the execution of Atahualpa, Pizarro installed as emperor Manco Inca Yupanqui, a son of Huayna Cápac, the last widely recognized ruler of the empire. Upon realizing he was only a puppet leader, Manco Inca assembled an army of tens of thousands of men to reconquer Cuzco, with fighting beginning in 1536. Using the massive stone walls and hilltop location of Sacsayhuaman as an Inca fortress, the army rained burning arrows down onto the thatched roofs of the city. Widespread fires and destruction, plus heavy casualties on both sides, continued for months. Eventually, when Inca soldier-farmers began leaving Sacsayhuaman to plant their crops and large numbers of Spanish reinforcements arrived, the Incas were finally forced to withdraw.

Manco Inca and his followers retreated first to the estate of Ollantaytambo, where they slowed the advancing Spanish army by flooding the plains surrounding Rió Urubamba. Again, the might of the Spaniards prevailed, however, and Manco Inca withdrew to a heavily forested base called Vilcabamba in the upper Amazon. There, they established a Neo-Inca state with a series of rulers reigning in the mountainous outpost. This state was a thorn in the side of the Spanish colonists for several decades. Finally, Spanish soldiers captured and executed Túpac Amaru, the last ruler, and destroyed Vilcabamba. The reign of the Incas disintegrated in 1572.

For the Indigenous Andeans, the changes brought by the Spanish colonial period led to the collapse of thousands of years of cultural brilliance. New diseases such as measles and smallpox, destruction during warfare, disruption of traditional lifestyles, and the damaging effects of forced labor had catastrophic effects. By the close of the sixteenth century, historians estimate an appalling decline of at least 50 percent in the regional Andean population that had existed prior to European contact.[11]

In recent decades, exquisite small gold and silver Inca sculptures of animals and people, some decorated with finely woven textiles and feathers, have been found in ritual settings on high Andean peaks. These elegant offerings provide poignant reminders of the legacy of art and vibrant culture that was destroyed.

Inca Cuzco Becomes Colonial Cuzco

As the victorious Spanish conquistadors divided central Cuzco into housing lots for themselves, they ordered the demolition of Inca structures. Laborers pulled down the shaped stone blocks from the Inca buildings for reuse in Spanish churches, convents, and residential and commercial structures. By the end of the sixteenth century, native masons had learned to emulate the Spanish style so well that hardly any trace of Indigenous influence remained. The character of the city was modified dramatically.

After the Spanish secured Sacsayhuaman following the 1537 siege, the stone blocks from its structures provided a convenient source of building materials. An early Spanish chronicler reported that virtually every Spanish home built in Cuzco contained blocks from Inca walls and buildings.[12] Rumors about the possibility of buried treasure within the complex also encouraged destructive excavations. Today, only the largest stone blocks remain at Sacsayhuaman. Paradoxically, builders didn't carry these away and reuse them because the Spanish saw the blocks as much too difficult to move.

As they altered Cuzco during this cultural transition, the Spaniards also endeavored to crush the "idolatrous" beliefs of the Incas, while fulfilling their own objectives. In one example, a Spanish official, Juan Polo de Ondegardo, recognized the sacred character of the Pacific coast sand in the Haucaypata plaza in 1559 when planning was underway to construct the Cuzco Cathedral next to it. To obtain high-quality construction material conveniently and economically for the project, to collect gold and silver items possibly buried beneath the sand, and to squash disfavored beliefs of the Incas, he ordered the sand removed and incorporated in construction cement.[13] The official recorded the Incas were greatly distressed by the removal of the sand from this important site. Archaeologists believe that for the Incas, however, sacredness was embedded in the object's material, so the significance could be independent of the shape it took or the use.[14] Thus, the sand incorporated within the mortar of the cathedral walls continued to be revered by the Incas—certainly not what the Spaniards expected.

Throughout central Cuzco today, as well as in the surrounding region, traces of the work of the Inca builders endure in stone block terrace walls and structures, including the immense Cuzco Cathedral that incorporates a chapel built on the foundations of an Inca palace and the Church of Santo Domingo anchored above the curved outer wall of the Coricancha. Outside Cuzco, the town of Chinchero has a colonial church built on Inca building foundations. Although the architecture of central Cuzco has protected status now, urban growth has and is continuing to destroy many other Inca structures in the region.

An archival 1913 book about travel in Peru includes an image of Cuzco showing the rounded shapes of blocks in an Inca wall beneath colonial structures (Figure 20.2). The accompanying description provides details:

> Along the steep streets of this portion of the city extensive remains of the foundations and walls of these palaces still remain, their giant stones and perfect masonry provoking the constant wonder of the traveller[sic]. Pictures of them give but a poor impression, for the heavy rustic finish of the face of each stone hides the perfection of the joints, which are so finely

FIGURE 20.2. Street in Cuzco with colonial structures built above Inca walls. Illustration by Ernest Clifford Peixotto, *Pacific Shores from Panama* (1913): 171.

fitted that, devoid of mortar as they are, the blade of a small pocket-knife can scarcely be inserted into any one of them.[15]

Disappearing Artifacts

The lands once inhabited by the Incas and their ancestors may top the list of the most intensively looted ancient centers of civilization on our planet.[16] The Spanish conquistadors began the practice when they realized that tombs of ancient Andean nobility could hold vast stores of silver and gold. Looting became synonymous with mining, and they rushed to divide Inca monuments into claim areas with titles assigned and registered in Spanish archives. Commercial exploitation of antiquities became an enormous business, and for centuries smugglers have been sending their finds out of the country.

The tragic result of all this plundering is that only a few gold and silver artifacts crafted by Inca artisans remain for us to admire today. Early in my research about the Incas, I learned that if it seems that photos of the same artifacts appear repeatedly, that is because they do. Virtually all the fabulous precious metal items collected for Atahualpa's ransom, as well as the pieces looted from temples and palaces by the conquistadors in their early explorations, were melted down into ingot blocks. The Spaniards saved only a few artifacts, including 18-carat gold life-sized figurines of a woman and a llama, and shipped these intact to King Philip of Spain. In recent decades, a few items left as offerings in high mountaintop shrines or buried in ancient constructions have come to light, including the small statues found beneath the Plaza de Armas in Cuzco.

The remote location of Machu Picchu protected this site, as the Spanish colonists apparently never discovered the citadel. The abundance of mummies, ceramics, and other artifacts found by Hiram Bingham in 1911 suggests that after being abandoned by the Incas, vegetation rapidly obscured the site and only a few local inhabitants knew of its location. Nonetheless, among all the artifacts that Bingham and his team retrieved in their expeditions, noticeably absent were any of the legendary gold or silver objects of the Incas. Many decades later, only a single gold bracelet was found buried within an ancient foundation wall.[17]

Shortly after my first trip to Peru, I came across information that most likely explains the mysterious disappearance of Machu Picchu gold. Several decades before Bingham arrived, researchers believe a German entrepreneur named Augusto Berns plundered Machu Picchu.[18] Inexplicably, in the late nineteenth century, Inca artifacts appeared in many European palaces and museums. In the 1860s, Herr Berns operated a lumber mill in the town of Aguas Calientes, directly below the archaeological site. His company held a mining concession for extracting wood and gold, allowing goods to be transferred out of the country. Machu Picchu was most likely the "gold mine" harvested, pointing to Berns as the source of the Inca treasures sold in Europe. By the time Bingham reached the city about fifty years later, these riches had vanished.

During the Bingham excavations at Machu Picchu between 1911 and 1915, the team sent thousands of Inca artifacts to Yale University with the understanding that the items would be returned to Peru. Some artifacts eventually were sent back, but most remained at the Yale Peabody Museum. A long and bitter custody battle between the esteemed academic institution and the government of Peru ensued.[19] Finally, Peru sued Yale in U.S. Federal courts in 2008. Thousands of Peruvian demonstrators gathered to demand that Yale return the collections, and Peruvian officials asked President Obama, and even the Pope in the Vatican, to help resolve the standoff. After high-level negotiations, the parties resolved the suit in November 2010 with the outcome that Yale agreed to return the artifacts. Three separate shipments and hundreds of boxes were used to transport the items back to Peru, where they are housed in Cuzco.

When I visited Peru in 2006, before Yale had agreed to return the artifacts, one of our tour guides complained bitterly about the artifacts being held. Interestingly, because of the nuances of Spanish to English pronunciation, our guide called the venerable university "Jail" instead of Yale—a word substitution that greatly amused the Americans in our group!

Transforming the Great Inca Road
In a twist of fate, the approximately 25,000 mi (40,234 km) Qhapaq Ñan, or Inca road network, provided the Spanish with access to unimaginable wealth and opportunity. The two major north–south roads, one beside the coast and the second in the highlands along the spine of the Andes Mountains, allowed the invaders to rapidly consolidate occupation of the far-flung lands of the once prosperous Inca Empire.

Initially, the Spaniards used llamas to move the goods required for their ventures. The mortality rate of these native animals was high, however, as they were not as hardy as the mules that eventually replaced them. Tens of thousands of sheep, hogs, cattle, and other Eurasian livestock were imported, especially for mining communities. These animals transported goods and powered machinery in mines, such as hoists. They provided meat and hides for shoes and clothing, while their fat supplied oils to lubricate machinery and tallow to make candles. Severe overgrazing and erosion followed the introduction of these sharp-hooved animals.[20]

One small irony that I particularly appreciate is that the horses of the conquistadors, raised on the open grasslands of Spain, wisely resisted walking on the steep stairways and across the narrow swinging bridges of the Inca roads. These delays must have been frustrating, if short-lived, for the Spaniards as they rushed to investigate and exploit the new lands.

Along the Inca Road, many Inca bridges continued to be used for several centuries. These bridges could extend across greater distances than any masonry bridge built in history before that time. Although the Spaniards attempted to introduce European bridge technology in the Andes, their efforts ended in failure. No superior design alternatives were available until engineers developed the technology for long-span iron and steel structures in the nineteenth century.[21]

During Inca times, keeping the roads and bridges in good working order was in the people's interest, as the network connected extended families and agricultural holdings. Maintenance of the road network was the responsibility of the local communities through mit'a tax labor. Deterioration began soon after the institution of Spanish rule. Colonial authorities attempted to compel the local communities to provide supplies and labor to maintain the road network without compensation, which naturally led to local resistance.[22] Many local roads and bridges also fell into ruin when illness, death, and forced resettlement of communities to other regions resulted in disuse.

As the centuries passed, an estimated 75 percent of the Inca network disappeared. Although some colonial endeavors required maintaining segments of the road system, the Spaniards ordered the destruction of other sections. Metal horseshoes and the metal-rimmed wheels of ox carts also caused serious damage to many more parts. Lack of maintenance and urban expansion erased other roadways as well.

From the coast to the high mountains, after Pizarro and his men marched into Cajamarca in 1532, the homeland of ancient Andean societies for thousands of years changed immensely. In replacing the Inca world, the Spanish colonists transformed the natural environment of the Central Andes, the Indigenous population and their societies, and the Inca road network. It was truly a *pachacuti*—an overturning of the world.

21

Looking Ahead

In another lifetime, I'd love to take a year to hike the entire length of the ancient Inca Road section that once rolled up and down along the spine of the Andes Mountains. It would be a grand adventure, since this north–south route covers over 3,000 mi (4,828 km) through spectacular surroundings. Much of the former roadway would be virtually unrecognizable, since we have lost major parts in the changes of the past centuries, so winding my way along the route would be challenging.

Many miles of Inca roads and trails were restored and opened to hikers beginning midway through the twentieth century when Peruvian authorities promoted the Andes as a global hiking destination. Today, the road network provides opportunities for some of the best hiking and mountaineering in the world. Thousands of tourists in boots with high-friction rubber "waffle" soles and local porters in sandals with soles of tire treads hike the ancient trails. One can appreciate the smooth rock slabs underfoot, polished by untold millions of ancient footsteps, while also admiring the engineering skills required to construct such a complex and extensive road network.

I have already had the good fortune and opportunity to hike along several tens of miles of these roadways in my visits to Peru. The most memorable was the multi-day hike on the Classic Inca Trail to Machu Picchu, on my first trip to Peru in 2005. Several hiking routes follow Inca paths to the lofty city of Machu Picchu, and hikers typically cover these in two to six days. My group began at the trailhead and security checkpoint named "Km 82," a trail section that covers about 27 mi (43 km) while crossing several high mountain passes.

For three days I admired stunning views, from the surrounding mountains to the varied rocks underfoot. The trail incorporates thousands of stone stair steps, meanders along narrow paths hugging cliff faces, and passes through tunnels in massive rock outcrops. Hikers pass by the silent remains of ancient stone storehouses and abandoned agricultural terraces, all accessible only from the ancient trail system and far from any modern road. Along the route, vegetation ranges from grass and brush to orchids, bromeliads, and a profusion of other tropical plants in "cloud forests" close to Machu Picchu. Together in a landscape of distant snow-covered mountains, deep valleys, lakes, and rivers, these sights make this journey unforgettable.

Five hundred years ago, the Incas would have needed to spend a week or more in travel time between Cuzco and Machu Picchu, with herders moving caravans of llamas burdened with supplies. Inca relay runners would have covered the terrain in a matter of hours. In recent years, runners have been taking part in a foot race marathon held on a 26.2 mi (42 km) segment of trail leading to Machu Picchu, and the fastest participants complete this route in under four hours.

Contemporary Concerns
Indigenous Andeans have endured tremendous social upheaval since the fall of the Inca Empire.[1] After hundreds of years of colonial rule, bloody independence wars raged from approximately 1810 to 1826. Ultimately, the Andean countries of Columbia, Ecuador, Peru, Bolivia, Chile, and Argentina were established, with multiple boundary adjustments made over the following decades. Territorial disputes between the Andean countries and adjoining South American countries, including Brazil, persisted into the twentieth century. Internal conflicts contributed to political instability and more bloodshed. Many revolutionary movements and military dictators have risen, struggled to hold power, and fallen, leaving a trail of atrocities in their wake.

During the twentieth and twenty-first centuries, several Andean countries have had relatively modest economic development and lagged compared to the growth of other countries. Likely causes include inequalities rooted in both pre-colonial and colonial times.[2] The Inca Empire was ruled by a small number of elites—about 100,000 out of a population of 12 million or more. Most people were involved in agricultural production, and while all reportedly had adequate food, clothing, and housing, they did not receive an education beyond what they needed to fulfill their labor duties to the state. The high level of educational inequality in the Inca Empire possibly contributed negatively to longer-term economic development patterns. In addition, national governments have a long tradition of neglecting the knowledge and institutions of Indigenous populations, based on a deeply entrenched history of disdain by the colonists.

Politically powerful people who control the land and trade are typically reluctant to implement changes that could challenge their dominance. In Andean countries, economic elites have a long history of resisting the modernization that would have benefitted a greater percentage of the population. They have hindered industrialization, stifled innovation, and neglected education for the Indigenous and the poor. This inequality has increasingly restrained the region's growth.

Outsiders have coveted the rich natural resources of the Andes and carried them away in a long and sordid history, with few benefits extended to the Indigenous people. Beginning with Atahualpa's ransom of gold and silver shipped to Spain, exploitation has continued into the twenty-first century with metallic ores mined by exceedingly profitable transnational corporations and the "white silver" of cocaine smuggled out to meet consumer demand in wealthy countries. Political scientists and economists recognize that reliance on specific commodities in an extractive economy leads to boom-bust economic cycles that weaken political institutions, essentially creating a "resource curse."[3] Blessed with an abundance of valuable natural resources, the Andeans also continue to suffer from the foreign attention these riches bring.

Major environmental and economic changes have taken place in the centuries since the fateful convergence of Spanish and Inca cultures. This story is not only one of tragedy, desecration, exploitation, and plunder but also a tale of survival and resilience. Many trials lie ahead for the Andean people, but also reasons to be hopeful. Lessons from the past can inform environmental conservation and cultural preservation, as well as shed light on paths forward for our societies.

A Changing Climate

The ancient Andeans needed to adapt to many climatic changes, but they did not face the significant and rapid warming of their environment that is currently underway. Particularly in high-altitude environments, climate change

FIGURE 21.1. Alpamayo in the Cordillera Blanca and lake held back by unstable glacial moraines. Photograph by author.

is presenting new challenges.[4] A large farming population in the highlands of Peru and Bolivia practices traditional agriculture and relies on rain-fed subsistence crops of quinoa and potatoes. Warming air and soil temperatures are forcing farmers to move fields for their cold weather-adapted crops to higher locations upslope, where the soils typically are less fertile and more difficult for laborers to access (the title of a research paper—"You Can't Grow Potatoes in the Sky"—captures this predicament[5]). Poor yields are forcing many people to leave the agricultural sector and migrate into towns seeking other work. We can view these migrants as among the first generation of climate refugees.

Throughout Andean countries, glaciers are retreating because of rising temperatures. A significant reduction in glacier mass is underway, and scientists predict the tropical glaciers in the Central Andes will shrink dramatically, with projected volume losses of between 78 and 97 percent by the end of this century.[6] The rapid retreat of glaciers is threatening water supplies essential to local populations. Water scarcity and uncertainty are serious issues facing the

Andeans, as glacier runoff in many regions is essential to support people, agriculture, energy production, and ecosystems.[7] The highland areas in southern Peru, Bolivia, and northern Chile are especially affected.

Glacier retreat causes other harm, too. The rapid melting of short and steep mountain glaciers has become a source of significant hazards to communities in high valleys, especially in the Cordillera Blanca, homeland of the Chavín culture. In this region of northern Peru, hundreds of picturesque blue lakes occupy glacier-cut valleys. Jumbled piles of rock in terminal moraines left behind by retreating glaciers create dams that hold many of the lakes. These precarious dams can burst suddenly, creating catastrophic floods and debris flows downstream. Also, avalanches and landslides composed of ice and rock can fall into lakes from unstable slopes above a lake, creating walls of water that overflow or breach the dams. These outburst floods are natural hazards, but the hazard level is significantly increasing because of the rapid glacier retreat associated with rises in existing lake volumes, as well as in the formation of new lakes[8] (Figure 21.1).

The Cordillera Blanca region suffered from two disastrous glacial dam failures in the past century. In 1941, Lago Palcacocha burst through its natural moraine dam high above the city, probably when an icefall into the lake produced a displacement wave that eroded the dam. As the floodwaters swept downward, an estimated 6,000 people died and about one third of the city of Huaraz was destroyed. Despite remediation work on the Palcacocha dams, another glacial outburst flood occurred in 2003, although the volume of water released would have been much larger if authorities had not made repairs.[9]

In 1945, a large debris flow raced down the Río Wacheqsa valley, burying portions of the Chavín de Huántar archaeological site and the adjacent modern town. The instigating factor was an upstream landslide that also fell into a glacial lake, displacing water that destroyed the morainal dam for the lake. Throughout the Ancash region, local authorities have worked to lower lake levels or reinforce natural dams, but the danger from these potential outbursts remains high.

Other developments have occurred in response to the hazards from glacial lake outburst floods. Research on glaciers and glacial lake engineering in the Cordillera Blanca resulted in widespread dissemination of information about this spectacularly scenic region, as well as development of infrastructure, including roads into remote and rugged canyons. Ultimately, these factors stimulated more tourism in Ancash than anywhere else within the glaciated Andes, along with explorations for mineral resources in remote regions. These changes have helped to boost local economies, but they also pose threats to the environment and its natural beauty.

Andean Mines and Metals Today
Mining provides the foundation for modern Andean economies. These South American countries are among the top producers of a dazzling and dizzyingly long list of metals ranging from antimony to barium, beryllium, bismuth, boron, copper, gold, indium, iodine, lead, molybdenum, nitrate, platinum, rhenium, selenium, silver, tellurium, tin, tungsten, zinc, and many more. Optimal conditions for the formation of these metallic ores occurred over tens of millions of years during the active tectonic episodes that constitute the geologic history of the Andes.

Revered by ancient Andean cultures, gold is a major export item from Peru. Gold mining ranges from small-scale local operations to massive open-pit quarries operated by multinational companies. Illegal mining also is widespread, with miners often working in challenging areas including the jungles of the Amazon and the highest mountains. These isolated places include Mount Ananea, home to the sprawling and impoverished settlement of La Rinconada, reportedly the highest human habitation on earth. At an elevation of 16,000 feet, La Rinconada is an exceedingly tough place for humans to live.

Miners collect "artisanal gold" from placer deposits in small operations in the lowlands of the Amazon Basin. In these rainforests, widespread deforestation and sedimentation of rivers are a disastrous result of mining. Mercury amalgamation continues to be used to process much of this gold, and the large amounts of mercury released into rivers and streams are causing serious environmental contamination.[10] In the highlands, thousands toil in "informal" mines with hand tools and labor practices little changed from centuries ago. Many women and children pick carefully through the rocky spoil piles from these mines, scavenging for any overlooked shiny bits. Driven by poverty, the mining frenzy increases as metal prices rise, with virtually all seekers harboring a hope for potential riches that are almost always elusive.

On the opposite end of the spectrum is the enormous open-pit Yanacocha gold mine in the Cajamarca region of northern Peru, one of the largest gold mines on earth. A joint venture of a Peruvian company, the World Bank, and U.S.-based Newmont Corporation, this mine has been continuously expanded since production began in 1993.[11] The operation has a long and sordid history, including severe environmental degradation and minimal sharing of economic benefits with the local residents of the region. Similar large-scale mining operations exist throughout the Andes, with the metals sent off to other continents and hundreds of millions of dollars in profits pocketed by people in major cities located thousands of miles away.

With globalization and the shift to an economic model rooted in commodity exports, Peru, like other Latin America countries, continues to be a major exporter of a wide variety of metals.[12] In this economic model, multinational mining corporations from advanced democracies like the United States and Canada, but also countries like China, invest in major mining projects. This activity has generated ongoing conflicts. Popular protest and environmental justice movements have spoken out against extractive industries and made demands that these corporations invest in the communities where they are exploiting resources. Slowly, positive changes may be occurring.

A Drug Culture of "White Silver" and Ayahuasca
Sacred plants once used by the ancient Andeans in their religious rituals have found a place in recreational drug use. The ancient people cultivated and used coca leaves for thousands of years. After the Spanish conquest, however, coca leaf usage went through significant changes, as the Catholic Church forbade the inclusion of coca in religious rituals. Nonetheless, coca production became an important industry in the Spanish colonial economy. Large plantations of these plants were established, and production of coca actually increased under Spanish rule. The reason? Mining company managers recognized the value of this stimulant for maximizing worker output, and so coca leaves were used to pay the Indigenous people forced to work in the dreadful conditions of mines.[13]

In approximately 1860, German chemists developed a chemical process to extract cocaine from coca leaves using solvents. Cocaine subsequently became a wonder drug for medicinal use, especially as an anesthetic, and even became a key ingredient in the new beverage Coca-Cola in the late 1800s (changed to cocaine-free in 1906). When the recreational use and abuse of cocaine grew over time, the addictive nature of the drug, as well as other adverse health effects, became clear. By the early twentieth century, many countries had outlawed cocaine.

Today Peru and a few other Andean countries allow people to grow, sell, and possess coca for traditional uses. Following long-standing cultural practices, millions of people drink coca tea or chew the leaves. Coca is as central to Andean culture as coffee or tea for European and Asian cultures. International drug control treaties, however, lump coca leaves together with heroin and cocaine. The latter is technically a "concentrate of coca leaf" and logically should be distinguished in this way. Efforts by the Andean countries to change international laws have been ongoing for decades, so far unsuccessfully.

Poverty drives many Andean farmers to grow coca leaf for cocaine production, as coca can bring in several times more income with reliable markets when compared with coffee, avocados, and other crops. The vast web of this clandestine and often violent "white silver" industry involves hundreds of thousands of people, from farmers to smugglers. Cocaine generates tens of billions of dollars annually in revenues, making it among the most valuable single commodity chains in world history. Although cocaine is available worldwide, its largest markets are in wealthy countries, with the majority going to consumers in Europe and the United States.

Besides coca, Peru has another recreational drug attraction. Many tourists from the United States and European countries who are seeking spiritual transformations consume the powerful hallucinogenic drug ayahuasca, in a form of "drug tourism." Derived from two or more plants that grow in the Amazon jungles, ayahuasca has a long history of traditional use in the Amazon Basin. Today, it is a thriving business in Peru. Indigenous shamans conduct ceremonies where participants consume this drug at "retreat centers" that are advertised for locations in both lowland rainforest towns and the popular tourist region in the highlands around Cuzco. Some people who have consumed ayahuasca report positive psychological benefits, but it can also have dangerous side effects.

Vulnerable Archaeological Sites
Increasing tourism in Peru and other parts of the Central Andes has important economic value but also brings new challenges. Decision-makers have put some protections into place. Andean countries today have many World Heritage Site landmarks, with legal protection administered by the United Nations Educational, Scientific, and Cultural Organization (UNESCO). Each designated site is judged to be of outstanding value because of cultural, historical, and/or natural significance, making it worthy of preservation for future

FIGURE 21.2. Celebration of Inti Raymi at Sacsayhuaman. Photograph by McKay Savage, 2012, available under a Creative Commons Attribution 2.0 Generic License.

generations. Archaeological sites of the Incas and their ancestors with World Heritage Site designations include the City of Cuzco, Machu Picchu, Chavín de Huántar, the lines and geoglyphs of the Nazca culture, Chan Chan (Chimú culture), Caral-Supe (Norte Chico), and the Great Inca Road/Qhapaq Ñan.

With more than one million tourists visiting Machu Picchu every year, officials have imposed a series of entry restrictions to reduce the degradation of the site from overcrowding. Still, some developments are concerning. One of these is a controversial new airport adjacent to the nearby city of Chinchero, where construction began in 2017.[14] The new airport, scheduled to open late in 2024, will accommodate large aircraft on international flights. The projected increase in the number of arriving tourists, plus noise and construction impacts, has prompted concern from UNESCO and many other groups in the region.

Not all challenges have obvious, short-term solutions. Climate change, especially prolonged rainstorms, threaten many archaeological sites.[15] Intense rainfall on the coast is damaging the enormous adobe structures at Caral and Chan Chan. At Moray in the highlands near Cuzco, a section of impressive circular terraces that stood solidly for 500 years was recently damaged when unusually intense rainfall triggered a landslide.

Other archaeological sites also need to be protected and defended from a variety of threats. Squatters are moving onto the 5,000-year-old ruins of Caral to build houses and plow fields to plant crops, and some have issued death threats to archaeologists and claimed they have exclusive rights to the land.[16] Archaeological site looting remains a major problem, fueled by high demands for antiquities in other countries. Damage to the area surrounding the Nazca lines has occurred from vehicles driving across them, and even from trampling by Greenpeace protestors who were spelling out a message to climate change conference attendees in 2014.[17] Urban expansion also threatens many sites, encouraged by rising land values surrounding important archaeological sites. Government efforts to control damage to archaeological sites are uneven. Sometimes, the authorities appear to be indifferent.

In sum, irreversible damage is occurring, and once destruction has occurred and information is lost, it is gone forever.

What's Ahead?

Despite the difficult history of the past few centuries, the legacy of the Incas continues in the proud people of the Andes. Quechua, the official language of Tawantinsuyu, is spoken by at least 8 to 10 million people today. A few million more people speak Aymara, the language of many ancient societies in the Altiplano region. These languages help to preserve the rich traditional knowledge of Andean cultural practices. Agricultural terraces built by the Incas and their ancestors continue to be used by farmers cultivating crops. The magnificent Inca stonework is widely admired, both because of the impressive engineering and the elegant aesthetics.

Andean culture today shows great pride in rich ancient traditions. You can see it in several popular reenactments of ceremonies originating with the Incas. These rituals include *Quyllor Rit'i*, held on the full moon before the winter solstice with pilgrimages to high mountain peaks to make offerings to the spirits that inhabit the landscape, and *Inti Raymi*, observed in June at Sacsayhuaman and other locations to celebrate the winter solstice and the New Year (Figure 21.2). The importance and value of local and Indigenous knowledge systems is increasingly being recognized by decision-makers, especially as these provide a source of information for sustainable management of fragile mountain ecosystems. We can learn lessons in creativity and resilience from these ancient societies.

If I could return to hike the length of the Inca Road in 50, or 100, or even 1,000 years, what will the lands formerly inhabited by the Incas and their ancestors look like? What resources will Andean countries export to the world in the future? Perhaps with more expansive political motivations, future generations will improve the lives of all Andean citizens by sharing more of the wealth found in their highly productive landscapes.

In the meantime, the ancient cultures live on in the languages and practices of modern Andeans, direct descendants of the proud Incas and their remarkable ancestors who flourished for thousands of years before them.

Notes

Chapter 1
1. Brian S. Bauer, *Ancient Cuzco: Heartland of the Inca* (University of Texas Press, 2010), 157.
2. Bauer, 150–152.
3. Bauer, 150–152.
4. George E. Ericksen, Jaime Fernández Concha, and Enrique Silgado, "The Cusco, Peru, Earthquake of May 21, 1950," *Bulletin of the Seismological Society of America* 44, no. 2A (1954): 97–112.
5. Bauer, *Ancient Cuzco*, 152.
6. Richard L. Burger and Lucy Salazar-Burger, "Machu Picchu Rediscovered: The Royal Estate in the Cloud Forest," *Discovery* 24, no. 2 (1993): 20–25.
7. Michael E. Moseley, *The Incas and Their Ancestors: The Archaeology of Peru*, rev. ed. (Thames & Hudson, 2001), 12–18.
8. Michael A. Malpass, *Ancient People of the Andes* (Cornell University Press, 2016), 2–3.
9. Merriam-Webster, s.v. "ancient," https://www.merriam-webster.com/dictionary/ancient.
10. John Haywood, *The Penguin Historical Atlas of Ancient Civilizations* (Penguin Books, 2005), 17.
11. Peter Watson, *The Great Divide: History and Human Nature in the Old World and the New* (Weidenfeld & Nicolson, 2012), 100–101. There are many examples of the limited exchanges between Indigenous Americans, including that the llama, guinea pig, and potato of the Andean highlands never reached the highlands of Mexico; the writing systems of Mesoamerica never reached the Andes.
12. Melinda A. Zeder et al., "Documenting Domestication: The Intersection of Genetics and Archaeology," *TRENDS in Genetics* 22, no. 3 (2006): 139–155.
13. Xinru Liu, *The Silk Road in World History* (Oxford University Press, 2010).
14. The ancient Indigenous societies of the Andes are often referred to as "precolumbian" or "precolonial." In practice, these terms are used to denote the entire history of the Indigenous cultures of the Americas until subjugated by Europeans. In literal terms, precolumbian means the time preceding Christopher Columbus's voyage that reached the Americas in 1492.
15. Gary Haynes, introduction to *American Megafaunal Extinctions at the End of the Pleistocene*, ed. Gary Haynes (Springer, 2009), 1.
16. Kurt Rademaker et al., "Paleoindian Settlement of the High-Altitude Peruvian Andes," *Science* 346, no. 6208 (2014): 466–469.

17 Mark Aldenderfer et al., "Four-Thousand-Year-Old Gold Artifacts from the Lake Titicaca Basin, Southern Peru," *Proceedings of the National Academy of Sciences* 105, no. 13 (2008): 5002–5005.
18 The radiocarbon dating method is based on living organisms taking up the ratio of carbon-14 to nitrogen-14 that is present in the environment. Once an organism has died, the carbon-14 begins to decay, and the amount measured can be used to calculate when death occurred. The method has an upper limit of about 50,000 years, or somewhat longer under specific conditions. During certain time periods, such as since 1950 when nuclear testing has been conducted, the amount of radiocarbon in the atmosphere has varied and so correction factors need to be applied.
19 James L. Luteyn and Steven P. Churchill, "Vegetation of the Andes," in *Imperfect Balance: Landscape Transformations in the Precolumbian Americas,* ed. David L. Lentz (Columbia University Press, 2000), 281–310.

Chapter 2

1 Victor Ramos, "Plate Tectonic Setting of the Andean Cordillera," *Episodes Journal of International Geoscience* 22, no. 3 (1999): 183–190; Martin Prinz, George E. Harlow, and Joseph Peters, eds., *Simon and Schuster's Guide to Rocks and Minerals* (Simon and Schuster, 1978).
2 Eldridge Moores and Robert J. Twiss, *Tectonics* (W. H. Freeman, 1995), 332–336.
3 Moores and Twiss, 332–336.
4 Christian A Meyer, Daniel Marty, and Matteo Belvedere, "Titanosaur Trackways from the Late Cretaceous El Molino Formation of Bolivia (Cal Orck'o, Sucre)," *Annales Societatis Geologorum Poloniae* 88, no. 2 (2018), 223–241.
5 Georg Petersen, *Mining and Metallurgy in Ancient Perú,* trans. William E. Brooks, Special Paper 467 (Geological Society of America, 2010), 15.
6 Moores and Twiss, *Tectonics*, 7.
7 Moores and Twiss, 7.
8 Moores and Twiss, 7.
9 Wolfgang Frisch, Martin Meschede, and Ronald C. Blakey, *Plate Tectonics: Continental Drift and Mountain Building* (Springer, 2011), 4.

Chapter 3

1 W. Jacquelyne Kious and Robert I. Tilling, *This Dynamic Earth: The Story of Plate Tectonics* (Diane Publishing/U.S. Geological Survey, 1996), 4.
2 Eldridge Moores and Robert J. Twiss, Tectonics (W. H. Freeman, 1995), 75–80.
3 S. L. De Silva and P. W. Francis, "Potentially Active Volcanoes of Peru: Observations Using Landsat Thematic Mapper and Space Shuttle Imagery," *Bulletin of Volcanology* 52, no. 4 (1990):287.
4 Moores and Twiss, *Tectonics*, 49–50.
5 Kious and Tilling, *This Dynamic Earth*, 59.
6 Moores and Twiss, *Tectonics*, 155.
7 Moores and Twiss, 332–336.

8 Stephan V. Sobolev et al., "Mechanism of the Andean Orogeny: Insight from Numerical Modeling," in *The Andes: Active Subduction Orogeny*, eds. Onno Oncken et al. (Springer, 2006), 513. The westward drift of the South American plate has increased from about 2 cm/year to 3 cm/year over the past 30 million years. Susan Rhea et al., *Seismicity of the Earth 1900–2007, Nazca Plate and South America*, Open-File Report 2010-1083-E (U.S. Geological Survey, 2010), abstract, https://pubs.usgs.gov/publication/ofr20101083E. The Nazca plate is subducting eastward at about 7–8 cm/year.
9 Moores and Twiss, *Tectonics*, 155.
10 Moores and Twiss, 86–89.
11 Wolfgang Frisch, Martin Meschede, and Ronald C. Blakey, *Plate Tectonics: Continental Drift and Mountain Building* (Springer, 2011), 12.
12 Scientists disagree as to whether the plates began moving as soon as the earth formed, or whether this action started much later—this is one of many topics of geologic history that are uncertain and controversial.
13 An interesting and useful aspect of newly forming rocks is the ability to record the position of magnetic north, providing what is known as paleomagnetic data. Metallic minerals that are in the process of solidifying in a rock are somewhat like chocolate chips in cookie dough. These metallic fragments, our chocolate chips, act as tiny compasses; while they can still move around, they line up to point towards magnetic north. Magma that hardens to become volcanic rock is ideal, so the large expanses of volcanic rock in the Central Andes provide valuable paleomagnetic data. Metallic fragments in sediments that eventually harden into sandstone and other types of sedimentary rock also align towards north. By collecting and recording the orientations of small samples from rock outcrops, and then taking them to a laboratory and measuring the offset of the aligned minerals relative to present magnetic north, researchers can determine the position of a rock when it first formed.
14 Victor A. Ramos and A. Aleman, "Tectonic Evolution of the Andes," in *Tectonic Evolution of South America*, eds. Umberto G. Cordani, Edison J. Milani, Antonio Thomaz Filho, and Diogenes de Almeida Campos (31st International Geological Congress, Rio de Janeiro, 2000), 645.
15 Moores and Twiss, *Tectonics*, 76–77.
16 Frish, Meschede, and Blakely, *Plate Tectonics*, 4.
17 Frish, Meschede, and Blakely, 154.
18 Frish, Meschede, and Blakely, 131–132.
19 Gideon Rosenbaum et al., "Subduction of the Nazca Ridge and the Inca Plateau: Insights into the Formation of Ore Deposits in Peru," *Earth and Planetary Science Letters* 239, no. 1–2 (2005), 18–32.
20 Michael Haschke et al., "Central and Southern Andean Tectonic Evolution Inferred from Arc Magmatism," in *The Andes: Active Subduction Orogeny*, eds. Oncken et al. (Springer, 2006), 337–353.

Chapter 4

1 Eldridge Moores and Robert J. Twiss, *Tectonics* (W. H. Freeman, 1995), 332.

2   Susan Rhea et al., *Seismicity of the Earth 1900–2007, Nazca Plate and South America*, Open-File Report 2010-1083-E (U.S. Geological Survey, 2010), abstract, https://pubs.usgs.gov/publication/ofr20101083E.
3   Robert L. Kovach, *Early Earthquakes of the Americas* (Cambridge University Press, 2004), 121.
4   Gabriel Veloza et al., "Open-Source Archive of Active Faults for Northwest South America," *GSA Today*, 22, no. 10 (2012): 4–7.
5   Scientists use several different magnitude scales to report the strength of an earthquake. These result in small differences in reported magnitudes. The moment magnitude scale (Mw) is most appropriate for medium to large earthquakes and is commonly used in the scientific literature and throughout this book. However, I have not confirmed that all the magnitudes I report are moment magnitudes, so I don't specify specific magnitude scales.
6   Seth Stein et al., "The Nazca–South America Convergence Rate and the Recurrence of the Great 1960 Chilean Earthquake," *Geophysical Research Letters* 13, no. 8 (1986): 713.
7   Diana Comte and Mario Pardo, "Reappraisal of Great Historical Earthquakes in the Northern Chile and Southern Peru Seismic Gaps," *Natural Hazards* 4, no. 1 (1991): 39, 41; Kovach, *Early Earthquakes*, 25, 121.
8   Polina Lemenkova, "Geomorphological Modelling and Mapping of the Peru-Chile Trench by GMT," *Polish Cartographical Review* 51, no. 4 (2019): 181–194.
9   Kovach, *Early Earthquakes*, 25.
10 Moores and Twiss, *Tectonics*, 256.
11 Kovach, *Early Earthquakes*, 25.
12 Cliff Frohlich, *Deep Earthquakes* (Cambridge University Press, 2006), 5, 497; Harry W. Green and Heidi Houston, "The Mechanics of Deep Earthquakes," *Annual Review of Earth and Planetary Sciences* 23, no. 1 (1995): 170.
13 Green and Houston, "Mechanics of Deep Earthquakes," 169–170.
14 Shallow earthquakes and deep earthquakes originate under different temperature and pressure conditions. From laboratory studies, scientists know that as temperature and pressure increase, rocks under stress fail by something called ductile creep—they essentially liquify and ooze out—instead of experiencing sudden brittle failure. Deep earthquakes occur where brittle failure appears to be impossible; nonetheless, they obviously still happen. As a seismologist colleague told me decades ago, "seismology is an infant science."
15 Frohlich, *Deep Earthquakes*, 5, 493.
16 David P. Schwartz, "Paleoseismicity and Neotectonics of the Cordillera Blanca Fault Zone, Northern Peruvian Andes," *Journal of Geophysical Research: Solid Earth* 93, no. B5, (1988): 4712–4730.
17 Melissa K. Giovanni et al, "Extensional Basin Evolution in the Cordillera Blanca, Peru: Stratigraphic and Isotopic Records of Detachment Faulting and Orogenic Collapse in the Andean Hinterland," *Tectonics* 29, no. 6, (2010): 1.
18 Schwartz, "Paleoseismicity," 4712.

19 Kovach, *Early Earthquakes*, 24–25.
20 Joseph Martinod et al., "Horizontal Subduction Zones, Convergence Velocity and the Building of the Andes," *Earth and Planetary Science Letters* 299, no. 3–4 (2010): 303–305.
21 Quentin Bletery et al., "Mega-Earthquakes Rupture Flat Megathrusts," *Science* 354, no. 6315 (2016): 1027–1031.
22 Marc-André Gutscher et al., "Geodynamics of Flat Subduction: Seismicity and Tomographic Constraints from the Andean Margin," *Tectonics* 19, no. 5 (2000): 814–833; Ramos, "Plate Tectonic Setting," 185.
23 Emile A. Okal, José C. Borrero, and Costas E. Synolakis, "Evaluation of Tsunami Risk from Regional Earthquakes at Pisco, Peru," *Bulletin of the Seismological Society of America* 96, no. 5 (2006): 1637.
24 Kovach, *Early Earthquakes*, 136.
25 C. Vigny et al., "The 2010 Mw 8.8 Maule Megathrust Earthquake of Central Chile, Monitored by GPS," *Science* 332, no. 6036, (2011): 1417.
26 Hermann M. Fritz et al, "Field Survey of the 27 February 2010 Chile Tsunami," *Pure and Applied Geophysics* 168, no. 11 (2011): 1989–1990.
27 Eric L. Geist et al., "Implications of the 26 December 2004 Sumatra–Andaman Earthquake on Tsunami Forecast and Assessment Models for Great Subduction-Zone Earthquakes," *Bulletin of the Seismological Society of America* 97, no. 1A (2007): S249–S270.
28 George Plafker, George E. Ericksen, and Jaime F. Concha, "Geological Aspects of the May 31, 1970, Peru Earthquake," *Bulletin of the Seismological Society of America* 61, no. 3 (1971): 543–578.
29 Plafker, Ericksen, and Concha, 543, 552; Lloyd S. Cluff, "Peru Earthquake of May 31, 1970: Engineering Geology Observations," *Bulletin of the Seismological Society of America* 61, no. 3 (1971): 511–533.
30 Cluff, 511.
31 Cluff, 511.

Chapter 5

1 Charles R. Stern, "Active Andean Volcanism: Its Geologic and Tectonic Setting," *Revista Geológica de Chile* 31, no. 2 (2004): 161–206.
2 S. L. De Silva and P. W. Francis, "Potentially Active Volcanoes of Peru: Observations Using Landsat Thematic Mapper and Space Shuttle Imagery," *Bulletin of Volcanology* 52, no. 4 (1990): 287.
3 Eldridge Moores and Robert J. Twiss, *Tectonics* (W. H. Freeman, 1995), 157–179.
4 Moores and Twiss, 157–161.
5 Stern, "Active Andean Volcanism," 161–206.
6 Wolfgang Frisch, Martin Meschede, and Ronald C. Blakey, *Plate Tectonics: Continental Drift and Mountain Building* (Springer, 2011), 114.
7 Johan Reinhard and Constanza Ceruti, "Sacred Mountains, Ceremonial Sites, and Human Sacrifice among the Incas," *Archaeoastronomy* 19 (2005): 2.

8. Reinhard and Ceruti, "Sacred Mountains," 2.
9. Victor A. Ramos and A. Aleman, "Tectonic Evolution of the Andes," in *Tectonic Evolution of South America*, eds. Umberto G. Cordani, Edison J. Milani, Antonio Thomaz Filho, and Diogenes de Almeida Campos (31st International Geological Congress, Rio de Janeiro, 2000), 158–159.
10. Stern, "Active Andean Volcanism," 161–206.
11. De Silva and Francis, "Potentially Active Volcanoes," 287; Stern, 161–206.
12. Stern, 161–206.
13. Charles C. Plummer and Diane H. Carlson, *Physical Geology*, 12th ed. (Sacramento State University and McGraw-Hill Higher Education, 2008), 97.
14. Kurt Rademaker et al., "Paleoindian Settlement of the High-Altitude Peruvian Andes," *Science* 346, no. 6208 (2014): 466–469; Sarah Ann Meinekat, Christopher E. Miller, and Kurt Rademaker, "A Site Formation Model for Cuncaicha Rock Shelter: Depositional and Postdepositional Processes at the High-Altitude Keysite in the Peruvian Andes," *Geoarchaeology* 37, no. 2 (2022): 304.
15. Rademaker et al., 466–469.
16. Giulio Bigazzi et al., "Obsidian-Bearing Lava Flows and Pre-Columbian Artifacts from the Ecuadorian Andes: First New Multidisciplinary Data," *Journal of South American Earth Sciences* 6, no. 1–2 (1992): 25.
17. Daniel H. Sandweiss et al., "Quebrada Jaguay: Early South American Maritime Adaptations," *Science* 281, no. 5384 (1998): 1830–1832.
18. Nicolas Tripcevich and Daniel A. Contreras, "Quarrying Evidence at the Quispisisa Obsidian Source, Ayacucho, Peru," *Latin American Antiquity* 22, no. 1 (2011): 131–134.
19. Richard L. Burger, Karen L. Mohr Chávez, and Sergio J. Chávez, "Through the Glass Darkly: Prehispanic Obsidian Procurement and Exchange in Southern Peru and Northern Bolivia," *Journal of World Prehistory* 14, no. 3 (2000): 274; Lucas C. Kellett, Mark Golitko, and Brian S. Bauer, "A Provenance Study of Archaeological Obsidian from the Andahuaylas Region of Southern Peru," *Journal of Archaeological Science* 40, no. 4 (2013): 1890.
20. Burger, Chávez, and Chávez, 272–275.
21. Burger, Chávez, and Chávez, 347–353.
22. Sandweiss et al., "Quebrada Jaguay," 1832; Rademaker et al., "Paleoindian Settlement," 467.
23. Burger, Chávez, and Chávez, "Through the Glass Darkly," 348.
24. Tripcevich and Contreras, "Quarrying Evidence," 121–136; Nicolas Tripcevich and Daniel A. Contreras, "Archaeological Approaches to Obsidian Quarries: Investigations at the Quispisisa Source," in *Mining and Quarrying in the Ancient Andes*, eds. Nicholas Tripcevich and Kevin J. Vaughn (Springer, 2013), 23–44.
25. Burger, Chávez, and Chávez, "Through the Glass Darkly," 348; Nicholas Tripcevich and Alex Mackay, "Procurement at the Chivay Obsidian Source, Arequipa, Peru," *World Archaeology* 43, no. 2 (2011): 271–274.
26. Burger, Chávez, and Chávez, 347.

27 Steven J. Fonte et al., "Pathways to Agroecological Intensification of Soil Fertility Management by Smallholder Farmers in the Andean Highlands," *Advances in Agronomy*, vol. 116 (Academic Press, 2012): 127–128.
28 Franz Zehetner, W. P. Miller, and L. T. West, "Pedogenesis of Volcanic Ash Soils in Andean Ecuador," *Soil Science Society of America Journal* 67, no. 6 (2003): 1797.
29 Zehetner, Miller, and West, 1808.
30 Stern, "Active Andean Volcanism," 161–206.
31 Stern, 161–206.
32 Brad S. Singer et al., "Dynamics of a Large, Restless, Rhyolitic Magma System at Laguna del Maule, Southern Andes, Chile," *GSA Today* 24, no. 12 (2014): 4–10; Brad S. Singer et al., "Geomorphic Expression of Rapid Holocene Silicic Magma Reservoir Growth beneath Laguna del Maule, Chile," *Science Advances* 4, no. 6 (2018): eaat1513.
33 Singer et al., "Dynamics," 4.
34 Jean-Claude Thouret et al., "Ubinas: The Evolution of the Historically Most Active Volcano in Southern Peru," *Bulletin of Volcanology* 67, no. 6 (2005): 557–589.
35 Marie-Christine Gerbe and Jean-Claude Thouret, "Role of Magma Mixing in the Petrogenesis of Tephra Erupted during the 1990–98 Explosive Activity of Nevado Sabancaya, Southern Peru," *Bulletin of Volcanology* 66, no. 6 (2004): 541–561.
36 Jean-Claude Thouret et al., "Geology of El Misti Volcano near the City of Arequipa, Peru," *Geological Society of America Bulletin* 113, no. 12 (2001): 1593–1610.
37 De Silva and Francis, "Potentially Active Volcanoes," 293.

Chapter 6

1 John I. Garver et al., "Uplift and Exhumation of the Northern Peruvian Andes," in *6th International Symposium on Andean Geodynamics, Extended Abstracts* (ISAG, Barcelona, 2005), 305–306.
2 Bijeesh Kozhikkodan Veettil and Ulrich Kamp, "Global Disappearance of Tropical Mountain Glaciers: Observations, Causes, and Challenges," *Geosciences* 9, no. 5 (2019): 196.
3 Joe Simpson, *Touching the Void* (Random House, 1998). In 1985, Joe Simpson and climbing partner, Simon Yates, successfully reached the summit of the previously unclimbed West Face of Siula Grande, but on the descent during a raging storm, Simpson fell and broke his leg badly. Yates tried to lower Simpson on ropes but lost contact with him during the storm. Eventually, to save his own life, Yates cut the rope that tied him to Simpson. The next day Yates searched vainly for Simpson but, not finding him, assumed he was dead. Incredibly, Simpson was alive but had fallen into a deep crevasse on a steep glacier; miraculously, he managed to work his way downward and exit the crevasse. He then spent the next three days and nights crawling across ice and rock with multiple injuries and frostbite. Incredibly, he survived and managed to reach the base camp only hours before Yates planned to leave.
4 Victor A. Ramos and A. Aleman, "Tectonic Evolution of the Andes," in *Tectonic Evolution of South America*, eds. Umberto G. Cordani, Edison J. Milani, Antonio

Thomaz Filho, and Diogenes de Almeida Campos (31st International Geological Congress, Rio de Janeiro, 2000), 635–685.

5   O. Adrian Pfiffner and Laura Gonzalez, "Mesozoic-Cenozoic Evolution of the Western Margin of South America: Case Study of the Peruvian Andes," *Geosciences* 3, no. 2 (2013): 262.

6   Ramos and Aleman, 655.

7   John I. Garver et al., "Implications for Timing of Andean Uplift from Thermal Resetting of Radiation-Damaged Zircon in the Cordillera Huayhuash, Northern Peru," *Journal of Geology* 113, no. 2 (2005): 133–135.

8   As discussed in Chapters 4 and 5, flat slab segments of the Andes today are characterized by earthquakes and steep slab segments by volcanic eruptions. Within the past 60 million years, however, segments of the subduction zone have alternated between shallow and steeply dipping. Victor A. Ramos and Andrés Folguera, "Andean Flat-Slab Subduction Through Time," *Geological Society, London, Special Publications* 327, no. 1 (2009): 31–54.

9   Teresa Eileen Jordan et al., "Uplift of the Altiplano-Puna Plateau: A View from the West," *Tectonics* 29, no. 5 (2010): 1–31.

10 F. A. Capitanio et al., "Subduction Dynamics and the Origin of Andean Orogeny and the Bolivian Orocline," *Nature* 480, no. 7375 (2011): 83.

11 Onno Oncken et al., "Deformation of the Central Andean Upper Plate System: Facts, Fiction, and Constraints for Plateau Models," in *The Andes,* eds. Onno Oncken et al. (Springer, 2006), 5.

12 Christian A. Meyer, Daniel Marty, and Matteo Belvedere, "Titanosaur Trackways from the Late Cretaceous El Molino Formation of Bolivia (Cal OUSGrck'o, Sucre)," *Annales Societatis Geologorum Poloniae*, vol. 88, no. 2 (2018): 223–241; Karen Moreno et al., "Large Theropod Dinosaur Footprint Associations in Western Gondwana: Behavioural and Palaeogeographic Implications," *Acta Palaeontologica Polonica* 57, no. 1 (2012): 73.

13 Andrew Leier et al., "Stable Isotope Evidence for Multiple Pulses of Rapid Surface Uplift in the Central Andes, Bolivia," *Earth and Planetary Science Letters* 371 (2013), 50.

14 Oncken, et al., "Deformation," 3.

15 Oncken et al., 22; Leier et al., "Stable Isotope Evidence," 49.

16 Joseph Martinod et al., "Horizontal Subduction Zones, Convergence Velocity and the Building of the Andes," *Earth and Planetary Science Letters* 299, no. 3–4 (2010): 304.

17 Jordan et al. "Uplift of the Altiplano-Puna," 3.

18 Oncken et al., "Deformation," 5. Researchers estimate about 160 mi (260 km) of shortening in the Altiplano segment and 75 mi (120 km) in the Puna segment.

19 Martinod et al, "Horizontal Subduction Zones," 314.

20 Martinod et al, 306.

21 Oncken et al., "Deformation," 22.

22 Martinod et al., "Horizontal Subduction Zones," 299–309.

23 Capitanio et al., "Subduction Dynamics," 84. Oceanic crust that has been accumulating for a long time has a greater thickness and higher density than younger crust. When older crust is subducted, it sinks more rapidly than younger crust.

24 Simon Lamb, *Devil in the Mountain: A Search for the Origin of the Andes,* (Princeton University Press, 2004), 298–300.
25 Oncken et al., "Deformation," 23.
26 Oncken et al., 3–27.
27 Martinod et al., "Horizontal Subduction Zones," 304–307. Although today the Altiplano-Puna plateau is underlain by a steeply dipping oceanic slab section, in the past this segment of the subduction zone was shallow-dipping. We know that above flat or shallow subducting segments, the amount of contact, and therefore friction, between two plates significantly increases and favors earthquake generation and the compressive forces that build mountains.
28 Richard W. Allmendinger et al., "Bending the Bolivian Orocline in Real Time," *Geology* 33, no. 11 (2005): 905.
29 Simon Lamb, "Active Deformation in the Bolivian Andes, South America," *Journal of Geophysical Research: Solid Earth* 105, no. B11 (2000): 25627–25653.
30 Oncken et al., "Deformation," 22.
31 Simon Lamb, *Devil in the Mountain*, 161–164.

Chapter 7

1 Charles C. Plummer and Diane H. Carlson, *Physical Geology*, 12th ed. (Sacramento State University and McGraw-Hill Higher Education, 2008), 205, 329.
2 Martin Jakobsson et al., "Post-Glacial Flooding of the Bering Land Bridge Dated to 11 cal ka BP Based on New Geophysical and Sediment Records," *Climate of the Past* 13, no. 8 (2017): 991–1005; Scott A. Elias, Susan K. Short, and Hilary H. Birks, "Late Wisconsin Environments of the Bering Land Bridge," *Palaeogeography, Palaeoclimatology, Palaeoecology* 136, no. 1–4 (1997): 293.
3 Jakobsson et al., "Post-Glacial Flooding," 991–1005.
4 Jakobsson et al., 991–1005.
5 Plummer and Carlson, *Physical Geology*, 329.
6 Jon M. Erlandson et al., "Ecology of the Kelp Highway: Did Marine Resources Facilitate Human Dispersal from Northeast Asia to the Americas?" *Journal of Island and Coastal Archaeology* 10, no. 3 (2015): 392–411; Todd J. Braje et al., "Finding the First Americans," *Science* 358, no. 6363 (2017): 592–594.
7 Erlandson et al., 392–411
8 David G. Anderson and Thaddeus G. Bissett, "The Initial Colonization of North America: Sea Level Change, Shoreline Movement, and Great Migrations," in *Mobility and Ancient Society in Asia and the Americas*, eds. Michael D. Frachetti and Robert N. Spengler III (Springer, 2015), 61.
9 The distinctive stone tools of this culture were first identified near Clovis, New Mexico, in the 1920s, which is why they are called Clovis points. Pressure-flaked from various types of rock, the two-sided points have a characteristic flute or channel groove at the base of the blade, possibly used as an attachment point to fasten a wood or bone shaft for a spear.

10. Jon M. Erlandson and Todd J. Braje, "Stemmed Points, the Coastal Migration Theory, and the Peopling of the Americas," in *Mobility and Ancient Society in Asia and the Americas*, eds. Michael D. Frachetti and Robert N. Spengler III (Springer, 2015), 49–58.
11. Tom D. Dillehay, "The Late Pleistocene Cultures of South America," *Evolutionary Anthropology: Issues, News, and Reviews* 7, no. 6 (1999): 206–216.
12. Tom D. Dillehay et al., "New Archaeological Evidence for an Early Human Presence at Monte Verde, Chile," *PloS One* 10, no. 11 (2015): e0141923.
13. Thomas D. Dillehay, "The Battle of Monte Verde," *Sciences* 37, no. 1 (1997): 28.
14. Dillehay et al., "New Archaeological Evidence," abstract, e0141923.
15. Tom D. Dillehay et al., "Monte Verde: Seaweed, Food, Medicine, and the Peopling of South America," *Science* 320, no. 5877 (2008): 784–786.
16. Todd J. Braje et al., "Finding the First Americans," *Science* 358, no. 6363 (2017): 592–594; Tom D. Dillehay et al., "A Late Pleistocene Human Presence at Huaca Prieta, Peru, and Early Pacific Coastal Adaptations," *Quaternary Research* 77, no. 3 (2012): 418.
17. Bastien Llamas et al., "Ancient Mitochondrial DNA Provides High-Resolution Time Scale of the Peopling of the Americas," *Science Advances* 2, no. 4 (2016): e1501385.
18. Dillehay, "Late Pleistocene Cultures," 209–210.
19. Matthew R. Bennett et al., "Evidence of Humans in North America during the Last Glacial Maximum," *Science* 373, no. 6562 (2021), 1528–1531.
20. Jeffrey S. Pigati et al., "Independent Age Estimates Resolve the Controversy of Ancient Human Footprints at White Sands," *Science* 382, no. 6666 (2023): 73–75.
21. Daniel H. Sandweiss and James B. Richardson III, "Central Andean Environments," in *Handbook of South American Archaeology*, eds. Helaine Silverman and William Isbell (Springer, 2008), 95.
22. Sarah Ann Meinekat, Christopher E. Miller, and Kurt Rademaker, "A Site Formation Model for Cuncaicha Rock Shelter: Depositional and Postdepositional Processes at the High-Altitude Keysite in the Peruvian Andes," *Geoarchaeology* 37, no. 2 (2022): 309.
23. Dillehay, "Late Pleistocene Cultures," 209.
24. Lorna G. Moore, Susan Niermeyer, and Stacy Zamudio, "Human Adaptation to High Altitude: Regional and Life-Cycle Perspectives," *American Journal of Physical Anthropology* 107, no. S27 (1998): 25–64.
25. Terence N. D'Altroy, *The Incas*, 2nd ed. (John Wiley & Sons. 2015), 46.
26. C. Earle Smith Jr., "Plant Remains from Guitarrero Cave," in *Guitarrero Cave*, ed. Thomas F Lynch (Academic Press, 1980), 87–119.
27. Rebecca Stone-Miller, *Art of the Andes: From Chavín to Inca*, 2nd ed. (Thames and Hudson, 2002), 17.
28. Edward A. Jolie et al., "Cordage, Textiles, and the Late Pleistocene Peopling of the Andes," *Current Anthropology* 52, no. 2 (2011): 285–296.
29. Jennifer A. Leonard et al., "Ancient DNA Evidence for Old World Origin of New World Dogs," *Science* 298, no. 5598 (2002): 1613–1616; Angela R. Perri et al., "Dog Domestication and the Dual Dispersal of People and Dogs into the Americas," *Proceedings of the National Academy of Sciences* 118, no. 6 (2021): e2010083118.

30 David L. Erickson et al., "An Asian Origin for a 10,000-Year-Old Domesticated Plant in the Americas," *Proceedings of the National Academy of Sciences* 102, no. 51 (2005): 18315–18320.
31 Logan Kistler et al., "Transoceanic Drift and the Domestication of African Bottle Gourds in the Americas," *Proceedings of the National Academy of Sciences* 111, no. 8 (2014): 2937–2941.
32 Leonard et al., "Ancient DNA Evidence," 1615.
33 Jonathan Haas and Winifred Creamer, "Why Do People Build Monuments? Late Archaic Platform Mounds in the Norte Chico," in *Early New World Monumentality*, eds. Richard L. Burger and Robert M. Rosenswig (University Press of Florida, 2012), 306–307.
34 Elizabeth Arkush and Charles Stanish, "Interpreting Conflict in the Ancient Andes: Implications for the Archaeology of Warfare," *Current Anthropology* 46, no. 1 (2005): 3–28.
35 D'Altroy, *Incas*, 114–115.

Chapter 8

1 Anthony John Stuart, "Late Quaternary Megafaunal Extinctions on the Continents: A Short Review," *Geological Journal* 50, no. 3 (2015): 338–363.
2 Michael O. Woodburne, "The Great American Biotic Interchange: Dispersals, Tectonics, Climate, Sea Level and Holding Pens," *Journal of Mammalian Evolution* 17, no. 4 (2010): 245–264.
3 Stuart, "Late Quaternary Megafaunal Extinctions," 345–352.
4 Stuart, 350–352.
5 Denis Vialou et al., "Peopling South America's Centre: The Late Pleistocene Site of Santa Elina," *Antiquity* 91, no. 358 (2017): 865–884.
6 Tom D. Dillehay, "The Late Pleistocene Cultures of South America," *Evolutionary Anthropology: Issues, News, and Reviews* 7, no. 6 (1999): 210.
7 Todd A. Surovell et al., "The La Prele Mammoth Site, Converse County, Wyoming, USA," in *Human-Elephant Interactions: From Past to Present*, eds. G. E. Konidaris et al. (Tübingen University Press, 2021), 303–320.
8 Paul L. Koch and Anthony D. Barnosky, "Late Quaternary Extinctions: State of the Debate," *Annual Review of Ecology, Evolution, and Systematics* 37 (2006): 217.
9 Felisa A. Smith et al., "Body Size Downgrading of Mammals over the Late Quaternary," *Science* 360, no. 6386 (2018): 310–313.
10 Matheus Souza Lima-Ribeiro et al., "Climate and Humans Set the Place and Time of Proboscidean Extinction in Late Quaternary of South America," *Palaeogeography, Palaeoclimatology, Palaeoecology* 392 (2013): 554.
11 Alberto L. Cione, Eduardo P. Tonni, and Leopoldo Soibelzon, "Did Humans Cause the Late Pleistocene–Early Holocene Mammalian Extinctions in South America in a Context of Shrinking Open Areas?," in *American Megafaunal Extinctions at the End of the Pleistocene*, ed. Gary Haynes (Springer, 2009), 125–144.

12 Kurt Rademaker et al., "Paleoindian Settlement of the High-Altitude Peruvian Andes," *Science* 346, no. 6208 (2014): 466–469.
13 Clark L. Erickson, "The Lake Titicaca Basin: A Precolumbian Built Landscape," in *Imperfect Balance: Landscape Transformation in the Precolumbian Americas*, ed. David L. Lentz (Columbia University Press, 2000), 320.
14 Jane C. Wheeler, "South American Camelids: Past, Present and Future," *Journal of Camelid Science* 5, no. 1 (2012): 13–14.
15 Wheeler, 13–14.
16 Guillermo L. Mengoni Goñalons and Hugo D. Yacobaccio, "The Domestication of South American Camelids," in *Documenting Domestication: New Genetic and Archaeological Paradigms*, eds. Melinda A. Zeder et al. (University of California Press, 2006), 228–244.
17 Goñalons and Yacobaccio, "Domestication of South American Camelids," 228–244.
18 Melody Shimada and Izumi Shimada, "Prehistoric Llama Breeding and Herding on the North Coast of Peru," *American Antiquity* 50, no. 1 (1985): 3–26.
19 Wheeler, "South American Camelids," 7, 11.
20 Aleksa K. Alaica, "Partial and Complete Deposits and Depictions: Social Zooarchaeology, Iconography and the Role of Animals in Late Moche Peru," *Journal of Archaeological Science: Reports* 20 (2018): 864–872.
21 John Wayne Janusek, *Ancient Tiwanaku*, vol. 9 (Cambridge University Press, 2008), 58–59.
22 Alaica, "Partial and Complete Deposits," 868.
23 Peter W. Stahl, "Animals, Domesticated," in *Encyclopedia of the Incas*, ed. Gary Urton and Adriana von Hagen (Rowman & Littlefield, 2016), 26, 28.
24 Stahl, "Animals, Domesticated," 26.
25 Peter Watson, *The Great Divide: History and Human Nature in the Old World and the New* (Weidenfeld & Nicolson, 2012), 111.
26 Watson, 110–111.

Chapter 9

1 Lonnie G. Thompson et al., "Pre-Incan Agricultural Activity Recorded in Dust Layers in Two Tropical Ice Cores," *Nature* 336, no. 6201 (1988): 763–765.
2 Karin D'Agostino et al., "Late-Quaternary Lowstands of Lake Titicaca: Evidence from High-Resolution Seismic Data," *Palaeogeography, Palaeoclimatology, Palaeoecology* 179, no. 1–2 (2002): 97–111.
3 Michael E. Moseley, T*he Incas and Their Ancestors: The Archaeology of Peru*, rev. ed. (Thames & Hudson, 2001), 26–30.
4 Moseley, 26
5 D'Agostino et al., "Late-Quaternary Lowstands," 105–110; Michael W. Binford et al., "Climate Variation and the Rise and Fall of an Andean Civilization," *Quaternary Research* 47, no. 2 (1997): 235–248; Scott L. Cross et al., "Late Quaternary Climate and Hydrology of Tropical South America Inferred from an Isotopic and Chemical Model of Lake Titicaca, Bolivia and Peru," *Quaternary Research* 56, no. 1 (2001): 7–8.

6 John Wayne Janusek, *Ancient Tiwanaku*, vol. 9 (Cambridge University Press, 2008), 48.
7 Daniel H. Sandweiss and Jeffrey Quilter, "Collation, Correlation, and Causation in the Prehistory of Coastal Peru," in *Surviving Sudden Environmental Change: Understanding Hazards, Mitigating Impacts, Avoiding Disasters,* eds. Emily McClung de Tapia, Jago Cooper, and Payson D. Sheets (University Press of Colorado, 2012), 117.
8 M. R. Strecker et al., "Tectonics and Climate of the Southern Central Andes," *Annual Review of Earth and Planetery Sciences* 35 (2007): 752.
9 Pierre Sepulchre et al., "Impacts of Andean Uplift on the Humboldt Current System: A Climate Model Sensitivity Study," *Paleoceanography* 24, no. 4 (2009), 10.
10 Sepulchre et al., 1.
11 Sepulchre et al., 1.
12 Francisco P. Chavez et al., "The Northern Humboldt Current System: Brief History, Present Status and a View Towards the Future," *Progress in Oceanography* 79, no. 2–4 (2008): 95–105.
13 Sepulchre et al., "Impacts of Andean Uplift," 1.
14 Daniel H. Sandweiss and James B. Richardson III, "Central Andean Environments," in *Handbook of South American Archaeology*, eds. Helaine Silverman and William Isbell (Springer, 2008), 93–104.
15 Chavez et al., "Northern Humboldt Current System," 95–105.
16 Daniel H. Sandweiss et al., "Variation in Holocene El Niño Frequencies: Climate Records and Cultural Consequences in Ancient Peru," *Geology* 29, no. 7 (2001): 603.
17 Daniel H. Sandweiss et al., "Mid-Holocene Climate and Culture Change in Coastal Peru," *Climate Change and Cultural Dynamics* (2007): 25–50.
18 Thomas Pozorski and Shelia Pozorski, "Preceramic and Initial Period Monumentality within the Casma Valley of Peru," in *Early New World Monumentality*, eds. Richard L. Burger and Robert M. Rosenswig (University Press of Florida, 2012): 364–398.
19 Peter Watson, *The Great Divide: History and Human Nature in the Old World and the New* (Weidenfeld & Nicolson, 2012), 112.
20 Pozorski and Pozorski, "Preceramic and Initial Period Monumentality," 364–398.
21 Chavez et al., "The Northern Humboldt Current System," 95–105.
22 Michael E. Moseley, and David K. Keefer, "Deadly Deluges in the Southern Desert: Modern and Ancient El Niños in the Osmore Region of Peru," in *El Niño, Catastrophism, and Culture Change in Ancient America,* eds. Daniel H. Sandweiss and Jeffery Quilter (Dumbarton Oaks Research Library and Collection, 2008): 129–144.
23 Sandweiss and Quilter, "Collation, Correlation, and Causation," 127.
24 Sandweiss and Quilter, 119.
25 Moseley and Keefer, "Deadly Deluges," 136.
26 Sandweiss and Quilter, "Collation, Correlation, and Causation," 127–128.
27 Moseley and Keefer, "Deadly Deluges," 136.

28. Sandweiss et al., "Holocene El Niño Frequencies," 603.
29. Donald T. Rodbell et al., "An ~15,000-year Record of El Niño-Driven Alluviation in Southwestern Ecuador," *Science* 283, no. 5401 (1999): 516–520.
30. Moseley and Keefer, "Deadly Deluges," 1; Sandweiss et al., "Holocene El Niño Frequencies," 603; Rodbell et al., "An ~15,000-Year Record," 519.
31. David B. Enfield, "Evolution and Historical Perspective of the 1997–1998 El Niño–Southern Oscillation Event," *Bulletin of Marine Science* 69, no. 1 (2001): 7–25.
32. Angela M. Bayer et al., "The 1997–1998 El Niño as an Unforgettable Phenomenon in Northern Peru: A Qualitative Study," *Disasters* 38, no. 2 (2014): 351–374.
33. Elin Mogollon-Pasapera et al., "Bartonella: Emerging Pathogen or Emerging Awareness?," *International Journal of Infectious Diseases* 13, no. 1 (2009): 3–8. Although the death of Huayna Capac, the Inca emperor, in 1524 has been attributed to smallpox, it may have been caused by bartonellosis. A major outbreak of this disease occurred in the central Andes in 1524–1525 and was widely spread by the many thousands of laborers working on public projects and armies of soldiers, all moving about the large expanse of Inca territory.
34. Sandweiss et al., "Holocene El Niño Frequencies," 603.
35. Sandweiss et al., "Mid-Holocene Climate," 25–50.
36. Sandweiss et al., "Holocene El Niño Frequencies," 605.
37. Paul Roscoe, "Catastrophe and the Emergence of Political Complexity: A Social Anthropological Model," in *El Nino, Catastrophism, and Culture Change in Ancient America*, eds. Daniel H. Sandweiss and Jeffery Quilter (Dumbarton Oaks Research Library and Collection, 2008): 59–75.
38. Roscoe, 59–75.

Chapter 10

1. Tom D. Dillehay, "The Late Pleistocene Cultures of South America," *Evolutionary Anthropology: Issues, News, and Reviews* 7, no. 6 (1999): 207.
2. Daniel H. Sandweiss, "Early Fishing and Inland Monuments: Challenging the Maritime Foundations of Andean Civilization," in *Andean Civilization: A Tribute to Michael E. Moseley*, eds. Joyce Marcus and Patrick Ryan Williams, Monograph 63 (Cotsen Institute of Archaeology Press, 2009): 50; Barbara Pickersgill, "Domestication of Plants in the Americas: Insights from Mendelian and Molecular Genetics," *Annals of Botany* 100, no. 5 (2007): 925–940.
3. Terence N. D'Altroy, "Andean Land Use at the Cusp of History," in *Imperfect Balance: Landscape Transformation in the Precolumbian Americas*, ed. David L. Lentz (Columbia University Press, 2000): 363–365.
4. Michael E. Moseley, *The Incas and Their Ancestors: The Archaeology of Peru*, rev. ed. (Thames & Hudson, 2001), 44.
5. Daniel H. Sandweiss and Jeffrey Quilter, "Collation, Correlation, and Causation in the Prehistory of Coastal Peru," in *Surviving Sudden Environmental Change: Understanding Hazards, Mitigating Impacts, Avoiding Disasters*, eds. Emily McClung de Tapia, Jago Cooper, and Payson D. Sheets (University Press of Colorado, 2012), 125.

6 D'Altroy, *Incas*, 361–364.
7 Kim MacQuarrie, *The Last Days of the Incas* (Simon and Schuster, 2008), 157.
8 Dillehay, "Late Pleistocene Cultures," 213–214.
9 Daniel H. Sandweiss and James B. Richardson III, "Central Andean Environments," in *Handbook of South American Archaeology*, eds. Helaine Silverman and William Isbell (Springer, 2008), 96.
10 Tom D. Dillehay, Herbert H. Eling, and Jack Rossen, "Preceramic Irrigation Canals in the Peruvian Andes," *Proceedings of the National Academy of Sciences* 102, no. 47 (2005): 17241–17244; Moseley, *The Incas and Their Ancestors*, 32.
11 Thomas Pozorski and Shelia Pozorski, "Preceramic and Initial Period Monumentality within the Casma Valley of Peru," in *Early New World Monumentality*, eds. Richard L. Burger and Robert M. Rosenswig (University Press of Florida, 2012): 388–389.
12 Michael A. Malpass, "Irrigation," in *Encyclopedia of the Incas*, eds. Gary Urton and Adriana von Hagen (Rowman & Littlefield, 2015), 166–167.
13 Jeanette E. Sherbondy, "Water and Power: The Role of Irrigation Districts in the Transition from Inca to Spanish Cuzco," in *Irrigation at High Altitudes: The Social Organization of Water Control Systems in the Andes*, eds. William P. Mitchell and David Guillet (Society for Latin American Anthropology and American Anthropological Association, 1993), 79.
14 Kevin Lane, "Water Technology in the Andes," in *Encyclopaedia of the History of Science, Technology, and Medicine in Non-Western Cultures*, ed. Helaine Selin (Springer, 2014), 8.
15 Donald A. Proulx, "Nasca Puquios and Aqueducts," University of Massachusetts, https://people.umass.edu/proulx/online_pubs/Zurich_Puquios_revised_small.pdf, first published in German in *Nasca: Geheimnisvolle Zeichen im Alten Peru*, edited by Judith Rickenbach (Museum Rietberg Zürich, 1999), 89–96; Katharina J. Schreiber and Josue Lancho Rojas, "The Puquios of Nasca," *Latin American Antiquity* 6, no. 3 (1995): 234–235.
16 Schreiber and Rojas, 229.
17 Jonathan A. Sandor and Neal S. Eash, "Ancient Agricultural Soils in the Andes of Southern Peru," *Soil Science Society of America Journal* 59, no. 1 (1995): 177–178.
18 Lane, "Water Technology in the Andes," 3.
19 Sergio J. Chávez, "Agricultural Terraces as Monumental Architecture in the Titicaca Basin: Their Origins in the Yaya-Mama Religious Tradition," in *Early New World Monumentality*, ed. Richard L. Burger and Robert M. Rosenswig (University Press of Florida, 2012): 431-453.
20 Michael A. Malpass, "Terracing," in *Encyclopedia of the Incas*, eds. Gary Urton and Adriana von Hagen (Rowman & Littlefield, 2015), 271–274; Kenneth. R. Wright and Alfredo V. Zegarra, *Machu Picchu: A Civil Engineering Marvel* (American Society of Civil Engineers Press, 2000), 52.
21 John Wayne Janusek, *Ancient Tiwanaku*, vol. 9 (Cambridge University Press, 2008), 186–193; Lane, "Water Technology in the Andes," 11.
22 Janusek, 186–187.

23 Clark L. Erickson and Kay L. Candler, "Raised Fields and Sustainable Agriculture in the Lake Titicaca Basin of Peru," in *Fragile Lands of Latin América,* ed. John O. Browder (Westview Press, 1989): 231–248.

24 Janusek, *Ancient Tiwanaku*, 183–184; Lane, "Water Technology in the Andes," 8.

25 Guano became an important export commodity for Peru in the 1800s when it was shipped to Europe. The substantial revenues generated from guano sales from 1845 into the early 1870s helped to bring a period of peace and prosperity known as the "Guano Age"; the eventual depletion of this resource forced an end to this era. Gregory T. Cushman, "'The Most Valuable Birds in the World': International Conservation Science and the Revival of Peru's Guano Industry, 1909–1965," *Environmental History* 10, no. 3 (2005): 477–478.

26 Paul Szpak et al., "Influence of Seabird Guano and Camelid Dung Fertilization on the Nitrogen Isotopic Composition of Field-Grown Maize (*Zea mays*)," *Journal of Archaeological Science* 39, no. 12 (2012): 3723.

27 Francisca Santana-Sagredo et al., "'White Gold' Guano Fertilizer Drove Agricultural Intensification in the Atacama Desert from AD 1000," *Nature Plants* 7, no. 2 (2021): 152–158.

28 Kenneth R. Wright et al., *Moray: Inca Engineering Mystery* (American Society of Civil Engineers, 2011), 5–6.

29 Wright et al., 6, 19.

30 Wright et al., 43–55.

31 Wright et al., 49–50.

32 John C. Earls and Gabriela Cervantes, "Inka Cosmology in Moray: Astronomy, Agriculture, and Pilgrimage," in *The Inka Empire*, edited by Izumi Shimada (University of Texas Press, 2021), 121–148.

33 Earls and Cervantes, 135, 143.

34 Michael A. Malpass, *Ancient People of the Andes* (Cornell University Press, 2016), 10–11.

Chapter 11

1 A. J. Chepstow-Lusty et al., "Tracing 4,000 Years of Environmental History in the Cuzco Area, Peru, from the Pollen Record," *Mountain Research and Development* (1998): 159–172.

2 Barbara Pickersgill, "Domestication of Plants in the Americas: Insights from Mendelian and Molecular Genetics," *Annals of Botany* 100, no. 5 (2007): 925–940.

3 C. Earle Smith Jr., "Plant Remains from Guitarrero Cave," in *Guitarrero Cave*, ed. Thomas F. Lynch (Academic Press, 1980), 87–119.

4 Rebeca Salvador-Reyes and Maria Teresa Pedrosa Silva Clerici, "Peruvian Andean Maize: General Characteristics, Nutritional Properties, Bioactive Compounds, and Culinary Uses," *Food Research International* 130 (2020): 108934. According to Salvador-Reyes and Clerici, the term "maize" is used for *Zea mays* domestic crops that are used locally, and the term "corn" is used for industrial or commercial-scale crops.

5 Katharina Neumann, Alexandre Chevalier, and Luc Vrydaghs, "Phytoliths in Archaeology: Recent Advances," *Vegetation History and Archaeobotany* 26, no. 1 (2017): 1–3.

6 The major reference sources used for this section are: Janusek, *Ancient Tiwanaku*, 38–46; Michael A. Malpass, "Farming" in *Encyclopedia of the Incas,* eds. Gary Urton and Adriana von Hagen (Rowman & Littlefield, 2015), 136–138; Christine A. Hastorf, "Foodstuffs, Domesticated," in *Encyclopedia of the Incas,* eds. Gary Urton and Adriana von Hagen (Rowman & Littlefield, 2015), 142–145; Sandweiss and Richardson, "Central Andean Environments," 93–104; D'Altroy, "Andean Land Use," 357–390.
7 Pickersgill, "Domestication of Plants," 925–935.
8 Donald Ugent, Tom Dillehay, and Carlos Ramirez, "Potato Remains from a Late Pleistocene Settlement in Southcentral Chile," *Economic Botany* 41, no. 1 (1987): 17–27.
9 Karl S. Zimmerer, "The Ecogeography of Andean Potatoes," *BioScience* 48, no. 6 (1998): 446.
10 Zimmerer, "Ecogeography of Andean Potatoes," 447.
11 John Wayne Janusek, *Ancient Tiwanaku*, vol. 9 (Cambridge University Press, 2008),40.
12 Daniel W. Gade, "Andes, Central," in *Encyclopedia of the Incas,* eds. Gary Urton and Adriana von Hagen (Rowman & Littlefield, 2015), 25.
13 Terence N. D'Altroy, "Andean Land Use at the Cusp of History," in *Imperfect Balance: Landscape Transformation in the Precolumbian Americas*, ed. David L. Lentz (Columbia University Press, 2000): 45.
14 Salvador-Reyes and Clerici, "Peruvian Andean Maize," 108934.
15 Claudia A. Bedoya et al., "Genetic Diversity and Population Structure of Native Maize Populations in Latin America and the Caribbean," *PloS one* 12, no. 4 (2017): e0173488.
16 Nicole A. Sublette Mosblech et al., "Anthropogenic Control of Late-Holocene Landscapes in the Cuzco Region, Peru," *Holocene* 22, no. 12 (2012): 1369.
17 D'Altroy, *Incas*, 401–405.
18 Brian S. Bauer, *Ancient Cuzco: Heartland of the Inca* (University of Texas Press, 2010), 144–146.
19 Janusek. *Ancient Tiwanaku*, 158.
20 Adriana von Hagen, "Chicha," *Encyclopedia of the Incas*, eds. Gary Urton and Adriana von Hagen (Rowman & Littlefield, 2015), 73–75.
21 von Hagen, "Chicha," 73–75.
22 von Hagen, 73–75.
23 Ruth Shady Solis, Jonathan Haas, and Winifred Creamer, "Dating Caral, a Preceramic Site in the Supe Valley on the Central Coast of Peru," *Science* 292, no. 5517 (2001): 723; Jeffery Quilter, "Architecture and Chronology at El Paraiso, Peru," *Journal of Field Archaeology* 12, no. 3 (1985): 294–296.
24 Henrik B. Lindskoug, "Fire Events, Violence and Abandonment Scenarios in the Ancient Andes: The Final Stage of the Aguada Culture in the Ambato Valley, Northwest Argentina," *Journal of World Prehistory* 29, no. 2 (2016): 155–214.
25 Janusek, *Ancient Tiwanaku*, 41.
26 John Ochsendorf, "Spanning the Andes," in *The Great Inka Road: Engineering an Empire*, eds. Ramiro Matos Mendieta and José Barreiro (National Museum of the American Indian/Smithsonian Books, 2015), 51–60.
27 Ochsendorf, "Spanning the Andes," 57.

28 Ochsendorf, 58.
29 Adriana von Hagen, "Bridges," in *Encyclopedia of the Incas,* eds. Gary Urton and Adriana von Hagen (Rowman & Littlefield, 2015), 57–58.
30 Brian S. Bauer, "Suspension Bridges of the Inca Empire," in *Andean Archaeology III: North and South*, eds. William Isbell and Helaine Silverman (Springer, 2006), 491.

Chapter 12
1 John Haywood, *The Penguin Historical Atlas of Ancient Civilizations* (Penguin Books, 2005), 14–17.
2 Richard L. Burger and Robert M. Rosenswig, eds., *Early New World Monumentality* (University Press of Florida, 2012).
3 Jonathan Haas and Winifred Creamer, "Why Do People Build Monuments? Late Archaic Platform Mounds in the Norte Chico," in *Early New World Monumentality*, eds. Richard L. Burger and Robert M. Rosenswig (University Press of Florida, 2012), 289.
4 Peter Watson, *The Great Divide: History and Human Nature in the Old World and the New* (Weidenfeld & Nicolson, 2012), 514.
5 These interpretations incorporate Western thoughts and traditions, but the ancient Andeans may have had completely different ideas and motivations.
6 Watson, *Great Divide*, 255.
7 Terence N. D'Altroy, "Labor Service," in *Encyclopedia of the Incas*, eds. Gary Urton and Adriana von Hagen (Rowman and Littlefield, 2015), 177–181; Michael A. Malpass, "Village Life" in *Encyclopedia of the Incas*, eds. Gary Urton and Adriana von Hagen (Rowman & Littlefield, 2015), 284–286. Although many ancient cultures used slavery as a labor force for monumental construction, in ancient Andean cultures, labor exchanges in networks of joint obligation and support were used. In the Inca Empire, members of the general public typically owed at least two to three months of service, or *mit'a*, annually for public service obligations. When not providing their mit'a, they lived in their home villages and farmed or practiced other occupational specialties.
8 Haas and Creamer, "Why Do People Build Monuments," 304.
9 Haas and Creamer, 305; Thomas Pozorski and Shelia Pozorski, "Preceramic and Initial Period Monumentality within the Casma Valley of Peru," in *Early New World Monumentality*, eds. Richard L. Burger and Robert M. Rosenswig (University Press of Florida, 2012): 390.
10 Haas and Creamer, 305–308.
11 Haas and Creamer, 302–303.
12 Haas and Creamer, 300; Richard L. Burger and Lucy C. Salazar, "Monumental Public Complexes and Agricultural Expansion on Peru's Central Coast during the Second Millennium BC," in *Early New World Monumentality,* eds. Richard L. Burger and Robert M. Rosenswig (University Press of Florida, 2012), 420.
13 Haas and Creamer, 308.
14 Haas and Creamer, 291–292.
15 Haas and Creamer, 296–297.
16 Haas and Creamer, 297.

17 Haas and Creamer, 301.
18 Haas and Creamer, 301.
19 Haas and Creamer, 297.
20 Jonathan Haas, Winifred Creamer, and Alvaro Ruiz, "Power and the Emergence of Complex Polities in the Peruvian Preceramic," *Archeological Papers of the American Anthropological Association* 14, no. 1 (2004): 37–52.
21 Michael A. Malpass, *Ancient People of the Andes* (Cornell University Press, 2016), 67–95.
22 Burger and Salazar, "Monumental Public Complexes," 399–401.
23 Burger and Salazar, 401–402.
24 Pozorski and Pozorski, "Preceramic and Initial Period Monumentality," 376–378.
25 Pozorski and Pozorski, 391.
26 Malpass, *Ancient People*, 96–115; Daniel H. Sandweiss et al., "Variation in Holocene El Niño Frequencies: Climate Records and Cultural Consequences in Ancient Peru," *Geology* 29, no. 7 (2001): 605.
27 John Wayne Janusek, *Ancient Tiwanaku*, vol. 9 (Cambridge University Press, 2008), 48–49.
28 Silvia Rodriguez Kembel and Herbert Haas, "Radiocarbon Dates from the Monumental Architecture at Chavín de Huántar, Perú," abstract, *Journal of Archaeological Method and Theory* 22, no. 2 (2015): 51.
29 Rebecca Stone-Miller, *Art of the Andes: From Chavín to Inca*, 2nd ed. (Thames and Hudson, 2002), 77–81.
30 Helaine Silverman, "A Nasca 8 Occupation at an Early Nasca Site: The Room of the Posts at Cahuachi," *Andean Past* 1, no. 1 (1987): 5–55; Nicola Masini et al., "Integrated Remote Sensing Approach in Cahuachi (Peru): Studies and Results of the ITACA Mission (2007–2010)," in *Satellite Remote Sensing: A New Tool for Archaeology*, Vol. 16, eds. Rosa Lasaponara and Nicola Masini (Springer 2012), 309–312.
31 Stone-Miller, *Art of the Andes*, 64–81; Rosa Lasaponara et al., "New Discoveries in the Piramide Naranjada in Cahuachi (Peru) Using Satellite, Ground Probing Radar and Magnetic Investigations," *Journal of Archaeological Science* 38, no. 9 (2011): 2038–2039.
32 Stone-Miller, 92–93.
33 Stone-Miller, 92–93.
34 Stone-Miller, 92–93.
35 Michael E. Moseley, *The Incas and Their Ancestors: The Archaeology of Peru*, rev. ed. (Thames & Hudson, 2001), 178–179.
36 Janusek, *Ancient Tiwanaku*, 107–168.
37 Alan L. Kolata, "The Urban Concept of Chan Chan," in *The Northern Dynasties: Kingship and Statecraft in Chimor*, eds. Michael E. Moseley and Alana Cordy-Collins (Dumbarton Oaks Research Library and Collection, 1990), 107–109.
38 Moseley, *Incas and Their Ancestors*, 80.
39 Ana Cecilia Mauricio et al., "The Earliest Adobe Monumental Architecture in the Americas," *Proceedings of the National Academy of Sciences* 118, no. 48 (2021), e2102941118.
40 Mauricio et al., e2102941118; Georg Petersen, *Mining and Metallurgy in Ancient Perú*, trans. William E. Brooks, Special Paper 467 (Geological Society of America, 2010), 21.

41 Juan Bariola et al., "Earthquake-Resistant Provision for Adobe Construction in Peru," in *Proceedings: Ninth World Conference on Earthquake Engineering, 1988, Tokyo-Kyoto, Japan,* (1989), 1153–57; Lorenzo Jurina and Monica Righetti, *Traditional Building in Peru* (ICOMOS International Wood Committee, 2001).

42 Haas and Creamer, "Why Do People Build Monuments?" 297.

43 Kenneth. R. Wright and Alfredo V. Zegarra, *Machu Picchu: A Civil Engineering Marvel* (American Society of Civil Engineers Press, 2000), 61–67.

44 Jurina and Righetti, *Traditional Building in Peru,* ICOMOS International Wood Committee, 2001.

45 Kembel and Haas, "Radiocarbon Dates," 354.

46 Jeffrey Quilter, "Architecture and Chronology at El Paraiso, Peru," *Journal of Field Archaeology* 12, no. 3 (1985): 294–296.

47 Hiroshi Fukuyama et al., "Shaking Table Test on Seismic Response Properties of 'Shicras,' Stones Wrapped in Vegetable Fiber Bags," *Journal of Disaster Research* 8, no. 3 (2013): 526–533; Hiroshi Fukuyama et al., "Research on Earthquake Response Reduction Properties and Its Repeatability of the Foundation Technology Used in the Sanctuaries Dating up to 5,000 Years Ago," *Journal of Japan Association for Earthquake Engineering* 16, no. 11 (2016): 11–25.

48 Ramiro Matos Mendieta, "The Living Road," in *The Great Inka Road: Engineering an Empire,* eds. Ramiro Matos Mendieta and José Barreiro (National Museum of the American Indian/Smithsonian Books, 2015): 153.

49 Adriana von Hagen, "Roads," in *Encyclopedia of the Incas,* eds. Gary Urton and Adriana von Hagen (Rowman & Littlefield, 2015): 242–245.

50 Clifford Schexnayder, Christine M. Fiori, and Gerardo Chang Recavarren, "Engineering the Inka Road," in *The Great Inka Road: Engineering an Empire,* eds. Ramiro Matos Mendieta and José Barreiro (National Museum of the American Indian/Smithsonian Books, 2015), 109–112.

51 Victoria Castro, "The Qhapaq Ñan and Its Landscapes," in *The Great Inka Road: Engineering an Empire,* eds. Ramiro Matos Mendieta and José Barreiro (National Museum of the American Indian/Smithsonian Books, 2015), 17.

52 von Hagen, "Roads," 245.

53 Adriana von Hagen, "Tambos," in *Encyclopedia of the Incas,* eds. Gary Urton and Adriana von Hagen (Rowman & Littlefield, 2015): 267–268.

54 von Hagen, "Roads," 242–245.

55 Burger and Salazar, *Monumental Public Complexes,* 426.

Chapter 13

1 Peter Watson, *Great Divide,* 193, based on work on narcotics from the Old World and New World by Weston La Barre.

2 Michael Dietler, "Alcohol: Anthropological/Archaeological Perspectives," *Annual Review of Anthropology* 35 (2006): 229–249; Watson, *Great Divide,* 174–179.

3 Michael E. Moseley, *The Incas and Their Ancestors: The Archaeology of Peru,* rev. ed. (Thames & Hudson, 2001), 166–169.

4 Vincenzo De Feo, "Ethnomedical Field Study in Northern Peruvian Andes with Particular Reference to Divination Practices," *Journal of Ethnopharmacology* 85, no. 2–3 (2003): 251.
5 De Feo, "Ethnomedical Field Study in Northern Peruvian Andes," 251.
6 Bonnie Glass-Coffin, "Shamanism and San Pedro Through Time: Some Notes on the Archaeology, History, and Continued Use of an Entheogen in Northern Peru," *Anthropology of Consciousness* 21, no. 1 (2010): 58–59.
7 Constantino Manuel Torres, "Archaeological Evidence for the Antiquity of Psychoactive Plant Use in the Central Andes," *Annuli dei Musei Civici Roverero* 11 (1995): 320.
8 Torres, 295–300.
9 Catherine J. Allen, "Coca," in *Encyclopedia of the Incas*, eds. Gary Urton and Adriana von Hagen (Rowman & Littlefield, 2015): 86.
10 Deborah Pacini and Christine Franquemont, eds., *Coca and Cocaine: Effects on People and Policy in Latin America*, Cultural Survival Report No. 23 (Cultural Survival and Latin American Studies Program, Cornell University, 1986), 6.
11 Pacini and Franquemont, 24.
12 Pacini and Franquemont, 8.
13 Allen, "Coca," 89.
14 Richard L. Burger, "The Construction of Values during the Peruvian Formative," in *The Construction of Value in the Ancient World*, Vol. 5, eds. John K. Papadopoulos and Gary Urton (Cotsen Institute of Archeology Press, 2012), 243.
15 Joanne Pillsbury, "The Thorny Oyster and the Origins of Empire: Implications of Recently Uncovered Spondylus Imagery from Chan Chan, Peru," *Latin American Antiquity* 7, no. 4 (1996): 318.
16 Burger, "Construction of Values during the Peruvian Formative," 254–255.
17 Valerie A. Andrushko et al., "Investigating a Child Sacrifice Event from the Inca Heartland," *Journal of Archaeological Science* 38, no. 2 (2011): 324; Dagmara M. Socha, Johan Reinhard, and Ruddy Chávez Perea, "Inca Human Sacrifices on Misti Volcano (Peru)," *Latin American Antiquity* 32, no. 1 (2021): 144.
18 Edward R. Swenson, "Cities of Violence: Sacrifice, Power and Urbanization in the Andes," *Journal of Social Archaeology* 3, no. 2 (2003): 256–296.
19 Maize eventually traveled from Mexico to the Andes in ancient times, but Andeans never adopted the hieroglyphic writing of the Mayas and Aztecs, and llamas were not used outside of South America. Watson, *Great Divide,* 100–101.
20 Watson, 161.
21 Elizabeth P. Benson and Anita G. Cook, eds., *Ritual Sacrifice in Ancient Peru* (University of Texas Press, 2001), 11–14.
22 Glenn M. Schwartz, "The Archaeological Study of Sacrifice," *Annual Review of Anthropology* 46 (2017): 227.
23 Schwartz, 225–227.
24 Socha, Reinhard, and Perea, "Inca Human Sacrifices on Misti Volcano," 139–140.

25 J. Marla Toyne et al., "Residential Histories of Elites and Sacrificial Victims at Huacas de Moche, Peru, as Reconstructed from Oxygen Isotopes," *Journal of Archaeological Science* 42 (2014): 15–28.
26 Gabriel Prieto et al., "A Mass Sacrifice of Children and Camelids at the Huanchaquito-Las Llamas site, Moche Valley, Peru," *PLoS One* 14, no. 3 (2019): e0211691; Elise Dufour et al., "Life History and Origin of the Camelids Provisioning a Mass Killing Sacrifice During the Chimú Period: Insight from Stable Isotopes," *Environmental Archaeology* 25, no. 3 (2020): 310–324.
27 Toyne et al., "Residential Histories of Elites and Sacrificial Victims at Huacas de Moche," 17–19.
28 Steve Bourget, *Sacrifice, Violence, and Ideology Among the Moche* (University of Texas Press, 2021), 32–137; Richard C. Sutter and Rosa J Cortez, "The Nature of Moche Human Sacrifice: A Bioarchaeological Perspective," *Current Anthropology* 46, no. 4 (2005): 521–549
29 Sutter and Cortez, 526.
30 Johan Reinhard and Constanza Ceruti, "Sacred Mountains, Ceremonial Sites, and Human Sacrifice among the Incas," *Archaeoastronomy* 19 (2005): 1–43.
31 Reinhard and Ceruti, 1–43.
32 Socha, Reinhard, and Perea, "Inca Human Sacrifices on Misti Volcano," 141.
33 Reinhard and Ceruti, "Sacred Mountains," 13–15.
34 Maria Constanza Ceruti, "Frozen Mummies from Andean Mountaintop Shrines: Bioarchaeology and Ethnohistory of Inca Human Sacrifice," *BioMed Research International* (2015), https://doi.org/10.1155/2015/439428.
35 Reinhard and Ceruti, "Sacred Mountains," 1–43.

Chapter 14

1 Rebecca Stone-Miller, *Art of the Andes: From Chavín to Inca*, 2nd ed. (Thames and Hudson, 2002), 42–43, 96–102, 156–161, 171, 214–215.
2 A. B. Johnson Jr. and B. Francis, *Durability of Metals from Archaeological Objects, Metal Meteorites, and Native Metals*, report no. PNL—3198, prepared for U.S. Department of Energy (Battelle Pacific Northwest Labs., 1980), iii.
3 Heather Lechtman, "Technologies of Power: The Andean Case," in *Configurations of Power*, eds. J. S. Henderson and P. J. Netherly (Cornell University Press, 1993), 251–252.
4 Nicholas J. Saunders, "'Catching the Light': Technologies of Power and Enchantment in Pre-Columbian Goldworking," in *Gold and Power in Ancient Costa Rica, Panama, and Colombia*, eds. Jeffrey Quilter and John W. Hoopes (Dumbarton Oaks Research Library and Collection, 2003), 15–16. Gold and silver were particularly important, but pearls, crystals, obsidian, and other shiny materials also were revered.
5 Jorge Oyarzún, "Andean Metallogenesis: A Synoptical Review and Interpretation," *Tectonic Evolution of South America*, eds. Umberto G. Cordani et al. (31st International Congress, Rio de Janeiro, 2000), 725–753.
6 Dion K. Weatherley and Richard W. Henley, "Flash Vaporization during Earthquakes Evidenced by Gold Deposits," *Nature Geoscience* 6, no. 4 (2013): 294–298.

7   Oyarzún, "Andean Metallogenesis," 725–753.
8   Georg Petersen, *Mining and Metallurgy in Ancient Perú,* trans. William E. Brooks, Special Paper 467 (Geological Society of America, 2010), 23.
9   Mark Aldenderfer et al., "Four-Thousand-Year-Old Gold Artifacts from the Lake Titicaca Basin, Southern Peru," *Proceedings of the National Academy of Sciences* 105, no. 13 (2008): 5002–5005.
10 Yuichi Matsumoto and Yuri Palomino, "Early Horizon Gold Metallurgy from Campanayuq Rumi in the Peruvian South-Central Highlands," *Ñawpa Pacha* 32, no. 1 (2012): 115–130.
11 Lechtman, "Technologies of Power," 263.
12 Terence N. D'Altroy, *The Incas,* 2nd ed. (John Wiley & Sons. 2015), 253–255.
13 Petersen, *Mining and Metallurgy,* 27.
14 Carol A. Schultze et al., "Direct Evidence of 1,900 Years of Indigenous Silver Production in the Lake Titicaca Basin of Southern Peru," *Proceedings of the National Academy of Sciences* 106, no. 41 (2009): 17280–17283.
15 Heather Lechtman, "Metallurgy," in *Encyclopedia of the Incas*, eds. Gary Urton and Adriana von Hagen (Rowman and Littlefield, 2015), 188–191.
16 D'Altroy, *Incas,* 255.
17 Petersen, *Mining and Metallurgy,* 28.
18 Pía Sapiains et al., "Supergene Copper and the Ancient Mining Landscapes of the Atacama Desert: Refining the Protocol for the Study of Archaeological Copper Minerals through the Case Study of Pukara de Turi," *Minerals* 11, no. 12 (2021): 1–27.
19 Lautaro Núñez et al., "The Temple of Tulán-54: Early Formative Ceremonial Architecture in the Atacama Desert," *Antiquity* 91, no. 358 (2017): 901–915.
20 Petersen, *Mining and Metallurgy,* 29.
21 William E. Brooks, Gabriela Schwörbel, and Luis Enrique Castillo, "Amalgamation and Small-Scale Gold Mining in the Ancient Andes," in *Mining and Quarrying in the Ancient Andes*, eds Nicholas Tripcevich and Kevin Vaughn (Springer, 2013), 336.
22 Brooks, Schwörbel, and Castillo, 335.
23 Colin A. Cooke et al., "Use and Legacy of Mercury in the Andes," *Environmental Science & Technology* 47, no. 9 (2013): 4181–4188.
24 Petersen, *Mining and Metallurgy,* 29–30.
25 John Wayne Janusek, *Ancient Tiwanaku,* vol. 9 (Cambridge University Press, 2008), 118.
26 Petersen, *Mining and Metallurgy,* 30–31.
27 William E. Brooks et al., "Lead in Ancient Peru: The Curamba Smelter and Lead Sling Bullets," *Journal of the Minerals, Metals and Materials Society* 64, no. 11 (2012): 1356–1364.
28 Petersen, *Mining and Metallurgy,* 32; Kevin J. Vaughn et al., "Hematite Mining in the Ancient Americas: Mina Primavera, a 2,000 Year Old Peruvian Mine." *Journal of the Minerals, Metals and Materials Society* 59, no. 12 (2007): 16–20.
29 Petersen, *Mining and Metallurgy,* 31.
30 Colin A. Cooke, Mark B. Abbott, and Alexander P. Wolfe, "Late-Holocene Atmospheric Lead Deposition in the Peruvian and Bolivian Andes," *Holocene* 18, no. 2 (2008): 353–359; Cooke et al., "Use and Legacy of Mercury," 4181–4188.

31 Cooke, Abbott, and Wolfe, 353–359.

Chapter 15

1. Rebecca Stone-Miller, *Art of the Andes: From Chavín to Inca*, 2nd ed. (Thames and Hudson, 2002), 9–12.
2. Richard L. Burger and Robert B. Gordon, "Early Central Andean Metalworking from Mina Perdida, Peru," *Science* 282, no. 5391 (1998): 1108.
3. Antonio de la Calancha, *Coronica Moralizada del Orden de San Augustin en el Peru con Sucesos Egenplares en Esta Monarquía* (Pedro Lacavalleria, 1638), 413–414, cited in Emily C. Floyd, "Medium Study-Tears of the Sun: The Naturalistic and Anthropomorphic in Inca Metalwork," *Conversations: An Online Journal of the Center for the Study of Material and Visual Cultures of Religion, Yale University* (2016), 22.
4. Mark Aldenderfer et al., "Four-Thousand-Year-Old Gold Artifacts from the Lake Titicaca Basin, Southern Peru," *Proceedings of the National Academy of Sciences* 105, no. 13 (2008): 5002–5005.
5. Burger and Gordon, "Early Central Andean Metalworking from Mina Perdida," 1110.
6. Burger and Gordon, 1108–1111.
7. Stone-Miller, *Art of the Andes*, 41–43.
8. Stone-Miller, 43.
9. Stone-Miller, 82.
10. Gerhard Hörz and Monika Kallfass, "The Treasure of Gold and Silver Artifacts from the Royal Tombs of Sipán, Peru: A Study on the Moche Metalworking Techniques," *Materials Characterization* 45, no. 4–5 (2000): 393.
11. Deborah Schorsch, "Silver-and-Gold Moche Artifacts from Loma Negra, Peru," *Metropolitan Museum Journal* 33 (1998): 109–136.
12. Hörz and Kallfass, "Treasure of Gold and Silver Artifacts," 391–420.
13. Stone-Miller, *Art of the Andes*, 97–98.
14. Roberto Cesareo et al., "Analysis of the Spectacular Gold and Silver from the Moche Tomb 'Señora de Cao,'" *X-Ray Spectrometry* 45, no. 3 (2016): 138.
15. Hörz and Kallfass, "Treasure of Gold and Silver Artifacts," 391–399.
16. Stone-Miller, *Art of the Andes*, 102.
17. Stone-Miller, 170–171.
18. Gonzalo Fernandez de Oviedo, *Sumario de las Historia Natural de las Indias* (Fondo de Cultura Económica, [1526]1950), quoted in Georg Petersen, *Mining and Metallurgy in Ancient Perú*, trans. William E. Brooks, Special Paper 467 (Geological Society of America, 2010), 57.
19. Heather Lechtman, "Metallurgy," in *Encyclopedia of the Incas*, eds. Gary Urton and Adriana von Hagen (Rowman and Littlefield, 2015), 190.
20. Colleen Zori, "Extracting Insights from Prehistoric Andean Metallurgy: Political Organization, Interregional Connections, and Ritual Meanings," *Journal of Archaeological Research* 27, no. 4 (2019): 501–556.
21. Stone-Miller, *Art of the Andes*, 185.

22. Diego Salazar et al., "Early Evidence (ca. 12,000 BP) for Iron Oxide Mining on the Pacific Coast of South America," *Current Anthropology* 52, no. 3 (2011): 463–475.
23. Salazar et al., 465.
24. Salazar et al., 463.
25. Carol A. Schultze, "Silver Mines of the Northern Lake Titicaca Basin," in *Mining and Quarrying in the Ancient Andes: Sociopolitical, Economic and Symbolic Dimensions*, eds. Nicholas Tripcevich and Kevin Vaughn (Springer, 2013), 231–251.
26. Carol A. Schultze at al., "Indigenous Silver Production in the Lake Titicaca Basin," 17280–17283.
27. Diego Salazar, César Borie, and Camila Oñate, "Mining, Commensal Politics, and Ritual under Inca Rule in Atacama, Northern Chile," in *Mining and Quarrying in the Ancient Andes: Sociopolitical, Economic and Symbolic Dimensions*, eds. Nicholas Tripcevich and Kevin Vaughn (Springer, 2013), 253–274.
28. Georg Petersen, *Mining and Metallurgy*, 23–26.
29. Petersen, 43.
30. Izumi Shimada and Alan K. Craig, "The Style, Technology and Organization of Sicán Mining and Metallurgy, Northern Peru: Insights from Holistic Study," *Chungará (Arica)* 45, no. 1 (2013): 3–31.
31. Kevin J. Vaughn and Nicholas Tripcevich, introduction to *Mining and Quarrying in the Ancient Andes: Sociopolitical, Economic and Symbolic Dimensions*, eds. Nicholas Tripcevich and Kevin Vaughn (Springer, 2013), 8.
32. William E. Brooks, Gabriela Schwörbel, and Luis Enrique Castillo, "Amalgamation and Small-Scale Gold Mining in the Ancient Andes," in *Mining and Quarrying in the Ancient Andes*, eds Nicholas Tripcevich and Kevin Vaughn (Springer, 2013), 213–229.
33. Pedro Cieza de León, *La Crónica General del Perú, Tomo I: Colección Urteaga Romero, Historiadores Clásicos del Perú, Tomo VII, Lima* (Libreria e Imprinta Gil,[1550]1924), 309, cited in Petersen, *Mining and Metallurgy*, 48.
34. Schultze at al., "Indigenous Silver Production," 17280–17283.
35. Colin A. Cooke, Mark B. Abbott, and Alexander P. Wolfe, "Late-Holocene Atmospheric Lead Deposition in the Peruvian and Bolivian Andes," *Holocene* 18, no. 2 (2008): 353–359.
36. Colin A. Cooke, Alexander P. Wolfe, and William O. Hobbs, "Lake-Sediment Geochemistry Reveals 1400 Years of Evolving Extractive Metallurgy at Cerro de Pasco, Peruvian Andes," *Geology* 37, no. 11 (2009): 1019–1022.
37. Brooks, Schwörbel, and Castillo, "Amalgamation and Small-Scale Gold Mining," 333–347.
38. Brooks, Schwörbel, and Castillo, 336–337.
39. Brooks, Schwörbel, and Castillo, 343. Metal workers blowing into these pipes would have produced narrow flames of around 2,700°F (1,500°C).
40. Colin A. Cooke et al., "Over Three Millennia of Mercury Pollution in the Peruvian Andes," *Proceedings of the National Academy of Sciences* 106, no. 22 (2009): 8830–8834.

41 Heather Lechtman, "Arsenic Bronze: Dirty Copper or Chosen Alloy? A View from the Americas," *Journal of Field Archaeology* 23, no. 4 (1996): 477–478. In the Old World, people began using arsenic bronze in the late fifth millennia CE and worked this alloy for almost 2,000 years before tin bronze was widely produced.

42 Lechtman, 477–478. Arsenic bronze was desirable for the traditional sheet metal production of Andean cultures, as this alloy has greater ductility than tin bronze.

43 The Sicán culture succeeded the Moche and flourished from about 750–1375 CE along the northern coast of modern Peru.

44 Petersen, *Mining and Metallurgy*, xix.

45 Kevin J. Vaughn and Nicholas Tripcevich, introduction to *Mining and Quarrying in the Ancient Andes: Sociopolitical, Economic and Symbolic Dimensions*, eds. Nicholas Tripcevich and Kevin Vaughn (Springer, 2013), 9–11.

46 Kevin J. Vaughn et al., "The Organization of Mining in Nasca during the Early Intermediate Period: Recent Evidence from Mina Primavera," in *Mining and Quarrying in the Ancient Andes: Sociopolitical, Economic and Symbolic Dimensions*, eds. Nicholas Tripcevich and Kevin Vaughn (Springer, 2013), 157–182.

Chapter 16

1 Rebecca Stone-Miller, *Art of the Andes: From Chavín to Inca*, 2nd ed. (Thames and Hudson, 2002), 9–10.

2 Stone-Miller, 17.

3 Gary Urton, "Weaving and Textiles" in *Encyclopedia of the Incas*, eds. Gary Urton and Adriana von Hagen (Rowman & Littlefield, 2015), 297–301.

4 Edward A. Jolie et al., "Cordage, Textiles, and the Late Pleistocene Peopling of the Andes," *Current Anthropology* 52, no. 2 (2011): 285–296.

5 Stone-Miller, *Art of the Andes*, 17.

6 Sam Byrne et al., "Were Chinchorros Exposed to Arsenic? Arsenic Determination in Chinchorro Mummies' Hair by Laser Ablation Inductively Coupled Plasma-Mass Spectrometry (LA-ICP-MS)," *Microchemical Journal* 94, no. 1 (2010): 29.

7 Stone-Miller, *Art of the Andes*, 43–44.

8 Richard L. Burger, "The Chavin Horizon: Stylistic Chimera or Socioeconomic Metamorphosis," *Latin American Horizons* (1993): 57–58.

9 Stone-Miller, *Art of the Andes*, 52–57.

10 Stone-Miller, 52.

11 Stone-Miller, 49.

12 Stone-Miller, 212–213.

13 Stone-Miller, 211–212.

14 Stone-Miller, 211–212.

15 Gary Urton, "Quipu," in *Encyclopedia of the Incas*, eds. Gary Urton and Adriana von Hagen (Rowman & Littlefield, 2015), 234–236.

16 Daniel H. Sandweiss, "Collaborative Research: Molluscan Radiocarbon as a Proxy for Upwelling in Holocene Peru," Grant Reports 349 (University of Maine Office of Research and Sponsored Programs, 2011), 4.

17 Urton, "Quipu," 234–236.
18 Daniel H. Sandweiss, "Early Fishing and Inland Monuments: Challenging the Maritime Foundations of Andean Civilization," in *Andean Civilization: A Tribute to Michael E. Moseley*, eds. Joyce Marcus and Patrick Ryan Williams, Monograph 63 (Cotsen Institute of Archaeology Press, 2009): 39–54.
19 Jean-François Millaire et al., "Statecraft and Expansionary Dynamics: A Virú Outpost at Huaca Prieta, Chicama Valley, Peru," *Proceedings of the National Academy of Sciences* 113, no. 41 (2016): E6020; Stone-Miller, *Art of the Andes*, 19–20.
20 Gary Urton, "Weaving and Textiles," 297–301.
21 Heidi King, *Peruvian Featherworks: Art of the Precolumbian Era* (Metropolitan Museum of Art, 2012), 14.
22 Adriana von Hagen, "Feathers," in *Encyclopedia of the Incas*, eds. Gary Urton and Adriana von Hagen (Rowman & Littlefield, 2015), 140–142.
23 Stone-Miller, *Art of the Andes*, 172.
24 von Hagen, "Feathers," 140–142.
25 von Hagen, 141.
26 Pedro Pizarro, *Relación* (Simon and Schuster, 2008), cited in MacQuarrie, *Last Days of the Incas*, 107–108.
27 Georg Petersen, *Mining and Metallurgy in Ancient Perú*, trans. William E. Brooks, Special Paper 467 (Geological Society of America, 2010), 9–10; William E. Brooks et al., "Mineral Pigments at Huaca Tacaynamo (Chan Chan, Peru)," *Bulletin de l'Institut Français d'Etudes Andines* 37, no. 3(2008): 441–450.
28 Burger, "Chavin Horizon," 57–58.
29 Margaret Young-Sánchez. *Tiwanaku: Ancestors of the Inca* (Denver Art Museum and University of Nebraska Press, 2004): 38–53.
30 Georg Petersen, *Mining and Metallurgy in Ancient Perú*, trans. William E. Brooks, Special Paper 467 (Geological Society of America, 2010), 3–8.
31 Ernst E. Wreschner et al., "Red Ochre and Human Evolution: A Case for Discussion [and Comments and Reply]," *Current Anthropology* 21, no. 5 (1980): 631–644.
32 Shortly after leaving Capital Reef National Park, I was fortunate to visit the exhibit, "The Red That Colored the World," at the Museum of International Folk Art in Santa Fe, New Mexico. The companion publication to that exhibit is the book, *A Red Like No Other*, which brings together an abundance of historical, scientific, and artistic information about cochineal. This book was the major reference source used for this section. Carmella Padilla and Barbara C. Anderson, eds, *A Red Like No Other: How Cochineal Colored the World* (Skira Rizzoli and Museum of International Folk Art, 2015).
33 Padilla and Anderson, *A Red Like No Other*, 90–92; Michael G. Campana, Nelly M. Robles Garcia, and Noreen Tuross, "America's Red Gold: Multiple Lineages of Cultivated Cochineal in Mexico," *Ecology and Evolution* 5, no. 3 (2015): 607–617.
34 Padilla and Anderson, *A Red Like No Other,* 109.
35 Elena Phipps and Nobuko Shibayama, "Tracing Cochineal through the Collection of the Metropolitan Museum," *Textile Society of America Symposium Proceedings* 44 (2010): 4.

36 Elena Phipps, "Shades of Red: Color and Culture in Andean Textiles" in *A Red Like No Other: How Cochineal Colored the World,* eds. Carmella Padilla and Barbara C. Anderson (Skira Rizzoli and Museum of International Folk Art, 2015), 112–113.

37 Carlos Marichal, "The Cochineal Commodity Chain: Mexican Cochineal and the Rise of Global Trade," in *A Red Like No Other: How Cochineal Colored the World,* eds. Carmella Padilla and Barbara C. Anderson (Skira Rizzoli and Museum of International Folk Art, 2015), 54.

38 Nicolasa Chávez, "Carmine and Earthly Delights: Cochineal in Cosmetics, Contemporary Craft, and the Strawberry Frappuccino," in *A Red Like No Other: How Cochineal Colored the World,* eds. Carmella Padilla and Barbara C. Anderson (Skira Rizzoli and Museum of International Folk Art, 2015), 266. Starbucks hit a public relations minefield in 2012 when an employee allegedly read the list of ingredients in their strawberry Frappuccino drinks, recognized cochineal, and blew the whistle. Public outrage (the "ewww!" factor), especially from vegans, ensued and Starbucks quickly pulled the pink drinks from the menu.

39 Stone-Miller, *Art of the Andes*, 17.

40 Stone-Miller, 45.

41 Stone-Miller, 46.

42 Stone-Miller, 65–73.

43 Stone-Miller, 31. These wheels were not used for throwing pots, as in a potter's wheel, but only for ease of applying wraparound decoration. They demonstrated that Andean people were not ignorant of the use of a wheel.

44 Stone-Miller, 103–117.

45 Donna McClelland, Donald McClelland, and Christopher B. Donnan, *Moche Fineline Painting from San José de Moro,* (Cotsen Institute of Archaeology Press, 2007), 1–208. The rollout drawings that are reproductions of Moche fine-line drawings on ceramic vessels are fascinating.

46 Stone-Miller, *Art of the Andes*, 103.

47 Tamara L. Bray, "Ceramics," in *Encyclopedia of the Incas*, eds. Gary Urton and Adriana von Hagen (Rowman & Littlefield, 2015), 70–73.

Chapter 17

1 Michael E. Moseley, *The Incas and Their Ancestors: The Archaeology of Peru*, rev. ed. (Thames & Hudson, 2001), 163–170.

2 Rebecca Stone-Miller, *Art of the Andes: From Chavín to Inca*, 2nd ed. (Thames and Hudson, 2002), 41.

3 Daniel A. Contreras, "Sociopolitical and Geomorphologic Dynamics at Chavín de Huántar, Peru" (PhD diss., Stanford University, 2007) 115.

4 Stone-Miller, *Art of the Andes*, 29.

5 Daniel A. Contreras, and David K. Keefer, "Implications of the Fluvial History of the Wacheqsa River for Hydrologic Engineering and Water Use at Chavín de Huántar, Peru," *Geoarchaeology: An International Journal* 24, no. 5 (2009): 615.

6 Sandweiss et al., "Variation in Holocene El Niño Frequencies," *Geology* 29, no. 7 (2001): 605.
7 Contreras and Keefer, "Fluvial History of the Wacheqsa River," 598.
8 Julio C. Tello, "Discovery of the Chavín Culture in Peru," *American Antiquity* 9, no. 1 (1943): 135.
9 Silvia Rodriguez Kembel and Herbert Haas, "Radiocarbon Dates from the Monumental Architecture at Chavín de Huántar, Perú," abstract, *Journal of Archaeological Method and Theory* 22, no. 2 (2015): 421–423.
10 An alternative carbon-14 chronology, indicating the site was established at about 950 BCE and abandoned by 400 BCE, is proposed by Richard Burger, building on a pottery chronology he initially established from excavation work in 1975. Richard L. Burger, "Understanding the Socioeconomic Trajectory of Chavín de Huántar: A New Radiocarbon Sequence and Its Wider Implications," *Latin American Antiquity* 30, no. 2 (2019): 373–392.
11 John W. Rick, "The Evolution of Authority and Power at Chavín de Huántar, Peru," *Archeological Papers of the American Anthropological Association* 14, no. 1 (2004): 80.
12 Contreras and Keefer, "Fluvial History of the Wacheqsa River," 590.
13 Contreras and Keefer, 593–594.
14 Contreras and Keefer, 593–594.
15 Stone-Miller, *Art of the Andes*, 29.
16 Moseley, *Incas and Their Ancestors*, 166–169.
17 *Strombus* is native to the warm ocean waters far to the north of Chavín, offshore from Ecuador.
18 Stone-Miller, *Art of the Andes*, 43–44.
19 Stone-Miller, 36.
20 Constantino Manuel Torres, "Archaeological Evidence for the Antiquity of Psychoactive Plant Use in the Central Andes," *Annuli dei Musei Civici Roverero* 11 (1995): 301.
21 Stone-Miller, *Art of the Andes*, 37.
22 Stone-Miller, 35–36.
23 Moseley, *Incas and Their Ancestors*, 165.
24 Contreras and Keefer, "Fluvial History of the Wacheqsa River," 589–618.
25 Contreras, "Sociopolitical and Geomorphologic Dynamics at Chavín de Huántar," 105–106.
26 John Edwin Cobbing et al. "Geología de los Cuadrángulos de Huaraz, Recuay, La Unión, Chiquián y Yanahuanca," Boletín A 76 (1996), Figures 4.1, 4.3; John Edwin Cobbing and Agapito Wilfredo Sánchez Fernández, *Mapa Geologico del Cuadrangulo de Recuay* (Ministerio de Energia y Minas and Instituto Geologico Minero y Metalurgico, 1996).
27 Contreras and Keefer, "Fluvial History of the Wacheqsa River," 598.
28 Daniel A. Contreras, "Reconstructing Landscape at Chavín de Huántar, Peru: A GIS-Based Approach," *Journal of Archaeological Science* 36, no. 4 (2009), 1014.
29 Contreras, "Sociopolitical and Geomorphologic Dynamics at Chavín de Huántar," 225.

30. Silvia Rodriguez Kembel and John W. Rick, "Building Authority at Chavín de Huántar: Models of Social Organization and Development in the Initial Period and Early Horizon," *Andean Archaeology* (2004): 65.
31. Robert J. W. Turner, Rosemary J. Knight, and John Rick, "Geological Landscape of the Pre-Inca Archaeological Site at Chavín de Huántar, Peru," *Current Research* (Geological Survey of Canada, 1999-D), 47–56.
32. Contreras, "Sociopolitical and Geomorphologic Dynamics at Chavín de Huántar," 112–114.
33. Contreras and Keefer, "Fluvial History of the Wacheqsa River," 614.
34. Contreras and Keefer, 593.
35. Contreras and Keefer, 589–618.
36. Contreras and Keefer, 592.
37. Contreras and Keefer, 612.
38. Contreras, "Sociopolitical and Geomorphologic Dynamics at Chavín de Huántar," 132.
39. Contreras and Keefer, "Fluvial History of the Wacheqsa River," 613–614.
40. Moseley, *Incas and Their Ancestors*, 163.
41. Burger, "Understanding the Socioeconomic Trajectory of Chavín de Huántar," 5.
42. Silvia Rodriguez Kembel, "The Architecture at the Monumental Center of Chavín de Huántar: Sequence, Transformations, and Chronology," in *Chavín: Art, Architecture, and Culture,* eds. Jeffrey Quilter and William J. Conklin (Cotsen Institute of Archaeology Press, 2008): 77; Kembel and Rick, "Building Authority at Chavín de Huántar," 54.
43. Sandweiss et al., "Variation in Holocene El Niño Frequencies," 604.
44. Kembel and Haas, "Radiocarbon Dates from the Monumental Architecture at Chavín de Huántar," 381, 406, 422.
45. Rick, "Evolution of Authority and Power at Chavín de Huántar," 74.

Chapter 18

1. John Wayne Janusek, *Ancient Tiwanaku*, vol. 9 (Cambridge University Press, 2008), 22–23, 104.
2. José M. Capriles and Juan Albarracin-Jordan, "The Earliest Human Occupations in Bolivia: A Review of the Archaeological Evidence," *Quaternary International* 301 (2013), 55.
3. Clark L. Erickson, "The Lake Titicaca Basin: A Precolumbian Built Landscape," in *Imperfect Balance: Landscape Transformation in the Precolumbian Americas*, ed. David L. Lentz (Columbia University Press, 2000), 320. Endemic to mid- and high-elevations of the Andes, *Polylepis* are wind-pollinated trees with thick and layered bark that are well-equipped to withstand harsh climatic conditions. The ancient Andeans highly valued these trees for fuel and building material. Due to overharvesting for firewood, clearing of woodlands for pastures, and destruction of seedlings by domesticated animals, only small and isolated stands of the trees remain in the Andes.

4   Gina M. Paduano et al., "A Vegetation and Fire History of Lake Titicaca since the Last Glacial Maximum," *Palaeogeography, Palaeoclimatology, Palaeoecology* 194, no. 1–3 (2003): 274–276.
5   Janusek, *Ancient Tiwanaku*, 65–106.
6   Janusek, 104.
7   Janusek, 96–97.
8   Janusek, 48.
9   Janusek, 186–193.
10 Janusek, 171, 179.
11 Janusek, 141–148.
12 Janusek, 222–225.
13 Janusek, 109–128.
14 Janusek, 134–135.
15 Janusek, 116.
16 Alan L. Kolata, "Mimesis and Monumentalism in Native Andean Cities," *RES: Anthropology and Aesthetics*, 29, no. 1 (1996): 230–231.
17 In many ancient Andean archaeological sites, deliberately broken ceramics, often containing food remains, are found in the graves of elites, as well as in burials of human sacrifice victims. This ritual smashing "shows the strong Andean orientation toward the afterlife and the conviction that art is animate and therefore mortal, but continues its efficacy on the Other Side" (Stone-Miller, *Art of the Andes*, 152).
18 Kolata, "Mimesis and Monumentalism in Native Andean Cities," 232–233.
19 Kolata, 223–236. The exotic color of the green pebbles is described in this reference. The pebbles may be volcanic andesite, as the green mineral chlorite can be abundant in these rocks, although I could not find specific information.
20 Janusek, *Ancient Tiwanaku*, 110–113.
21 John Wayne Janusek et al., "Building Taypikala: Telluric Transformations in the Lithic Production of Tiwanaku," in *Mining and Quarrying in the Ancient Andes: Sociopolitical, Economic and Symbolic Dimensions,* eds. Nicholas Tripcevich and Kevin Vaughn (Springer, 2013), 65–97.
22 Kolata, "Mimesis and Monumentalism in Native Andean Cities," 227–228.
23 Janusek, *Ancient Tiwanaku*, 145, 155.
24 Janusek et al., "Building Taypikala," 69–70.
25 Janusek et al., 76–77.
26 Janusek et al., 76.
27 Rebecca Stone-Miller, *Art of the Andes: From Chavín to Inca*, 2nd ed. (Thames and Hudson, 2002), 133–134.
28 Janusek et al., "Building Taypikala," 83–87.
29 Janusek et al., 85–87.
30 Janusek, *Ancient Tiwanaku*, 134–135.
31 Janusek et al., "Building Taypikala," 91–92.
32 Janusek et al., 87–88.

33 Janusek, *Ancient Tiwanaku*, 239–240.
34 Janusek, 143–249.
35 Information about Wari and Tiwanaku relationships in this section is from Janusek, 250–288.
36 Janusek, 292–298; Patrick Ryan Williams, "Rethinking Disaster-Induced Collapse in the Demise of the Andean Highland States: Wari and Tiwanaku," *World Archaeology* 33, no. 3 (2002): 371–372.
37 Janusek, 292–298.
38 Leslie A. Friedman, "The Making of Place: Myth and Memory at the Site of Tiwanaku, Bolivia," in *Finding the Spirit of Place: Between the Tangible and the Intangible*, 16th International Council on Monuments and Sites General Assembly and International Symposium, Quebec, Canada (Sept 29–Oct 4, 2008), 1–10.

Chapter 19

1 Paul R. Steele, *Handbook of Inca Mythology* (ABC-CLIO, 2004), 188–192; Terence N. D'Altroy, *The Incas*, 2nd ed. (John Wiley & Sons. 2015), 70–73.
2 Brian S. Bauer, *Ancient Cuzco: Heartland of the Inca* (University of Texas Press, 2010), 89.
3 Stella Nair, "Estates, Royal," in *Encyclopedia of the Incas,* eds. Gary Urton and Adriana von Hagen (Rowman & Littlefield, 2015), 127.
4 Michael E. Moseley, *The Incas and Their Ancestors: The Archaeology of Peru*, rev. ed. (Thames & Hudson, 2001), 9.
5 John Haywood, *The Penguin Historical Atlas of Ancient Civilizations* (Penguin Books, 2005), 134.
6 Tamara L. Bray, "Feasts, State-Sponsored," in *Encyclopedia of the Incas,* eds. Gary Urton and Adriana von Hagen (Rowman & Littlefield, 2015), 138–140.
7 Terence N. D'Altroy, "Labor Service," in *Encyclopedia of the Incas*, eds. Gary Urton and Adriana von Hagen (Rowman and Littlefield, 2015), 177–181.
8 Noble David Cook, "Diseases, Foreign," in *Encyclopedia of the Incas,* eds. Gary Urton and Adriana von Hagen (Rowman & Littlefield, 2015), 116–118.
9 D'Altroy, *Incas*, 449–459.
10 D'Altroy, 467.
11 Moseley, *Incas and Their Ancestors*, 7; Bauer, *Ancient Cuzco*, 91.
12 Moseley, 32.
13 Adriana von Hagen, "Roads," in *Encyclopedia of the Incas*, eds. Gary Urton and Adriana von Hagen (Rowman & Littlefield, 2015), 242–245.
14 Adriana von Hagen, "Antisuyu," in *Encyclopedia of the Incas,* eds. Gary Urton and Adriana von Hagen (Rowman & Littlefield, 2015), 31–32.
15 Adriana von Hagen, "Collasuyu," in *Encyclopedia of the Incas,* eds. Gary Urton and Adriana von Hagen (Rowman & Littlefield, 2015), 90–92.
16 Adriana von Hagen, "Cuntisuyu," in *Encyclopedia of the Incas,* eds. Gary Urton and Adriana von Hagen (Rowman & Littlefield, 2015), 104–105.

17 Adriana von Hagen, "Chinchaysuyu," in *Encyclopedia of the Incas,* eds. Gary Urton and Adriana von Hagen (Rowman & Littlefield, 2015), 75–76.
18 D'Altroy. *Incas,* 9–12.
19 No one really knows the population of the Inca Empire, but an estimate of around 10 to 14 million is reported in many sources.
20 Krzysztof Makowski, "Religion," in *Encyclopedia of the Incas,* eds. Gary Urton and Adriana von Hagen (Rowman & Littlefield, 2015), 239–240.
21 Kenneth. R. Wright and Alfredo V. Zegarra, *Machu Picchu: A Civil Engineering Marvel* (American Society of Civil Engineers Press, 2000), 15–16; Kenneth R. Wright, Alfredo V. Zegarra, and William L. Lorah, "Ancient Machu Picchu Drainage Engineering," *Journal of Irrigation and Drainage Engineering* 125, no. 6 (1999), 23–25.
22 Helmut Tributsch, "On the Reddish, Glittery Mud the Inca Used for Perfecting Their Stone Masonry," *Journal of Earth Sciences & Environmental Studies,* 3, no. 1 (2017): 309–324.
23 Jean-Pierre Protzen, "Quarrying and Stonecutting," in *Encyclopedia of the Incas,* eds. Gary Urton and Adriana von Hagen (Rowman & Littlefield, 2015), 225–230.
24 Wright and Zegarra, *Machu Picchu,* 62.
25 Stella Nair, "Architecture," in *Encyclopedia of the Incas,* eds. Gary Urton and Adriana von Hagen (Rowman & Littlefield, 2015), 37–41.
26 Protzen, "Quarrying and Stonecutting," 226.
27 Lisbet Bengtsson, *Prehistoric Stonework in the Peruvian Andes: A Case Study at Ollantaytambo,* GOTARC Series B, No. 10; Etnologiska Studier 44 (Department of Archaeology, Göteborg University, Sweden, 1998), 41–85.
28 Dennis Ogburn, "Power in Stone: The Long-Distance Movement of Building Blocks in the Inca Empire," *Ethnohistory* 51, no. 1 (2004): 101–135. At least 450 blocks, weighing up to about 1,543 lb (700 kg), were transported, probably by thousands of men carrying each stone on a litter. The movement of this stone showcased the vast amount of labor that the Incas controlled and may have been intended to dissuade potentially rebellious people in the outer provinces from resisting the state.
29 Protzen, "Quarrying and Stonecutting," 227.
30 Protzen, 227.
31 Wright and Zegarra, *Machu Picchu,* 108.
32 Protzen, "Quarrying and Stonecutting," 228–229.
33 Bauer, *Ancient Cuzco,* 103–104.
34 Rebecca Stone-Miller, *Art of the Andes: From Chavín to Inca,* 2nd ed. (Thames and Hudson, 2002), 193.
35 Tributsch, "On the Reddish, Glittery Mud," 309.
36 Wright and Zegarra, *Machu Picchu,* 62.
37 Pedro Sancho de la Hoz, *An Account of the Conquest of Peru (1534),* trans. Philip A. Means (Cortés Society, [1534]1917), quoted in Bauer, *Ancient Cuzco,* 110.
38 Bauer, 143–146.
39 Bauer, 139.

40 Bauer, 139–157.
41 Bauer, 111–117.
42 Juan Polo de Ondegardo, *On the Errors and Superstitions of the Indians, Taken from the Treatise and Investigation Done by Licentiate Polo* (1571), trans. A. Brunel, John V. Murra, and Sidney Muirden (Human Relations Area Files, Yale University, 1965), quoted in Bauer, 113.
43 Bauer, 112–115.
44 Bauer, 98–105.
45 Adriana von Hagen, "Sacsahuaman" in *Encyclopedia of the Incas,* eds. Gary Urton and Adriana von Hagen (Rowman & Littlefield, 2015), 250–251.
46 Bauer, *Ancient Cuzco*, 99.
47 Elizabeth Arkush, "Fortifications," in *Encyclopedia of the Incas,* eds. Gary Urton and Adriana von Hagen (Rowman & Littlefield, 2015), 148.
48 D'Altroy, *Incas*, 224.
49 D'Altroy, 414.
50 Mariusz Ziółkowski et al., "When Did the Incas Build Machu Picchu and Its Satellite Sites? New Approaches Based on Radiocarbon Dating," *Radiocarbon* 63, no. 4 (2021): 1133–1148.
51 Wright and Zegarra, *Machu Picchu*, 5.
52 Wright and Zegarra, 19.
53 Wright, Zegarra, and Lorah, "Ancient Machu Picchu Drainage Engineering," 9.
54 Wright, Zegarra, and Lorah, 5–9.
55 Wright and Zegarra, *Machu Picchu*, 36–40.
56 D'Altroy, *Incas*, 2, 143–144.

Chapter 20

1 Terence N. D'Altroy, *The Incas*, 2nd ed. (John Wiley & Sons. 2015), 450–459.
2 D'Altroy, 456. Pizarro's secretary wrote that the room was about 20 ft x 15.75 ft (6.2 m x 4.8 m), and the gold was to reach a white line set at half its height, or about 8.2 ft (2.5 m).
3 D'Altroy, 31. The metal quantities described in this reference are: "the royal fifth of 2,600 lb of gold and 5,200 [lb] of silver (MacQuarrie 2007:124), using a July 2012 price of $1,570/oz for gold and $26/oz for silver."
4 Jason W. Moore, "'This Lofty Mountain of Silver Could Conquer the Whole World': Potosí and the Political Ecology of Underdevelopment, 1545–1800," *Journal of Philosophical Economics* 4, no. 1 (2010): 58–103. Much of the new wealth was used by Spanish King Philip II in his European war strategies— a quest to fight back the Protestantism creeping into Europe and to preserve the true faith of Catholicism.
5 Nicholas A. Robins, *Mercury, Mining, and Empire: The Human and Ecological Cost of Colonial Silver Mining in the Andes* (Indiana University Press, 2011); Nicholas A. Robins et al., "Estimations of Historical Atmospheric Mercury Concentrations from Mercury Refining and Present-Day Soil Concentrations of Total Mercury in Huancavelica, Peru," *Science of the Total Environment* 426 (2012): 146–154.

6 Information about Potosí in this section is from Peter J. Bakewell, *Miners of the Red Mountain: Indian Labor in Potosí, 1545–1650* (University of New Mexico Press, 1984); Peter J. Bakewell and Jacqueline Holler, *A History of Latin America to 1825*, Vol. 8. (John Wiley & Sons, 2009); Moore, "This Lofty Mountain of Silver," 58–103.
7 Moore, 58–103.
8 Moore, 58–103.
9 Robins, *Mercury, Mining, and Empire*, ix.
10 D'Altroy, *Incas*, p. 459–467.
11 David N. Cook, *Demographic Collapse: Indian Peru, 1520–1620*, Cambridge University Press, 1981, cited in D'Altroy, 468.
12 Garcilaso in 1609, cited in Carolyn S. Dean, "Creating a Ruin in Colonial Cusco: Sacsahuamán and What Was Made of It," *Andean Past* 5, no. 1 (1998): 163.
13 Brian S. Bauer, *Ancient Cuzco: Heartland of the Inca* (University of Texas Press, 2010), 112–115.
14 Thomas B. F. Cummins, "A Tale of Two Cities: Cuzco, Lima, and the Construction of Colonial Representation," in *Converging Cultures: Art and Identity in Spanish America* (Brooklyn Museum and Harry N. Abrams, 1996), cited in Carolyn Dean, *A Culture of Stone: Inka Perspectives on Rock* (Duke University Press, 2010), 161.
15 Ernest C. Peixotto, *Pacific Shores from Panama* (Charles Scribner's Sons, 1913), 170.
16 Michael E. Moseley, *The Incas and Their Ancestors: The Archaeology of Peru*, rev. ed. (Thames & Hudson, 2001), 17.
17 Kenneth. R. Wright and Alfredo V. Zegarra, *Machu Picchu: A Civil Engineering Marvel* (American Society of Civil Engineers Press, 2000), 52.
18 Dan Collyns, "Machu Picchu Ruin 'Found Earlier,'" *BBC News*, June 6, 2008, http://news.bbc.co.uk/2/hi/americas/7439397.stm.
19 Diane Orson, "Yale Returns Machu Picchu Artifacts to Peru," *All Things Considered*, NPR, December 15, 2010, https://www.npr.org/2010/12/15/132083890/yale-returns-machu-picchu-artifacts-to-peru.
20 Moore, "This Lofty Mountain of Silver," 58–103.
21 John Ochsendorf, "Spanning the Andes," in *The Great Inka Road: Engineering an Empire*, eds. Ramiro Matos Mendieta and Jos. Barreiro (National Museum of the American Indian/Smithsonian Books, 2015), 58.
22 Carmen Arellano, "From Inka Road to Royal Road," in *The Great Inka Road: Engineering an Empire,* eds. Ramiro Matos Mendieta and José Barreiro (National Museum of the American Indian and Smithsonian Books, 2015), 147.

Chapter 21

1 Marie Arana, *Silver, Sword, and Stone: Three Crucibles in the Latin American Story* (Simon and Schuster, 2019).
2 John H. Coatsworth, "Inequality, Institutions and Economic Growth in Latin America," *Journal of Latin American Studies* 40, no. 3 (2008): 545–569; Dácil-Tania Juif and Joerg Baten, "On the Human Capital of Inca Indios before and after the Spanish

Conquest: Was There a 'Pre-Colonial Legacy,'" *Explorations in Economic History* 50, no. 2 (2013): 227–241.
3. Javier Arellano-Yanguas, "Aggravating the Resource Curse: Decentralisation, Mining and Conflict in Peru," *Journal of Development Studies* 47.4, (2011), 617–638.
4. USAID, Climate Change Risk Profile—Peru (2017), https://www.climatelinks.org/sites/default/files/asset/document/2017_Climate%20Change%20Risk%20Profile_Peru.pdf.
5. Matthew Sayre, Tammy Stenner, and Alejandro Argumedo, "You Can't Grow Potatoes in the Sky: Building Resilience in the Face of Climate Change in the Potato Park of Cuzco, Peru," *Culture, Agriculture, Food and Environment* 39, no. 2 (2017), 105.
6. Tina Schoolmeester et al., *The Andean Glacier and Water Atlas: The Impact of Glacier Retreat on Water Resources* (UNESCO and GRID-Arendal, 2018), 9.
7. Mark Carey, *In the Shadow of Melting Glaciers: Climate Change and Andean Society* (Oxford University Press, 2010), 5–6.
8. Adam Emmer et al., "Glacier Retreat, Lakes Development and Associated Natural Hazards in Cordillera Blanca, Peru," in *Landslides in Cold Regions in the Context of Climate Change* (Springer, 2014), 231–252.
9. Emmer et al., 239, 248.
10. Gerardo Martinez et al., "Mercury Contamination in Riverine Sediments and Fish Associated with Artisanal and Small-Scale Gold Mining in Madre de Dios, Peru," *International Journal of Environmental Research and Public Health* 15, no. 8 (2018): 1584.
11. Ruth Preciado Jeronimo, Edwin Rap, and Jeroen Vos, "The Politics of Land Use Planning: Gold Mining in Cajamarca, Peru," *Land Use Policy* 49 (2015): 104–117.
12. Maritza Paredes, "The Glocalization of Mining Conflict: Cases from Peru," *Extractive Industries and Society* 3, no. 4 (2016): 1046–1057.
13. Catherine J. Allen, "Coca," in *Encyclopedia of the Incas*, eds. Gary Urton and Adriana von Hagen (Rowman & Littlefield, 2015): 89.
14. Dan Collyns, "'It Would Destroy It': New International Airport for Machu Picchu Sparks Outrage," *Guardian*, May 15, 2019, https://www.theguardian.com/cities/2019/may/15/archaeologists-outraged-over-plans-for-machu-picchu-airport-chinchero; Douglas Broom, "Peru Is Building a New International Airport near Machu Picchu—and Archaeologists Are Worried," *World Economic Forum*, May 23, 2019, https://www.weforum.org/agenda/2019/05/peru-is-building-a-new-international-airport-near-machu-picchu-and-archaeologists-are-worried.
15. Renáta Adamcová et al., "Adobe Material of the Temple of the Sun, Pachamac, Peru: Engineering Geological Classification and Sustainability Assessment as a Challenge," *Acta Geologica Slovaca* 12, no. 2 (2020): 153–160.
16. Dan Collyns, "Squatters Issue Death Threats to Archaeologist Who Discovered Oldest City in the Americas," *Guardian*, January 3, 2021, https://www.theguardian.com/world/2021/jan/03/squatters-ancient-ruins-peru-death-threats-archeologist-caral.
17. Dan Vergano, "Mystery Surrounds Delicate Nasca Lines Threatened by Greenpeace," *National Geographic*, December 12, 2014, https://www.nationalgeographic.com/culture/article/141212-nazca-lines-greenpeace-archaeology-science.

Bibliography

Adamcová, Renáta, Magdaléna Kondrcová, Franz Ottner, and Karin Wriessnig. "Adobe Material of the Temple of the Sun, Pachamac, Peru: Engineering Geological Classification and Sustainability Assessment as a Challenge." *Acta Geologica Slovaca* 12, no. 2 (2020): 153–160.

Alaica, Aleska K. "Partial and Complete Deposits and Depictions: Social Zooarchaeology, Iconography and the Role of Animals in Late Moche Peru." *Journal of Archaeological Science: Reports* 20 (2018): 864–872.

Aldenderfer, Mark, Nathan M. Craig, Robert J. Speakman, and Rachel Popelka-Filcoff. "Four-Thousand-Year-Old Gold Artifacts from the Lake Titicaca Basin, Southern Peru." *Proceedings of the National Academy of Sciences* 105, no. 13 (2008): 5002–5005.

Allen, Catherine J. "Coca." In *Encyclopedia of the Incas*, edited by Gary Urton and Adriana von Hagen, 86–90. Rowman & Littlefield, 2015.

Allmendinger, Richard W., Robert Smalley Jr., Michael Bevis, Holly Caprio, and Benjamin Brooks. "Bending the Bolivian Orocline in Real Time." *Geology* 33, no. 11 (2005): 905–908.

Anderson, David G., and Thaddeus G. Bissett. "The Initial Colonization of North America: Sea Level Change, Shoreline Movement, and Great Migrations." In *Mobility and Ancient Society in Asia and the Americas*, edited by Michael D. Frachetti and Robert N. Spengler III, 59–88. Springer, 2015.

Andrushko, Valerie A., Michele R. Buzon, Arminda M. Gibaja, Gordon F. McEwan, Antonio Simonetti, and Robert A. Creaser. "Investigating a Child Sacrifice Event from the Inca Heartland." *Journal of Archaeological Science* 38, no. 2 (2011): 323–333.

Arana, Marie. *Silver, Sword, and Stone: Three Crucibles in the Latin American Story*. Simon and Schuster, 2019.

Arellano, Carmen. "From Inka Road to Royal Road." In *The Great Inka Road: Engineering an Empire*, edited by Ramiro Matos Mendieta and José Barreiro, 141–148. National Museum of the American Indian/Smithsonian Books, 2015.

Arellano-Yanguas, Javier. "Aggravating the Resource Curse: Decentralisation, Mining and Conflict in Peru." *Journal of Development Studies* 47, no. 4 (2011): 617–638.

Arkush, Elizabeth. "Fortifications." In *Encyclopedia of the Incas*, edited by Gary Urton and Adriana von Hagen, 145–149. Rowman & Littlefield, 2015.

Arkush, Elizabeth, and Charles Stanish. "Interpreting Conflict in the Ancient Andes: Implications for the Archaeology of Warfare." *Current Anthropology* 46, no. 1 (2005): 3–28.

Bakewell, Peter J. *Miners of the Red Mountain: Indian Labor in Potosí, 1545–1650*. University of New Mexico Press, 1984.

Bakewell, Peter, and Jacqueline Holler. *A History of Latin America to 1825*. Vol. 8. John Wiley & Sons, 2009.

Bariola, Juan, Julio Vargas, Daniel Torrealva, and G. Ottazi. "Earthquake-Resistant Provision for Adobe Construction in Peru." *Proceedings: Ninth World Conference on Earthquake Engineering, 1988, Tokyo-Kyoto, Japan*, (1989): 1153–1157.

Bauer, Brian S. *Ancient Cuzco: Heartland of the Inca*. University of Texas Press, 2010.

Bauer, Brian S. "Suspension Bridges of the Inca Empire." In *Andean Archaeology III: North and South*, edited by William Isbell and Helaine Silverman, 468–493. Springer, 2006.

Bayer, Angela M., Heather E. Danysh, Mijail Garvich, Guillermo Gonzálvez, William Checkley, María Alvarez, and Robert H. Gilman. "The 1997–1998 El Niño as an Unforgettable Phenomenon in Northern Peru: A Qualitative Study." *Disasters* 38, no. 2 (2014): 351–374.

Bedoya, Claudia A., Susanne Dreisigacker, Sarah Hearne, Jorge Franco, Celine Mir, Boddupalli M. Prasanna, Suketoshi Taba, Alain Charcosset, and Marilyn L. Warburton. "Genetic Diversity and Population Structure of Native Maize Populations in Latin America and the Caribbean." *PloS one* 12, no. 4 (2017): e0173488.

Bengtsson, Lisbet. *Prehistoric Stonework in the Peruvian Andes: A Case Study at Ollantaytambo*. GOTARC Series B, No. 10; Etnologiska Studier 44. Department of Archaeology, Göteborg University, Sweden, 2000.

Bennett, Matthew R., David Bustos, Jeffrey S. Pigati, Kathleen B. Springer, Thomas M. Urban, Vance T. Holliday, Sally C. Reynolds et al. "Evidence of Humans in North America during the Last Glacial Maximum." *Science* 373, no. 6562 (2021): 1528–1531.

Benson, Elizabeth P., and Anita G. Cook, eds. *Ritual Sacrifice in Ancient Peru*. University of Texas Press, 2001.

Bigazzi, Giulio, Mauro Coltelli, N. J. C. Hadler, A. M. Osorio Araya, Massimo Oddone, and Ernesto Salazar. "Obsidian-Bearing Lava Flows and Pre-Columbian Artifacts from the Ecuadorian Andes: First New Multidisciplinary Data." *Journal of South American Earth Sciences* 6, no. 1–2 (1992): 21–32.

Binford, Michael W., Alan L. Kolata, Mark Brenner, John W. Janusek, Matthew T. Seddon, Mark Abbott, and Jason H. Curtis. "Climate Variation and the Rise and Fall of an Andean Civilization." *Quaternary Research* 47, no. 2 (1997): 235–248.

Bletery, Quentin, Amanda M. Thomas, Alan W. Rempel, Leif Karlstrom, Anthony Sladen, and Louis De Barros. "Mega-Earthquakes Rupture Flat Megathrusts." *Science* 354, no. 6315 (2016): 1027–1031.

Bourget, Steve. *Sacrifice, Violence, and Ideology Among the Moche: The Rise of Social Complexity in Ancient Peru*. University of Texas Press, 2021.

Braje, Todd J., Tom D. Dillehay, Jon M. Erlandson, Richard G. Klein, and Torben C. Rick. "Finding the First Americans." *Science* 358, no. 6363 (2017): 592–594.

Bray, Tamara L. "Ceramics." In *Encyclopedia of the Incas*, edited by Gary Urton and Adriana von Hagen, 70–73. Rowman & Littlefield, 2015.

Bray, Tamara L. "Feasts, State-Sponsored." In *Encyclopedia of the Incas*, edited by Gary Urton and Adriana von Hagen, 138–140. Rowman & Littlefield, 2015.

Brooks, William E., Luisa Vetter Parodi, Armando V. Farfán, and David Dykstra. "Lead in Ancient Peru: The Curamba Smelter and Lead Sling Bullets." *Journal of the Minerals, Metals and Materials Society* 64, no. 11 (2012): 1356–1364.

Brooks, William E., Victor Piminchumo, Héctor Suárez, John C. Jackson, and John P. McGeehin. "Mineral Pigments at Huaca Tacaynamo (Chan Chan, Peru)." *Bulletin de l'Institut Français d'Études Andines* 37, no. 3(2008): 441–450.

Brooks, William E., Gabriela Schwörbel, and Luis Enrique Castillo. "Amalgamation and Small-Scale Gold Mining in the Ancient Andes." In *Mining and Quarrying in the Ancient Andes: Sociopolitical, Economic and Symbolic Dimensions,* edited by Nicholas Tripcevich and Kevin Vaughn, 213–229. Springer, 2013.

Broom, Douglas. "Peru Is Building a New International Airport Near Machu Picchu—and Archaeologists Are Worried." *World Economic Forum*, May 23, 2019. https://www.weforum.org/agenda/2019/05/peru-is-building-a-new-international-airport-near-machu-picchu-and-archaeologists-are-worried.

Burger, Richard L. "The Chavin Horizon: Stylistic Chimera or Socioeconomic Metamorphosis." *Latin American Horizons* (1993): 41–82.

Burger, Richard L. "The Construction of Values during the Peruvian Formative." In *The Construction of Value in the Ancient World*, Vol. 5, edited by John K. Papadopoulos and Gary Urton, 288–305. Cotsen Institute of Archeology Press, 2012.

Burger, Richard L. "Understanding the Socioeconomic Trajectory of Chavín de Huántar: A New Radiocarbon Sequence and Its Wider Implications." *Latin American Antiquity* 30, no. 2 (2019): 373–392.

Burger, Richard L., and Robert B. Gordon. "Early Central Andean Metalworking from Mina Perdida, Peru." *Science* 282, no. 5391 (1998): 1108–1111.

Burger, Richard L., Karen L. Mohr Chávez, and Sergio J. Chávez. "Through the Glass Darkly: Prehispanic Obsidian Procurement and Exchange in Southern Peru and Northern Bolivia." *Journal of World Prehistory* 14 (2000): 267–362.

Burger, Richard L., and Robert M. Rosenswig, eds. *Early New World Monumentality*. University Press of Florida, 2012.

Burger, Richard L., and Lucy C. Salazar. "Monumental Public Complexes and Agricultural Expansion on Peru's Central Coast during the Second Millennium BC." In *Early New World Monumentality,* edited by Richard L. Burger and Robert M. Rosenswig. University Press of Florida, (2012): 399–430.

Burger, Richard L., and Lucy Salazar-Burger. "Machu Picchu Rediscovered: The Royal Estate in the Cloud Forest." *Discovery* 24, no. 2 (1993): 20–25.

Byrne, Sam, Dula Amarasiriwardena, Basel Bandak, Luke Bartkus, Jennifer Kane, Joseph Jones, Jorge Yañez, Bernardo Arriaza, and Lorena Cornejo. "Were Chinchorros Exposed to Arsenic? Arsenic Determination in Chinchorro Mummies' Hair by Laser Ablation Inductively Coupled Plasma-Mass Spectrometry (LA-ICP-MS)." *Microchemical Journal* 94, no. 1 (2010): 28–35.

Campana, Michael G., Nelly M. Robles Garcia, and Noreen Tuross. "America's Red Gold: Multiple Lineages of Cultivated Cochineal in Mexico." *Ecology and Evolution* 5, no. 3 (2015): 607–617.

Capitanio, F. A., Claudio Faccenna, Sergio Zlotnik, and D. R. Stegman. "Subduction Dynamics and the Origin of Andean Orogeny and the Bolivian Orocline." *Nature* 480, no. 7375 (2011): 83–86.

Capriles, José M., and Juan Albarracin-Jordan. "The Earliest Human Occupations in Bolivia: A Review of the Archaeological Evidence." *Quaternary International* 301 (2013): 46–59.

Carey, Mark. *In the Shadow of Melting Glaciers: Climate Change and Andean Society*. Oxford University Press, 2010.

Castro, Victoria. "The Qhapaq Ñan and Its Landscapes." In *The Great Inka Road: Engineering an Empire,* edited by Ramiro Matos Mendieta and José Barreiro, 13–20. National Museum of the American Indian/Smithsonian Books, 2015.

Ceruti, Maria Constanza. "Frozen Mummies from Andean Mountaintop Shrines: Bioarchaeology and Ethnohistory of Inca Human Sacrifice." *BioMed Research International,* 2015: https://doi.org/10.1155/2015/439428.

Cesareo, Roberto, R. Franco Jordan, Arabel Fernandez, Angel Bustamante, J. Fabian, Sandra del Pilar Zambrano, Sorala Azeredo et al. "Analysis of the Spectacular Gold and Silver from the Moche Tomb 'Señora de Cao.'" *X-Ray Spectrometry* 45, no. 3 (2016): 138–154.

Chavez, Francisco P., Arnaud Bertrand, Renato Guevara-Carrasco, Pierre Soler, and Jorge Csirke. "The Northern Humboldt Current System: Brief History, Present Status and a View Towards the Future." *Progress in Oceanography* 79, no. 2–4 (2008): 95–105.

Chávez, Nicolasa. "Carmine and Earthly Delights—Cochineal in Cosmetics, Contemporary Craft, and the Strawberry Frappuccino." In *A Red Like No Other: How Cochineal Colored the World*, edited by Carmella Padilla and Barbara C. Anderson, 266–275. Skira Rizzoli and Museum of International Folk Art, 2015.

Chávez, Sergio J. "Agricultural Terraces as Monumental Architecture in the Titicaca Basin: Their Origins in the Yaya-Mama Religious Tradition." In *Early New World Monumentality,* edited by Richard L. Burger and Robert M. Rosenswig, 431–453. University Press of Florida, 2012.

Chepstow-Lusty, A. J., K. D. Bennett, J. Fjeldså, A. Kendall, W. Galiano, and A. Tupayachi Herrera. "Tracing 4,000 Years of Environmental History in the Cuzco Area, Peru, from the Pollen Record." *Mountain Research and Development* (1998): 159–172.

Cione, Alberto L., Eduardo P. Tonni, and Leopoldo Soibelzon. "Did Humans Cause the Late Pleistocene–Early Holocene Mammalian Extinctions in South America in a Context of Shrinking Open Areas?" In *American Megafaunal Extinctions at the End of the Pleistocene*, edited by Gary Haynes, 125–144. Springer, 2009.

Cluff, Lloyd S. "Peru Earthquake of May 31, 1970; Engineering Geology Observations." *Bulletin of the Seismological Society of America* 61, no. 3 (1971): 511–533.

Coatsworth, John H. "Inequality, Institutions and Economic Growth in Latin America." *Journal of Latin American Studies* 40, no. 3 (2008): 545–569.

Cobbing, Edwin John, and Agapito Sánchez. *Mapa Geologico del Cuadrangulo de Recuay*, scale 1:100,000. Ministerio de Energia y Minas and Instituto Geologico Minero y Metalurgico, 1996.

Cobbing, Edwin John, Agapito Sánchez, William Martínez, and Héctor Zárate. "Geología de los Cuadrángulos de Huaraz, Recuay, La Unión, Chiquián y Yanahuanca." Boletín A 76, 1996.

Collyns, Dan. "'It Would Destroy It': New International Airport for Machu Picchu Sparks Outrage." *Guardian*, May 15, 2019. https://www.theguardian.com/cities/2019/may/15/archaeologists-outraged-over-plans-for-machu-picchu-airport-chinchero.

Collyns, Dan. "Machu Picchu Ruin 'Found Earlier.'" *BBC News*, June 6, 2008. http://news.bbc.co.uk/2/hi/americas/7439397.stm.

Collyns, Dan. "Squatters Issue Death Threats to Archaeologist Who Discovered Oldest City in the Americas." *Guardian*, January 3, 2021. https://www.theguardian.com/world/2021/jan/03/squatters-ancient-ruins-peru-death-threats-archeologist-caral.

Comte, Diana, and Mario Pardo. "Reappraisal of Great Historical Earthquakes in the Northern Chile and Southern Peru Seismic Gaps." *Natural Hazards* 4, no. 1 (1991): 23–44.

Contreras, Daniel A. "Reconstructing Landscape at Chavín de Huántar, Peru: A GIS-based Approach." *Journal of Archaeological Science* 36, no. 4 (2009):1006–1017.

Contreras, Daniel A. "Sociopolitical and Geomorphologic Dynamics at Chavín de Huántar, Peru." PhD diss., Stanford University, 2007.

Contreras, Daniel A., and David K. Keefer. "Implications of the Fluvial History of the Wacheqsa River for Hydrologic Engineering and Water Use at Chavín de Huántar, Peru." *Geoarchaeology: An International Journal* 24, no. 5 (2009): 589–618.

Cook, Noble David. "Diseases, Foreign." In *Encyclopedia of the Incas*, edited by Gary Urton and Adriana von Hagen, 116–118. Rowman & Littlefield, 2015.

Cooke, Colin A., Mark B. Abbott, and Alexander P. Wolfe. "Late-Holocene Atmospheric Lead Deposition in the Peruvian and Bolivian Andes." *Holocene* 18, no. 2 (2008): 353–359.

Cooke, Colin A., Prentiss H. Balcom, Harald Biester, and Alexander P. Wolfe. "Over Three Millennia of Mercury Pollution in the Peruvian Andes." *Proceedings of the National Academy of Sciences* 106, no. 22 (2009): 8830–8834.

Cooke, Colin A., Holger Hintelmann, Jay J. Ague, Richard Burger, Harald Biester, Julian P. Sachs, and Daniel R. Engstrom. "Use and Legacy of Mercury in the Andes." *Environmental Science & Technology* 47, no. 9 (2013): 4181–4188.

Cooke, Colin A., Alexander P. Wolfe, and William O. Hobbs. "Lake-Sediment Geochemistry Reveals 1400 Years of Evolving Extractive Metallurgy at Cerro de Pasco, Peruvian Andes." *Geology* 37, no. 11 (2009): 1019–1022.

Cordani, Umberto G., Edison J. Milani, Antonio T. Filho, and Diogenes de Almeida Campos, eds. *Tectonic Evolution of South America*. 31st International Geological Congress, Rio de Janeiro, August 6–17, 2000.

Cross, Scott L., Paul A. Baker, Geoffrey O. Seltzer, Sherilyn C. Fritz, and Robert B. Dunbar. "Late Quaternary Climate and Hydrology of Tropical South America Inferred from an Isotopic and Chemical Model of Lake Titicaca, Bolivia and Peru." *Quaternary Research* 56, no. 1 (2001): 1–9.

Cummins, Thomas B. F. "A Tale of Two Cities: Cuzco, Lima, and the Construction of Colonial Representation." In *Converging Cultures: Art and Identity in Spanish America*, edited by Diane Fane, 157–170. Brooklyn Museum and Harry N. Abrams, 1996.

Cushman, Gregory T. "'The Most Valuable Birds in the World': International Conservation Science and the Revival of Peru's Guano Industry, 1909–1965." *Environmental History* 10, no. 3 (2005): 477–509.

D'Agostino, Karin, Geoffrey Seltzer, Paul Baker, Sherilyn Fritz, and Robert Dunbar. "Late Quaternary Lowstands of Lake Titicaca: Evidence from High-Resolution Seismic Data." *Palaeogeography, Palaeoclimatology, Palaeoecology* 179, no. 1–2 (2002): 97–111.

D'Altroy, Terence N. "Andean Land Use at the Cusp of History." In *Imperfect Balance: Landscape Transformation in the Precolumbian Americas*, edited by David L. Lentz, 357–390. Columbia University Press, 2000.

D'Altroy, Terence N. *The Incas*. 2nd ed. John Wiley & Sons, 2015.

D'Altroy, Terence N. "Labor Service." In *Encyclopedia of the Incas*, edited by Gary Urton and Adriana von Hagen, 177–181. Rowman & Littlefield, 2015.

Dean, Carolyn. *A Culture of Stone: Inka Perspectives on Rock*. Duke University Press, 2010.

Dean, Carolyn S. "Creating a Ruin in Colonial Cusco: Sacsahuamán and What Was Made of It." *Andean Past* 5, no. 1 (1998): 161–183.

De Feo, Vincenzo. "Ethnomedical Field Study in Northern Peruvian Andes with Particular Reference to Divination Practices." *Journal of Ethnopharmacology* 85, no. 2–3 (2003): 243–256.

De Silva, S. L., and P. W. Francis. "Potentially Active Volcanoes of Peru: Observations Using Landsat Thematic Mapper and Space Shuttle Imagery." *Bulletin of Volcanology* 52, no. 4 (1990): 286–301.

Diamond, Jared. *Guns, Germs, and Steel: The Fates of Human Societies*. W. W. Norton & Company, 1997.

Dietler, Michael. "Alcohol: Anthropological/Archaeological Perspectives." *Annual Review of Anthropology* 35 (2006): 229–249.

Dillehay, Tom D. "The Battle of Monte Verde." *Sciences* 37, no. 1 (Jan/Feb 1997): 28–33.

Dillehay, Tom D. "The Late Pleistocene Cultures of South America." *Evolutionary Anthropology: Issues, News, and Reviews* 7, no. 6 (1999): 206–216.

Dillehay, Tom D., Duccio Bonavia, Steve L. Goodbred, Mario Pino, Victor Vásquez, and Teresa Rosales Tham. "A Late Pleistocene Human Presence at Huaca Prieta, Peru, and Early Pacific Coastal Adaptations." *Quaternary Research* 77, no. 3 (2012): 418–423.

Dillehay, Tom D., Herbert H. Eling, and Jack Rossen, "Preceramic Irrigation Canals in the Peruvian Andes." *Proceedings of the National Academy of Sciences* 102, no. 47 (2005): 17241–17244.

Dillehay, Tom D., Carlos Ocampo, José Saavedra, Andre Oliveira Sawakuchi, Rodrigo M. Vega, Mario Pino, Michael B. Collins et al. "New Archaeological Evidence for an Early Human Presence at Monte Verde, Chile." *PloS One* 10, no. 11 (2015): e0141923.

Dillehay, Tom D., Carlos Ramírez, Mario Pino, Michael B. Collins, Jack Rossen, and Jimena Daniela Pino-Navarro. "Monte Verde: Seaweed, Food, Medicine, and the Peopling of South America." *Science* 320, no. 5877 (2008): 784–786.

Dufour, Elise, Nicolas Goepfert, Manon Le Neün, Gabriel Prieto, and John W. Verano. "Life History and Origin of the Camelids Provisioning a Mass Killing Sacrifice during the Chimú Period: Insight from Stable Isotopes." *Environmental Archaeology* 25, no. 3 (2020): 310–324.

Earls, John C., and Gabriela Cervantes. "Inka Cosmology in Moray: Astronomy, Agriculture, and Pilgrimage." In *The Inka Empire*, edited by Izumi Shimada, 121–148. University of Texas Press, 2021.

Elias, Scott A., Susan K. Short, and Hilary H. Birks. "Late Wisconsin Environments of the Bering Land Bridge." *Palaeogeography, Palaeoclimatology, Palaeoecology* 136, no. 1–4 (1997): 293–308.

Emmer, Adam, Vít Vilímek, Jan Klimeš, and Alejo Cochachin. "Glacier Retreat, Lakes Development and Associated Natural Hazards in Cordillera Blanca, Peru." In *Landslides in Cold Regions in the Context of Climate Change*, edited by Wei Shan, Ying Guo, Fawu Wang, Hikdeaki Marui, and Alexander Strom, 231–252. Springer, 2014.

Enfield, David B. "Evolution and Historical Perspective of the 1997–1998 El Niño-Southern Oscillation Event." *Bulletin of Marine Science* 69, no. 1 (2001): 7–25.

Ericksen, George E., Jaime Fernández Concha, and Enrique Silgado. "The Cusco, Peru, Earthquake of May 21, 1950." *Bulletin of the Seismological Society of America* 44, no. 2A (1954): 97–112.

Erickson, Clark L. "The Lake Titicaca Basin: A Precolumbian Built Landscape." In *Imperfect Balance: Landscape Transformation in the Precolumbian Americas*, edited by David L. Lentz, 311–356. Columbia University Press, 2000.

Erickson, Clark L., and Kay L. Candler. "Raised Fields and Sustainable Agriculture in the Lake Titicaca Basin of Peru." In *Fragile Lands of Latin América*, edited by John O. Browder, 231–248. Westview Press, 1989.

Erickson, David L., Bruce D. Smith, Andrew C. Clarke, Daniel H. Sandweiss, and Noreen Tuross. "An Asian Origin for a 10,000-Year-Old Domesticated Plant in the Americas." *Proceedings of the National Academy of Sciences* 102, no. 51 (2005): 18315–18320.

Erlandson, Jon M., and Todd J. Braje. "Stemmed Points, the Coastal Migration Theory, and the Peopling of the Americas." In *Mobility and Ancient Society in Asia and the Americas*, edited by Michael D. Frachetti and Robert Spengler III, 49–58. Springer, 2015.

Erlandson, Jon M., Todd J. Braje, Kristina M. Gill, and Michael H. Graham. "Ecology of the Kelp Highway: Did Marine Resources Facilitate Human Dispersal from Northeast

Asia to the Americas?" *Journal of Island and Coastal Archaeology* 10, no. 3 (2015): 392–411.

Floyd, Emily C. "Medium Study-Tears of the Sun: The Naturalistic and Anthropomorphic in Inca Metalwork." *Conversations: An Online Journal of the Center for the Study of Material and Visual Cultures of Religion, Yale University* (2016): 1–36, https://mavcor.yale.edu/sites/default/files/article_pdf/floyd_emily_medium_study.pdf.

Fonte, Steven J. Vanek, Pedro Oyarzun, Soroush Parsa, D. Carolina Quintero, Idupulapati M. Rao, and Patrick Lavelle. "Pathways to Agroecological Intensification of Soil Fertility Management by Smallholder Farmers in the Andean Highlands." *Advances in Agronomy* 116 (2012): 125–184.

Friedman, Leslie A. "The Making of Place: Myth and Memory at the site of Tiwanaku, Bolivia." In *Finding the Spirit of Place: Between the Tangible and the Intangible*. 16th International Council on Monuments and Sites General Assembly and International Symposium, Quebec, Canada (Sept 29–Oct 4, 2008): 1–10.

Frisch, Wolfgang, Martin Meschede, and Ronald C. Blakey. *Plate Tectonics: Continental Drift and Mountain Building*. Springer, 2011.

Fritz, Hermann M., Catherine M. Petroff, Patricio A. Catalán, Rodrigo Cienfuegos, Patricio Winckler, Nikos Kalligeris, Robert Weiss et al. "Field Survey of the 27 February 2010 Chile Tsunami." *Pure and Applied Geophysics* 168 (2011): 1989–2010.

Frohlich, Cliff. *Deep Earthquakes*. Cambridge University Press, 2006.

Fukuyama, Hiroshi, Masami Fujisawa, Akio Abe, Toshikazu Kabeyasawa, and Zen Shirane. "Research on Earthquake Response Reduction Properties and Its Repeatability of the Foundation Technology Used in the Sanctuaries Dating up to 5,000 Years Ago." *Journal of Japan Association for Earthquake Engineering* 16, no. 11 (2016): 11–25.

Fukuyama, Hiroshi, Masami Fujisawa, Akio Abe, Toshikazu Kabeyasawa, Zen Shirane, Taiki Saito, and Zenon Aguilar. "Shaking Table Test on Seismic Response Properties of 'Shicras,' Stones Wrapped in Vegetable Fiber Bags." *Journal of Disaster Research* 8, no. 3 (2013): 526–533.

Gade, Daniel W. "Andes, Central." In *Encyclopedia of the Incas*, edited by Gary Urton and Adriana von Hagen, 21–26. Rowman & Littlefield, 2015.

Garver, John I., M. Montario, S. E. Perry, P. W. Reiners, and Joan M. Ramage. "Uplift and Exhumation of the Northern Peruvian Andes." In *6th International Symposium on Andean Geodynamics, Extended Abstracts*, 305–307. ISAG, Barcelona, 2005.

Garver, John I., P. W. Reiners, L. J. Walker, Joan M. Ramage, and S. E. Perry. "Implications for Timing of Andean Uplift from Thermal Resetting of Radiation-Damaged Zircon in the Cordillera Huayhuash, Northern Peru." *Journal of Geology* 113, no. 2 (2005): 117–138.

Geist, Eric L., Vasily V. Titov, Diego Arcas, Fred F. Pollitz, and Susan L. Bilek. "Implications of the 26 December 2004 Sumatra-Andaman Earthquake on Tsunami Forecast and Assessment Models for Great Subduction-Zone Earthquakes." *Bulletin of the Seismological Society of America* 97, no. 1A (2007): S249–S270.

Gerbe, Marie-Christine and Jean-Claude Thouret. "Role of Magma Mixing in the Petrogenesis of Tephra Erupted during the 1990–98 Explosive Activity of Nevado Sabancaya, Southern Peru." *Bulletin of Volcanology* 66, no. 6 (2004): 541–561.

Giovanni, Melissa K., Brian K. Horton, Carmala N. Garzione, Brendan McNulty, and Marty Grove. "Extensional Basin Evolution in the Cordillera Blanca, Peru: Stratigraphic and Isotopic Records of Detachment Faulting and Orogenic Collapse in the Andean Hinterland." *Tectonics* 29, no. 6, (2010): 1–21.

Glass-Coffin, Bonnie. "Shamanism and San Pedro Through Time: Some Notes on the Archaeology, History, and Continued Use of an Entheogen in Northern Peru." *Anthropology of Consciousness* 21, no. 1 (2010): 58–82.

Goñalons, Guillermo L. Mengoni, and Hugo D. Yacobaccio. "The Domestication of South American Camelids." In *Documenting Domestication: New Genetic and Archaeological Paradigms*, edited by Melinda A. Zeder, Daniel G. Bradley, Bruce D. Smith, and Eve Emshwiller, 228–244. University of California Press, 2006.

Green, Harry W., and Heidi Houston. "The Mechanics of Deep Earthquakes." *Annual Review of Earth and Planetary Sciences* 23, no. 1 (1995): 169–213.

Gutscher, Marc-André, Wim Spakman, Harmen Bijwaard, and E. Robert Engdahl. "Geodynamics of Flat Subduction: Seismicity and Tomographic Constraints from the Andean Margin." *Tectonics* 19, no. 5 (2000): 814–833.

Haas, Jonathan, and Winifred Creamer. "Why Do People Build Monuments? Late Archaic Platform Mounds in the Norte Chico." In *Early New World Monumentality*, edited by Richard L. Burger and Robert M. Rosenswig, 289–312. University Press of Florida, 2012.

Haas, Jonathan, Winifred Creamer, and Alvaro Ruiz. "Power and the Emergence of Complex Polities in the Peruvian Preceramic." *Archeological Papers of the American Anthropological Association* 14, no. 1 (2004): 37–52.

Haschke, Michael, Andreas Günther, Daniel Melnick, Helmut Echtler, Klaus-Joachim Reutter, Ekkehard Scheuber, and Onno Oncken. "Central and Southern Andean Tectonic Evolution Inferred from Arc Magmatism." In *The Andes: Active Subduction Orogeny*, edited by Onno Oncken, Guillermo Chong, Gerhard Franz, Peter Giese, Hans-Jürgen Götze, Victor A. Ramos, Manfred R. Strecker, and Peter Wigger, 337–353. Springer, 2006.

Hastorf, Christine A. "Foodstuffs, Domesticated." In *Encyclopedia of the Incas*, edited by Gary Urton and Adriana von Hagen, 142–145. Rowman & Littlefield, 2015.

Haynes, Gary. *American Megafaunal Extinctions at the End of the Pleistocene*. Springer, 2009.

Haywood, John. *The Penguin Historical Atlas of Ancient Civilizations*. Penguin Books, 2005.

Hörz, Gerhard, and Monika Kallfass. "The Treasure of Gold and Silver Artifacts from the Royal Tombs of Sipán, Peru—A Study on the Moche Metalworking Techniques." *Materials Characterization* 45, no. 4–5 (2000): 391–419.

Jakobsson, Martin, Christof Pearce, Thomas M. Cronin, Jan Backman, Leif G. Anderson, Natalia Barrientos, Göran Björk et al. "Post-Glacial Flooding of the Bering Land Bridge Dated to 11 cal ka BP Based on New Geophysical and Sediment Records." *Climate of the Past* 13, no. 8 (2017): 991–1005.

Janusek, John Wayne. *Ancient Tiwanaku*. Vol. 9. Cambridge University Press, 2008.

Janusek, John Wayne, Patrick Ryan Williams, Mark Golitko, and Carlos Lémuz Aguirre. "Building Taypikala: Telluric Transformations in the Lithic Production of Tiwanaku." In *Mining and Quarrying in the Ancient Andes: Sociopolitical, Economic and Symbolic Dimensions,* edited by Nicholas Tripcevich and Kevin Vaughn, 65–97. Springer, 2013.

Jeronimo, Ruth Preciado, Edwin Rap, and Jeroen Vos. "The Politics of Land Use Planning: Gold Mining in Cajamarca, Peru." *Land Use Policy* 49 (2015): 104–117.

Johnson, A. B., Jr., and B. Francis. *Durability of Metals from Archaeological Objects, Metal Meteorites, and Native Metals.* Report No. PNL-3198. Prepared for US Department of Energy by Battelle Pacific Northwest Labs, 1980. https://doi.org/10.2171/5406419.

Jolie, Edward A., Thomas F. Lynch, Phil R. Geib, and James M. Adovasio. "Cordage, Textiles, and the Late Pleistocene Peopling of the Andes." *Current Anthropology* 52, no. 2 (2011): 285–296.

Jordan, Teresa Eileen, Peter L. Nester, N. Blanco, G. D. Hoke, F. Dávila, and A. J. Tomlinson. "Uplift of the Altiplano-Puna Plateau: A View from the West." *Tectonics* 29, no. 5 (2010): 1–31.

Juif, Dácil-Tania, and Joerg Baten. "On the Human Capital of Inca Indios before and after the Spanish Conquest: Was There a 'Pre-Colonial Legacy'?" *Explorations in Economic History* 50, no. 2 (2013): 227–241.

Jurina, Lorenzo, and Monica Righetti. *Traditional Building in Peru.* ICOMOS International Wood Committee, 2001.

Kellett, Lucas C., Mark Golitko, and Brian S. Bauer. "A Provenance Study of Archaeological Obsidian from the Andahuaylas Region of Southern Peru." *Journal of Archaeological Science* 40, no. 4 (2013): 1890–1902.

Kembel, Sylvia Rodriguez. "The Architecture at the Monumental Center of Chavín de Huántar: Sequence, Transformations, and Chronology." In *Chavín: Art, Architecture, and Culture,* edited by Jeffery Quilter and William J. Conklin, 35–81. Cotsen Institute of Archaeology Press, 2008.

Kembel, Silvia Rodriguez, and Herbert Haas. "Radiocarbon Dates from the Monumental Architecture at Chavín de Huántar, Perú." *Journal of Archaeological Method and Theory* 22 (2015): 345–427.

Kembel, Sylvia Rodriguez, and John W. Rick. "Building Authority at Chavín de Huántar: Models of Social Organization and Development in the Initial Period and Early Horizon." In *Andean Archaeology,* edited by Helaine Silverman, 51–76. Blackwell Publishers, 2004.

King, Heidi. *Peruvian Featherworks: Art of the Precolumbian Era.* Metropolitan Museum of Art and Yale University Press, 2012.

Kious, W. Jacquelyne, and Robert I. Tilling. *This Dynamic Earth: The Story of Plate Tectonics.* Diane Publishing/U.S. Geological Survey, 1996.

Kistler, Logan, Álvaro Montenegro, Bruce D. Smith, John A. Gifford, Richard E. Green, Lee A. Newsom, and Beth Shapiro. "Transoceanic Drift and the Domestication of African Bottle Gourds in the Americas." *Proceedings of the National Academy of Sciences* 111, no. 8 (2014): 2937–2941.

Koch, Paul L., and Anthony D. Barnosky. "Late Quaternary Extinctions: State of the Debate." *Annual Review of Ecology, Evolution, and Systematics* 37 (2006): 215–250.

Kolata, Alan L. "Mimesis and Monumentalism in Native Andean Cities." *RES: Anthropology and Aesthetics* 29, no. 1 (1996): 223–236.

Kolata, Alan L. "The Urban Concept of Chan Chan." In *The Northern Dynasties: Kingship and Statecraft in Chimor*, edited by Michael E. Moseley and Alana Cordy-Collins, 107–109. Dumbarton Oaks Research Library and Collection, 1990.

Kovach, Robert L. *Early Earthquakes of the Americas*. Cambridge University Press, 2004.

Lamb, Simon. "Active Deformation in the Bolivian Andes, South America." *Journal of Geophysical Research: Solid Earth* 105, no. B11 (2000): 25627–25653.

Lamb, Simon. *Devil in the Mountain: A Search for the Origin of the Andes*. Princeton University Press, 2004.

Lane, Kevin. "Water Technology in the Andes." In *Encyclopaedia of the History of Science, Technology, and Medicine in Non-Western Cultures*, edited by Helaine Selin, 1–24. Springer, 2014.

Lasaponara, Rosa, Nicola Masini, Enzo Rizzo, and Giuseppe Orefici. "New Discoveries in the Piramide Naranjada in Cahuachi (Peru) Using Satellite, Ground Probing Radar and Magnetic Investigations." *Journal of Archaeological Science* 38, no. 9 (2011): 2031–2039.

Lechtman, Heather. "Arsenic Bronze: Dirty Copper or Chosen Alloy? A View from the Americas." *Journal of Field Archaeology* 23, no. 4 (1996): 477–514.

Lechtman, Heather. "Metallurgy." In *Encyclopedia of the Incas*, edited by Gary Urton and Adriana von Hagen, 188–191. Rowman & Littlefield, 2015.

Lechtman, Heather. "Technologies of Power: The Andean Case." In *Configurations of Power—Holistic Anthropology in Theory and Practice*, edited by J. S. Henderson, and P. J. Netherly, 244–280. Cornell University Press, 1994.

Leier, Andrew, Nadine McQuarrie, Carmala Garzione, and John Eiler. "Stable Isotope Evidence for Multiple Pulses of Rapid Surface Uplift in the Central Andes, Bolivia." *Earth and Planetary Science Letters* 371 (2013): 49–58.

Lemenkova, Polina. "Geomorphological Modelling and Mapping of the Peru-Chile Trench by GMT." *Polish Cartographical Review* 51, no. 4 (2019): 181–194.

Leonard, Jennifer A., Robert K. Wayne, Jane Wheeler, Raúl Valadez, Sonia Guillén, and Carles Vila. "Ancient DNA Evidence for Old World Origin of New World Dogs." *Science* 298, no. 5598 (2002): 1613–1616.

Lima-Ribeiro, Matheus Souza, David Nogués-Bravo, Levi Carina Terribile, Persaram Batra, and José Alexandre Felizola Diniz-Filho. "Climate and Humans Set the Place and Time of Proboscidean Extinction in Late Quaternary of South America." *Palaeogeography, Palaeoclimatology, Palaeoecology* 392 (2013): 546–556.

Lindskoug, Henrik B. "Fire Events, Violence and Abandonment Scenarios in the Ancient Andes: The Final Stage of the Aguada Culture in the Ambato Valley, Northwest Argentina." *Journal of World Prehistory* 29, no. 2 (2016): 155–214.

Liu, Xinru. *The Silk Road in World History*. Oxford University Press, 2010.

Llamas, Bastien, Lars Fehren-Schmitz, Guido Valverde, Julien Soubrier, Swapan Mallick, Nadin Rohland, Susanne Nordenfelt et al. "Ancient Mitochondrial DNA Provides High-Resolution Time Scale of the Peopling of the Americas." *Science Advances* 2, no. 4 (2016): e1501385.

Luteyn, James L., and Steven P. Churchill. "Vegetation of the Tropical Andes: An Overview." In *Imperfect Balance: Landscape Transformation in the Precolumbian Americas*, edited by David L. Lentz, 281–310. Columbia University Press, 2000.

MacQuarrie, Kim. *The Last Days of the Incas*. Simon and Schuster, 2008.

Makowski, Krzysztof. "Religion." In *Encyclopedia of the Incas*, edited by Gary Urton and Adriana von Hagen, 237–242. Rowman & Littlefield, 2015.

Malpass, Michael A. *Ancient People of the Andes*. Cornell University Press, 2016.

Malpass, Michael A. "Farming." In *Encyclopedia of the Incas,* edited by Gary Urton and Adriana von Hagen, 136–138. Rowman & Littlefield, 2015.

Malpass, Michael A. "Irrigation." In *Encyclopedia of the Incas*, edited by Gary Urton and Adriana von Hagen, 166–167. Rowman & Littlefield, 2015.

Malpass, Michael A. "Terracing." In *Encyclopedia of the Incas*, edited by Gary Urton and Adriana von Hagen, 271–274. Rowman & Littlefield, 2015.

Malpass, Michael A. "Village Life." In *Encyclopedia of the Incas*, edited by Gary Urton and Adriana von Hagen, 284–286. Rowman & Littlefield, 2015.

Mann, Charles C. *1491: New Revelations of the Americas before Columbus*. 2nd ed. Vintage Books, 2011.

Marichal, Carlos. "The Cochineal Commodity Chain: Mexican Cochineal and the Rise of Global Trade." In *A Red Like No Other: How Cochineal Colored the World,* edited by Carmella Padilla and Barbara C. Anderson, 54–67. Skira Rizzoli and Museum of International Folk Art, 2015.

Martinez, Gerardo, Stephen A. McCord, Charles T. Driscoll, Svetoslava Todorova, Steven Wu, Julio F. Araújo, Claudia M. Vega, and Luis E. Fernandez. "Mercury Contamination in Riverine Sediments and Fish Associated with Artisanal and Small-Scale Gold Mining in Madre de Dios, Peru." *International Journal of Environmental Research and Public Health* 15, no. 8 (2018): 1584, https://doi.org/10.3390/ijerph15081584.

Martinod, Joseph, Laurent Husson, Pierrick Roperch, Benjamin Guillaume, and Nicolas Espurt. "Horizontal Subduction Zones, Convergence Velocity and the Building of the Andes." *Earth and Planetary Science Letters* 299, no. 3–4 (2010): 299–322.

Masini, Nicola, Rosa Lasaponara, Enzo Rizzo, and Giuseppe Orefici. "Integrated Remote Sensing Approach in Cahuachi (Peru): Studies and Results of the ITACA Mission (2007–2010)." In *Satellite Remote Sensing: A New Tool for Archaeology,* Vol. 16, edited by Rosa Lasaponara and Nicola Masini, 307–344. Springer, 2012.

Matsumoto, Yuichi, and Yuri Palomino. "Early Horizon Gold Metallurgy from Campanayuq Rumi in the Peruvian South-Central Highlands," *Ñawpa Pacha* 32, no. 1 (2012): 115–130.

Mauricio, Ana Cecilia, Rolf Grieseler, Andrew R. Heller, Alice R. Kelley, Francisco Rumiche, Daniel H. Sandweiss, and Willem Viveen. "The Earliest Adobe Monumental

Architecture in the Americas." *Proceedings of the National Academy of Sciences* 118, no. 48 (2021): e2102941118.

McClelland, Donna, Donald McClelland, and Christopher B. Donnan. *Moche Fineline Painting from San José de Moro*. Cotsen Institute of Archaeology Press, 2007.

Meinekat, Sarah Ann, Christopher E. Miller, and Kurt Rademaker. "A Site Formation Model for Cuncaicha Rock Shelter: Depositional and Postdepositional Processes at the High-Altitude Keysite in the Peruvian Andes." *Geoarchaeology* 37, no. 2 (2022): 304–331.

Mendieta, Ramiro Matos. "The Living Road." In *The Great Inka Road: Engineering an Empire,* edited by Ramiro Matos Mendieta and José Barreiro, 153–163. National Museum of the American Indian/Smithsonian Books, 2015.

Meyer, Christian A., Daniel Marty, and Matteo Belvedere. "Titanosaur Trackways from the Late Cretaceous El Molino Formation of Bolivia (Cal Orck'o, Sucre)." *Annales Societatis Geologorum Poloniae* 88, no. 2 (2018): 223–241.

Millaire, Jean-François, Gabriel Prieto, Flannery Surette, Elsa M. Redmond, and Charles S. Spencer. "Statecraft and Expansionary Dynamics: A Virú Outpost at Huaca Prieta, Chicama Valley, Peru." *Proceedings of the National Academy of Sciences* 113, no. 41 (2016): E6020.

Mogollon-Pasapera, Elin, Laszlo Otvos Jr., Antonio Giordano, and Marco Cassone. "Bartonella: Emerging Pathogen or Emerging Awareness?" *International Journal of Infectious Diseases* 13, no. 1 (2009): 3–8.

Moore, Jason W. "This Lofty Mountain of Silver Could Conquer the Whole World: Potosí and the Political Ecology of Underdevelopment, 1545–1800." *Journal of Philosophical Economics* 4, no. 1 (2010): 58–103.

Moore, Lorna G., Susan Niermeyer, and Stacy Zamudio. "Human Adaptation to High Altitude: Regional and Life-Cycle Perspectives." *American Journal of Physical Anthropology* 107, no. S27 (1998): 25–64.

Moores, Eldridge M., and Twiss, Robert J. *Tectonics*. W. H. Freeman, 1995.

Moreno, Karen, Silvina De Valais, Nicolás Blanco, Andrew J. Tomlinson, Javier Jacay, and Jorge O. Calvo. "Large Theropod Dinosaur Footprint Associations in Western Gondwana: Behavioural and Palaeogeographic Implications." *Acta Palaeontologica Polonica* 57, no. 1 (2012): 73–83.

Moseley, Michael E. *The Incas and Their Ancestors: The Archaeology of Peru*. Rev. ed. Thames & Hudson, 2001.

Moseley, Michael E., and David K. Keefer. "Deadly Deluges in the Southern Desert: Modern and Ancient El Niños in the Osmore Region of Peru." In *El Niño, Catastrophism, and Culture Change in Ancient America,* edited by Daniel H. Sandweiss and Jeffery Quilter, 129–144. Dumbarton Oaks Research Library and Collection, 2008.

Nair, Stella. "Architecture." In *Encyclopedia of the Incas*, edited by Gary Urton and Adriana von Hagen, 37–41. Rowman & Littlefield, 2015.

Nair, Stella. "Estates, Royal." In *Encyclopedia of the Incas*, edited by Gary Urton and Adriana von Hagen, 127–130. Rowman & Littlefield, 2015.

Neumann, Katharina, Alexandre Chevalier, and Luc Vrydaghs. "Phytoliths in Archaeology: Recent Advances." *Vegetation History and Archaeobotany* 26, no. 1 (2017): 1–3.

Núñez, Lautaro, Isabel Cartajena, Carlos Carrasco, Patricio López Mendoza, Patricio de Souza, Francisco Rivera, Boris Santander, and Rodrigo Loyola. "The Temple of Tulán-54: Early Formative Ceremonial Architecture in the Atacama Desert." *Antiquity* 91, no. 358 (2017): 901–915.

Ochsendorf, John. "Spanning the Andes." In *The Great Inka Road: Engineering an Empire*, edited by Ramiro Matos Mendieta and José Barreiro, 51–60. National Museum of the American Indian/Smithsonian Books, 2015.

Ogburn, Dennis. "Power in Stone: The Long-Distance Movement of Building Blocks in the Inca Empire." *Ethnohistory* 51, no. 1 (2004): 101–135.

Okal, Emile A., José C. Borrero, and Costas E. Synolakis. "Evaluation of Tsunami Risk from Regional Earthquakes at Pisco, Peru." *Bulletin of the Seismological Society of America* 96, no. 5 (2006): 1634–1648.

Oncken, Onno, David Hindle, Jonas Kley, Kirsten Elger, Pia Victor, and Kerstin Schemmann. "Deformation of the Central Andean Upper Plate System—Facts, Fiction, and Constraints for Plateau Models." In *The Andes: Active Subduction Orogeny*, edited by Onno Oncken, Guillermo Chong, Gerhard Franz, Peter Giese, Hans-Jürgen Götze, Victor A. Ramos, Manfred R. Strecker, and Peter Wigger, 3–27. Springer, 2006.

Orson, Diane. "Yale Returns Machu Picchu Artifacts to Peru." *All Things Considered*, NPR, Dec 15, 2010. https://www.npr.org/2010/12/15/132083890/yale-returns-machu-picchu-artifacts-to-peru.

Oyarzún, Jorge. "Andean Metallogenesis: A Synoptical Review and Interpretation." In *Tectonic Evolution of South America*, edited by Umberto G. Cordani, Edison J. Milani, Antonio T. Filho, and Diogenes de Almeida Campos, 725–753. 31st International Congress, Rio de Janeiro, August 6–17, 2000.

Pacini, Deborah, and Christine Franquemont, eds. *Coca and Cocaine: Effects on People and Policy in Latin America*. Cultural Survival Report No. 23. Cultural Survival and Latin American Studies Program, Cornell University, 1986.

Padilla, Carmella, and Barbara C. Anderson, eds. *A Red Like No Other: How Cochineal Colored the World: An Epic Story of Art, Culture, Science, and Trade*. Skira Rizzoli and Museum of International Folk Art, Santa Fe, New Mexico, 2015.

Paduano, Gina M., Mark B. Bush, Paul A. Baker, Sherilyn C. Fritz, and Geoffrey O. Seltzer. "A Vegetation and Fire History of Lake Titicaca since the Last Glacial Maximum." *Palaeogeography, Palaeoclimatology, Palaeoecology* 194, no. 1–3 (2003): 259–279.

Paredes, Maritza. "The Glocalization of Mining Conflict: Cases from Peru." *Extractive Industries and Society* 3, no. 4 (2016): 1046–1057.

Peixotto, Ernest C. *Pacific Shores from Panama*. Charles Scribner's Sons, 1913.

Perri, Angela R., Tatiana R. Feuerborn, Laurent A.F. Frantz, Greger Larson, Ripan S. Malhi, David J. Meltzer, and Kelsey E. Witt. "Dog Domestication and the Dual Dispersal of

People and Dogs into the Americas." *Proceedings of the National Academy of Sciences* 118, no. 6 (2021): e2010083118.

Petersen, Georg. *Mining and Metallurgy in Ancient Perú.* Translated by William E. Brooks. Special Paper 467. Geological Society of America, 2010.

Pfiffner, O. Adrian, and Laura Gonzalez. "Mesozoic-Cenozoic Evolution of the Western Margin of South America: Case Study of the Peruvian Andes." *Geosciences* 3, no. 2 (2013): 262–310.

Phipps, Elena. "Shades of Red: Color and Culture in Andean Textiles." In *A Red Like No Other: How Cochineal Colored the World,* edited by Carmella Padilla and Barbara C. Anderson, 106–117. Skira Rizzoli and Museum of International Folk Art, 2015.

Phipps, Elena, and Nobuko Shibayama. "Tracing Cochineal through the Collection of the Metropolitan Museum." *Textile Society of America Symposium Proceedings* 44 (2010): 1–10.

Pickersgill, Barbara. "Domestication of Plants in the Americas: Insights from Mendelian and Molecular Genetics." *Annals of Botany* 100, no. 5 (2007): 925–940.

Pigati, Jeffrey S., Kathleen B. Springer, Jeffrey S. Honke, David Wahl, Marie R. Champagne, Susan R. H. Zimmerman, Harrison J. Gray, et al. "Independent Age Estimates Resolve the Controversy of Ancient Human Footprints at White Sands." *Science* 382, no. 6666 (2023), 73–75.

Pillsbury, Joanne. "The Thorny Oyster and the Origins of Empire: Implications of Recently Uncovered *Spondylus* Imagery from Chan Chan, Peru." *Latin American Antiquity* 7, no. 4 (1996): 313–340.

Plafker, George, George E. Ericksen, and Jaime F. Concha. "Geological Aspects of the May 31, 1970, Perú Earthquake." *Bulletin of the Seismological Society of America,* 61, no. 3 (1971): 543–578.

Plummer, Charles C., and Diane H. Carlson. *Physical Geology.* 12th ed. Sacramento State University and McGraw-Hill Higher Education, 2008.

Pozorski, Thomas, and Shelia Pozorski. "Preceramic and Initial Period Monumentality within the Casma Valley of Peru." In *Early New World Monumentality,* edited by Richard L. Burger and Robert M. Rosenswig, 364–398. University Press of Florida, 2012.

Prieto, Gabriel, John W. Verano, Nicolas Goepfert, Douglas Kennett, Jeffrey Quilter, Steven LeBlanc, Lars Fehren-Schmitz et al. "A Mass Sacrifice of Children and Camelids at the Huanchaquito-Las Llamas Site, Moche Valley, Peru." *PLoS One* 14, no. 3 (2019): e0211691.

Prinz, Martin, George E. Harlow, and Joseph Peters, eds. *Simon and Schuster's Guide to Rocks and Minerals.* Simon and Schuster, 1978.

Protzen, Jean-Pierre. "Quarrying and Stonecutting." In *Encyclopedia of the Incas*, edited by Gary Urton and Adriana von Hagen, 225–230. Rowman & Littlefield, 2015.

Proulx, Donald A. "Nasca Puquios and Aqueducts." University of Massachusetts. https://people.umass.edu/proulx/online_pubs/Zurich_Puquios_revised_small.pdf. First published in German in *Nasca: Geheimnisvolle Zeichen im Alten Peru,* edited by Judith Rickenbach, 89–96. Museum Rietberg Zürich, 1999.

Quilter, Jeffery. "Architecture and Chronology at El Paraiso, Peru." *Journal of Field Archaeology* 12, no. 3 (1985): 294–296.
Rademaker, Kurt, Gregory Hodgins, Katherine Moore, Sonia Zarrillo, Christopher Miller, Gordon R. M. Bromley, Peter Leach, David A. Reid, Willy Yépez Álvarez, and Daniel H. Sandweiss. "Paleoindian Settlement of the High-Altitude Peruvian Andes." *Science* 346, no. 6208 (2014): 466–469.
Ramos, Victor A. "Plate Tectonic Setting of the Andean Cordillera." *Episodes Journal of International Geoscience* 22, no. 3 (1999): 183–190.
Ramos, Victor A., and A. Aleman. "Tectonic Evolution of the Andes." In *Tectonic Evolution of South America*, edited by Umberto G. Cordani, Edison J. Milani, Antonio Thomaz Filho, and Diogenes de Almeida Campos, 453–480. 31st International Geological Congress, Rio de Janeiro, 2000.
Ramos, Victor A., and Andrés Folguera. "Andean Flat-Slab Subduction through Time." *Geological Society, London, Special Publications* 327, no. 1 (2009): 31–54.
Reinhard, Johan, and Constanza Ceruti. "Sacred Mountains, Ceremonial Sites, and Human Sacrifice among the Incas." *Archaeoastronomy* 19 (2005): 1–43.
Rhea, Susan, Gavin Hayes, Antonio Villaseñor, Kevin P. Furlong, Arthur C. Tarr, and Harley Benz. *Seismicity of the Earth 1900–2007, Nazca Plate and South America*. Abstract. Open-File Report 2010-1083-E. U.S. Geological Survey, 2010. https://pubs.usgs.gov/publication/ofr20101083E.
Rick, John W. "The Evolution of Authority and Power at Chavín de Huántar, Peru." *Archeological Papers of the American Anthropological Association* 14, no. 1 (2004): 71–89.
Robins, Nicholas A. *Mercury, Mining, and Empire: The Human and Ecological Cost of Colonial Silver Mining in the Andes*. Indiana University Press, 2011.
Robins, Nicholas A., Nicole Hagan, Susan Halabi, Heileen Hsu-Kim, Ruben Dario Espinoza Gonzales, Mark Morris, George Woodall et al. "Estimations of Historical Atmospheric Mercury Concentrations from Mercury Refining and Present-Day Soil Concentrations of Total Mercury in Huancavelica, Peru." *Science of the Total Environment* 426 (2012): 146–154.
Rodbell, Donald T., Geoffrey O. Seltzer, David M. Anderson, Mark B. Abbott, David B. Enfield, and Jeremy H. Newman. "An ~15,000-year Record of El Niño-Driven Alluviation in Southwestern Ecuador." *Science* 283, no. 5401 (1999): 516–520.
Roscoe, Paul. "Catastrophe and the Emergence of Political Complexity: A Social Anthropological Model." In *El Nino, Catastrophism, and Culture Change in Ancient America*, edited by Daniel S. Sandweiss, and Jeffrey Quilter, 59–75. Dumbarton Oaks Research Library and Collection, 2008.
Rosenbaum, Gideon, David Giles, Mark Saxon, Peter G. Betts, Roberto F. Weinberg, and Cecile Duboz. "Subduction of the Nazca Ridge and the Inca Plateau: Insights into the Formation of Ore Deposits in Peru." *Earth and Planetary Science Letters* 239, no. 1–2 (2005): 18–32.
Salazar, Diego, César Borie, and Camila Oñate. "Mining, Commensal Politics, and Ritual under Inca Rule in Atacama, Northern Chile." In *Mining and Quarrying*

in the Ancient Andes: Sociopolitical, Economic and Symbolic Dimensions, edited by Nicholas Tripcevich and Kevin Vaughn, 253–274. Springer, 2013.

Salazar, Diego, Donald Jackson, Jean Louis Guendon, Hernán Salinas, Diego Morata, Valentina Figueroa, Germán Manríquez, and Victoria Castro. "Early Evidence (ca. 12,000 BP) for Iron Oxide Mining on the Pacific Coast of South America." Current Anthropology 52, no. 3 (2011): 463–475.

Salvador-Reyes, Rebeca, and Maria Teresa Pedrosa Silva Clerici. "Peruvian Andean Maize: General Characteristics, Nutritional Properties, Bioactive Compounds, and Culinary Uses." Food Research International 130 (2020): 108934.

Sandor, Jonathan A., and Neal S. Eash. "Ancient Agricultural Soils in the Andes of Southern Peru." Soil Science Society of America Journal 59, no. 1 (1995): 177–178.

Sandweiss, Daniel H. Collaborative Research: Molluscan Radiocarbon as a Proxy for Upwelling in Holocene Peru. Grant Reports 349. University of Maine Office of Research and Sponsored Programs, 2011.

Sandweiss, Daniel H. "Early Fishing and Inland Monuments: Challenging the Maritime Foundations of Andean Civilization." In Andean Civilization: A Tribute to Michael E. Moseley, edited by Joyce Marcus and Patrick Ryan Williams, Monograph 63, 39–54. Cotsen Institute of Archaeology Press, 2009.

Sandweiss, Daniel H., Kirk A. Maasch, C. Fred T. Andrus, Elizabeth J. Reitz, James B. Richardson III, Melanie Riedinger-Whitmore, and Harold B. Rollins. "Mid-Holocene Climate and Culture Change in Coastal Peru." Climate Change and Cultural Dynamics (2007): 25–50.

Sandweiss, Daniel H., Kirk A. Maasch, Richard L. Burger, James B. Richardson III, Harold B. Rollins, and Amy Clement. "Variation in Holocene El Niño Frequencies: Climate Records and Cultural Consequences in Ancient Peru." Geology 29, no. 7 (2001): 603–606.

Sandweiss, Daniel H., Heather McInnis, Richard L. Burger, Asunción Cano, Bernardino Ojeda, Rolando Paredes, María del Carmen Sandweiss, and Michael D. Glascock. "Quebrada Jaguay: Early South American Maritime Adaptations." Science 281, no. 5384 (1998): 1830–1832.

Sandweiss, Daniel H., and Jeffrey Quilter. "Collation, Correlation, and Causation in the Prehistory of Coastal Peru." In Surviving Sudden Environmental Change: Understanding Hazards, Mitigating Impacts, Avoiding Disasters, edited by Jago Cooper and Payson Sheets, 117–139. University Press of Colorado, 2012.

Sandweiss, Daniel H., and James B. Richardson III. "Central Andean Environments." In The Handbook of South American Archaeology, edited by Helaine Silverman and William Isbell, 93–104. Springer, 2008.

Santana-Sagredo, Francisca, Rick J. Schulting, Pablo Méndez-Quiros, Ale Vidal-Elgueta, Mauricio Uribe, Rodrigo Loyola, Anahí Maturana-Fernández et al. "'White Gold' Guano Fertilizer Drove Agricultural Intensification in the Atacama Desert from AD 1000." Nature Plants 7, no. 2 (2021): 152–158.

Sapiains, Pía, Valentina Figueroa, Frances Hayashida, Diego Salazar, Andrew Menzies, Cristián González, Rodrigo Loyola et al. "Supergene Copper and the Ancient

Mining Landscapes of the Atacama Desert: Refining the Protocol for the Study of Archaeological Copper Minerals through the Case Study of Pukara de Turi." *Minerals* 11, no. 12 (2021): 1–27, https://doi.org/10.3390/min11121402.

Saunders, Nicholas J. "'Catching the Light': Technologies of Power and Enchantment in Pre-Columbian Goldworking." In *Gold and Power in Ancient Costa Rica, Panama, and Colombia,* edited by Jeffrey Quilter and John W. Hoopes, 15–47. Dumbarton Oaks Research Library and Collection, 2003.

Sayre, Matthew, Tammy Stenner, and Alejandro Argumedo. "You Can't Grow Potatoes in the Sky: Building Resilience in the Face of Climate Change in the Potato Park of Cuzco, Peru." *Culture, Agriculture, Food and Environment* 39, no. 2 (2017): 100–108.

Schexnayder, Clifford, Christine M. Fiori, and Gerardo Chang Recavarren. "Engineering the Inka Road." In *The Great Inka Road: Engineering an Empire,* edited by Ramiro Matos Mendieta and José Barreiro, 109–112. National Museum of the American Indian/Smithsonian Books, 2015.

Schoolmeester, Tina, Kari Synnove Johansen, Björn Alfthan, Elaine Baker, Malena Hesping, and Koen Verbist. *The Andean Glacier and Water Atlas: The Impact of Glacier Retreat on Water Resources.* UNESCO and GRID-Arendal, 2018.

Schorsch, Deborah. "Silver-and-Gold Moche Artifacts from Loma Negra, Peru." *Metropolitan Museum Journal* 33 (1998): 109–136.

Schreiber, Katharina J., and Josue Lancho Rojas. "The Puquios of Nasca." *Latin American Antiquity* 6, no. 3 (1995): 229–254.

Schultze, Carol A. "Silver Mines of the Northern Lake Titicaca Basin." In *Mining and Quarrying in the Ancient Andes: Sociopolitical, Economic and Symbolic Dimensions,* edited by Nicholas Tripcevich and Kevin Vaughn, 231–251. Springer, 2013.

Schultze, Carol A., Charles Stanish, David A. Scott, Thilo Rehren, Scott Kuehner, and James K. Feathers. "Direct Evidence of 1,900 Years of Indigenous Silver Production in the Lake Titicaca Basin of Southern Peru." *Proceedings of the National Academy of Sciences* 106, no. 41 (2009): 17280–17283.

Schwartz, David P. "Paleoseismicity and Neotectonics of the Cordillera Blanca Fault Zone, Northern Peruvian Andes." *Journal of Geophysical Research: Solid Earth* 93, no. B5 (1988): 4712–4730.

Schwartz, Glenn M. "The Archaeological Study of Sacrifice." *Annual Review of Anthropology* 46 (2017): 223–240.

Sepulchre, Pierre, Lisa C. Sloan, Mark Snyder, and Jerome Fiechter. "Impacts of Andean Uplift on the Humboldt Current System: A Climate Model Sensitivity Study." *Paleoceanography* 24, no. 4 (2009): 1–11, https://doi.org/10.1029/2008PA001668.

Sevink, Jan. *The Cordillera Blanca Guide: A Unique Landscape Explained + Trips.* University of Amsterdam and The Mountain Institute, 2009.

Sherbondy, Jeanette E. "Water and Power: The Role of Irrigation Districts in the Transition from Inca to Spanish Cuzco." In *Irrigation at High Altitudes: The Social Organization of Water Control Systems in the Andes,* edited by William P. Mitchell and David Guillet,

69–97. Society for Latin American Anthropology and American Anthropological Association, 1993.

Shimada, Izumi, and Alan K. Craig. "The Style, Technology and Organization of Sicán Mining and Metallurgy, Northern Peru: Insights from Holistic Study." *Chungará (Arica)* 45, no. 1 (2013): 3–31.

Shimada, Melody, and Izumi Shimada. "Prehistoric Llama Breeding and Herding on the North Coast of Peru." *American Antiquity* 50, no. 1 (1985): 3–26.

Silgado, Enrique. "The Ancash, Peru, Earthquake of November 10, 1946." *Bulletin of the Seismological Society of America* 41, no. 2 (1951): 83–100.

Silverman, Helaine. "A Nasca 8 Occupation at an Early Nasca Site: The Room of the Posts at Cahuachi." *Andean Past* 1, no. 1 (1987): 5–55.

Simpson, Joe. *Touching the Void*. Random House, 1998.

Singer, Brad S., Nathan L. Andersen, Hélène Le Mével, Kurt L. Feigl, Charles DeMets, Basil Tikoff, Clifford H. Thurber et al. "Dynamics of a Large, Restless, Rhyolitic Magma System at Laguna del Maule, Southern Andes, Chile." *GSA Today* 24, no. 12 (2014): 4–10.

Singer, Brad S., Hélène Le Mével, Joseph M. Licciardi, Loreto Córdova, Basil Tikoff, Nicolas Garibaldi, Nathan L. Andersen, Angela K. Diefenbach, and Kurt L. Feigl. "Geomorphic Expression of Rapid Holocene Silicic Magma Reservoir Growth beneath Laguna del Maule, Chile." *Science Advances* 4, no. 6 (2018): eaat1513.

Smith, C. Earle, Jr. "Plant Remains from Guitarrero Cave." In *Guitarrero Cave: Early Man in the Andes*, edited by Thomas F. Lynch, 87–119. Academic Press, 1980.

Smith, Felisa A., Rosemary E. Elliott Smith, S. Kathleen Lyons, and Jonathan L. Payne. "Body Size Downgrading of Mammals Over the Late Quaternary." *Science* 360, no. 6386 (2018): 310–313.

Sobolev, Stephan V., Andrey Y. Babeyko, Ivan Koulakov, and Onno Oncken. "Mechanism of the Andean Orogeny: Insight from Numerical Modeling." In *The Andes: Active Subduction Orogeny*, edited by Onno Oncken, Guillermo Chong, Gerhard Franz, Peter Giese, Hans-Jürgen Götze, Victor A. Ramos, Manfred R. Strecker, and Peter Wigger, 513–535. Springer, 2006.

Socha, Dagmara M., Johan Reinhard, and Ruddy Chávez Perea. "Inca Human Sacrifices on Misti Volcano (Peru)." *Latin American Antiquity* 32, no. 1 (2021): 138–153.

Solis, Ruth Shady, Jonathan Haas, and Winifred Creamer. "Dating Caral, a Preceramic Site in the Supe Valley on the Central Coast of Peru." *Science* 292, no. 5517 (2001): 723–726.

Stahl, Peter W. "Animals, Domesticated." In *Encyclopedia of the Incas*, edited by Gary Urton and Adriana von Hagen, 26–31. Rowman & Littlefield, 2015.

Steele, Paul R. *Handbook of Inca Mythology*. ABC-CLIO, 2004.

Stein, Seth, Joseph F. Engeln, Charles DeMets, Richard G. Gordon, Dale Woods, Paul Lundgren, Don Argus, Carol Stein, and Douglas A. Wiens. "The Nazca–South America Convergence Rate and the Recurrence of the Great 1960 Chilean Earthquake." *Geophysical Research Letters* 13, no. 8 (1986): 713–716.

Stern, Charles R. "Active Andean Volcanism: Its Geologic and Tectonic Setting." *Revista Geológica de Chile* 31, no. 2 (2004): 161–206.

Steward, Julian H., ed. *Handbook of South American Indians.* Bureau of American Ethnology Bulletin 143. Smithsonian Institution, 1946.

Stone-Miller, Rebecca. *Art of the Andes: From Chavín to Inca.* Thames and Hudson, 1995.

Strecker, M. R., R. N. Alonso, B. Bookhagen, B. Carrapa, G. E. Hilley, E. R. Sobel, and M. H. Trauth. "Tectonics and Climate of the Southern Central Andes." *Annual Review of Earth and Planetery Sciences* 35 (2007): 747–787.

Stuart, Anthony John. "Late Quaternary Megafaunal Extinctions on the Continents: A Short Review." *Geological Journal* 50, no. 3 (2015): 338–363.

Sublette Mosblech, Nicole A., Alex Chepstow-Lusty, Bryan G. Valencia, and Mark B. Bush. "Anthropogenic Control of Late-Holocene Landscapes in the Cuzco Region, Peru." *Holocene* 22, no. 12 (2012): 1361–1372.

Surovell, Todd A., Spencer R. Pelton, Madeline E. Mackie, Chase M. Mahan, Matthew J. O'Brien, Robert L. Kelly, and Vance Haynes Jr. "The La Prele Mammoth Site, Converse County, Wyoming, USA." In *Human-Elephant Interactions: From Past to Present,* edited by G. E. Konidaris, R. Barkai, V. Tourloukis, and K. Harvati, 303–320. Tübingen University Press, 2021.

Sutter, Richard C., and Rosa J Cortez. "The Nature of Moche Human Sacrifice: A Bioarchaeological Perspective." *Current Anthropology* 46, no. 4 (2005): 521–549.

Swenson, Edward R. "Cities of Violence: Sacrifice, Power and Urbanization in the Andes." *Journal of Social Archaeology* 3, no. 2 (2003): 256–296.

Szpak, Paul, Jean-François Millaire, Christine D. White, and Fred J. Longstaffe. "Influence of Seabird Guano and Camelid Dung Fertilization on the Nitrogen Isotopic Composition of Field-Grown Maize (*Zea Mays*)." *Journal of Archaeological Science* 39, no. 12 (2012): 3721–3740.

Tello, Julio C. "Discovery of the Chavín Culture in Peru." *American Antiquity* 9, no. 1 (1943): 135–160.

Thompson, Lonnie G., Mary E. Davis, Ellen Mosley-Thompson, and K-B. Liu. "Pre-Incan Agricultural Activity Recorded in Dust Layers in Two Tropical Ice Cores." *Nature* 336, no. 6201 (1988): 763–765.

Thouret, Jean-Claude, Anthony Finizola, Michel Fornari, Annick Legeley-Padovani, Jaime Suni, and Manfred Frechen. "Geology of El Misti Volcano near the City of Arequipa, Peru." *Geological Society of America Bulletin* 113, no. 12 (2001): 1593–1610.

Thouret, Jean-Claude, Marco Rivera, Gerhard Wörner, Marie-Christine Gerbe, Anthony Finizola, Michel Fornari, and Katherine Gonzales. "Ubinas: The Evolution of the Historically Most Active Volcano in Southern Peru." *Bulletin of Volcanology* 67, no. 6 (2005): 557–589.

Torres, Constantino Manuel. "Archaeological Evidence for the Antiquity of Psychoactive Plant Use in the Central Andes." *Annuli dei Musei Civici Roverero* 11 (1995): 291–326.

Toyne, J. Marla, Christine D. White, John W. Verano, Santiago Uceda Castillo, Jean François Millaire, and Fred J. Longstaffe. "Residential Histories of Elites and Sacrificial

Victims at Huacas de Moche, Peru, as Reconstructed from Oxygen Isotopes." *Journal of Archaeological Science* 42 (2014): 15–28.

Tributsch, Helmut. "On the Reddish, Glittery Mud the Inca Used for Perfecting Their Stone Masonry." *Journal of Earth Sciences & Environmental Studies* 3, no. 1 (2017): 309–324.

Tripcevich, Nicholas, and Daniel A. Contreras. "Archaeological Approaches to Obsidian Quarries: Investigations at the Quispisisa Source." In *Mining and Quarrying in the Ancient Andes: Sociopolitical, Economic and Symbolic Dimensions,* edited by Nicholas Tripcevich and Kevin Vaughn, 23–44. Springer, 2013.

Tripcevich, Nicholas, and Daniel A. Contreras. "Quarrying Evidence at the Quispisisa Obsidian Source, Ayacucho, Peru." *Latin American Antiquity* 22, no. 1 (2011): 121–136.

Tripcevich, Nicholas, and Alex Mackay. "Procurement at the Chivay Obsidian Source, Arequipa, Peru." *World Archaeology* 43, no. 2 (2011): 271–297.

Tripcevich, Nicholas, and Kevin Vaughn, eds. *Mining and Quarrying in the Ancient Andes: Sociopolitical, Economic and Symbolic Dimensions.* Springer, 2013.

Turner, Robert J. W., Rosemary J. Knight, and John Rick. "Geological Landscape of the Pre-Inca Archaeological Site at Chavín de Huántar, Peru." *Current Research* (Geological Survey of Canada, 1999-D): 47–56.

Ugent, Donald, Tom Dillehay, and Carlos Ramirez. "Potato Remains from a Late Pleistocene Settlement in Southcentral Chile." *Economic Botany* 41 (1987): 17–27.

Urton, Gary. "Quipu." In *Encyclopedia of the Incas,* edited by Gary Urton and Adriana von Hagen, 234–236. Rowman & Littlefield, 2015.

Urton, Gary. "Weaving and Textiles." In *Encyclopedia of the Incas*, edited by Gary Urton and Adriana von Hagen, 297–301. Rowman & Littlefield, 2015.

Urton, Gary, and Adriana von Hagen, eds. *Encyclopedia of the Incas*. Rowman & Littlefield, 2015.

USAID. Climate Change Risk Profile—Peru (2017). https://www.climatelinks.org/sites/default/files/asset/document/2017_Climate%20Change%20Risk%20Profile_Peru.pdf.

Vaughn, Kevin J., Moises Linares Grados, Jelmer W. Eerkens, and Matthew J. Edwards. "Hematite Mining in the Ancient Americas: Mina Primavera, a 2,000 Year Old Peruvian Mine." *Journal of the Minerals, Metals and Materials Society* 59, no. 12 (2007): 16–20.

Vaughn, Kevin J., and Nicholas Tripcevich. Introduction to *Mining and Quarrying in the Ancient Andes: Sociopolitical, Economic and Symbolic Dimensions*, edited by Nicholas Tripcevich and Kevin Vaughn, 3–19. Springer, 2013.

Vaughn, Kevin J., Hendrik Van Gijseghem, Verity H. Whalen, Jelmer W. Eerkens, and Moises Linares Grados. "The Organization of Mining in Nasca during the Early Intermediate Period: Recent Evidence from Mina Primavera." In *Mining and Quarrying in the Ancient Andes: Sociopolitical, Economic and Symbolic Dimensions,* edited by Nicholas Tripcevich and Kevin Vaughn, 157–182. Springer, 2013.

Veettil, Bijeesh Kozhikkodan, and Ulrich Kamp. "Global Disappearance of Tropical Mountain Glaciers: Observations, Causes, and Challenges." *Geosciences* 9, no. 5 (2019): 196.

Veloza, Gabriel, Richard Styron, Michael Taylor, and Andrés Mora. "Open-Source Archive of Active Faults for Northwest South America." *GSA Today* 22, no. 10 (2012): 4–10.

Vergano, Dan. "Mystery Surrounds Delicate Nasca Lines Threatened by Greenpeace." *National Geographic*, December 12, 2014. https://www.nationalgeographic.com/culture/article/141212-nazca-lines-greenpeace-archaeology-science.

Vialou, Denis, Mohammed Benabdelhadi, James Feathers, Michel Fontugne, and Agueda Vilhena Vialou. "Peopling South America's Centre: The Late Pleistocene Site of Santa Elina." *Antiquity* 91, no. 358 (2017): 865–884.

Vigny, C., A. Socquet, S. Peyrat, J. C. Ruegg, M. Métois, R. Madariaga, S. Morvan, M. Lancieri, R. Lacassin, J. Campos, and D. Carrizo. "The 2010 Mw 8.8 Maule Megathrust Earthquake of Central Chile, Monitored by GPS." *Science* 332, no. 6036 (2011): 1417–1421.

von Hagen, Adriana. "Antisuyu." In *Encyclopedia of the Incas*, edited by Gary Urton and Adriana von Hagen, 31–32. Rowman & Littlefield, 2015.

von Hagen, Adriana. "Bridges." In *Encyclopedia of the Incas*, edited by Gary Urton and Adriana von Hagen, 57–58. Rowman & Littlefield, 2015.

von Hagen, Adriana. "Chicha." In *Encyclopedia of the Incas*, edited by Gary Urton and Adriana von Hagen, 73–75. Rowman & Littlefield, 2015.

von Hagen, Adriana. "Chinchaysuyu" In *Encyclopedia of the Incas*, edited by Gary Urton and Adriana von Hagen, 75–76. Rowman & Littlefield, 2015.

von Hagen, Adriana. "Collasuyu." In *Encyclopedia of the Incas*, edited by Gary Urton and Adriana von Hagen, 90–92. Rowman & Littlefield, 2015.

von Hagen, Adriana. "Cuntisuyu." In *Encyclopedia of the Incas*, edited by Gary Urton and Adriana von Hagen, 104–105. Rowman & Littlefield, 2015.

von Hagen, Adriana. "Feathers." In *Encyclopedia of the Incas*, edited by Gary Urton and Adriana von Hagen, 140–142. Rowman & Littlefield, 2015.

von Hagen, Adriana. "Roads." In *Encyclopedia of the Incas*, edited by Gary Urton and Adriana von Hagen, 242–245. Rowman & Littlefield, 2015.

von Hagen, Adriana. "Sacsahuaman." In *Encyclopedia of the Incas*, edited by Gary Urton and Adriana von Hagen, 250–251. Rowman & Littlefield, 2015.

von Hagen, Adriana. "Tambos." In *Encyclopedia of the Incas*, edited by Gary Urton and Adriana von Hagen, 267–268. Rowman & Littlefield, 2015.

Watson, Peter. *The Great Divide: History and Human Nature in the Old World and the New*. Weidenfeld & Nicolson, 2012.

Weatherley, D. K., and R. W. Henley. "Flash Vaporization during Earthquakes Evidenced by Gold Deposits." *Nature Geoscience* 6, no. 4 (2013): 294–298.

Wheeler, Jane C. "South American Camelids: Past, Present and Future." *Journal of Camelid Science* 5, no. 1 (2012): 1–24.

Williams, Patrick Ryan. "Rethinking Disaster-Induced Collapse in the Demise of the Andean Highland States: Wari and Tiwanaku." *World Archaeology* 33, no. 3 (2002): 361–374.

Woodburne, Michael O. "The Great American Biotic Interchange: Dispersals, Tectonics, Climate, Sea Level and Holding Pens." *Journal of Mammalian Evolution* 17, no. 4 (2010): 245–264.

Wreschner, Ernst E., Ralph Bolton, Karl W. Butzer, Henri Delporte, Alexander Häusler, Albert Heinrich, Anita Jacobson-Widding et al. "Red Ochre and Human Evolution: A Case for Discussion [and Comments and Reply]." *Current Anthropology* 21, no. 5 (1980): 631–644.

Wright, Kenneth R., Ruth M. Wright, Alfredo V. Zegarra, and Gordon McEwan. *Moray: Inca Engineering Mystery*. American Society of Civil Engineers Press, 2011.

Wright Kenneth R., and Alfredo V. Zegarra. *Machu Picchu: A Civil Engineering Marvel*. American Society of Civil Engineers Press, 2000.

Wright, Kenneth R., Alfredo V. Zegarra, and William L. Lorah. "Ancient Machu Picchu Drainage Engineering." *Journal of Irrigation and Drainage Engineering 125*, no. 6 (1999): 360–369.

Young-Sánchez, Margaret. *Tiwanaku: Ancestors of the Inca*. Denver Art Museum and University of Nebraska Press, 2004.

Zeder, Melinda A., Eve Emshwiller, Bruce D. Smith, and Daniel G. Bradley. "Documenting Domestication: The Intersection of Genetics and Archaeology." *TRENDS in Genetics* 22, no. 3 (2006): 139–155.

Zehetner, Franz, W. P. Miller, and L. T. West. "Pedogenesis of Volcanic Ash Soils in Andean Ecuador." *Soil Science Society of America Journal* 67, no. 6 (2003): 1797–1809.

Zimmerer, Karl S. "The Ecogeography of Andean Potatoes." *Bioscience* 48, no. 6 (1998): 445–454.

Ziółkowski, Mariusz, Jose Bastante Abuhadba, Alan Hogg, Dominika Sieczkowska, Andrzej Rakowski, Jacek Pawlyta, and Sturt W. Manning. "When Did the Incas Build Machu Picchu and Its Satellite Sites? New Approaches Based on Radiocarbon Dating." *Radiocarbon* 63, no. 4 (2021): 1133–1148.

Zori, Colleen. "Extracting Insights from Prehistoric Andean Metallurgy: Political Organization, Interregional Connections, and Ritual Meanings." *Journal of Archaeological Research* 27, no. 4 (2019): 501–556.

Index

Page numbers in *italics* refer to figures and tables

Aconcagua, *30*, 39, 155
Africa, 28, 156
African culture, 10–11, 81
Alexander the Great, 232
Amazon Basin, 15, 93, 94, 118, 143, 146. *See also* Andes Mountains; animals; Incas
Andean cultures, *13*; and adaptation, 11, 52, 79, 121, 126, 213; and afterlife, 11, 138, 149, 152, 183, 218; age ranges of, 12, 213; and agricultural terraces, 271; and agriculture, 11, 24, 55, 64, 79, 82, 90, 91, 92, 96, 97, 100, 103, 104–15, 117, 133, 150, 179, 185, 189, 190, 207, 215–16, 217, 226, 227, 233; and Altiplano people, 119, 213–14, 215, 216–17, 227–28; and ancient Andeans, 11, 12, 13, 14, 15, 18–21, 24, 45, 52, 53–54, 79–82, 91, 96–97, 100, 102, 103–5, 106, 111, 114–15, 117, 121, 128, 151–55, 163, 166, 173–74, 181, 212–13, 215, 230, 268; and archaeological sites, 82, 98, 131–32, 173–74, 177, 181, 185, 186, 229, 230; and architecture, 8, 64, 82, 131–42, 163, 189, 214; artifacts of, 11, 52, 54, 80, 101, 111, 154, 155, 162–63, 164, 168, 170, 175–76, 178, 179, 181, 186, 191, 209, 214, 217, 226; art objects of, 11, 19, 21, 52, 64, 81, 82, 89, 91, 137, 138, 148, 150, 156, 162, 164, 166, *167*, 168, 169, 170, 171–72, 180–88, *183*, 194, 198, 213, 218, 256; and Asia, 103, 155, 156; and astronomical carvings, 223; and

Atacama Desert, 107, 162, 181–82; and burials, 159, 160–61, 162, 164, 183, 186, 187, 192, 193–94, 203; and Casma valley cultures, 134; and Central Andes, 168, 177, 189–90, 198–200, 225, 226; and ceramics, 122–23, 144, 150, 154, 164, 168, 175, 177, 178, 179, 180, 187, 189–94, 198, 214, 226; and ceremonial complexes, 11, 101, 112, 114, 155, 202–3, 205, 207–9, 213–14, 218; and Chavín culture, 13, 14, 61, 101, 135, 146–47, 162, 167, 169–70, 178, 181, 182, 187–88, 191, *192*, 194, 197–99, 202–5, 209–11, 266; and *chicha*, 122–23, 152, 216–217; and children, 152, 153, 154, 155, 186; and Chimu people, 12, 100, 138–39, 153, 178, 186; and Chinchorros, 181–82; and climate change, 97–102, 134–35; and clothing, 73, 88, 105, 115, 152, 156, 170, 182, 183–84, 186, 187, 222, 223; and conflicts, 82, 100, 134, 227–28, 232–33; construction techniques of, 24, 112–15, 128, 131–34, 135, 202; and different environments, 203; and dualism of universe, 170, 189, 202; economic systems of, 97, 232; and Europeans, 7, 8, 11, 232–33; extent of, 13, 15, 226; and feasts, 214, 217, 218, 226, 227; and fishing, 96–97, 104, 124; and flooding, 101, 102, 198; and foods, 82, 90–91, 92, 96, 97, 102, 103–5, 115, 116, 120–22, 126, 130–31, 133, 183, 190,

333

210, 227; and fuel, 73, 103–4; and geoglyphs, 135–37; and gold, 267; and harvest of salt, 20, 105; and herders, 55, 104, 227; and historical records, 8, 214; and human sacrifices, 151–55, 186, 192, 218; and hunter-gatherer societies, 10, 19, 51–52, 73, 79–80, 97, 104, 117, 126, 213; and hunting, 11, 51, 80, 97, 104; and Inca culture, 91, 106, 110, 112, 113–14, 122–26, 128, 130, 139, 146–47, 150–55, 161, 162, 164, 166, 175, 178, 179, 180, 181, 184, 185–87, 189, 194, 230–42; and Indigenous knowledge, 271–72; and interaction with different groups, 53–54, 82, 104–5, 125, 134, 137, 143–44, 226, 231–33, 235; and irrigation agriculture, 133, 226; and Killke people, 243; and Lake Titicaca, 216, 227; and Lambayeque (Sican), *176*, 178; and land, 24, 73, 100, 103, 106, 116; and languages, 12, 235, 271; and leaders' authority, 129–30, 131, 133, 134, 235; and marine resources, 105, 233; and metallurgical techniques, 178; migration of, 103–4; and Moche culture, 12, 90, 91, 100, 111, 124, 137–38, 146–48, 151, 153, 170–71, 177, 189, 190, 191–94; and modern Andeans, 11, 146, 272; and mountain ecosystems, 272; and mummies, 8, 90, 149, 155, 171, 181–82; and music, 168, 179, 251; and narcotics, 118, 146–50; and Nazca people, 100, 107, 135–37, 148, 189, 191; and Norte Chico people, 12, 97–98, 100–101, 106, 123, 128, 131–33, 150, 185, 186; and Paracas culture, 182–83; political development of, 134, 172, 181; and population, 97, 104, 116, 120, 126, 215, 216, 256; and pottery, 180, 186, 189–91; and qochas, 111, 115, 216; and Quechua, 12, 90, 120, 123, 128, 184, 271; and *quipus*, 10, *184*, 184–85; and relationship with environment, 15, 24, 25, 51–52, 58, 59–60, 69, 73, 82, 95, 100–102, 104, 105, 166, 181; religious practices of, 90, 101, 102, 121, 122–23, 130, 131, 143, 145, 146–49, 151–54, 155, 168, 179, 182, 184, 208, 209, 210, 214, 217, 224, 268; resilience of, 15, 45, 102, 264, 272; ritual drugs in, 148–49; and rituals, 52, 90, 102, 115, 121, 122–23, 130, 134, 137, 143, 145, 147–49, 151–55, 163, 166, 168, 179, 181, 184, 192, 202, 205, 208–10, 214, 217, 220, 221, 224, 268, 271; and rocks, 17, 20–21, 23, 51, 52, 202; and ruling lineages, 218, 231–32; and sacred nature of mines, 179; and sacred plants, 268; and sacrifices, 90, 102, 147, 151–55, 156, 178, 192, 218, 235; settlements of, 73, 79–80, 99, 124, 190, 209, 210, 217, 226–27; and shamans, 148, 191, 192, 198, 204, 205, 269; and social stratification, 150, 160, 166, 170–71, 172, 178, 182–83, 184, 185, 192–93, 217, 227; and societal development, 81–82, 105, 115, 126, 134; Spanish chroniclers of, 175, 184, 185, 186–87, 231; and Spanish rule, 268; and *Spondylus* shell, 150–51, 154, 179, 209; and starvation, 100; structures of, 11, 24, 45, 153–54, 155, 186, 211; and Tawantinsuyu, 271; and textiles, 11, 80, 81, 88, 91, 101, 115, 137, 144, 148, 150, 154, 162, 168, 171, 179–88, 189, 198, 203, 213, 214, 224, 226; and Tiwanaku culture, 13, 14, 64, 90, 110, 111, 122–24, 138, 146–47, 163, 164, 176, 177, 188, 194, 213–14, 216–29; and tools, 10, 11, 21, 51, 52, 80, 82, 91, 103, 163, 168, 179, 191; and trading, 52–53, 54, 78, 90, 97, 104–15, 118, 120, 122, 125, 143–44, 149, 150, 162–63, 180, 186, 214, 215, 226; and tropical shells, 147, 150; and use of animals, 11, 54, 81–82,

87, 88, 89–90, 91, 103, 104, 105, 191; and uses of coca leaves, 146, 149–50; and volcanoes, 11, 154; and Wari culture, 164, 177; and water, 92–93, 94, 95, 96–98, 105–7, 110, 111, 113–14, 115, 136, 208–9; and women, 123, 152, 154, 159, 166, 171, 187, 259; and writing systems, 3, 7, 10, 12, 184–85. *See also* Andean monuments; animals; Incas; Moche culture; Nazca culture; Uru people; Wari culture

Andean monuments: from adobe, 136–40, 141, 221; and agricultural terraces, 131, 199, 230; and Akapana, 217, 218, *219*, 221, 224–25; and architecture, 134, 217, 218, 219–21, 223, 225; and astronomical events, 220; as burial sites, 137, 218; and Cahuachi ceremonial center, 136, 137; and Central Andes, 210; and ceremonial complexes, 136–38, 197–99, 200, 207, 211, 218–21; and Chimu kings and commoners, 138–39; as civic centers, 131, 132; construction of, 128–31, 133–34, 137, 207–8, 218, 219–21, 224–25, 230; and depictions of violence, 134; destruction of, 227, 228–29; and drainage systems, 218, 220, 221; and earthquakes, 140–42; and engineering skill, 225; and environmental hazards, 199; and environmental knowledge, 208; and Gateway of the Sun, *222*, 223; and Huajje, 173; and human labor, 128, 130, 131, 140, 142, 207–8, 218, 223, 224, 225; and Inca culture, 139, 140, 142–44, 228, 230, 233, 236–48; on Isla del Sol (Island of the Sun), 144; and Kalasasaya, 217, 219–21, 223, 225; and Kimsachata range, 218–19, 224; and Lake Titicaca, 221, 225; longevity of, 140–42, 144–45, 189; materials of, 137, 138, 139–42, 218, 219, 220, 221, 224–25; of the Moche people, 137–38; and Nazca Lines, 128, 135–37; and Norte Chico people, 140; and Ollantaytambo, 131; and Pacific coast, 144, 210; and pilgrims, 138, 221; and platform mounds, 135, 136–37, 140, 201, 217, 221; and public spaces, 225; and Pumapunku, 217, 221, 224–25; and pyramids, 134, 136, 138, 142, 144, 153, 168, 173, 218, 219; reasons for, 128–31; and religious and political leaders, 211, 217, 221, 225; religious practices at, 145, 153, 220; and Rio Casma site, 134; and Rio Tiwanaku, 221, 225; and sacred power, 144–45; and Sacsayhuaman walls, 21, 128, 131, 240, 243, 248; and *shicra* bags, 142; and shrines, 143, 218; and Spaniards, 228; stone sculptures of, 221–23; and Sunken Temple, 217, 219, 220, 221; and temple structures, 128, 129–30, 137, 142, 144, 217, 219–21, 230; and terraced mounds, 132, 134, 221; and Tiwanaku city, 224, 225, 228, 229; and Tiwanaku culture, 144, 213, 217–29; and trade via roads, 143–44; and water, 217, 218–19, 220, 221. *See also* Chavín de Huántar; Incas; Nazca culture; Sacsayhuaman; terraces

Andes Mountains: age of, 6; and agriculture, 105–6, 110, 111–12, 114, 117–22, 126; and Alpamayo mountain, 61; and Altiplano, 82, 90, 94, 111, 138, 164, 212–14; and Altiplano-Puna plateau, 59–60, 63–64, 65, 66, 95; and Amazon Basin, 267; and Amazon River, 62, 94; ancient architectural monuments in, 32, 36, 45; and ancient cultures, 11, 12, 13, 14, 18, 24, 34, 40, 48, 59–60, 78–80, 83; and andesite rocks, 18, 50; archaeological sites in, 79, 80, 97, 106, 150, 168, 213; and

336 INDEX

bridge technology, 261; and Central Andes, 15, 20, 21, 22–25, 28, 29, 32, 34, 36, 44–45, 47, 52, 59–69, 73, 75, 79, 81, 87, 92–99, 104, 105, 106, 107, 109, 112, 115, 117, 123, 124, 126, 128, 129, 130, 134, 140, 148, 150, 156, 159–60, 174–75, 213, 232, 251, 261, 265–66, 269; and Central Volcanic Zone, 48, 50, 154; and ceramics, 80, 111; and climate change, 264–67; climate of, 7, 8, 9, 11, 15, 51–52, 59–60, 67–68, 73, 74, 79, 80, 87, 92–102, 103, 104, 105, 106, 116, 118–19, 126, 129, 130, 134–35, 174, 199, 203; and coastal deserts, 166; and Cordillera Blanca, 61–62, 63, 88, 197, 199, 209, 211, *265*, 266; and Cordillera Negra, 62, 63; Cordillera ranges of, 59, 61–63, 65, 93, 94, 95, 135, 199, 233; and earthquakes, 6, 7, 11, 24, 32, 33, 34, 36–37, 41, 44–45, 50, 106, 211; and environmental diversity, 116, 117–19, 126; features of, 5–7, 22–24, 59–69, 88; and floods, 101, 129; formation of, 24, 28, 29, 31; geography of, 12, 15, 59, 61–63, 116; height of, 5, 7, 16, 27, 29, 50, 52, 61, 62, 63, 64, 66, 74, 88, 94, 103–4, 111, 118–19, 120, 143, 155, 174, 198, 199, 213, 216; and hiking, 262–63; history of, 95, 159, 267; and Huascaran mountain, 61; and Huayhuash regions, 62; and Huayna Picchu, 244; and ice, 6–7, 74, 92; and Inca roads, 143, 260, 262; Incas in, 3, 5, 7, 8, 9, 10, 124–26, 151, 175, 178; Indigenous people of, 7, 8, 9–10, 15, 59–60, 90, 120, 126, 213, 261, 263, 264; and Lake Titicaca, 13, 21, 63–64, 65, 94, *95*, 109, 110, 111, 124, 135, 138, 144, 151, 160, 173, 175, 176–77, 213; and landslides, 6, 7, 63; location of, 5, 9, 25, 116; and Machu Picchu, 244; and maize, 121–22; and mining, 267–68; natural resources of, 264; and obsidian, 87, 103, 214; and Peru-Chile Trench, 68; and Pleistocene archaeological sites, 79–80; precipitation in, 92, 93–94, 97, 101, 105–6, 111, 119, 121, 135, 150, 199, 210; Pucuncho Basin of, 79, 87; and *puna* zone, 119; *quecha* zone of, 119; resources of, 82, 91; and settlement sites, 83, 94; and societal development, 10, 11, 24, 79, 80–81; and Southern Volcanic Zone, 56; and subduction zones, 67–68; and tectonic episodes, 267; temperature of, 52, 59, 80, 94, 119; and volcanic rocks, 18, 52, 67; volcanic zones in, 48, 50, 67; and volcanoes, 7, 11, 24, 25, 46–50, 52; and water, 93–98, 111, 112, 134, 135; and World Heritage Sites, 269–70; Yerupaja in, 62. *See also* Andean cultures; earth

animals: and adaptation, 87; and alpacas, 51, 55, *61*, 83, 87, 88–89, 90, 91, 104, 105, 111, 119, 153, 164, 182, 203, 213, 216, 217; and Amazon Basin, 180; and Amazon rainforest, 186; and Andean societies, 90–91, 96–97, 104, 105, 186; and art designs, 181, 185, 186, 191; and bats, 187; and bears, 83, 84; and birds, 86, 91, 96, 98, 186; butchering of, 86; and camelids, 51, 85, 86, *87*, 87–90, 96, 116, 122, 153, 180, 182, 188, 189, 210, 214, 252; and camels, 84, 87; and carnivores, 84, 91; and cats, 83, 84, 85; and Chavín artists, 203; and deer, 51, 81–82, 86, 87, 116, 183, 210; and dogs, 80, 81, 84; domestication of, 11, 80, 81, 87, 88, 90, 91, 103, 126, 213; and elephants, 84, 85; and Eurasian livestock, 260; extinctions of, 86–87; and fertilizer, 109; and fish and bird migration, 111; as food, 81–82, 87, 88, 90–91; and fossils, 83; and geoglyphs, 136;

and *Glyptodon*, 85; grazing of, 60, *61*, 74, 85, 87, 96, 213, 216; and ground sloths, 11, 83, 84, 85, 86; and guanacos, 81, 83, 86, 87–88; and guano, 111–12; and guinea pigs, 90–91, 104, 152, 210; and herbivores, 85–86, 91; herds of, 85, 87, 88, 90; hides of, 52, 77, 87; and horses, 84, 85, 86, 88, 252, 260–61; hunting of, 86, 87; intercontinental exchanges of, 84; and jaguars, 148; and llamas, 51, 54, 55, 83, 87, 88–89, *89*, 90, 91, 104, 105, 107, 111, 119, 143, 152, 153, 154, 156, 164, 175, 178, 203, 209, 213, 214, 216, 217, 223, 241, 259, 260, 263; and mammals, 81–86, 91, 96, 98, 116; and mammoths, 84, 86; and marine creatures, 98, 105, 116; and mastodons, 11, 85, 86; and megafauna, 86; and migration, 74, 75, 79, 81–82, 84; and mining, 260; and opossums, 84; and osteoderms, 86; pasturing of, 208; and plants, 81, 85; and Pleistocene animals, 84–87; and reproduction, 79, 90; and reptiles, 86; sculptures of, 156; selective breeding of, 87, 88–89; of South America, 84–91; tracks of, 66; and trading, 90; and vicunas, 82, 83, 86, 87–88; and wolves, 81; wool from, 90, 182, 185, 188, 189, 203, 214. *See also* earth
anoxia, 7, 79
Asia, 5, 11, 74, 75, 78, 84. *See also* Andean cultures
Atlantic Ocean, 11, 28, 62, 67, 81, 93. *See also* South America
Aztec culture, 10, 11, 128, 152, 189

bartonellosis, 100
Beringia land bridge, 74, 75
Berns, Augusto, 259
Bingham, Hiram, III, 8, 54, 259, 260

Bolivia: and agriculture, 265; and Altiplano-Puna plateau, 59–60, 214–15; archaeological sites in, 142; and Bolivian Orocline, 29, 64–66, 68–69; ceremonial sites in, 48; and Chivay obsidian, 54; and city of Tiwanaku, 213; and construction of La Paz, 228; and deep earthquakes, 36; and dinosaur footprints, 20; and foods, 91;; and Inca culture, 231; Lago Poopo in, 215; and Lake Titicaca, 214–15, 225–26; mercury contamination of, 255; northern region of, 15, 20, 68; and Potosi mines, 253–55; and Salar de Uyuni, 215; and tin sources, 163; and Tiwanaku culture, 138; and valley of Callejon de Huaylas, 63. *See also* Tiwanaku (city)
Burger, Richard L., 200

Canada, 74, 78, 268
Central America, 10, 75, 128
Cerro Blanco, 137
Cerro Rico, 253, *254*, 255
Chavín culture, 13, 14, 61, 101, 135, 142. *See also* Andean cultures; Chavín de Huántar
Chavín de Huántar, *201*, *202*, *206*; and Amazon River, 199; archaeological site of, 36, 182–83, 197, 199, 200, 201–2, 266; architecture of, 201–5, 207; art objects of, 150–51, 182, 198, 200, 201, 203–5; building of, 128, 206–8, 209, 211; and ceramic vessels, 209–10; ceremonial site of, 202–3, 205, 207, 208, 209, 211; and Chavín cult, 198; and Chimu Formation, 206, 207; dates of construction of, 200; drainage system of, 202–3; and floods, 199, 200, 210, 211; and landslides, 200, 207–9; location of, 129, 197, 198–99, 202, 206, 209; and pilgrims, 101, 135,

198, 209, 211; and precipitation, 202; and religion, 182, 210, 211; and Rios Wacheqsa and Mosna, 199, 200, 202, 205, 208; and rituals, 205, 207, 208, 209; and sacred waters, 197, 199; and sculpture El Lanzon, 205; as seat of religious power, 198, 208; temples of, 142, 148, 150–51, 200, 201–5, 207, 208, 209, 210, 211; and tenon heads, 203, 204–5; and town of Chavín, 198, 200; and visitors, 200–201; water system of, 221; as a World Heritage Site, 270

Chimu Empire (Kingdom of Chimor), 138–39, 171, 172, 270. *See also* Andean cultures

China, 143, 268

Church of Santo Domingo, 4, 5, 251, 257

Clovis projectile points, 75

cocaine, 264, 268–69. *See also* plants

cochineal red dye, 188–89

Columbia, 36, 231, 263

Cordillera Blanca fault zone, 36, *37*, 59

Coricancha: as center of Inca Empire, 3, 241; and Church of Santo Domingo, 4; curved stone wall of, 3, *4*, 4, 7, 45, 140, 141, 251, 257; descriptions of, 8; location of, 122

Cuzco: and Alca obsidian, 54; and andesite, 239; archaeological sites in, 7–8, 45, 143, 144, 242; architecture of, 251, 256;; and bird feathers, 186; Cathedral of, 90, 240, 251, 257; and Central Andes, 93; and Chimu artisans, 172; and Chinchero, 106, 257; and chunos, 121; and Church of Santo Domingo, 251, 257; city of, 3, 8, 21, 91, 146, 212, 231, 233, 241–42, 251, 256–58, 270; and Coricancha, 122, 241; drainage system of, 241; earthquakes in, 4, 5, 38; elevation of, 7; Haucaypata in, 242, 251; imperial complex in, 230, 241; and Inca artifacts, 260; Inca rebellion in, 255–56; and Killke societies, 231; location of, 60, 129; and Machu Picchu, 263; and Moray's location, 112, 271; and mummies, 235; Plaza de Armas in, 180, 242, 251, 259; and religious structures, 235, 242; and Sacsayhuaman walls, 128; and sun deity, 231; and temple complex, 21, 241; and tourism, 8

da Vinci, Leonardo, 90

deities: and *chicha* consumption, 123; and control of water, 136, 137, 153; and control of weather, 102, 105, 115, 129–30, 134, 137, 147, 198, 203, 210; and Coricancha, 241; and earthquake deities, 37, 48, 198, 203; and human sacrifices, 152, 153, 154, 178; of the Incas, 241; and Inti (god of the Sun), 122, 161; and monumental temples, 101, 129–30, 198; of mountains and mines, 179; offerings to, 21, 48, 80, 123, 145, 147, 149, 150, 154, 155, 179, 184, 198, 235, 259, 271; and polytheism, 129; and religious items, 157, 178; and rituals, 102, 123, 130, 137, 143, 154–55, 179, 184; and sacrifices, 48, 102, 123, 137, 143, 152, 154–55; and sculpture El Lanzon, 205; and Sun god, 152, 161, 231; and Viracocha, 231

Dillehay, Tom, 77

earth: and activity in Andes region, 6–7, 24–25, 33, 37, 46, 48, 50, 56–58, 62, 107, 198, 199; age of, 5–6; Antarctic region of, 96; and batholiths, 67; and climate change, 56, 63, 74, 75, 78, 86–87, 92, 97, 98, 210, 211, 215, 227, 264; and coastal erosion, 78; and continental plates, 64, 67, 68, 74; and continent formation, 28, 68; core of, 25; crust of, 22, 25, 26, 27, 29, 36, 37,

40, 56, 66–67; and destruction, 32; dinosaurs on, 20, 24, 28, 62, 66, 86; and earthquakes, 23, 24, 26, 27, 29, 31, 32, 33, 36–37, 78, 99; and environmental contamination, 267; and flooding, 98, 99, 100, 139, 144, 147, 152, 153; and glacial action, 62, 63, 74, 265–66; heat energy of, 25; and Inca Empire, 233, 235; landforms on, 24, 59–69, 74; and landslides, 6, 7, 32, 40, 44–45, 99, 129, 144, 198, 207, 210–11, 266; and La Rinconada, 267; and magma, 17, 27, 47–48, 67; and mantle, 25, 26, 27, 29, 34, 47, 48, 50; and marine creatures, 86, 97, 98, 100; and migration routes, 74; mountain chains of, 5–7, 24, 27, 28, 29, 30, 61–63, 66, 68–69, 95, 159; and natural hazards, 266; and Nazca plate, 50; and oceanic crust, 22, 26–27, 29, 34; and oceanic plates, 33, 64, 67, 68; and oceans, 5, 22, 29, 30–31, 41, 62, 74, 75, 97, 98, 99, 100, 103; and paleoclimate data, 99; Pleistocene Ice Age of, 36, 50, 54, 74, 80, 81, 86, 97, 214–15; and rising temperatures, 265–66; settlement sites on, 50, 73, 75–80, 86, 97–98, 99; shape of, 47, 100; structure of, 22, 23, 25, 27, 28; and subduction zones, 27, 28–31, 33, 34, 47, 50, 64; surface of, 20, 22, 25, 100; and tectonic plates, 24–31, 33; temperature of, 25; and Tibetan Plateau, 27, 63; and tsunamis, 152; and volcanoes, 23, 25, 26, 27, 29, 155; and water, 216; and winds, 99, 107, 158. *See also* earthquakes; plate tectonics; volcanoes

earthquakes: of 1650 (in Cuzco), 4, 45; of 1950 (in Cuzco), 45; and Alaskan earthquake, 44; and ancient Andeans, 37, 44, 45, 59; and Andes mountains, 6, 7, 23, 31, 32, 36–37, 44–45, 50, 197; and art, 166; and buildings, 44, 45, 140–42; cause of, 26, 33, 34, 40, 41; and Chavín de Huántar, 208, 210–11; destruction from, 3, 4, 32–33, 34, 44–45, 166, 211; and disaster in Ancash (May 1970), 41–44, 45; fatalities from, 41, 44; and flat slab plate interfaces, 39; focal depths of, 34, 36; and gold, 159; and great quakes, 33–36, 39, 40; and hazards, 32, 44–45, 129, 137, 197; historical records of, 32, 34, 40; and Incas, 231, 251; and landslides, 32, 40, 44–45, 199, 208; magnitudes of, 68; and Maule earthquake, 40; and mountain building, 24, 29, 31; and Nazca plate, 27, 33, 34; and Peru-Chile Trench, 34, *38*; and plate tectonics, 33–34, 36, 38–39; and resistance of buildings, 241; and sacrifices, 152; and shaking intensity, 44, 45; societal impact of, 34, 36, 37; and South American plate, 34; and subduction zones, 34, 36, 38, 39–41; and Sumatra-Andaman earthquake, 41, 44; and surface-faulting earthquakes, 36–37; and tectonic plates, 41; and tsunamis, 32, 33, 39–41; and Valdivia earthquake, 33, 40; and Wadati-Benioff zone, 34. *See also* Andes Mountains; earth; volcanoes

Ecuador, 180, 231, 239, 263

Einstein, Albert, 69

El Niño, 98–102, 133, 135, 139, 147, 153. *See also* Pacific Ocean

El Niño-Southern Oscillation (ENSO), 98

Eurasia, 73, 80, 81, 91

Europe, 74, 143, 156, 164, 189, 253. *See also* Incas

European culture, 10–11, 232, 233, 236, 241, 252. *See also* Spanish conquistadors

genetic data, 78, 81, 117

Genghis Khan, 232
geology: and Altiplano-Puna plateau, 29, 64, 65, 66–67, 68; and altitude, 20, 29, 66, 67; and Andes region, 5–7, 16, 18–19, 20, 24, 29, 31, 44, 64, 66–69, 197, 199–200; and Chavín de Huántar, 205–6, 209; and data, 36–37, 66; and earthquakes, 44, 159, 199; and fossils, 20, 24, 28, 66; and geoglyphs, 135–36, 137; and glacial moraines, 36, 199; and hazards, 126; and karst topography, 112; and Laguna del Maule volcanic field, 56; and landslides, 197, 205–26; and metallic zones, 159; and minerals, 28, 55, 165; and mountains, 5–7, 18, 20, 22–23, 29, 31, 156; and natural disaster assessment, 41; and ocean's floor, 36; and oroclines, 64, 66; and Oyon Formation, 206; and quartz formation, 19; and water, 92–94. *See also* earthquakes; metals; rocks
Great Pyramids of Giza, 128
Greenpeace, 271
Guitarrero Cave, 12, 80, 117, 181

Himalayas, 5, 27
Holocene, 74, 86
Huajje site, 173
Huascaran mountain, 39, 41, *43*, 44, 45, 59. *See also* Andes Mountains
Huayna Picchu, 127, 244
hunter-gatherers, 10, 51–52, 73, 77, 86, 103. *See also* Andean cultures

Incas, *234*; and adaptation, 241; administrative systems of, 232, 235; and agriculture, 110, 112, 114, 115, 122, 230, 232, 233, 261, 263, 271; and the Altiplano, 233; and Amazon Basin, 233, 256; and ancestors, 230, 231, 271, 272; and Andean societies, 10, 15, 105, 115, 230, 231, 271; and archaeological sites, 9, *9*, 11, 21, 45, 164, 230, 236, 270; architecture of, 112–13, 139, 172, 235, 237; and art designs, 181, 194; artifacts of, 180, 259, 260; art objects of, 235, 241, 253, 256, 259; and Atacama Desert, 172, 173; and Atahualpa, 232, 248, 252–53, 255, 259, 264; and base of Vilcabamba, 256; and bird feathers, 186; and bridges, 261; and building muyus, 112–13, 248; and capital Cuzco, 139, 143, 172, 233, 235, 239, 241–42; and *chicha*, 122–23, 194; and civil war, 232; class system of, 115, 139, 144, 184, 235–36; and clothing, 187, 189, 235, 263–64; and conquest of Kingdom of Chimor, 171, 172; construction techniques of, 236–37, 239–44; and control of resources, 82, 111, 113, 115, 144, 187, 194, 232, 243, 244; and culture, 11, *13*, 19, 114, 115, 122–23, 179, 194, 231, 235, 242, 251–52; downfall of, 232–33, 248, 252, 256; and education, 264; emperor of, 82, 161, 186, 187, 231, 232, 247, 248, 252, 255; Empire of, 3, 4, 7, 10, 12, 19, 38, 48, 82, 105, 110, 112, 122, 124–25, 127, 130, 139, 142, 143–44, 152, 161, 171, 172, 177, 178, 184, 194, 228, 230, 231–36, 241, 247–48, 251, 252, 260, 263–64; engineering skills of, 113–14, 125–26, 139, 143, 144, 236, 241–47, 271; and Europeans, 232, 241, 248; feasts of, 105, 110, 123, 144, 194; festivals of, 122, 123, 242, 251; and food, 263–64; and grinding mills, 175; highland estates of, 128, 144; and history as a *pachacuti*, 247, 248; and Huascar, 232; and Huayna Capac, 231, 232, 255; and human labor, 236, 237, 239–40, 242, 247; and human sacrifices, 179; and Inti (god of the Sun), 122; and irrigation, 175, 230, 233; and Isla del Sol (Island of the Sun), 186; labor system of, 232, 237, 239, 255, 261; and Lake Titicaca, 186, 231, 233; and Machu Picchu, 8, 16, 45, 110, 230, 236, 259; and maize, 119, 122, 144, 194; and Manco Inca Yupanqui, 255, 256; metallurgy of, 166; and metal separation, 175; and metalworkers, 171–72, 177; militarism of, 82, 125, 143; and mining, 178, 254; and Misti volcano's eruption, 58; monuments of, 259; and Moray's construction, 112–15; and mummies, 155, 182; nobility of, 232; and Ollantaytambo, 231, 236, 237–38, 240, 244, 248, 256; and Pachacuti Inca Yupanqui (Supreme Inca), 231, 247; and Pisac, 231; and population, 230, 232, 233, 235; and potatoes, 119, 120; and public celebrations, 232; and puquio water collection, 115; and qochas, 115; quarries of, 236, 237–39; and Quechua, 12, 56, 112, 142, 231; and *quipus*, 185; and religion, 112, 114, 115, 122, 123, 143, 146–47, 150, 151, 153–54, 155, 161, 235, 257; and respect for gold, 161, 241; and rituals, 145, 146–47, 154, 155, 162, 235, 256, 271; road networks of, 128, 131, 142–44, 172, 230, 233, 234, 235, 260, 261, 270; rope bridges of, 124–26; rulers of, 131, 139, 161, 231–32, 235; and Sacred Valley, 233, 243–44; and sacrifices, 48, 90, 152, 153–55, 235; and Sacsayhuaman, 240, 242–43, 255–56, 271; and sanctuary Coricancha, 3–5, 241; shrines of, 48, 122, 151, 153–55, *155*, 186, 235, 242; and social stratification, 263–64; Spanish accounts of, 231, 242; and Spanish conquest, 8, 11, 19, 232–33, 256, 264; Spanish rule of, 261; and *Spondylus* shell, 233; and stonework, 3–4, 9, 19, 103, 113–14, 139, 140, 143, 235–37, 239–40, 241, 242, 243, 251, 257–58, 271; storehouses of, 105, 144, 232, 235, 244; structures of, 256, 257; and Sun god, 161; and Tawantinsuyu realm, 233–35, 248; and terraces, 233, 235, 243, 247, 248, 257; and textiles, 256; and Tiwanaku city, 228; tools of, 3, 8, 113, 172, 236, 239, 248; and Topa Inca Yupanqui, 231; and trading, 150; and Tupac Amaru, 256; and unification of groups, 235; and use of animals, 236; and walls of Sacsayhuaman, 128. *See also* Andes Mountains; Coricancha; Cuzco; Machu Picchu; Sacsayhuaman

Indian Ocean, 41

Indonesia, 41

irrigation systems, 106–7, 110, 111, 113, 115, 131. *See also* Incas; Norte Chico people; plants

Japan, 26, 40, 142

Kelp Highway, 75, 77, 81

King Philip (of Spain), 259

Lumbreras, Luis, 200

Machu Picchu, *19*, *89*; and agriculture, 247; archaeological site of, 259–60; Chivay obsidian at, 54–55; city of, 244, 246, 247; drainage system of, 247; estates of, 231, 236; foundation of, 45, 244, 247; and Gate of the Sun, 127; and gold, 259; granite at, 18–19, 141, 246; and hammerstones, 239; and Inca relay runners, 263; Inca Trail to, 262–63; location of, 9, 129, 229, 243, 245, 259; and mining, 259; as a monument, 9, 128, 131, 140, 247; and natural beauty, 244, 247; precipitation at,

247; and royal family of Incas, 244–45; stone walls of, 237; and terraces, 110, 127, *141*, 237, 247; tools from, 172; trail to, 16, 127; and visitors, 8, 9, 127–28, 270; water supply of, 246–47; as a World Heritage site, 247, 270

Maya civilization, 10, 128

metals: and alloys, 160, 161, 163, 166, 169–71, 178; and ammunition, 164; and Andean metallurgy, 156–57, 161, 163, 164–66, 168–72; and bronze, 163, 178; and Central Andes, 158–62, 164, 174, 178; and cinnabar, 162, 177–78, 187, 188, 253; and copper, 156, 157, 159, 160, 161–62, 163, 166, 168, 171–72, 175, 177, 178, 187, 214, 233, 267; deposits of, 30, 60, 156, 157–59, 162, 163, 165, 172, 174, 177, 178, 253–54, 267; and gilding process, 171–72; and gold, 3, 11, 19, 21, 64, 78, 118, 144, 150, 154, 156, 157, 158–62, 163, 165, 166, 167, 168, 169, 170–74, 176, 177, 183, 186, 194, 223, 229, 241, 242, 252, 256, 257, 258, 259, 267; and high temperature smelting, 175–76, 178; and igneous rocks, 160; and iron, 156, 159, 164, 173, 178, 187, 261; jewelry made from, 137, 156, 160, 170–71, 183, 259; and lake sediment studies, 164–65; and lead, 156, 157, 159, 161, 163–64, 172, 176–77, 187; and mercury, 150, 156, 159, 162–63, 172, 177, 253, 254, 255; and metal art, 156, 169–71, 172, 189; and metallic ores, 30, 156, 157, 160, 161, 162, 163, 164, 165, 172, 173, 174–75, 177, 178, 179, 253, 264, 267; and metal separation, 175–77; and minerals, 163, 164, 165, 170, 173, 174–75, 179, 187; and mining, 264, 267–68; and quartz, 160, 173; and religious items, 178–79; and San Ramon mine, 173; and seven metals of antiquity, 159, 165; and silica, 64, 159; and silver, 11, 21, 144, 150, 154, 156, 157, 159, 160, 161, 162, 163, 166, 169–73, 175, 176, 177, 186, 194, 229, 241, 242, 252–59; and South American countries, 267; and Spanish conquistadors, 11, 150, 172, 178, 252–55; and tectonic plates, 157–58; and tin, 156, 157, 159, 161, 163, 178, 233, 255, 267; and tools, 161, 162, 172, 173, 178; and zinc, 159, 161, 267. *See also* mining

Mexico: Aztec Empire in, 10, 128, 152; and human sacrifices, 151, 152; and maize, 121; massive structures in, 128; and Muscovy ducks, 91; as New Spain, 254; and Oaxaca region, 188; and smallpox, 232

Middle East, 11

migration, 73–75, 77, 78–79, 80, 81, 84. *See also* Andean cultures; animals

Mina Perdida site, 168

mining, 42, 54, 150, 162, 167–68, 172–74. *See also* Machu Picchu; metals; Spanish conquistadors

Moche culture: and adobe brick structures, 137–38; and ceramics, 111, 124, 151, 177, 191–94; and ceremonial complexes, 137; dates of, 12, 137; and human sacrifices, 153, 193; and metalworkers, 170; pottery of, 91, 100, 148, 190; and religious rituals, 90, 146–47; role of women in, 171; and Royal Tombs of Sipan, 193–94; and Temple of the Moon, 138; and Temple of the Sun, 137, 138; tombs of, 170–71, 193, 194

Monte Verde site, 12, *76*, 77, 78, 86, 120

monumentality, 9–10, 128, 129, 132, 207, 230

Moray, 112–15, 248, 271

Mount Khapia, 220, 225

Mount Llullaillaco, 155

Mount Saint Helens, 55

Mount Whitney, 50

National Geographic, 8, 165
Nazca culture: and Cahuachi ceremonial center, 136, 137; and geoglyphs, 270; and Nazca Lines, 135–36, 137, 191, 270; pottery of, 100, 148, 191; and puquio water collection, 107, *108*; and Rio Nazca, 137
New Zealand, 26, 40
Norte Chico people: and agriculture, 106, 133; architecture of, 98, 123, 128, 132–33, 142; and bird feathers, 186; and burial mounds, 150; and Caral site, 132, 133, 185, 270; dates of, 12; and feasts, 132; and human labor, 132; and irrigation, 106, 133; land of, 131–33; and marine resources, 100–101, 133; and platform mounds, 140; and political systems, 133; pyramid mounds of, 132–33; and river valleys, 132, 133; settlements of, 97–98, 132–33; and tropical shells, 150
North America: and animal extinctions, 86–87; and animal migrations, 84; archaeological sites in, 75–78; and Bering Strait, 74, 84; and Clovis culture, 77–78; human footprints in, 78; and ice sheets, 74–75; and islands, 30; and Isthmus of Panama, 84; and migrants, 73, 74, 75, 77–78; and Native Americans, 78; Rocky Mountains in, 75; and Wyoming butchery site, 86

Obama, Barack, 260
obsidian, 21, 50–55, 58, 78, 79–80, 82. *See also* Andes Mountains, volcanoes
orogeny (mountain-building), 22, 24, 28–31, 67, 68. *See also* earth

Pachacuti Inca Yupanqui, 231, 244–45, 247

Pacific Ocean: and Andes region, 15, 24, 62, 94, 98, 105–6, 116, 233; atmospheric circulation over, 95; and climate change, 97; coast of, 107, 142–43; crustal pieces in, 30; and earthquakes, 26, 34, 40; and El Niño, 210, 215; fish from, 81, 91, 144; foods from, 60, 144; and Humboldt Current (Peru Current), 95–98, 101; and Inca Empire, 230; and lahars (mud flows), 56; and marine migration routes, 75; and Nazca plate, 34; and oceanic crust, 34; and Pacific plate, 28; and Peru-Chile Trench, 34; and rivers, 79, 105–6; and submarine landslides, 40; and tsunamis' origins, 40; and upwelling of water, 97, 98; and volcanoes, 26, 40; and water temperature, 96, 98, 101, 210; and winds, 96, 98. *See also* El Niño
Pacific Ring of Fire, 26, *26*, 28
paints and pigments, 187–88, 189, 190, 191, 223
Paracas Peninsula, 203
Peru: agriculture in, 45, 56, 103, 114, 265, 269, 271; and the Altiplano, 20, 59, 212–13, 215, 217; Ancash region of, 41–44, 266–67; as an Andean country, 263; and Andean cultures, 7–8, 13, 15, 226; Andes region of, 30, 48, 50, 54; archaeological sites in, 54, 78, 114, 142–43, 155, 160–61, 223, 226, 269–71; Arequipa in, 50, 56, 57, 58, 155; and avalanche (1970), 42, 43, 45; Cajamarca city in, 232; and Caral site, 271; and Central Andes, 170, 269; central part of, 54, 134, 162, 177; ceremonial sites in, 48; and Cerro de Pasco region, 177; Chimbote in, 41, 44; and Chinchero, 270; and city of Chan Chan, 271; and city of Trujilo, 137, 138, 153, 171; and climate change,

270–71; climate of, 96, 215–16, 266–67; and coca, 146, 269; Cordillera Blanca in, 88, 135, 266; and deforestation, 267; and Don Francisco de Toledo, 254, 255; and earthquakes, 3, 4, 7, 36, 38–41, 44–45, 197; export items of, 267, 268; and fishing, 98; and floods, 266; government of, 260, 271; highland areas in, 266, 271; Huancavelica in, 178, 253, 255; Huaraz in, 36, 37, 59, 61, 146, 197, 198, 199, 266; and Huari (city), 226; and Inca culture, 164, 231, 260; Indigenous people of, 213, 215; and Lago Palcacocha, 266; and Lake Titicaca, 212, 214–15, 216, 217; Lima in, 7, 14, 59, 60, *76*, 98, 146, 168, 203; and looting, 271; mercury contamination of, 255; and Mina Primavera, 179; Moquegua Valley of, 226–27; Moray in, 113, *113*, 271; Nazca in, 108, 137; and Nazca lines, 271; northern region of, 13, 20, 32, 34, 36, 39, 41, 54, 59, 80, 88, 96, 97, 100, 111, 117, 128, 134, 135, 137, 138, 170, 171, 181, 191, 266; and Peruvian flat slab segment, 39, 50; precipitation in, 100, 107, 113, 114, 215, 270–71; Pucuncho Basin of, 50, 54, 79, 87; and Puno, 212; Quebrada Jaguay in, 54; Ranrahirca in, 41–42; and Rio Apruimac, 125; Rio Santa in, 43, 62, 80; and Royal Tombs of Sipan, 169, 170, 171; Sacred Valley in, 103, 109; southern region of, 48, 50, 54, 59, 63, 68, 128, 153, 191, 226; and tourism, 269, 270; and town of Chavín, 199, 200; Tumbes in, 100; and valley of Callejon de Huaylas, 45, 63, 80; visitors to, 10, 262; and water temperature, 100; Yanacocha mine in, 267–68; and Yucay, 103; Yungay in, 41–42, 43, 44, 45. *See also* Andean cultures; Cuzco; Huascaran mountain; Moray

Philippines, 26

plants, *121*; acids from, 236; and agriculture, 118–19, 208; altered states from, 147–48; and Amazon Basin, 269; and Andean cultures, 11, 50, 52, 60, 80, 97, 103, 104, 106, 114, 116, 118–26, 146–50, 213; and aquatic plants, 109, 110, 111; and art designs, 181, 241; and avocados, 118; and biodiversity, 116; and bird guano, 112, 122; as boat material, 124; and bottle gourds, 80–81, 104, 179; and *chicha*, 223, 226; and climate, 92, 98–99, 130; and coca leaf, 118, 146–50, 154, 179, 214, 233, 268, 269; and cotton, 81, 97, 104, 106, 111, 116, 118, 180, 182, 184, 188, 203; and deforestation, 213; and ditch grass seeds, 78; domestication of, 80, 81, 103, 104, 116–17, 120, 126, 185; and fiber bags, 123, *124*; fibers of, 80, 216; as food, 80, 90, 104, 105, 106, 116, 117–22, 123, 216; and fossils, 28; and fruits, 116, 117, 118, 144; and geoglyphs, 136; and grains, 105, 117, 119, 126, 144, 214, 216, 265; and grasslands, 82, 87, 88; growth of, 55–56, 60, 87, 104–6, 109, 110, 114, 117, 118–20, 213, 216; and hallucinogenic drugs, 204, 269; and irrigation, 118, 119, 122, 126; and *lomas* (small hills), 96; and maize, 111, 117, 118, 119, 121–22, 144, 154, 183, 214, 216–17, 226, 227; and medicinal plants, 118, 149150; and mescaline, 148, 203, 217; and microclimates, 109, 110, 114, 120; and narcotics, 14–150, 217; and peppers, 117, 118, 214; and planting platforms, 110; and pollen, 66, 78, 92, 213; and potatoes, 119–121, 144, 214, 216, 265; and primitive land plants, 5; and raised fields, 110–11, 216, 217, 227;

remains of, 8, 20, 50, 78, 106, 136; and reproduction, 79; and river valleys, 131; and roofs of buildings, 123–24; and San Pedro Cactus, 148–49, 203, 204, 217; and seaweed, 77; and soil formation, 55; and sunken gardens, 107; and totora, 216; and tropical plants, 263; and tubers, 119, 120–21, 216, 227; and vegetables, 117, 118, 119, 120–22, 123, 126, 214; and *vilca* pods, 148, 149; and water, 110, 111, 118, 119, 120, 121–22; and *yunga* zone, 118

plate tectonics, 24–31, 33, 34, 41, 62, 69. *See also* earthquakes; metals; rocks; South America; volcanoes

Pleistocene Ice Age, 36, 50, 54, 63, 74, 78. *See also* Andes Mountains; earth

Pluto (mythical ruler of the underworld), 18

Potosi mines, 253–55

Qhapaq Nan (Inca Road), 142–44, 260, 261, 262, 270, 272. *See also* Incas

radiocarbon age dates, 50, 77, 78, 99, 173

Rick, John W., 200

rocks: age of, 22–23, 68, 69; and Amazonian craton, 69; ancient shelters in, 50, 51, 54, 79–80, 87; of the Andes, 17, 18, 21–23, 50, 51, 69, 224–25; and andesite, 18, 21, 50, 51, 112–13, 114, 141, 173, 218, 220, 223, 224–25, 237, 239; and archaeological sites, 21, 22, 50, 239; in avalanches, 41–43, 44, 63, 199; and basalt, 18, 21, 22, 173; as building materials, 21–22, 82, 139, 140, 141–42, 207, 218, 220, 221, 237–39, 247; and chemical rocks, 20; and chrysocolla, 137; classification of, 17, 21; and climate, 20, 95; and coal, 20, 206, 207; and construction of drains, 114; and continental rocks, 69; and crystals, 18; and Cuzco region, 237; and dacite, 18; densities of, 22; and earthquakes, 19, 26, 33, 39, 44; and elevation of land and oceans, 22; erosion of, 160; formation of, 17, 18, 19, 20, 22, 31, 33, 62, 157; fragmentation of, 19–20, 23; and gemstones, 188; and granite, 18–19, 21, 22, 27, 29, 36, 45, 62, 63, 141, 157, 159, 173, 175, 202, 207, 208, 237, 246, 247; and hammerstones, 172, 173; and igneous rocks, 16–23, 50, 141, 163, 237; and Inca road, 143; and "iron hat" color, 161; and landslides, 45, 63, 247; and limestone, 20, 21, *21*, 112, 113, 202, 207, 237; and magma, 18, 20; and marble, 20; and marine fossils, 66; and metals, 157, 162; and metamorphic rocks, 17, 20–23, 31, 175, 239; and minerals, 22, 23, 66, 158, 167; and mining dangers, 254; and mountain building, 22, 29, 66; and natural quarries, 18–19, 140; and obsidian, 21, 209; and oceanic rocks, 27–28, 29, 47; and plate tectonics, 29, 30–31, 140; and platform mounds, 136; and plutonic rocks, 18, 31; and quarries, 173, 223–24, 225, 246, 247; and quartz, 19, 27, 157, 159, 167–68; and quartzite, 20–21, 207; and rock art, 50, 84, 221; and Rumicollca quarry, 237; and salt, 20; and sandstone, 20, 21, 65–66, 206, 207, 218, 220, 221, 223, 224, 225; and sedimentary rocks, 17, 19–23, 31, 36, 62, 65–66, 163, 206, 237; and shale, 66; and *shicra* bags, 142; and silica, 240; and silicic ignimbrites, 67; strength of, 44; and subduction, 62, 63; and tectonic plates, 62; and tools, 51; valuable metals in, 60, 253; various locations of, 16, 20, 22, 23, 30–31, 67; and volcanic rocks, 17, 21, 22, 31, 51, 52, 55,

58, 63, 67, 112–13, 162, 209, 224, 225, 237, 253; and volcanoes, 20, 46, 47, 57, 158; and water, 158, 159; and young rocks, 27–28. *See also* geology
Roman Empire, 143, 164

Sacsayhuaman, 21, 128, 131, 235, 237, 242–43. *See also* Incas; Spanish conquistadors
Siberia, 75
Silk Routes, 11, 143
Simpson, Joe, 62
Siula Grande, 62
South America, *6*; and accreted terrains, 30, 159; and agriculture, 111–12; and ancient Andeans, 30, 64, 77, 80, 99, 111; and ancient artifacts, 77, 80, 111; and Andes mountains, 9, 18, 20, 23, 63, 68–69; archaeological sites in, 75–78, 86, 142; Argentina in, 39, 47, 48, 56, 63, 68, 142, 154, 226, 231, 263; and Atacama Desert, 111–12, 16;and Atlantic Ocean, 94; Bolivian Orocline in, 29, 64–66, 68–69; Brazil in, 78, 81, 263; Chile in, 33, 34, 38, 39, 40, 47, 48, 56, 59, 63, 68, 77, 78, 85, 86, 96, 107, 111, 120, 142, 153–54, 162, 173, 182, 226, 231, 263, 266; climate of, 107; and Clovis culture, 77–78; coast of, 34, 40, 81, 96, 98, 107; continental plate of, 27, 29–30; and deep earthquakes, 36; and Ecuador, 96, 99, 142; Huaynaputina in, 56; and human sacrifices, 151; human settlements in, 11, 75–82, 86, 99; isostatic uplift in, 29; and megafauna loss, 87; and migration of people, 73, 74, 75, 77–78, 79, 80, 81; movement of, 67, 68, 69; and Native Americans, 78, 81; and Nazca plate, 26, 27, 28, 33, 34, 39; Pacific Coast of, 73; and Peru-Chile Trench, 47, 68; and Pleistocene megafauna, 84–86; precipitation in, 98; and seismicity of coastal and Andean regions, 35; and South American plate, 39, 50, 63, 67, 68, 69, 84; and subduction zones, 30–31, 34, 38–39, 62, 63, 66, 67, 68; western part of, 5, 12, 18, 20, 25, 26, 29, 30–31, 33; and wild potatoes, 120. *See also* Monte Verde site
Spain, 253, 254, 255, 259, 260, 264
Spanish conquistadors: accounts of, 8, 187, 241; advance of, 113, 245–46; and agriculture, 252; and Andean societies, 251–53, 256, 261; architecture of, 256; and Atahualpa, 252–53; and Cajamarca, 261; and Cathedral of Cuzco, 240; and Catholic Church, 268; and Catholicism, 148–49; and coca plantations, 150, 268; and Cuzco, 256–58; and destruction of Inca culture, 8, 185, 243–44, 256–57, 261; and destruction of land, 253, 255; and diseases, 11, 255, 256; and execution of Tupac Amaru, 256; and exploration, 4, 5, 19; and forced labor, 252–56; and Francisco Pizarro, 232, 248, 252, 253, 255, 261; and gold, 19, 172, 252, 253; and Inca palaces and land, 253; and Inca roads, 260, 261; and Indigenous culture, 8, 138, 148–49, 187, 252–59, 260, 261; and King of Spain, 189; loot of, 8, 172, 252, 253, 258–59; and mining, 252, 253–55, 259; religious beliefs of, 148–49, 252; and Sacsayhuaman, 256, 257; and smallpox, 232, 256; and Tiwanaku city, 228; and use of animals, 260
Spanish Dominicans, 4, 5, 45
Stanford University, 200
supercontinents, 28

Tello, Julio C., 200

terraces, 107, 109–13, 114, 115, 135, 199. *See also* Andean monuments; Machu Picchu; Norte Chico people
Tiwanaku (city), 21, 64, 138, 213, 214, 217–23. *See also* Andean monuments
Tiwanaku culture. *See* Andean cultures

United Nations Educational, Scientific, and Cultural Organization (UNESCO), 269, 270
United States: Alaska in, 26, 30, 39, 50, 75; Appalachian Mountains in, 6; California in, 24, 32, 40, 75, 78, 146, 157; and Channel Islands, 78; Federal courts of, 260; Grand Canyon in, 34; and the Gulf Stream, 96; and Hawaiian Islands, 17, 26, 46; and ice sheets, 74; and Kilauea volcano, 17; and mining, 268; and Native Americans, 188; New Mexico in, 78; San Andreas fault in, 24; Utah in, 188; Washington State in, 55; width of, 5
Uru people, 216

volcanoes: and active volcanoes, 46–48, 50, *53*, 55–58, 154, 155; and Alca source, *53*, 54; and ancient Andeans, 11, 46, 48, 52, 55, 58, 59; and Andes mountains, 7, 31, 47, 48, 50, 52–58, 157; and archaeological sites, 52, 54; ash plumes from, 55–56; and Chivay source, *53*, 54–55; and crop production, 57; destruction from, 56, 58, 166; and early Paleogene, 62; eruptions of, 20, 46, 47, 48, 50, 55, 56, 57, 58, 62, 67, 147, 152, 154, 225; fertile land from, 55–56, 58; and flat slab plate segments, 39; and food, 55; and granitic batholiths, 62; and hazards, 129; height of, 47; and hot springs, 199; and Huaynaputina, *53*, 56; and Laguna del Maule volcanic field, 56; and lahars (mud flows), 56; and lava, 46, 48, 50, 52, 55, 58, 62, 154; and Llullaillaco, *53*, 47; and magma, 29, 46, 47–48, 50, 56, 62, 67, 157; and Misti volcano, 50, *53*, *57*, 57–58, 155; and Mount Llullaillaco, *53*, 155; and obsidian, 50–51, 52, 54, 58; and Ojos del Salado, 47; and Quispisisa source, *53*, 54; and Sabancaya volcano, *53*, 57; and silica, 50, 52; and soil formation, 55, 56; and Southern Volcanic Zone, 56; and subduction zones, 47, 48, 50; and tectonic plates, 50; and Ubinas volcano, *53*, 57; and volcanic arcs, 47; and volcanic zones, 48, *49*, 50; and water, 47–48

Wari culture, 226, 227, 231
weaving, 185–86, 191, 203
White Sands National Park, 78
World Bank, 267

Yale Peabody Museum, 260
Yale University, 200, 260

Zapata, Marcos, 90